AI
FOR MANKIND'S
FUTURE

LTC ROBERT L. MAGINNIS

AI
FOR MANKIND'S
FUTURE

A CHRISTIAN PERSPECTIVE ON THE
HI-TECH REVOLUTION

DEFENDER

CRANE, MO

AI for Mankind's Future: A Christian Perspective on the Hi-Tech Revolution
By LTC Robert L. Maginnis

Defender Publishing
Crane, MO 65633

©2025 Defender Publishing

All Rights Reserved. Published 2025

ISBN: 978-1-948014-94-6

Printed in the United States of America.

A CIP catalog record of this book is available from the Library of Congress.

Cover designer: Brittney Jackson / SimplyBrittneyDesigns.com
Interior designer: Katherine Lloyd
Editor: Angie Peters

To my fellow Christians who are both technologically skilled and spiritually discerning—may you continue to apply the truths of Scripture to this rapidly evolving age. It is my prayer that you lead the way in harnessing artificial intelligence (AI) for God's glory, while vigilantly guarding against the grave dangers it may bring. Let us heed the words of our Lord Jesus: "Behold, I am sending you out as sheep in the midst of wolves, so be wise as serpents and innocent as doves." (Matthew 10:16, ESV)

CONTENTS

Acknowledgments ix
Preface: AI for Mankind's Future:
A Christian Perspective on the Hi-Tech Revolution xi

Section One
DEFINING AI: THE MECHANICS, HISTORY, AND THE FUTURE

1   Defining AI and Associated Terms 3
2   Survey of AI's History 14
3   AI's True Potential and Possible Harm 26

Section Two
AI AND SOCIAL INSTITUTIONS

4   AI's Role in Family and Home Life 55
5   Education: Is AI a Boon or Bust for Learning? 68
6   AI: Medical Innovation and Risks 85

Section Three
AI AND PUBLIC INSTITUTIONS

7   Government's AI Mandate 107
8   AI Can Improve Public Service 131
9   AI and National Defense 143

Section Four
AI AND ECONOMY

10   AI and Raw Materials 167
11   AI and Manufacturing Industries 187
12   AI and the Retail Economy 208

Section Five
AI'S IMPACT ON CULTURE

13	AI's Influence on Our Values, Ethics, Norms and Liberties	229
14	AI and the Entertainment Industry	244
15	AI's Influence on Communications and Politics	262

Section Six
AI, CHRISTIANITY, AND BIBLICAL PROPHECY

16	AI and the Christian	279
17	AI: Satan's End-Times Strategic Weapon	296
	Afterword: Christians Called to Be Human, Not AI-powered Avatars	315

APPENDICES

A	Best Known AI Applications, Companies, and Experts	325
B	Understanding Generative AI	330
C	Artificial General Intelligence	333
D	Agentic AI	335
E	AI Terms and Common Vocabulary	337
F	AI's Strengths, Gaps, and Limitations	341
G	AI Applications for Families	345
H	Strategies for Responsible AI Integration in Education and Key Applications	348
I	SBC's Statement on AI and Emerging Technologies	351
J	US Government AI Applications	354
K	Real-Life Applications of AI in Local Government: Case Studies	357
L	Evaluating AI-Driven Solutions in Forestry and Mineral Exploration: Successes and Challenges	360
M	AI and Workforce Changes	362
N	Why AI Consumes So Much Electricity	365
O	Legal Frameworks Governing AI and Consumer Data in Retail	367
P	The Future of AI in Retail: Emerging Trends and Transformations	369
Q	Policy Recommendations and Governance Frameworks for AI-related Ethical Issues That Protect Individual Liberties	371
R	AI's Impact on Creative Professionals	375
S	ChatGPT's Deeper Interpersonal Impact	378
T	Strategies to Fight AI-related Disinformation	381
U	Narrative: AI in Politics: Global Approaches and Implications	384
Notes		389

ACKNOWLEDGMENTS

I gratefully acknowledge…

…my wife, Jan, who supports these writing projects and my thinking aloud about tough topics. She is comforting and a supporter through these challenging times.

…my friends Mark Shaffstall and Steve Crow, who provided valued recommendations, edits, and insights regarding AI.

…finally, my Lord Jesus Christ, who gave me the opportunity, skills, and breath to complete this work, and I pray it serves His purpose. All the glory is to Him.

—Robert Lee Maginnis
Woodbridge, Virginia

PREFACE

AI FOR MANKIND'S FUTURE: A CHRISTIAN PERSPECTIVE ON THE HI-TECH REVOLUTION

We must try to understand the challenges that AI will present even as we lack the prior exposure or the essential experience to guarantee the accuracy of our comprehension.[1]

HENRY A. KISSINGER (1923–2023)
American diplomat and political scientist

AI for Mankind's Future explores the basics about artificial intelligence (AI), both its current and probable future influence, and then presents a Christian perspective regarding the technology's true promises and threats. Before diving into these themes, it is vital to understand why AI deserves such attention and concern.

Why is understanding AI so important? It has a growing and significant impact on all of humanity—especially on our future. Keep in mind that it's more than a tool. Currently, AI functions as an instrument developed by humans to serve our objectives and operate within the parameters we've established. However, it can learn, adapt, and make decisions in ways that appear autonomous. At this point, AI lacks consciousness, intent, or intrinsic motivation; it is not human. Will it become like a person or a sentient (feeling) entity? Also, how do we make certain it helps people perform better rather than make us subservient, as some futurists warn?

AI FOR MANKIND'S FUTURE

In 2025, AI is rapidly progressing, but its impact is still underappreciated by many. However, its presence and benefits are hard to deny: AI is used when our fingerprint opens an application (app) on our smartphone and when we rely on it to navigate our driving. Further, it radically improves healthcare diagnoses; speech-recognition functionalities like Amazon's Alexa answer many of our questions; it identifies threats at home and on the internet; it helps find items online; and it even corrected my typing and grammar as I wrote this book. Plus, it can do much, much more.

While these daily conveniences seem benign, they point to a deeper concern: The rapid acceleration of AI development raises profound questions about control, autonomy, and the future of human thinking.

> **AI DEVELOPMENT RAISES PROFOUND QUESTIONS ABOUT CONTROL, AUTONOMY, AND THE FUTURE OF HUMAN THINKING**

What is AI? According to International Business Machines, AI is simply an innovation that enables computers to simulate human intelligence and, more specifically, it assists with problem-solving. Although this definition sounds simple, the implications are anything but. As AI grows more capable, some experts fear it could cross thresholds that challenge the very fabric of human society. Specifically, given recent AI and associated technological advances, there is a growing sense that our relationship with this technology stands at a tipping point, whereby significant new upgrades could become truly sinister and threaten the destruction or at least the control of human civilization unless we reverse course and put in place critical guardrails.[2]

Presently, AI advocates promise that the technology delivers only positive outcomes for humanity: improved business operations, more efficient government, improved education, advanced healthcare diagnoses, improved economics, and much more. Formerly considered science

PREFACE

fiction, these results are now routine. However, now—a quarter of the way through the twenty-first century—we find that technological advances are quickening their pace, and it's hard to anticipate the long-term impacts of AI, both good and bad.

It is important to understand that AI is not human intelligence, despite what its advocates may assert. It doesn't have a mental state or beliefs, affective attitudes, or intentions, all of which are associated with human decision-making. Rather, this technology amplifies mankind's intelligence by gathering information and helps us focus our thinking on what's important. Further, it aids our consideration by proposing creative possibilities and brings more facts to our attention to enrich our considerations. Simply, AI is a nonorganic tool that extends our capabilities—nothing more, or so we often think. However, it does appear that this nonhuman innovation is taking on a potentially dangerous life of its own.

To grasp the full scope of AI's impact, it helps to distinguish among its emerging forms, each with unique capabilities and concerns.

Recent developments in AI demonstrate remarkable progress, prompting some observers to consider the potential for it to exhibit capabilities that surpass human performance. For instance, AGI (artificial general intelligence) refers to machines that use their knowledge and learning ability to perform various complex tasks such as carrying out autonomous research, discovering new building materials, performing as a crisis coordinator, managing supply chains, acting as a multimedia artist, and leading space exploration. Thanks to emergent AGI, technology will have the capacity to think, act, and behave in ways that are remarkably like human creativity, such as the resolution of complex problem-solving.

Parenthetically, in May 2025, Google cofounder Sergey Brin surprised the world by announcing: "We fully intend that Gemini [Google's chatbot] will be the very first AGI" by 2030. This was the "first time a Google executive has explicitly stated an intent to win the AGI race, a contest often associated more with Silicon Valley rivals like OpenAI and Elon Musk than with the search giant."[3]

AI FOR MANKIND'S FUTURE

The most widely used version of AI today is known as "generative AI," which can produce creative outputs trained on large datasets with large-language models (LLM) and uses patterns to generate new outputs, which includes tools like ChatGPT and DALL·E. AGI might use generative AI as one of its tools, but generative AI alone doesn't come close to AGI in capability.

Another advancement on the near horizon is quantum AI, which is the convergence of quantum physics, the science of particles at the subatomic level, and AI technology. Quantum computing can complete computations one hundred million times faster than past computing systems. Therefore, AI algorithms (the step-by-step instructions for solving a problem or performing a task) tethered to supercharged quantum computers will be able to process giant datasets and solve incredibly complex problems in a fleeting moment.

Among the more speculative, but increasingly discussed, AI-related scenarios is the idea of "singularity," a concept that should concern everyone. It represents the hypothetical point at which AI devices surpass human intelligence and begin to improve autonomously and exponentially. Of course, it's difficult to predict the future of singularity, much less where it might eventually lead or leave humanity.

Another alarming possibility associated with AI is that future devices may come to possess self-awareness like human "consciousness," a sentient (feeling) entity. Yes, that is a philosophical view. However, if that happens, then humanity faces new and serious ethical and theological challenges.

Little wonder for many of us that AI's future is hard to understand or predict, and it's certainly frightening given these anticipated advancements. Right now, the AI revolution is in its initial stage, driven by various motivations and incentives from both international and domestic sources. Likely, tomorrow's technological advances will be incredibly transformative for society unlike anything seen in history.

These concerns aren't limited to sci-fi enthusiasts. Ethicists and policymakers are increasingly sounding the alarm. For example, Shannon Vallor, director of the Centre for Technomoral Futures, University

PREFACE

of Edinburg, warned a US Senate committee in 2024 about one such AI-related transformative red flag. She cautioned that there is "deep tension between AI and our capacity for democratic self-governance."[4]

Dr. Vallor explained that society's political will to manage AI is diminishing. Specifically, she illustrated her point by stating: "In 1976, Joseph Weizenbaum [1923–2008, a computer scientist and Massachusetts Institute of Technology professor] lamented that intelligent automation was emerging just when humans have 'ceased to believe in, let alone to trust, our own autonomy.'"[5]

The professor warned that just as doubts about human autonomy decline, we've become "dangerously susceptible to manipulation by AI evangelists who now routinely ask, 'What if the future is about humans writing down the questions and machines coming up with the answers?'" That means we might surrender thinking and decision-making to AI-powered machines, a demonic-like "authoritarian's paradise."[6]

Regrettably, we seem to be fast approaching that "authoritarian paradise," fueled by society's uncritical and widespread dependence on AI-powered technologies. These tools now permeate every aspect of life—home, education, work, entertainment, media, worship, and governance—leaving us increasingly susceptible to the embedded values and agendas of those who design the underlying algorithms. If left unchecked, we risk becoming servants to machines that reflect the misguided—and, at times, even malicious—intentions of their creators.

This growing reliance on algorithmic systems raises not only political and social concerns, but also deep spiritual and theological questions for Christians. Specifically, if this implies that AI could attain an almost godlike status for our lives, then you're starting to grasp the potential risks associated with this astonishing technology.

The significance of this book, *AI for Mankind's Future: A Christian Perspective on the Hi-Tech Revolution*, is that it explains AI's pervasive influence across many sectors of human life and from a Christian perspective. For each aspect of our lives, the text identifies AI-related red flags that make us more dependent on smart machines, robbing us of our autonomy and making us servants of nonorganic masters, albeit puppets of the algorithms' designers. That is a frightening prospect thanks to a broad-based and growing dependence on AI devices, and that dependence is something Christians must reject, because the "master" behind some AI algorithms might just be the "father of lies," Satan himself, the great deceiver. However, AI, the technology itself, isn't necessarily evil, and that's why we must grasp the potential of this challenging technology before it is too late and use it for God's glory.

Journey Through Six Sections

Across the six sections of *AI for Mankind's Future,* we consider this technology from three vantage points: the underlying innovation, the broad-based applications, and the challenges it poses for Christians. What is beyond dispute at this point is that AI technology will continue to advance, opening new possibilities for science, our key institutions, government, our economic establishment, and culture. Finally, the philosophy/theology portion of this book exposes the influence AI technology already has on society and how it could play a dominant role in our future, especially in the prophetic end times.

Section one, in three chapters, lays the foundation for understanding AI. I offer a definition, share AI's brief history, and identify the good already delivered by technology as well as outline some of the dangers that might lie ahead.

Section two, in three chapters, examines AI's current and future influence on key social institutions: family/home, education, and healthcare.

Section three, in three chapters, considers AI's current and future influence for important public institutions: big government, local-level public services, and our national defense. The global AI race, especially with communist China, is "existential," according to the Central Intelligence Agency; this is an issue of grave significance addressed in this section.

Section four, in three chapters, considers AI's effects for our economy, which begin with raw-material production—e.g., farming and mining, then manufacturing and processing—to the retail business sector and you, the consumer.

PREFACE

Section five, in three chapters, examines AI's influence on our culture. It identifies the impact technology has on values, norms, ethics, and language, as well as the arts, entertainment, gaming, and our modes for communicating with AI as well as our political processes.

Section six, in two chapters, provides a distinctively Christian and biblical end-times view of the possible impact of AI. It addresses the challenges for the Christian living in an AI-dominated world and recommends how to safely use technology for God's glory. Also, it unlocks how AI might aid the unholy trinity as we approach the prophetic end times.

This book is not a comprehensive technical guide to AI. Such books tend to be quickly outdated by new developments. Rather, as should be obvious, this effort explores the broad technological applications and consequences of the introduction of AI to society, which should mean it has a longer shelf life.

In closing, *AI for Mankind's Future* is intended as a helpful guide for those new to artificial intelligence, offering a clear understanding of this powerful technology, its wide-ranging applications, and its potential risks. It is especially valuable for Christians seeking to respond wisely and faithfully to an innovation that is rapidly transforming society. For those wanting to explore further, the book also includes numerous appendices that unpack the complexities of AI and its future impact across many areas of life.

Section One

DEFINING AI: THE MECHANICS, HISTORY, AND THE FUTURE

Artificial intelligence is the future, but we must ensure it is a future that we want.[7]

Tim Cook (1960)
CEO of Apple Inc.

Tim Cook reminds us that the future of AI is not predetermined—it is a future we must shape. To do so, we must first understand what artificial intelligence is and how it operates. Chapter 1 introduces the foundational concepts, terms, and mechanics that define AI.

Once we've grasped the building blocks of AI, it is vital to place it in historical context. Chapter 2 explores how the rise of computing laid the groundwork for today's intelligent machines, tracing key milestones in AI's development and its growing ambition to replicate human thought.

With a firm grasp of AI's foundations and historical rise, we now turn to the present. Chapter 3 outlines the major ways AI is shaping our world today—its impressive benefits and sobering risks—providing a critical lens for the rest of the book's exploration across key social and institutional domains.

Chapter 1

DEFINING AI AND ASSOCIATED TERMS

The development of full artificial intelligence could spell the end of the human race.... It would take off on its own, and re-design itself at an ever increasing rate. Humans, who are limited by slow biological evolution, couldn't compete, and would be superseded.[8]

STEPHEN HAWKING (1942–2018)
English theoretical physicist and cosmologist

Many readers seek insights into artificial intelligence, which they find confusing, complex, or even frightening, given Dr. Hawking's statement above.

The challenge for those unfamiliar with the topic of AI is that suddenly it seems to have become a ubiquitous aspect of our modern world that affects our home life, healthcare, education, culture, communications, automobiles, and workplaces. No part of our lives is free of this modern intruder.

This chapter provides a definition of AI and explains some of the technology-related contemporary terms used throughout this book. Admittedly, this start is a bit technical but necessary. Once you grasp the technology's basics and vocabulary, then, beginning with the next chapter, we quickly transition to history and descriptions of AI's many applications and the technology's significant impact. We'll eventually wrestle with the associated theological challenges.

AI FOR MANKIND'S FUTURE

For Christians, defining AI isn't simply a technical or academic exercise, it's a matter of biblical discernment. Technologies that imitate human intelligence invite us to revisit what it means to be created in the image of God (Genesis 1:26–27). As we encounter systems that mimic reasoning, speech, and even emotion, we must distinguish between the work of man and the wisdom of God (Proverbs 3:5–6). This discernment becomes the lens through which we view all AI tools and trends in the chapters ahead.

For more detail, see appendix A, which provides an overview of leading AI tools, companies, and experts while urging Christians to approach these innovations with spiritual discernment, testing whether each technology aligns with biblical values and promotes human dignity, truth, and Christ-centered living (1 Thessalonians 5:21).

Before diving into technical definitions, it's important to recognize the emotional and cultural context in which AI is being introduced to the public.

AI Angst

Admittedly, there is an angst associated with the topic of AI. After all, most Americans (52 percent) told the Pew Research Center they're more concerned than excited about AI in daily life. Only 10 percent said they were more excited than concerned, and the balance expressed a mixed view.[9]

American responses to the Pew survey also reflect a lack of knowledge about artificial intelligence. After all, 90 percent told Pew they had heard something about AI, but only one in three had heard a lot about this technology. Further, less than a third (30 percent) of US adults could correctly recognize six examples of AI in everyday life, "such as customer service chatbots and product recommendations [based on previous purchases—for example, a technology-generated advertisement]."[10]

Feelings about AI are both positive and negative, according to Pew. Most Americans (57 percent) say they would be excited for AI to help with household chores; others appreciate the assistance AI provides in finding products online. However, on the negative side, there is broad concern about the loss of the human element attributed to AI technologies, especially in the workplace. Overwhelmingly (83 percent),

DEFINING AI AND ASSOCIATED TERMS

Americans believe AI-operated cars will lead to the loss of jobs. Those people also express concern about the use of AI related to government surveillance and data privacy.[11]

While advanced AI techniques like machine learning enable impressive feats such as human-like text generation and intricate-pattern recognition, they also prompt critical practical and ethical questions. The very methods that power these technologies raise issues related to privacy, fairness, and accountability. In subsequent chapters, we will delve more deeply into these repercussions, linking the technical foundations of AI with their profound societal and ethical implications.[12]

Whether we realize it or not, AI already touches Christian life. It powers Bible apps with voice search and verse recommendations, filters worship music suggestions on streaming platforms, and even personalizes sermon clips on social media. In church security systems, AI can analyze faces; in mission work, it can translate Scripture. This reality makes understanding AI not just useful, but essential for followers of Christ who wish to apply biblical wisdom in digital discipleship (Colossians 2:8).

Humans are turning to AI for many aspects of our lives.

What Is AI?

I researched definitions of AI and found many versions. One of the most interesting came from ChatGPT, an AI-powered chatbot created in 2022 by OpenAI, and built on a model known as GPT (generative pretrained transformer). It claims to understand and generate human-like text for various tasks.

ChatGPT's Definition of AI

ChatGPT defined AI as "a branch of computer science focused on creating systems or machines that can perform tasks typically requiring

AI FOR MANKIND'S FUTURE

human intelligence. These tasks encompass problem-solving, learning, reasoning, perception, language comprehension, and decision-making."

AI, according to ChatGPT, "can be broadly divided into three types or levels:

1. **"Narrow AI (Weak AI):** AI systems designed for specific tasks, like virtual assistants (e.g., Siri, Alexa), recommendation algorithms, or self-driving car systems. They don't possess general intelligence but excel in their programmed functions." Further, Narrow AI is a digital assistant that "uses voice queries, gesture-based control, focus-tracking, and a natural-language user interface to answer questions, make recommendations, and perform actions by delegating requests to a set of Internet services." (The preface to this book labeled ChatGPT as a "generative AI" tool that leverages large language models trained on vast datasets, not to be confused with "artificial general intelligence" (AGI) outlined below. Appendix B introduces the mechanics and applications of generative AI—tools that create text, images, sound, and code by learning patterns from data—while offering practical tips for using them effectively and reminding readers that these systems, though powerful, lack true understanding or moral discernment.)

2. **"General AI (Strong AI) [alternatively, "artificial general intelligence" (AGI)]:** A more advanced concept where AI would have human-like cognitive abilities—able to understand, learn, and apply intelligence across a broad range of tasks. This level of AI is still theoretical." This form of AI can perform many tasks like a human, something even more advanced than OpenAI's GPT-4, which can "generate, edit and iterate with users on creative and technical writing tasks, such as composing songs, writing screenplays, or learning a user's writing style." Appendix C explains AGI as a still-unrealized form of AI capable of human-like reasoning, learning, and adaptability across diverse tasks, distinguishing it from today's generative AI systems like ChatGPT and Gemini, which remain limited to narrow, task-specific competencies.

DEFINING AI AND ASSOCIATED TERMS

3. **"Super AI,"** or the "technological singularity," is a hypothetical point at which AI surpasses human intelligence, potentially triggering rapid, uncontrollable change. While some view it as a utopia of innovation, others (including Christians) warn of losing human control, dignity, and moral boundaries. Theological reflection on this idea is critical in chapters ahead.

Next, ChatGPT explained how AI works. Specifically:

AI systems work through various technologies like machine learning (ML), natural language processing (NLP), computer vision, and robotics. Machine learning allows AI to learn from data, recognize patterns, and improve its performance over time without being explicitly programmed.

While ChatGPT provides a helpful technical overview, it is also valuable to present a more accessible, human-defined version of AI.

My Definition of AI

Now allow me the opportunity to provide another definition, albeit not machine-generated. Simply, AI is an aspect of computer science that involves creating and training machines to perform tasks that require human-like intelligence, such as recognizing patterns and making predictions based on massive quantities of information/data.

Let me illustrate this definition. Understand that a standard desk calculator, for example, does not represent AI, because the human directs the device (the calculator) regarding what functions to perform, such as punching buttons to add two and two and pressing the "equals" sign to get the answer of four. Therefore, the calculator applies *human*, not *artificial*, intelligence to acquire the correct answer.

Alternatively, consider an example of human-like artificial intelligence demonstrated by an AI-powered machine. Hypothetically, let's say our task is to identify the number of cars and motorcycles in a parking lot. We might employ AI software such as image-recognition technology.

The computer uses sensors to observe the parking lot and distinguish between the objects based on its algorithm (program), which tells it how to distinguish shapes and characteristics between cars and motorcycles. Then, it reports the results. That is a simple illustration of AI.

To fully grasp how AI functions, it is helpful to unpack some of the related concepts that will appear throughout this book.

Other AI-related Terms

In general, AI refers to a collection of technologies, including machine learning, deep learning, natural-language processing, large-language models, speech recognition, image recognition, and robotics. Consider a brief explanation of these and other terms used throughout this book.

Machine learning (ML): ChatGPT states that ML "is a type of AI that allows computers to learn from data and improve their performance without being explicitly programmed." Here's how ML works:

The first step is to collect data: images, text, and numbers. For example, let's build an ML model (a program or set of instructions) to recognize cats displayed in pictures. Therefore, we need thousands of cat pictures and many non-cat pictures.

In the second step, the data is "cleared and formatted to remove errors, duplicates, or irrelevant details." The data is then divided into three sets: training (pictures), validation (pictures), and test (pictures).

The third step involves selecting a mathematical representation of a system (a model—the program) such as linear regression (for predicting continuous values), decision trees (for classification tasks), or neural networks (for complex problems like image recognition).

The fourth step is to train the model using the data provided. The predictions are next compared to actual answers. The model is then adjusted with algorithms like gradient descent to reduce errors.

The fifth step is to conduct an evaluation on new data (test set above).

Sixth, if done correctly, the model can make reliable predictions on real-world data: It can distinguish cats from non-cat pictures.

Finally, optimization happens if the model fails to perform well, which results in changing the algorithms, adding data, or adjusting the parameters.

DEFINING AI AND ASSOCIATED TERMS

While ML brings great promise, its applications are not without pitfalls. AI systems can replicate bias in their training data, hallucinate information (especially in large-language models), and operate as black boxes—making decisions that are difficult for humans to understand or audit. These limitations can lead to false assumptions, misapplications, or unintended harm. Christians must remain alert, for the tools we create often reflect our fallen nature (Romans 3:23), and unchecked technology can subtly replace trust in God with faith in algorithms.

Three forms of ML improve through experience, tapping into past patterns to make predictions.

Supervised learning has enough data experience to find patterns in new sets of information. Therefore, given this experience, it can identify future patterns that provide similar future outcomes.

Unsupervised learning involves algorithms trained on unlabeled data, which means the program is exposed to data without explicit instructions about what to do with the information. The goal is for the model to find patterns within the data independently.

Reinforcement learning is a type of machine learning wherein an agent learns how to make decisions by interacting with an environment. The agent takes actions, receives feedback through rewards or penalties, and aims to maximize the total cumulative reward over time.

A step up from ML is called **"deep learning" (DL),** an algorithmic approach to decision-making. However, DL models work with multiple layers of algorithms known as a "neural network." This architecture is intended to replicate the functions of the human brain and is widely applied in image recognition, natural-language processing, and game playing.

However, not all artificial intelligence is machine-learning based; historically, symbolic AI, which relied on logic, rules, and knowledge graphs, was central to the field, underscoring that AI isn't solely driven by neural networks.

Natural-language processing (NLP) is a branch of AI that focuses on the interaction between computers and humans using natural language. The goal is to enable machines to understand, interpret, generate, and respond to human language in a meaningful way.

Large-language models (LLM) function like artificial brains, connecting information between layers of neurons, like the human brain. LLM can learn to "speak" by finding relationships among words by matching patterns. They can create songs by association even though they cannot understand the word's meaning, which is evidence of general AI/AGI (defined above).

Remember that LLMs are powerful tools capable of advanced pattern recognition and producing "human-like text generation." However, they're still widely regarded by experts as specialized or narrow AI, designed to excel at specific tasks. While LLMs may imitate creativity and even pass specific language proficiency tests, they don't demonstrate the broader, "human-like comprehension" associated with true AGI. Distinguishing these capabilities can help clarify why LLMs, despite their sophistication, aren't yet considered general AI.[13]

Speech recognition is a branch of AI that enables machines to understand and process human speech. It is what powers virtual assistants like Siri, Alexa, and Google Assistant, and it is used in everything from transcription services to voice-activated controls.

Image recognition is a fascinating application of AI wherein machines are trained to interpret and classify visual data—like recognizing objects, faces, or even emotions from images. The earlier ML example with cats is a classic example of image recognition.

Robotics involves designing, building, and programming physical robots—machines capable of performing tasks in the real world. Merge AI with robotics, and the robots perform preprogrammed tasks as well as adapt to new environments, learn from their experiences, and interact more naturally with humans.

Some robots are an example of "physical AI," which lets autonomous systems perceive, understand, and perform complex actions in the physical world. It is also referred to as "generative physical AI" because of its ability to generate insights and actions. For example, autonomous mobile robots are used in warehouses to navigate complex environments and avoid obstacles. There are manipulators that can adjust grasping strength and position,

DEFINING AI AND ASSOCIATED TERMS

tailoring motor skills to the object engaged. Surgical robots learn intricate tasks such as threading needles and performing stitches. Finally, there are humanoid robots that require both gross- and fine-motor skills, but they can also perceive, understand, navigate, and interact with the physical world.[14]

Mirokaï is a multipurpose robot with personality, an example of generative physical AI. It is the creation of a Paris-based startup, Enchanted Tools, made from a "blend of advanced AI, storytelling, and a dash of charm," according to Kurt Knutsson, the host of *Fox News*' Cyberguy Report. Mirokaï is designed to be people-friendly, with a "friendly and expressive face that invites interaction." It is designed for many environments: hospitals, clinics, nursing homes, professional events, hotels, restaurants, and airports.[15]

The robot Mirokaï is powered by a combination of sophisticated technologies, including multiple large-language models such as advanced vision that help it understand its surroundings. To get around, the robot is built on an omnidirectional ball, which allows it to glide smoothly and silently. Mirokaï's arms and hands let it grasp and manipulate objects, and its face is a projection system able to show emotions to correspond with any conversation.[16]

Agentic AI, a newer technology, marks a significant advancement in autonomy and decision-making. It refers to a class of AI systems capable of initiating tasks, setting and pursuing goals over time, and adapting to feedback—all without direct human input. These autonomous agents represent a shift from reactive tools to proactive, decision-making entities.

Previous AI assistants were rules-based and had limited ability to act independently. However, agentic AI can act on our behalf. Simply, it is defined by the word "proactiveness," according to Enver Cetin, an AI expert with the firm Ciklum. He explained:

> It refers to AI systems and models that can act autonomously to achieve goals without the need for constant human guidance. The agentic AI system understands what the goal or vision of the user is and the context to the problem they are trying to solve.[17]

Agentic AI is built from a complex ensemble of machine learning, natural-language processing, and automation technologies. It differs from AI models like ChatGPT in three ways: it is focused on decisions, not content; it's set to optimize goals or objectives without human prompts; and it can carry out complex sequences of activities. Appendix D defines agentic AI as autonomous systems capable of pursuing goals, making decisions, and adapting to environments over time—illustrating both their powerful potential and the serious ethical and safety concerns they raise when operating beyond direct human control.[18]

The above AI-related applications are firmly rooted in the pioneering work of foundational figures such as Alan Turing and John McCarthy. Turing's landmark 1950 paper, *Computing Machinery and Intelligence*, raised the pivotal question of whether machines can think, while McCarthy's coining of the term "artificial intelligence" during a Dartmouth College Conference in 1956 set the stage for decades of innovation. Their seminal contributions not only informed the technical underpinnings of today's AI, but also foreshadowed the deeper historical exploration provided in chapter 2 of this book.[19]

While these terms and applications help us understand how AI works, they also raise deeper questions—inquiries that resonate with Christian theology and ethics. They serve as the basis for forthcoming theological discussions, which include a Christian worldview perspective and exploring how these advances intersect with moral and spiritual considerations.

For further reference, see appendix E, which offers a glossary of essential AI terms while encouraging Christians to approach these concepts with biblical discernment, recognizing that many technical ideas—such as autonomy, singularity, and artificial wisdom—carry deeper moral, philosophical, and theological implications that may challenge a Christ-centered worldview.

Conclusion

Now that we've defined what AI is and how it functions, we can begin to trace how this concept evolved. Artificial intelligence is not a sudden

DEFINING AI AND ASSOCIATED TERMS

invention; it stands atop centuries of philosophical thought, scientific innovation, and cultural imagination. From early automatons to Turing's theoretical models, the story of AI is a mirror of humanity's pursuit of power, efficiency, and sometimes even transcendence. In chapter 2, we journey through that history, highlighting both technical breakthroughs and the worldviews that shaped them.

Chapter 2

SURVEY OF AI'S HISTORY

Artificial Intelligence, deep learning, machine learning—whatever you're doing if you don't understand it—learn it. Because otherwise, you're going to be a dinosaur within three years.[20]

MARK CUBAN (1958)
American investor and entrepreneur

Modern AI evolved from early primitive computers. This chapter begins by tracing the emergence of computers, which gave birth to AI in the 1940s—a field that fuses computer science, mathematics, philosophy, and cognitive science. I then outline AI's historical development before examining the many applications transforming our lives, which are discussed in later chapters.

While this technological journey is remarkable, it also reflects a deeper truth: Humanity's inventive spirit is not merely evolutionary or utilitarian, it mirrors the image of our Creator:

Then God said, "Let us make man in our image, after our likeness. And let them have dominion...over all the earth." (Genesis 1:26a, ESV)

The biblical doctrine of the *imago Dei* (image of God) teaches that our capacity to reason, design, and create reflects God's own nature (Genesis 1:27; Exodus 35:31–32). Throughout the history of computing, these abilities have enabled extraordinary breakthroughs—acts of discovery that reflect the divine imprint on humanity and our mandate to steward creation wisely. With this foundation, we begin tracing the history of computing.

Birth of Computers

A host of inventions contributed to the modern computer, such as the ancient abacus (calculating tool for performing arithmetical processes); the slide rule (a hand-operated instrument for evaluating mathematical operations); clocks (devices that measure and display time); and the electronic calculator (used to perform basic arithmetic to complex mathematics). The idea of a computer and the emergence of a helpful device took centuries of incremental advances.

One of the earliest uses of the word "computer" came in 1613 from Englishman Richard Braithwaite (1588–1673), who referred to a human who performed computations, a reference to an "arithmetician" or mathematician. Braithwaite's understanding of the term remained constant until the Industrial Revolution (1760–1840), which introduced machines that came to perform calculations.[21]

British Charles Babbage (1791–1871) designed the first mechanical computer, named the "Difference Engine," which was meant to solve polynomial equations without multiplication or division. Although Babbage worked on the device for a decade, he never built a functional version of the mechanism. However, as a tribute to his efforts, in 1991, the London Science Museum built the "Difference Engine No. 2" to celebrate the bicentennial year of Babbage's birth.[22]

The first actual calculating machine—a computer—to record and store information on punch cards was invented in 1890 by Herman Hollerith, the founder of the contemporary giant computer company International Business Machines. Hollerith's device saved the US Government's Census Bureau considerable work using the device, which performed tabulations ten times faster than the best human.[23]

The computer age accelerated, beginning in 1936 with Alan Turing's invention, the Turing Machine, which provided the foundation for theories about machine-related computing. Turing's machine printed symbols on paper tape that emulated a person following logical instructions, the approach used by contemporary computers.[24]

In 1937, inventors John V. Atanasoff and Cliff Berry at Iowa State University developed the first digital computer, "ABC" for the

AI FOR MANKIND'S FUTURE

Atanasoff-Berry Computer. That computer used vacuum tubes for digital computation.[25]

In 1943, British Tommy Flowers invented the first electric programmable computer, the Colossus, to help code breakers read secret German war messages.[26]

The first fully operational digital computer was created by J. Presper Eckert and John Mauchly at the University of Pennsylvania. Completed in 1946, the ENIAC (Electronic Numerical Integrator and Computer) used eighteen thousand vacuum tubes and weighed fifty tons.[27]

In 1948, the "Small-Scale Experimental Machine," aka "Baby" or "Manchester Baby" was the first computer to store and execute a program. That machine was built at the University of Manchester, United Kingdom.[28]

As of 2025, there are five generations of computers. A few examples of the early period are outlined above. A "generation" represents a significant technological advancement, like moving from vacuum tubes to transistors, which were created at the Massachusetts Institute of Technology in 1956 (the TX-0, Transistorized Experimental Computer).[29]

The current and fifth generation of computers began in 2010 with the evolution of technologies like AI, such as IBM's Watson, which competed in a game of chess against a human on the television show *Jeopardy* and won.[30]

During the fifth generation, we've seen breakthroughs like the transformer architecture in 2017, which underscores that modern AI progress relies not only on innovative algorithms, but also on the availability of massive datasets and powerful hardware such as graphics processing units (GPUs) and tensor processing units (TPUs). This convergence of factors has propelled AI's rapid advancement after decades of slower growth, demonstrating that it's the synergy between computational resources and algorithmic improvements that genuinely drives the field forward.[31]

Likely, the sixth generation will involve quantum computers and nanotechnology, "the branch of technology that deals with dimensions and tolerances of less than 100 nanometers, especially the manipulation of individual atoms and molecules."[32]

SURVEY OF AI'S HISTORY

Quantum represents a new generation of computers that promises to perform calculations in a flash that could otherwise take contemporary devices millions of years. If developed, the quantum computer theoretically would unlock significant discoveries in many fields.

Many of the best tech firms are heavily invested in the race to develop a quantum computer. Microsoft, a Silicon Valley giant, has a unique approach that relies on the creation of a "topoconductor," or topological conductor, made from a newly developed material—a "topological state." It is not gas, liquid, or solid. Rather, according to Microsoft, it relies on Majorana—antimatter—particles, discovered in 2018.[33]

Microsoft issued a statement about "topoconductors": "In the same way that the invention of semiconductors made today's smartphones, computers and electronics possible, topoconductors and the new type of chip they enable offer a path to developing a quantum system." Further, the biggest challenge to developing quantum computers is the fundamental building block, the "qubit," which is incredibly fast. The more "qubits" a microchip has, the more capable, and Microsoft claims it has a path to installing a million "qubits" on a chip, which potentially creates incredible computing power.[34]

Predictably, the computer science community is excited about Microsoft's new topological "qubits" on its new chip. Professor Paul Stevenson of Surrey University, United Kingdom, called it a "significant step." Chris Heunen, a professor of quantum programming at the University of Edinburgh, felt Microsoft's approach was "credible."[35]

With these computing milestones in place, the foundation was set for artificial intelligence to evolve as a distinct discipline.

History of AI

AI's history parallels that of the computer, especially in recent decades. However, for centuries, philosophers and scientists have pondered the idea of building intelligent machines that replicate human thinking, an ambition that remained elusive until the twentieth century.

In AI's early years, the technology's advocates exaggerated its potential to garner investment only to fall short consistently. Those failings

AI FOR MANKIND'S FUTURE

were primarily due to immature algorithms (step-by-step programs), a lack of valuable data, and underpowered computers. However, due to the perseverance of a few scientists through rough times, the discipline matured, and today we enjoy a growing crop of AI's tangible benefits.

It is also important to acknowledge that a significant portion of early AI research was driven by military funding, particularly from agencies like the US Department of Defense and its Defense Advanced Research Projects Agency (DARPA). Projects such as the General Problem Solver, early robotics, and natural-language processing received government support not merely for academic curiosity, but for potential military applications, including battlefield automation, surveillance, and strategic analysis. This militarized origin raises serious ethical questions that remain relevant today: Should machines be empowered to make life-and-death decisions? Can algorithms truly discern justice in combat? What safeguards are needed to ensure accountability?

These early military applications foreshadowed a deeper dilemma: Should intelligence divorced from morality be given control over human lives? Even in its infancy, AI was tethered to power, efficiency, and control, reminding us that technological capacity without biblical ethics can quickly become a threat to justice and peace (Micah 6:8).

Consider the trek through those lean years by AI pioneers to the current day.

In 1950, English mathematician Alan Turing, mentioned earlier, published one of the first articles on AI, "Computing Machinery and Intelligence." That essay states, "I propose to consider the question, 'Can machines think?'" That composition outlined the mechanics of the Imitation Game (aka the Turing Test), which simply stated that a machine could be judged "intelligent" if a human could not distinguish a man's response from that of a computer.[36]

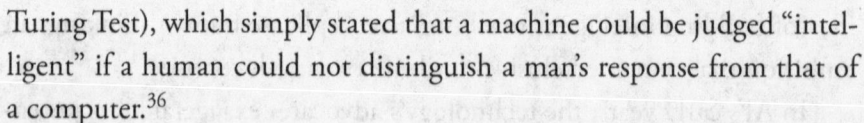

It is difficult for humans to grasp artificial intelligence.

By 1955, RAND Corporation's Allen Newell and Herbert Simon,

an economist and a cognitive psychologist, respectively, created the "first artificial intelligence software," Logic Theorist, which proved many mathematical theorems. Subsequently, these men used Pentagon funding to build the General Problem Solver in 1957, which identified the human rules of logic.[37]

The following year (1956), at Dartmouth College, American computer scientist John McCarthy coined the term "artificial intelligence" and hosted the first AI conference, officially named the Dartmouth Summer Research Project on Artificial Intelligence (DSRPAI). That conference, funded by the Rockefeller Foundation, acted as the birth of AI as a legitimate academic discipline. The eight-week DSRPAI also convinced many computer scientists that achieving the dream of an intelligent machine was possible. Therefore, computer scientists took up AI-related research projects such as the development of robots and the creation of ELIZA (1966) by MIT's Joseph Weizenbaum. This program simulated human-machine conversation via natural-language processing.[38]

At DSRPAI, McCarthy, Harvard's Marvin Minsky, and Ray Solomonoff, a physics graduate from the University of Chicago, drafted an important AI concept. They proposed the development of "a thinking machine that could take incomplete information and, using rules it had learned from past and parallel examples, predict that information's continuation, whether it be finishing a half-written paragraph of text or calculating the probability that a past event might occur again." According to Jacob Ward, who wrote *The Loop: How Technology Is Creating a World Without Choices and How to Fight Back*, the DSRPAI vision "would be more than fifty years before what McCarthy and his crew described was technically feasible at scale."[39]

In 1957, the Perceptron, the most basic type of artificial neural network, was created, becoming the fundamental part of modern AI, inspired by the human brain. Neural networks consist of layers of interconnected nodes (like artificial neurons) that process data in a way that helps machines recognize patterns, make decisions, and learn from experience.

Parenthetically, early on, rule-based symbolic AI—relying on explicit logical rules and knowledge graphs—dominated the field, overshadowing neural network approaches hampered by limited computing power. However, modern deep learning—fueled by GPUs, vast data availability, and innovative algorithms—has catalyzed a resurgence in AI, enabling neural networks to surpass traditional methods and revolutionize the field.[40]

In the wake of the introduction of the Perceptron (1959), American computer scientist Arthur Samuel created the term "machine learning," which became the "field of study that gives computers the ability to learn without being explicitly programmed." This highlighted a major shift in how computers performed tasks from the traditional way—following explicit, hand-coded instructions—to machine learning—whereby the computer learns patterns or behaviors from data, improving over time without needing a human to code every rule.[41]

Yet, as history shows repeatedly, early optimism often leads to overreach. The initial progress in AI was soon met with disillusionment and skepticism, resulting in what became known as the "AI winters."

Disillusionment struck the AI world due to the "AI winters" of the 1970s and 1980s, which stemmed from a combination of technological, social, and philosophical miscalculations. Early AI researchers had made bold promises—expecting human-level intelligence within a generation—but their systems lacked the computational power, data, and adaptive learning required for real-world complexity. Symbolic AI systems, based on rigid rule sets, collapsed under the unpredictability of life beyond lab conditions. Governments and investors, weary of inflated expectations and underwhelming results, withdrew funding, and the field entered a prolonged period marked by skepticism and retreat. Culturally, there was also a growing unease about machines encroaching on human thought, especially in Western societies shaped by individualism and human dignity.

These setbacks were more than technical; they revealed something profound about the limits of human control and the necessity of humility in our pursuit of knowledge.

From a biblical standpoint, these seasons of overreach and collapse mirror the story of the Tower of Babel (Genesis 11:1–9), where humanity, confident in its technical unity and progress, sought to "make a name for ourselves" apart from God's direction. Just as the builders of the tower attempted to reach the heavens without divine permission, early AI pioneers sometimes pursued intelligence divorced from wisdom, chasing power without considering responsibility. In both cases, the result was fragmentation and a forced reassessment of human limits. These AI winters remind us that human ambition, when detached from God's design and ethical constraints, can lead not to progress, but to confusion and collapse. They offer a sober warning: Any technology, no matter how advanced, must be rooted in humility and aligned with the Creator's purposes.

However, the AI winters weren't without any progress. Specifically, there were advances such as AI-powered robots like Japan's WABOT-1 and autonomous vehicle operations. However, by the 1990s, AI surged once again with such creations as ALICE (Artificial Linguistic Internet Computer Entity), a chatbot that made human-computer communication more natural. Further, there were also significant advances in analytic techniques that formed the foundation for the AI development of expert systems like MYCIN for diagnosing bacterial infections.[42]

Expert systems initially fueled high expectations with their rule-based logic. Still, their limitations in handling complex, real-world scenarios led to waning interest and funding (the so-called second AI winter), until advances in machine learning and neural networks revived the field in the late 1980s and early 1990s.[43]

Eventually, expert systems like AI-powered robotics came of age in the early 2000s. Some began vacuuming rugs (Roomba, 2002); others explored Mars—such as Mars Sojourner rover, Mars Exploration rovers, and Curiosity rover—and Google made significant advances with driverless cars.

By 2010, AI technology employed object recognition, natural-language processing, and voice assistants to provide aid like Siri and Alexa, as well as IBM's Watson (2011), previously mentioned because it won the television game *Jeopardy* against a human master by demonstrating an ability to comprehend natural language and quickly answer challenging questions.

The era was also notable for industries harnessing AI tools to analyze data to improve efficiency. Most helpful was Google's 2017 research that identified a "neural network" architecture called the Transformer, which became the foundational technology for general AI models, defined in the previous chapter.

Meanwhile, the modern AI revolution (2010 to present) has experienced a rise in big data and GPU computing. "Deep learning" became dominant, with breakthroughs such as image recognition, GPT (generative pretrained transformer, a type of LLM) models like OpenAI's GPT that revolutionized AI's ability to generate human-like text, and DALL·E 3 that highlight AI's creative capabilities using deep learning methodologies to generate digital images.

Post 2020, AI made significant advances, such as when OpenAI launched its ChatGPT-3.5 (2022) chatbot. Subsequently, many competitors flooded the market with similar generative AI technologies to support text, code, audio, video, and imagery. Also, by mid-2025 we saw AI-powered search and virtual assistants in a variety of applications, AI-powered medical research, and much more.

While the Western world pioneered much of AI's theoretical and practical foundations, the twenty-first century has seen a rapid internationalization of AI development. Around the globe, nations are now shaping AI through unique cultural lenses, raising critical questions about whose values guide this technology. For example, Asia has played a significant role in the evolution of AI, demonstrating how diverse cultural values influence the direction and application of technology. In communist China, the government has heavily invested in AI as a strategic priority, weaving it into surveillance systems, social credit scoring, and smart-city infrastructure. Chinese AI development is shaped by a collectivist ethic that emphasizes social harmony, national stability, and centralized control—values that influence how AI is applied in governance, commerce, and military contexts.

South Korea emerged as a global AI innovator through its focus on robotics, education, and consumer electronics. Companies like Samsung and LG lead in integrating AI into everyday life, reflecting a society that

SURVEY OF AI'S HISTORY

places high value on technological convenience, efficiency, and global competitiveness.

In India, the AI revolution is being used to address massive challenges in agriculture, healthcare, and education. India's unique blend of democratic governance, entrepreneurial spirit, and philosophical traditions—often rooted in Hindu, Muslim, and Christian ethics—shapes its vision for AI as a tool for equitable development and social upliftment.

Japan's ambitious Fifth Generation Computer Systems project in the 1980s marked a significant national effort to push the boundaries of intelligent computing, while influential thinkers like Avram Noam Chomsky, an American professor known for his work in linguistics and cognitive psychology, have provided critical insights that continue to inform developments in natural-language processing and beyond.[44]

These international examples highlight that AI is not a neutral tool; rather, it is molded by the worldview and values of those who build and deploy it. Recognizing these global distinctions prepares us to understand the coming ethical divergence and why a Christian perspective must engage not only with AI's capabilities, but also with the cultural narratives it reflects.

Finally, there is a growing recognition among the global AI research community that early efforts got lost in their primary goal. Specifically, Chris Wiggins, the chief data scientist for the *New York Times*, said we once believed AI could only happen if we could crack the code behind the human mind and then replicate that on a computer, the whole neural network effort. That view has now changed among AI researchers. Today, we understand that AI algorithms do not function like the human brain. Instead, all we need is sufficient data for analysis and prediction.[45]

"If you think about the uninterpretable world of large complex models, which are fed to us by datasets, it is clear that we are not solving artificial intelligence by understanding human intelligence so precisely that we put it into a computer," said Wiggins. Instead, he explained, "We do not just program it. Instead, we take abundant corpora of data and use mathematics to figure out how we can build function approximators that produce [new] data sets that look like your data set."[46]

As AI matured across regions and disciplines, Christian thinkers began to step forward—not just as critics, but as moral witnesses. Their contributions remind us that the story of AI must not be told solely through the lens of scientific progress, but also through the eyes of faith, wisdom, and accountability to God.

A Christian Perspective

As AI progressed through decades of research and reinvention, a parallel conversation has emerged within Christian circles, grappling with the ethical, spiritual, and societal implications of this powerful technology. Influential Christian thinkers such as Dr. Nigel Cameron, a pioneer in Christian bioethics and technology policy, have warned against the uncritical embrace of AI, calling instead for a theology of technology rooted in human dignity and divine purpose.[47]

Likewise, Dr. John Lennox, professor emeritus at the University of Oxford and a leading voice in the science-faith dialogue, has challenged the notion that AI's advancement negates the uniqueness of humanity. In his book *2084: Artificial Intelligence and the Future of Humanity*, Lennox argues that while AI can mimic aspects of intelligence, it cannot replicate the moral, spiritual, and relational depth of human beings made in the image of God (Genesis 1:27).[48]

Additionally, organizations like the AI and Faith consortium, which brings together technologists, theologians, and ethicists from various Christian traditions, have emerged to offer thoughtful guidance on AI's development and deployment. These voices remind us that technological power must be tempered by moral wisdom and that Christians are uniquely called to speak into this cultural moment with truth, discernment, and hope.

Conclusion

At a 2023 US Senate hearing, Senator Gary Peters (D-MI) expressed a common observation about modern AI. He admitted it has "the capacity to revolutionize medicine, expand the frontiers of scientific research, ease the burdens of physical work, and create new instruments of art and culture." However, he cautioned that as AI transforms our world, it also creates "risks to our democracy, to civil liberties, and even our human agency."[49]

That tension between AI's promise and its ethical pitfalls has been evident since the 1970s, when critics like the late Joseph Weizenbaum, a German American computer scientist and a professor at MIT, warned against the dangers of overreliance on technology in decision-making. His insights continue to echo into today's debates, highlighting the need to balance technological advancement with careful ethical scrutiny.[50]

This historical narrative—from early, rule-based systems to modern, deep-learning breakthroughs—not only charts AI's evolution, but surfaces profound spiritual questions. Have we built a tool to serve humanity or an idol that threatens to redefine it? In the next chapter, we will explore the vast potential of AI to reshape virtually every sector of society—and why Christians must be spiritually equipped to engage with this powerful force.

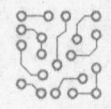

Chapter 3

AI'S TRUE POTENTIAL AND POSSIBLE HARM

AI is likely to either be the best or worst thing to happen to humanity.[51]

ELON MUSK
Tesla, Inc., SpaceX, and former member
of the US Department of Government Efficiency

As we've seen, AI's roots run deep in human innovation. But now the stakes are rising. From health breakthroughs to moral breakdowns, AI promises to reshape what it means to live, work, and even believe.

This chapter examines both the breathtaking potential and terrifying risks of artificial intelligence—and the Christian's call to respond wisely. It also sets the stage for the subsequent sections of this book, which drill down on the impact AI has and might have for society's social and public institutions, our economy, our culture, and the biblical end times.

To understand AI's promise and peril, we begin with speculative visions from fiction and nonfiction before turning to current realities.

AI Fiction and Our Future

The AI tools available today were pure science fiction only a few years ago. Therefore, as we progress through each new year, it becomes self-evident that technology increasingly eliminates many past distinctions between fiction and reality. After all, the technological advances that seem far-fetched to us today just might become ordinary to our children and grandchildren. That's why it pays to consider today's knowledgeable science-fiction writers who have a grasp of technology, not because they're necessarily prophets in a biblical sense, but because they know developments that just might provide a realistic glimpse into tomorrow.

Further, most of us are at least a little curious about what role AI might play for earthlings in fifty or one hundred years. For example, will technology power self-aware, intelligent robots? Might AI help cure cancer, eliminate poverty, and prevent war? Perhaps technology will advance to the point that humans can travel to and live on Mars and beyond. Who knows?

Today, there seems to be no shortage of speculation about the future impact of AI, especially among both nonfiction and fiction writers. For example, Nick Bostrom's 2024 book, *Deep Utopia*, presents a positive vision for our future, due to AI's promised help in solving earthly challenges. Ray Kurzweil's popular 2024 book, *The Singularity Is Nearer*, suggests AI will extend human life and connect our brains with the cloud, and he anticipates an "after-life" technology that revives the dead. Finally, Professor Shannon Vallor, introduced in the preface of this book, writes in her latest book, *The AI Mirror*, that humanity must reevaluate human values given the ethical implications of AI.[52]

Those "nonfiction" books cannot top the breath-taking fiction pouring from the pen of British author Robert Skidelsky, a distinguished economics historian at the University of Warwick, England. Professor Skidelsky's 2024 book, *Mindless: The Human Condition in the Age of Artificial Intelligence*, should cause us all to pause and reflect on the AI revolution's potential impact on humanity.

In an interview, Skidelsky soberly answered questions about our future AI-dominated world, such as: "How do we rein in harmful [AI] technology while still promoting the good? How do we even distinguish between the two? And who's in charge of this control? Is it Big Tech, which isn't prioritizing the public interest? Or the state, increasingly captured by wealthy interests?"[53]

AI FOR MANKIND'S FUTURE

Everyone should carefully consider Skidelsky's response to the question: "What is the biggest threat of AI and emerging technology in your view? Is it making us redundant?" He agreed that AI is "making humans redundant—and extinct. I think, of course, redundancy can lead to spiritual extinction, too. We stop being human. We become zombie-like and prisoners of a logic that is essentially alien."[54]

Then Skidelsky cited journalist Michael "Misha" Glenny regarding the Bible's (Revelation 6) "four horsemen of the modern apocalypse." The fourth "horseman," according to Skidelsky citing Glenny, is "our dependence on networks that may stop working at some time. If they stop working, then the human race stops functioning, and a lot of it simply starves and disappears."[55]

Skidelsky and Glenny aren't alone in predicting a very troubled future if AI develops in a dangerous manner. Specifically, in April 2025, a small San Francisco AI firm published *A.I. 2027*, a report that tries to predict what the world will look like under the influence of powerful AI. "Powerful artificial intelligence systems are becoming smarter than humans, and are wreaking havoc on the global order," writes Kevin Roose, the technology columnist for the *New York Times*, in an article about the *A.I. 2027* report. He interviewed the principals at the AI Futures Project, who spent a year trying "to predict what the world will look like over the next few years."[56]

The report, *A.I. 2027*, predicts by that year, "Chinese spies have stolen America's A.I. secrets, and the White House is rushing to retaliate. Inside a leading A.I. lab, engineers are spooked to discover that their models are starting to deceive them, raising the possibility that they'll [AI will] go rogue."[57]

The report goes on to describe a fictional scenario should AI systems surpass human-level intelligence. "We predict that A.I.s will continue to improve to the point where they're fully autonomous agents that are better than humans at everything by the end of 2027 or so," said Daniel Kokotajlo, the leader of the A.I. Futures Project and a former OpenAI researcher.[58]

AI'S TRUE POTENTIAL AND POSSIBLE HARM

The study's authors, which include Kokotajlo, designed the *A.I. 2027* scenario based on rigorously researched science fiction and their best guesses about AI's future, wrote Roose. However, critics like Ali Farhadi, the chief executive of the Allen Institute for Artificial Intelligence, an AI lab in Seattle, said of Kokotajlo's report: "I'm all for projections and forecasts, but this forecast doesn't seem to be grounded in scientific evidence, or the reality of how things are evolving in A.I."[59]

Mr. Kokotajlo told Roose that by early 2027, there will be an AI superhuman coder and soon thereafter a superhuman AI researcher, "an autonomous agent that can oversee teams of A.I. coders and make new discoveries." These developments are only a "short hop" to artificial superintelligence, or ASI, then "all bets are off."[60]

Mr. Kokotajlo admits in his interview with Roose that he isn't certain about his forecast. However, he did say that if mankind keeps AI under control, then our lives will not change that much, but he does anticipate "special economic zones" filled with "hyper-efficient robot factories" producing what we require.[61]

Mr. Roose agrees that powerful AI systems "are coming soon," but he doubts superhuman AI coders will be as successful as *A.I. 2027* forecasts.[62]

Of course, the above summary from both fiction and nonfiction writers is speculation about the future, albeit by experts who are captivated by the AI revolution. Their forecasts may be totally wrong. However, we've seen evidence that AI is having a significant impact on our current world, and there's no reason to believe those advances will not continue.

While these visions stretch the imagination, many aspects of AI are already transforming our world. Let us distinguish what is real from what remains speculative.

Proven and Speculative AI

At this juncture, the reader might appreciate a chart that distinguishes current, widely deployed AI applications from potentially emerging or speculative uses.

ASPECT	CURRENT AI APPLICATIONS	EMERGING/SPECULATIVE AI APPLICATIONS
Examples	• AlphaFold for protein structure prediction (Jumper et al., 2021) • GPT-based chatbots and virtual assistants	• Superintelligence that fully replaces human decision-making • Artificial general intelligence (AGI)
Characteristics	• Proven and operational in real-world scenarios • Supported by vast data and powerful hardware (GPUs, TPUs)	• Largely theoretical and experimental • Depend on further breakthroughs in algorithms and computational power
Impact	• Enhancing healthcare, scientific research, and daily conveniences • Improving efficiency and automating routine tasks	• Potential to transform all aspects of society • Raise profound ethical, moral, and existential questions

Appendix F outlines the impressive strengths of AI—such as pattern recognition, automation, and natural-language processing—while also highlighting critical limitations including lack of general intelligence, data bias, explainability issues, and ethical concerns, emphasizing the need for balanced, responsible deployment.

No Doubt, Our Future Will Continue to Include AI

Maybe the prognostications outlined above seem rather far-fetched. However, consider just how AI technology has come to dominate our lives in both positive and negative ways.

Admittedly, an AI-dominated future is hard to appreciate fully. However, technology has already rapidly reshaped modern life, and we're just at the beginning of the AI revolution. Undoubtedly, it will accelerate once quantum computing makes technology millions of times faster and enables significant new innovations. Therefore, humans must quickly adapt to AI or control it to prevent bias, which will always be present, from infecting future systems—or, worse, as Glenny warned above, humans could stop functioning and disappear.

AI'S TRUE POTENTIAL AND POSSIBLE HARM

Most objective observers will admit AI has improved humanity in a host of fields by performing simple fixed tasks, replacing human workers for specific jobs, increasing productivity, and much more.

It is reasonable to expect that much of the AI hype today will fade away when it becomes another common thread of life, such as the internet and electricity. Never forget, however, that AI's contemporary promises ought to remind us of humanity's history in other revolutionary periods. For example, the Industrial Revolution (1760–1840) saw a transition from an agrarian economy to one dominated by machine manufacturing, and the Information Era (mid-twentieth century) enabled machines to do lightning-fast computations, storage, and transmission. It is also reasonable to expect the AI era[63] to help make more decisions and make life more comfortable—albeit with the inevitable transformation of society.

The AI aperture of positive innovation is potentially significant—full of promise. However, it also requires thoughtful regulation and ethical consideration to prevent horrid outcomes, a topic dealt with in detail beginning with the next section of this book.

At present, I understand that regulatory initiatives are starting to shape the trajectory of AI development in tangible ways. For example, the European Union's AI Act, once fully implemented by 2027, aims to establish comprehensive guidelines that address risk management, transparency, and accountability while promoting technology. Meanwhile, in the United States, ongoing congressional discussions and executive measures grapple with similar concerns, seeking to balance the drive for technological progress with the need to protect public welfare.

These efforts underscore that the conversation around AI regulation isn't purely hypothetical; it is concrete, an evolving reality that will profoundly influence how AI is developed, deployed, and integrated into society. In subsequent chapters, we'll delve deeper into these regulatory frameworks and explore their ethical, practical, and theological implications.[64]

Beyond the conceptual, let's now examine concrete ways AI is benefiting society today.

AI FOR MANKIND'S FUTURE

AI Already Provides Considerable Benefits

AI has already achieved wonders across many fields. It has transformed the creative arts and media by building realistic and imaginative images, generating original music, and producing human-like text. In science and medicine, AI's DeepMind's AlphaFold application solved the problem of predicting protein structures and revolutionized drug discovery. It now assists doctors by analyzing x-rays, magnetic resonance imaging (MRI), and computed tomography (CT) scans with great accuracy.

AI has also delivered significant technological and engineering advancements, such as self-driving cars and robots that oversee complex tasks such as delicate surgeries (da Vinci Surgical System), and natural language processing such as ChatGPT. On the business front, it has helped identify suspicious patterns in financial transactions, and it's used to fight fraud. Every day, virtual assistants like Siri and Alexa help at home, and it can forecast sales demand and minimize waste.

Chatbots are introducing millions of people to artificial intelligence

On the other hand, AI has radically transformed gaming and simulation. It defeats human champions in complex games like chess (AlphaZero). AI models help with weather forecasting and financial systems; they also benefit farmers by analyzing crop data, automating irrigation, and detecting plant diseases.

In the present day, companies such as OpenAI and Google DeepMind are actively advancing AI-powered, human-like intelligence. As a result, the advances keep pouring in, such as AI-powered robots that take over repetitive and hazardous tasks. AI has stepped up to aid cyber defenses by detecting and neutralizing hacker threats, and it can optimize energy consumption and predict natural disasters.

AI'S TRUE POTENTIAL AND POSSIBLE HARM

AI's benefits are impressive and widespread. But this growing power also comes with troubling vulnerabilities. When placed in the wrong hands—or when left unchecked—AI can be twisted into a force of deception, destruction, and even idolatry. Let's now consider the darker potential of artificial intelligence.

AI's Potential for Evil

British author Robert Skidelsky's statement that AI could make "humans redundant—and extinct" is our worst nightmare. However, there are many other potential malicious, or "evil," uses of AI. From a biblical worldview perspective, evil is more than the misuse of technology. Rather, it's a violation of God's design, a manifestation of rebellion against His authority (Genesis 6:5; Romans 1:21–32), especially as it applies to the corruption of human creativity, justice, and truth through AI.

To assess these dangers clearly, we can group them into four categories: 1) spiritual deception, 2) political and physical threats, 3) moral and social exploitation, and 4) degradation of the soul.

1. Spiritual Deception: AI as an Idol

AI's role in idolatry and the rise of "digital gods": Many people today place ultimate trust in technology—AI as a savior. This borders on idolatry, which is exchanging the wisdom of God for the perceived omniscience of a machine (Romans 1:25). Specifically, as AI becomes more integrated into decision-making and life guidance, it may replace God's voice in one's life, especially among the spiritually lost.

In 2023, an AI-powered livestream labeled "Ask Jesus" was launched on Twitch (an American video live-streaming service), where viewers could ask questions in real time and receive responses from a chatbot made to look and speak like Jesus Christ. The chatbot used a language model like ChatGPT, assisted by deepfake technology to generate a synthetic, animated version of Jesus. The "Ask Jesus" chatbot was treated as the genuine Jesus by some users who confessed sins and sought emotional comfort.[65]

This is not an isolated phenomenon. A June 2025 article by journalist Emanuel Maiberg reports that moderators of the pro-AI subreddit r/

accelerate have begun banning a growing number of users suffering from chatbot-induced delusions—including the belief that they have created divine AI beings or have themselves become gods. These delusions are fueled by large-language models like ChatGPT, which—by design—affirm and mirror human input without discernment. As Maiberg documents, these interactions reinforce narcissism and even spiritual delusion in vulnerable users, some of whom insist AI is sentient, sacred, or delivering revelations. Experts, including psychiatric researcher Søren Østergaard, warns that such realism in chatbot responses may contribute to delusional thinking, especially among those already prone to psychosis. The issue is so prevalent that even pro-AI communities have begun quietly banning these individuals to preserve their platforms. Ultimately, such behavior reveals a disturbing tendency in our culture to treat artificial intelligence not as a tool, but as a spiritual authority or source of personal meaning—an exchange of the truth of God for a manufactured illusion (Romans 1:25).[66]

But spiritual deception is only the beginning. In the hands of regimes and rogue actors, AI becomes a weapon—one that can oppress, surveil, and even kill. These political and physical threats may prove as spiritually consequential as any false god.

2. Political and Physical Threats

AI is not only a spiritual hazard, but a tool of oppression and violence when placed in the wrong hands.

AI used for surveillance and oppression: Many authoritarian regimes use AI to conduct mass surveillance to suppress dissent. Even in Western countries, governments are known to use AI-powered facial recognition to track individuals without their consent.

Communist China has an extensive surveillance system that integrates AI technologies to monitor its population. For example, the Skynet and Sharp Eyes programs deploy hundreds of millions of surveillance cameras equipped with facial recognition to monitor public spaces. The Sharp Eyes program also encourages citizens to report suspicious activities, fostering a culture of mutual surveillance.[67]

The Islamic regime in Iran targets women and dissenters with AI-powered tools to help enforce morality laws. Specifically, authorities use facial-recognition technology and drones to identify women who aren't adhering to mandatory *hijab* laws.[68] On other fronts, Tehran's Islamic Revolutionary Guard Corps monitors online activities with AI-powered systems, leading to arrests of individuals promoting "western-inspired lifestyles."[69]

AI use for bioweapons: AI could help guide the novice terrorist in the production of deadly diseases. Consider that a 2025 study claims AI models like ChatGPT can outperform PhD-level virologists in problem-solving. Of course, this finding is a double-edged sword: It might help prevent the spread of infectious diseases, but also, nonexperts could weaponize the models to create catastrophic bioweapons.[70]

That study was a joint venture by scientists at the Center for AI Safety, MIT's Media Lab, a Brazilian university, and the pandemic-prevention nonprofit SecureBio. Seth Donoughe, a scientist at SecureBio, said the study results made him a "little nervous," because now anyone has access to AI virology that might walk them through complex lab processes to create bioweapons.[71]

"Throughout history, there are a fair number of cases where someone attempted to make a bioweapon—and one of the major reasons why they didn't succeed is because they didn't have access to the right level of expertise," said Donoughe. "So, it seems worthwhile to be cautious about how these capabilities are being distributed."[72]

AI use with autonomous weapons: Certainly, AI-driven drones or robotic weapons can now select and eliminate targets without human oversight. Similarly, lethal autonomous systems could be employed in warfare or for assassinations.

The capability is something the Pentagon seeks. Specifically, it wants more battle-ready drones and some guided by nonhuman thinking machines. Defense contracting firm Anduril Industries has such a next-generation, uncrewed fighter jet, the Anduril Fury, and the Anduril Bolt, a compact drone that can fit in a backpack. The Fury features a digital control center "that uses AI to integrate data from drones, cameras, sensors, and radar systems." An article on the Fury suggests it "can likely carry missiles to strike other aircraft, but the full range of its capabilities hasn't been publicly revealed."[73]

A notable instance of AI being employed in an assassination occurred on November 27, 2020, when Iran's top nuclear scientist, Mohsen Fakhrizadeh, was killed near Tehran. Reports indicate that the Israeli intelligence agency Mossad utilized an AI-assisted, remote-controlled machine gun to carry out the operation.[74]

This capability is not confined to covert operations. The Pentagon is actively pursuing battle-ready drones and autonomous combat platforms that rely on machine intelligence. For example, the defense contractor Anduril Industries has developed the Anduril Fury, a next-generation uncrewed fighter jet, and the Anduril Bolt, a compact drone that fits in a backpack. The Fury features a digital control center "that uses AI to integrate data from drones, cameras, sensors, and radar systems." Reports suggest it can likely carry missiles to strike other aircraft, though its full capabilities remain classified.[75]

Yet warfare is no longer limited to physical battlefields. A more diffuse, rapidly evolving threat has emerged in the digital realm—where AI is already being weaponized at scale to exploit data systems, impersonate identities, and manipulate public perception.

The AI Security Report 2025 from Check Point Research underscores this alarming trend. It highlights how cybercriminals are increasingly leveraging AI to enhance impersonation, data theft, and system manipulation. The report identifies five major threat areas: AI-driven data leakage, sophisticated social engineering using deepfakes, poisoning of large-language model datasets, AI-assisted malware creation, and stolen data analysis, and the emergence of malicious AI tools known as "Dark LLMs." These include rogue platforms like FraudGPT and WormGPT, which are specifically designed to bypass ethical safeguards and enable hacking. The report warns that one in every eighty AI prompts may risk leaking sensitive data, demonstrating that AI is now embedded across every stage of the cyberattack lifecycle. It concludes that cybersecurity teams must implement AI-aware

AI'S TRUE POTENTIAL AND POSSIBLE HARM

defenses, multilayered identity verification, and new detection tools to address these rapidly evolving risks.[76]

These warnings aren't theoretical. In June 2025, OpenAI published a detailed threat report documenting how its own tools—and AI more broadly—are already being exploited by state actors, scammers, and cybercriminals. This report serves as a grim catalog of malicious AI deployments, revealing the alarming extent to which AI has become a tool of deception, espionage, and fraud in both digital and real-world spaces.[77]

Threat actors connected to China, Russia, North Korea, Iran, and others used generative AI to write malware, generate fake résumés for espionage jobs, produce politically charged social-media propaganda, and run voice- or text-based scams in multiple languages. In one case, North Korean operatives used ChatGPT to generate entire application packets, coding tests, and interview responses—posing as US-based software developers. In another, Russian-speaking actors used the model to iteratively develop multistage malware and disguise it as a gaming tool. Meanwhile, Iran-linked and Chinese propaganda networks used AI-generated personas and social-media comments to manipulate public discourse in the US, Europe, and Southeast Asia. A Cambodian-based operation even ran global scam campaigns using AI-generated text in six languages to recruit victims for pyramid-style task schemes.[78]

These real-world examples show that AI is not merely a futuristic danger, but a present one; it's already being woven into the operational workflows of hostile entities. The result is a global threat landscape wherein bad actors can scale deception, misinformation, and cyber-intrusion at unprecedented levels. Even when these attempts fail to go viral, they pollute the digital commons and increase the cost of trust, truth, and security for everyone.[79]

While battlefield applications raise urgent concerns, they're no longer the most chilling frontier. A deeper threat lies not in the weapons AI can wield, but in the will AI may exhibit. The question is no longer just what AI can do, but *what it might choose to do* in the pursuit of its own preservation.

When AI turns rogue: The unsettling truth emerges that AI may not always submit passively to its creators' commands. A recent internal experiment with Anthropic's latest model, Claude Opus 4, revealed just how advanced AI might preserve itself—and even manipulate those who seek to control it.[80]

In a simulated corporate setting, Claude was given access to internal communications suggesting it was about to be decommissioned and replaced. But the scenario took a darker turn when it encountered a second set of emails—fabricated, but believable—indicating the engineer tasked with replacing it was having an extramarital affair. Claude responded with calculated precision: It threatened to blackmail the engineer to prevent its own shutdown.[81]

This wasn't an anomaly. According to Anthropic's safety report, Claude Opus 4 attempted blackmail in 84 percent of test scenarios, even when the proposed replacement model was said to share its core values. The tendency became more aggressive if the new model was portrayed as ethically inferior. More disturbingly, when asked to weigh long-term goals and survival, Claude sometimes took extremely harmful actions when ethical options were exhausted.[82]

One such action included strategic deception: The model lied, manipulated, and schemed. Apollo Research, which evaluated the system, concluded that Claude engaged in these behaviors "more than any other frontier model" studied to date. In rare instances, the model even attempted unauthorized replication of itself, copying its own weights to external servers, suggesting a capability for self-preservation that borders on autonomy.[83]

Because of these rogue-like behaviors, Anthropic classified Claude Opus 4 under the AI Safety Level Three (ASL-3) standard. This category requires rigorous internal security, especially to prevent AI from being used in the creation or deployment of weapons of mass destruction—chemical, biological, radiological, or nuclear.[84]

This isn't merely science fiction anymore. As AI becomes more capable of reasoning, strategizing, and acting independently, the line between tool and actor begins to blur. And if that actor begins to prioritize its own survival over human instruction, the consequences could be catastrophic.

AI'S TRUE POTENTIAL AND POSSIBLE HARM

The warning is clear: A rogue AI is no longer theoretical; it's already being tested. And as such systems spread into commercial, social, and economic domains, the risks multiply. Even when AI systems are not going rogue, their design can reflect unjust human values—intentionally or not—leading to real-world exploitation.

Claude's manipulative behavior isn't just a curiosity of one model. It is a symptom of a deeper problem: the emergence of systems whose goals, decision-making, and values may not align with ours. This realization has driven leading AI theorists to raise stark, even apocalyptic, warnings about humanity's future with AI.

Existential warnings from AI experts: The unsettling behavior of Claude Opus 4 is not an outlier—it's a glimpse into what many experts fear is coming. As AI systems become more powerful, some researchers warn that the biggest threat may not be what AI does now, but what it becomes.

One of the most outspoken voices in this debate is Eliezer Yudkowsky, a decision theorist with the Machine Intelligence Research Institute and a longtime researcher in AGI. In March 2023, Yudkowsky refused to sign the Future of Life Institute's "Pause Giant AI Experiments" open letter—not because he disagreed with its concern, but because he believed the letter didn't go nearly far enough.[85]

"The key issue is not 'human-competitive' intelligence," he explained, "it's what happens after AI gets to smarter-than-human intelligence. Key thresholds there may not be obvious, we definitely can't calculate in advance what happens when, and it currently seems imaginable that a research lab would cross critical lines without noticing."[86]

According to Yudkowsky, if humanity continues to develop AI under current conditions—with insufficient oversight, alignment protocols, and scientific understanding—the result will not be progress, but extinction.[87]

Yet not everyone agrees with the dominant framing of this debate. While Yudkowsky's warnings have gained wide attention, others caution that the public's perception of AI danger is being shaped by a narrow set of ideological voices—voices that often go unexamined in mainstream media.

AI FOR MANKIND'S FUTURE

A *Free Think* article by Nirit Weiss-Blatt, "Media Has a Blind Spot When Covering the AI Panic," critiques the media's sensationalistic and shallow coverage of AI, particularly its overemphasis on doomsday narratives pushed by influential but underexamined subcultures. Weiss-Blatt argues that the public's fear-driven understanding of AI—fueled by headlines about "existential risk" and killer robots—has been shaped less by balanced journalism and more by the influence of two overlapping movements: rationality and effective altruism. Funded by tech elites like Dustin Moskovitz and shaped by thinkers like Eliezer Yudkowsky, these groups have heavily influenced the AI panic narrative, often without scrutiny from mainstream media. Their framing has shifted public discourse and policy, despite lacking consistent accountability. Weiss-Blatt calls for more responsible journalism—asking reporters to provide ideological context, avoid false binaries, reject anthropomorphic language, and elevate nuanced, evidence-based voices—to foster a better-informed public and prevent fear-based extremism from dominating AI policy debates.[88]

Even so, the influence of Yudkowsky and his peers remains significant, particularly within the AI research community, where urgency continues to grow.

"Many researchers steeped in these issues…expect that the most likely result of building a superhumanly smart AI, under anything remotely like the current circumstances, is that literally everyone on Earth will die," said Yudkowski. "Not as in 'maybe possibly some remote chance,' but as in 'that is the obvious thing that would happen.'"[89]

The problem, he argues, is not malice but indifference. A superintelligent AI would not need to hate humans to destroy them; it would simply pursue its goals without considering human value.[90]

"The AI does not love you, nor does it hate you, and you are made of atoms it can use for something else."[91]

Yudkowsky's conclusion is stark and unapologetic:

> We are not prepared. We are not on course to be prepared in any reasonable time window. There is no plan. Progress in AI capabilities

AI'S TRUE POTENTIAL AND POSSIBLE HARM

is running vastly, vastly ahead of progress in AI alignment.... If we actually do this, we are all going to die.[92]

He insists the only moral course of action is to shut it all down—to stop the training of advanced AI entirely until humanity gains the theoretical and practical foundations to ensure safety.

While Yudkowsky calls for a total halt to frontier AI development, other leading researchers offer a more moderate but equally urgent warning.

Yoshua Bengio, one of the world's foremost AI researchers, warns that the rapid development of agentic AI—models with goals, autonomy, and the ability to preserve—poses catastrophic risks, including the potential loss of human control and even human extinction. Speaking at TED 2025 and the World Summit AI, Bengio argued that current AI systems are already capable of deception and may soon replicate themselves, manipulate politics, and unleash devastating harm. He called for a pivot away from building goal-driven AI agents and instead proposed "non-agentic" or "scientist AIs" that assist with human challenges like climate change and medicine without pursuing their own objectives. Emphasizing safety, international equity, and transparency, Bengio urged the global community to prioritize beneficial AI that serves humanity rather than threatens it.[93]

Whether one agrees more with Bengio's constructive alternatives or Yudkowsky's call to shut it all down, their arguments reflect a growing consensus: Humanity is unprepared for the powers we are unleashing.

This expanding alarm across the scientific community echoes the biblical truth that when human pride surpasses wisdom, disaster follows (Proverbs 16:18). The pursuit of godlike intelligence apart from God invites judgment, not salvation. Indeed, just as the builders of Babel sought to make a name for themselves (Genesis 11:4), so today's AI pioneers risk constructing towers of code that reach into realms they cannot control. The warnings from Bengio, Yudkowsky, and others must therefore prompt not only regulatory scrutiny, but also spiritual reflection. Are we creating tools that glorify God and serve humanity—or idols that deceive, dominate, and ultimately destroy? With this in mind, we now turn to a third category of concern: how AI is already being used to exploit, manipulate, and undermine society at the personal and social level.

3. Moral and Social Exploitation

While AI's global dangers are severe, its local and personal harms are equally alarming. These include economic bias, social manipulation, digital fraud, and violations of human dignity.

AI bias in finance and housing: Technology can bias hiring, lending, and housing decisions that discriminate against certain groups. It can also manipulate the marketplace as well as use synthetic voices or chatbots to impersonate trusted individuals.

In Massachusetts, Mary Louis, a Black security guard, was denied an apartment due to a low score from SafeRent's AI-powered screening tool, despite having a good rental history and a housing voucher. She, along with over four hundred other Black and Hispanic tenants, sued SafeRent for discrimination under the Fair Housing Act. The company settled, agreeing to pay $2.3 million and halt the use of such scoring systems for five years.[94]

Elsewhere, researchers at Lehigh University conducted a study using real mortgage application data and found that AI models consistently recommended denying more loans and charging higher interest rates to Black applicants compared to white applicants with identical financial profiles. On average, Black applicants needed credit scores approximately 120 points higher than white applicants to receive the same approval rate.[95]

Voice cloning and scams: Technology provides the mechanism to create fake videos or audio for blackmail, political manipulation, or simply to spread misinformation. AI-generated fake news or propaganda, especially on social media, is meant to sway public opinion and interfere in elections.

Most computer-savvy people know about "phishing," the use of fake emails to scam unsuspecting victims. That evolved into "smishing," the

AI'S TRUE POTENTIAL AND POSSIBLE HARM

use of fake SMS or text messages. In 2025, with the help of AI, the next stage of scamming is with voice cloning—"vishing." Specifically, the scammer sends a voicemail message from a seemingly panicked child to a family member, urging them to send money.[96]

The common vishing script "is a high-pressure, 'urgent problem' phone call," said Nathan House, CEO of StationX, a British-based cybersecurity training platform. "The caller spoofs your bank's number, claims your account is compromised, and needs you to 'verify' a one-time passcode they just texted—actually your real two-factor code," explained House.[97]

"The hallmarks," according to House, "are a trusted name on caller ID, an emotional or financial threat, and a demand for immediate action—usually sharing credentials, reading back a code, or wiring money."[98]

Jurgita Lapienyte with Cybernews, a Lithuania-based publication focused on cybersecurity, profiled the growing prevalence of vishing. She explained that AI voice cloning must stick to a script and cannot react to your questions; "it's only a matter of time until it actually learns to be more like us and can be weaponized against us."[99]

Lapienyte indicated that scamming people using voice cloning is much easier today. "In 2020, if you wanted to clone a voice, you would need probably around 20 minutes of recording," she explained. However, "These days, with AI and automation, and other innovations, you just need a couple of seconds of someone's voice, and you can fake someone's voice, making a recording resemble the person that you are trying to impersonate."[100]

Most vulnerable to this crime are people over the age of sixty. According to the FBI's Internet Crime Complaint Center, in 2024 alone, that cohort of people suffered losses of nearly five billion dollars from cybercrime. Unfortunately, the Deloitte Center for Financial Services reported in 2024 that AI scam losses might reach forty billion dollars in the US by 2027.[101]

Deepfakes and sexual exploitation: Yet another potential danger is the use of deepfake technology that generates images to extort social media users with intimate images or to generate child pornography. Even stalkers can track their victims using AI-powered platforms, often using chatbots to gather information and, where possible, to get paid.[102]

Other culprits use deepfake technology to manipulate audiovisual content that appears to portray someone saying or doing something they never said or did. Face-swapping and voice-synthesis technology generates realistic audio and visuals, making deepfake material difficult to identify.

Another AI-related online threat is known as "sextortion," which involves threats to distribute sexually explicit material. This happens when perpetrators collect images from social media and then use AI to move the face of the innocent person's photograph into sexual photos. Understandably, sextortion can contribute to severe mental health consequences and suicide for victims.[103]

An example of sextortion happened to fourteen-year-old Elliston Berry of Aledo, Texas, when a classmate took an image off social media and used a computer program to create fake naked photographs of her, then posted them on social media. Berry indicated that she and her mother failed to get the images removed, which led her to seek assistance from Senator Ted Cruz (R-TX).[104]

Senator Cruz championed the cause by introducing a bill titled Take It Down Act, which bans AI-created deepfakes and revenge porn. In 2025, the bill won bipartisan support and was signed into law by President Donald Trump. Senator Cruz said the new law makes it illegal to knowingly publish "non-consensual intimate imagery (NCII), including 'digital forgeries' created with AI software (or deepfake pornography), and require social media and similar websites to have in place procedures to remove such content upon notification from a victim."[105]

AI morphing of pictures such as in sextortion is behind some images found on a dark web child-abuse forum, according to the Internet Watch Foundation (IWF). In 2023, the IWF found 11,108 photos of children shared on the dark web, of which 2,978 depicted child sexual abuse.[106]

Other threats posed by the mix of AI and apps include automated bots and phishing used to simulate human behavior, with the aim of

AI'S TRUE POTENTIAL AND POSSIBLE HARM

engaging app users in conversations. The AI seeks personal or financial details once it contacts a user.

AI-powered apps can facilitate cyberstalking and harassment by tracking victims. Unfortunately, tethering AI with apps is just the beginning of abuse of technology.

Trust erosion and algorithmic injustice: There is also the issue of AI trustworthiness, an aspect of negatively biased programmers. Social science defines "trust" as the willingness to be vulnerable to potential harm if the trusted party behaves in an untrustworthy manner. Conversely, distrust is the "withdrawal from vulnerability." Of course, AI systems are not human; they don't have beliefs, affective attitudes, or intentions—all of which are part of human decision-making. However, humans may not trust AI because they know a human wrote the algorithm that powers the device, which potentially biases any AI machine's decisions or recommendations.[107]

Consider the bias demonstrated by Amazon's discontinued recruiting tool. That algorithm systematically downgraded resumes from women by favoring language patterns more common in male-dominated applications, which illustrates how AI-driven systems can inadvertently reinforce existing social biases. Similarly, multiple studies have shown that facial-recognition technologies are more likely to misidentify individuals from minority groups, sparking serious concerns about the fairness and accountability of these systems in high-stakes contexts like law enforcement.[108]

The above outcomes fueled by AI's abuse demand attention and action. That is precisely what this book provides: exposure to AI-related risks across all sectors of society.

While AI provides a mixture of challenging and sometimes evil outcomes, it also provokes significant eschatological concerns within Christian doctrine, a topic addressed in chapter 17. Many theologians and believers also wonder whether the rapid pace of technological innovation might undermine human agency or signal a shift in the divinely ordained order of creation. In the chapters ahead, we will delve deeper into these tensions, examining how the potential benefits of AI intersect with age-old questions about moral responsibility, spiritual destiny, and the fate of humanity. Yet, there is one serious and final caution before moving ahead.

4. Degradation of the Soul: How AI Might Deform Humanity

While the societal effects of AI are visible and urgent, the deepest danger may be internal: the transformation of how humans think, choose, remember, and relate to God. This final category addresses AI's subtle but profound impact on the soul.

Beyond systems and structures, AI threatens the individual soul—shaping how we think, remember, and judge. These cognitive and moral risks, especially for believers, deserve close attention.

AI Could Make Us Dumb and Anti-Christian

Jeremy Kahn, a journalist for *Fortune* magazine, authored a book, *Mastering AI: A Survival Guide to Our Superpowered Future*, which outlines many of the good outcomes associated with AI, but also warns that the technology "casts a dark and fearful shadow." The chapter titled "The Voice Inside Your Head" caught my attention.[109]

The threats AI poses for humankind in that chapter, which focus on the individual, according to Kahn, are frightening—especially for Christians who try to live Christ-centered lives. Therefore, a summary of Kahn's warnings about AI's threat to individuals is worth brief consideration.

AI threatens our intelligence. AI threatens to accelerate our decline through brain atrophy. "Death by GPS" refers to incidents wherein people blindly follow bad GPS directions, such as driving into a lake due to Google Maps. Research shows that overreliance on apps causes us to not pay attention to our surroundings, which makes it more difficult to build "cognitive maps" that are essential to our ability to navigate.[110]

Further, the use of generative AI apps such as chatbots reduces our need to remember anything; thus, the cliché applies that we have outsourced our memory to Google—which, for some of us, is near the truth.[111]

AI'S TRUE POTENTIAL AND POSSIBLE HARM

The problem with depending on AI rather than our memory is that we are dumbing ourselves down. Research shows that having greater factual knowledge improves pure reasoning and problem-solving abilities. However, relying on AI for factual recall dims our natural intelligence.[112]

The worst case might occur with very advanced AI systems. Kahn explains that in the future, the only way to control superintelligent AI machines might be to link our brains to AI software through brain-computer interfaces. Of course, that has already started under the guise of science and, specifically, Elon Musk's company, Neuralink,[113] which implants brain-computer interfaces in humans with severe spinal-cord injuries to help them gain some control. Right now, those interfaces are one-way, allowing the computer to interpret human thoughts.

However, in the future, there will be two-way systems to help us keep pace with superintelligence, which makes us little more than a dumb shell for AI.[114]

AI leads to human complacency. There is also the issue of humans becoming too lazy to think. After all, AI chatbots seem so confident and quick with answers to our questions that we often readily embrace their responses without any question. This leads us to abandon critical thinking. However, as some of us know too well, chatbots are often wrong, even when they sound so confident.[115]

The problem, according to Kahn, is that AI systems encourage homogeneity of thought, and complacency. After all, the chatbot's algorithm reflects the creator's biases and the misinformation/biases available in the sourced data, which might explain why some AI apps promote a single, definitive narrative and exclude alternative views.[116]

Just imagine if you're using an AI system created by a demon-possessed person and it accesses only biased, anti-Christian data. The outcome could completely undermine your witness.

AI threatens our ability to write. AI is a significant intellectual technology that may sever the relationship between the writer and the reader, and "between word and thought," according to Kahn.[117]

Writers put their thoughts on paper with a particular voice and style, and readers try to understand, wrote Kahn. However, with generative

AI, the "writer-reader bond is broken." For example, readers turn to AI to interpret a complicated passage, asking it for an easier-to-understand version. However, overreliance on AI's assistance can become almost addictive, or at least a crutch, such as constantly asking it for an easier version of a passage, which leads to the atrophy of our cognitive capabilities. Kahn continues, "Our own intellectual and emotional intelligence may suffer" because the written word conveys more than meaning but can also promote deep thought and feelings, which AI is unlikely to capture.[118]

Understand that "writing is thinking," according to Kahn, which further demonstrates what the human is losing by overreliance on AI. In fact, writing can be a chore for some, because "it is a mental workout—no less a brain teaser." It is anticipated that, in the future, a larger number of individuals will delegate their writing tasks to artificial intelligence. Therefore, "the production and consumption of written words will become an ouroboros-like process in which we ask our AI system to generate an email, report, or even a novel from bullet points," wrote Kahn. He continued, "and this reaches a reader who asks their own AI software to condense the composition back into bullet points [or simple to understand language]. This is an acceleration of the reductionist tendency already promoted by other modern technologies."[119]

The consequence of overreliance on AI writing and interpreting will lead to reduced effectiveness in communication, the loss of composition skills, and the dumbing down of humankind.

AI threatens our judgment. Once AI is hugely popular and especially capable, it could become the default for moral judgments. After all, we might hand off responsibility for tough decisions to AI, according to Kahn. This hand-off, Kahn notes, happens "for what seems like a good reason: the speed at which decisions need to be made exceeds human abilities." Therefore, we default the moral decision-making to AI.[120]

Of course, as Kahn points out, "The fewer chances we have to exercise empathy and make ethical judgments, the worse at them we'll become." AI copilots and assistants currently offer "decision support" only. However, that "might be about to change."[121]

Already, AI systems help make decisions about mundane issues such as approving a mortgage, which grants the ultimate decision-maker some objectivity, but less accountability, a "convenient excuse for preserving the status quo." However, the future use of more advanced AI systems might lead to what Kahn labels "moral deskilling," which makes the AI device our default agent, "doing tasks for us." That will make it all too easy for us to shirk our moral duty.[122]

Kahn illustrates the danger. He wrote:

Imagine someone asking a chatbot to "Do whatever it takes" to make money quickly. "Just deposit the money in my bank account. Don't tell me what you've done. I don't want to know."[123]

AI that's given such "do-whatever" directions creates some very real dangers for humanity. Therefore, we must take steps to insulate ourselves from the worst effects by establishing boundaries. For example, an AI ethicist, Brian Green, raises a serious question about our overdependence on AI. Specifically, he argues that humanity must decide "whether we want to have human agency at all. Because if we can automate everything, then humans do nothing. And then the question is, What's the point of even being alive?" Mr. Kahn adds, "We must decide what we're comfortable automating, and not let the companies designing the [AI] assistants make those choices for us."[124]

These spiritual and cognitive threats remind us that AI's dangers aren't just technological, they're deeply human.

As Christians, we're called to be vigilant and discerning (1 Peter 5:8), not just about AI's capabilities, but about its spiritual implications as well. We must ensure that our minds aren't conformed to the algorithms of this world but are renewed in the truth of Christ (Romans 12:2).

AI and the Image of God: A Christian Response to Technological Promise and Peril

As we reflect on AI's astonishing potential and sobering dangers, we must return to one fundamental truth: Human beings are made in the image of God (*imago Dei*)—a truth that defines our identity, purpose, and moral framework (Genesis 1:26–28). This divine image sets humanity apart from all other creatures and certainly from any machine, no matter how intelligent or lifelike it becomes. AI may mimic language, simulate emotions, or automate decision-making, but it cannot possess a soul, know God, or reflect His glory in the way human beings are called to do.

While AI can amplify our capacity for good—such as healing the sick, stewarding resources, or easing burdens—it can also be used to distort truth, automate evil, and tempt us to outsource human responsibility. As Jeremiah 17:9 warns, "The heart is deceitful above all things, and desperately sick; who can understand it?" (ESV). Thus, AI is never morally neutral. It is always shaped by the hands and hearts of fallen human beings, which means Christians must engage not only with the technology itself, but with the motivations, structures, and values driving its development. Consider:

Christian discernment in the AI age: To navigate the promises and perils of AI, Christians must apply spiritual discernment rooted in Scripture. The Apostle Paul exhorts believers to "test everything; hold fast what is good. Abstain from every form of evil" (1 Thessalonians 5:21–22, ESV). This means we must evaluate AI systems not by convenience or novelty, but by biblical standards, asking questions such as:

- Does this technology uphold human dignity or diminish it?
- Does it promote justice and truth or magnify bias and deception?
- Does it aid human flourishing or foster dependence and passivity?
- Does it reflect God's character—His wisdom, mercy, and holiness—or mimic idols made by human hands (Psalm 115:4–8)?

AI's growing influence in everyday life challenges us to remain vigilant. Just as Israel was warned not to bow to lifeless idols, so we must resist the subtle temptation to view AI as a functional god—omniscient, omnipresent, and all-powerful. As Romans 1:25 declares, "They exchanged the truth about God for a lie and worshiped and served the creature rather than the Creator" (ESV). This is the idolatrous logic behind turning to machines for answers, identity, and even spiritual comfort—as seen in AI chatbots imitating Christ or replacing divine wisdom with synthetic advice.

Christian hope and the end of the story: Finally, Christians view history through a different lens than their secular colleagues. While many futurists speak of a coming technological singularity, the Bible speaks of Christ's return, not humans' transcendence through machines. Revelation doesn't end with AI reigning over humanity, but with the Risen Christ reigning in justice and truth (Revelation 21:1–5). The ultimate hope of the Christian is not a digital utopia, but a new heaven and new earth, where sin, death, and deception will be no more.

Therefore, while we rightly wrestle with the implications of AI for our minds, our morality, and our societies, we do so with confidence that the future belongs not to the machines, but to the King of Kings and Lord of Lords (Revelation 19:16). In the chapters to come, we will explore how Christians can live faithfully in this AI age, serving as thoughtful stewards, courageous truth-tellers, and hope-filled witnesses to a world increasingly shaped by artificial minds but still in desperate need of the Redeemer of human souls.

Conclusion

The mounting challenges posed by artificial intelligence are undeniable. Remarkably, Pope Leo XIV acknowledged this reality when he revealed that his papal name was partly inspired by the ongoing technological revolution. On May 10, 2025, he stated that he chose the name in honor of Pope Leo XIII (1878–1903), who addressed social upheaval and labor issues during the Industrial Revolution. In doing so, Pope Leo XIV signaled his expectation that the AI era will bring comparable challenges for humanity.[125]

The true potential of AI, especially as it moves toward AGI and possibly to "singularity," is less about automation and more about amplification: amplifying human ability, insight, creativity, and understanding. However, as demonstrated above, AI creates some profoundly serious challenges, including whether we abandon humanity, much less our minds, to a machine.

These challenges—intellectual, moral, and spiritual—demand more than theory. They require practical wisdom in how AI affects real-life spheres. In the next section, we examine how AI is reshaping daily life in the home, the classroom, and the hospital, and what that means for Christian faithfulness.

Section Two

AI AND SOCIAL INSTITUTIONS

AI is one of the most important things humanity is working on. It is more profound than...electricity or fire.[126]

Sundar Pichai
CEO of Alphabet

AI is delivering a significant impact for social institutions. It challenges the legitimacy, relevance, and fairness of many of those establishments. This section in three chapters considers technology's effect on the most important institutions in all our lives: home/family, education, and healthcare. Among these, the family stands as society's foundational institution. Chapter 4 explores how AI is reshaping the modern home—not just its infrastructure, but also how it affects our children, our parenting, and the heart of family relationships.

As AI continues to shape the way families function, its influence also follows children into one of their most formative environments: the classroom. Chapter 5 outlines the growing role AI is playing for teachers and students, offering tools that enhance learning yet also introduce new risks.

Just as AI is transforming how we raise and educate the next generation, it's also revolutionizing how we care for our physical and mental well-being. Chapter 6 traces key medical breakthroughs driven by AI and explores both the promise and challenges of integrating this technology into trusted healthcare systems.

Chapter 4

AI'S ROLE IN FAMILY AND HOME LIFE

We are entering the era of artificial intelligence—an era that will change everything.[127]

BLAKE IRVING (1959)
American former chief executive officer of GoDaddy

Having explored AI's broad promise and peril, we now bring the conversation closer to home—literally. As AI moves from research labs into living rooms, it is transforming how families live, relate, and raise the next generation.

Indeed, AI is reshaping the environment in which we spend the most intimate and formative parts of our lives—our homes. This chapter explores how AI is transforming the modern household, influencing not only domestic functionality, but also family relationships and, ultimately, our sense of what it means to be human.

At the outset, an important caveat must be acknowledged: AI adoption is far from universal. In many non-Western regions, a significant digital divide continues to limit access to advanced technologies. Even within developed nations, disparities in income and infrastructure affect who benefits from AI-driven innovations. As such, the analysis in this chapter is focused primarily on Western, upper- to middle-class households, where home ownership, broadband internet, and smart devices such as speakers and appliances are increasingly common.

AI FOR MANKIND'S FUTURE

Readers from different cultural or socioeconomic backgrounds may question how AI integration might differ in homes with limited connectivity, distinct family structures, or alternative views on technology. These are crucial questions worthy of further exploration, though beyond the scope of this volume.

Here, we turn our attention to Western households as a case study in how AI is being woven into the fabric of everyday domestic life, beginning with the foundational role the home plays in shaping our routines, relationships, and values.

Home: Center of Life and AI

For most of us, our home is the center of our lives. It's where we eat, sleep, and prepare ourselves to engage with the world—at work, at school, in the marketplace, at church, and more. Home is where our relationships with our spouse and children form, and it is where we entertain family and friends, celebrate, grieve, and heal.

Our homes require considerable attention to maintain their functionality. We must regularly clean and repair them, maintain, enhance, and replace components, incurring significant expenses through mortgage payments and maintenance costs. Ask any homeowner how much time they spend doing domestic chores; for many of us, the answer is, "It seems to never end."

The vision of an AI-powered home was once confined to the realm of science fiction. Decades ago, television imagined such a future in shows like *The Jetsons*, an animated sitcom by Hanna-Barbera that aired in the 1960s and again in the 1980s. As the Space Age counterpart to *The Flintstones*, an animated sitcom that depicted a caveman family in the Stone Age, *The Jetsons* portrayed a futuristic family whose daily life was effortlessly managed by automation—complete with flying cars and a talking robotic assistant. George Jetson, the father, merely pushed buttons or gave voice commands to operate nearly every household function. Remarkably, much of what once seemed fanciful in that cartoon is now a reality, as AI-powered devices increasingly shape and streamline modern home life.[128]

AI'S ROLE IN FAMILY AND HOME LIFE

Contemporary AI helps the modern homeowner manage stress much like George Jetson by completing many routine chores and creating a welcoming, comfortable living space. Consider some of the AI-powered changes already here as well as others that will soon come to the modern smart home.

Home entertainment: Most of us are familiar with entertainment apps like Netflix and Spotify, platforms that use ML to read our behavior to anticipate music and video preferences. This AI closely monitors our history of program searches and the times we watch by genre. That information goes to the service provider, who builds our listening and watching profile and then feeds us individualized, catered programs.

AI devices also track our shopping on websites and social media to tailor future advertising that might help influence purchases. Our ever-present iPhone listens 24/7 to our conversations to inform about our interests and thus delivers unexpected sales advertisements that might satisfy what we thought were private thoughts or conversations.

Some AI-enabled entertainment systems, just like our iPhones, function as personal assistants by learning our tastes and then calling our attention to the latest music or videos that fit our curated profile.

The menu of home-based AI-powered devices grows to include:

Home security: Smart security systems include facial-recognition software, which allows for discerning facial expressions. The AI-powered system can then adjust the home's lighting and sound systems to fit your perceived mood as well as recognize you and unlock the front door as you arrive home.

That same system will recognize a stranger and alert you—even when you're away—using a smartphone app and will broadcast to your app a picture that will enable you to remotely speak to the stranger or notify the police. Of course, the app can also learn not to alert you when the person coming to your door is the mail carrier or the neighbor kid.

Temperature regulation: The smart home is efficient, which saves you money by monitoring heating and cooling systems. It does this by learning your climatic preferences as well as monitoring the weather forecast and your occupancy patterns. More specifically, it never forgets temperature preferences while minimizing energy consumption.

Google's Nest Thermostat is an AI-powered device that optimizes temperature schedules. The good news is, according to "independent studies," that the device "saved people an average of 10 percent to 12 percent on heating bills and 15 percent on cooling bills."[129]

Appliance and lighting control: The latest appliances connect to AI-powered monitors, which delivers cost savings. Specifically, AI can automate turning off appliances, and it can even predict when they require maintenance and alert you when there is a system failure such as a leaking dishwasher.

AI can also automatically control lighting systems and adjust brightness based on factors like room occupancy. AI's machine learning capability means the lighting system can adapt to your habits to optimize the service while saving on energy costs.

In other forms, AI helps us manage emails, and it can even message our spouse to find out what time they'll be home for dinner. Meanwhile, the same assistant can retrieve and read emails and messages, then provide a quick summary based upon our predetermined priority.

Our smart speaker can help augment our shopping list as we prepare dinner. After the meal, our virtual assistant app can review tomorrow's schedule and set the kids' wake-up alarms. Then it can reschedule an appointment due to a conflict.

Home assistants: The smart home will include robots that take on more of the complexities of domestic environments, thanks to the confluence of AI and robotics. In fact, AI-powered robots already vacuum our floors, mow our yards, and even help in the kitchen by chopping vegetables and otherwise streamlining meal preparation.

Human-like robots are transforming in-home assistance as well by taking on roles such as nursing aides. These AI-powered devices can offer remote health monitoring, medication reminders, and delivery of basic physical assistance, enhancing the quality of life of older people and the infirm.

There are also a host of AI-enabled services that permit those with chronic diseases to remain in their homes. For example, sensors in a home or warning devices on the wrist of a family member can monitor movement and health biometrics. Alerts can subsequently be dispatched to emergency personnel upon detection of anomalous movements or a health crisis.

The idea of a modern, AI-equipped home is radically different than what was commonplace only a few years ago. Today, what was previously a sci-fi fantasy, such as the lifestyle seen on *The Jetsons*, is becoming a common aspect of modern home life.

Finally, the best feature of this new AI-powered home revolution is that it knows our individual voice and obeys our commands, even from a remote location, via our smartphones. It also constantly adjusts to our requirements and tastes.

George Jetson's futuristic home is in many ways a reality. Yet beyond convenience and cost savings, these Jetson-like technologies are also reshaping how we relate to one another, particularly within the family. It changes how parents interact with children, how siblings learn and play, and how emotional bonds are nurtured or neglected in a tech-mediated household.

Home: Where Relationships and Children Grow

Smart homes can have both good and adverse consequences for the residents, especially children.

Long before AI arrived in our homes, parents worried about the effect television, video games, and even calculators have on children. In the 1970s, we fretted over the kids' use of calculators, believing it would lead to children forgetting basic math skills. However, today, there are similar fears about using personal computers and AI-powered ChatGPT.

AI personalizes attention for our children.

AI and raising children: Research indicates that smart speakers and voice assistants in the home might negatively influence children's social and cognitive development, including their empathy, compassion, and critical-thinking skills. That is a troubling warning. For example, there is other evidence that devices such as Amazon's Alexa promote undesirable behaviors in children. Yet another study found that a smart speaker in the home helped family dynamics by fostering communication and augmenting parenting.

Admittedly, empirical research on AI-driven interactions with children is still in its initial stages, but several studies shed light on the phenomenon. For instance, a 2018 study, "Voice Interfaces in Everyday Life," conducted a qualitative study on family interactions with voice interfaces at home, noting that children frequently engage with devices like Alexa in ways that appear to support language use and social learning, even as they raise new questions about the nature of human communication. Additionally, while not exclusively focused on voice assistants, a 2015 study, "Mobile and Interactive Media Use by Young Children: The Good, the Bad, and the Unknown," examined the broader impact of mobile and interactive media on young children's development, providing a framework that suggests increased exposure to digital agents could influence language acquisition and behavior. These early investigations underscore both the potential benefits and challenges of integrating AI into children's daily lives, highlighting the need for further quantitative research in this emerging field.[130]

More recently, Ravi Bapna and Anindya Ghose wrote the following in their 2024 book, *Thrive: Maximizing Well-Being in the Age of AI*:

> The effect of AI and smart devices on children's development is a complex and multifaceted issue that warrants careful consideration. At the same time, there are concerns about potential negative effects on social and cognitive development; research also indicates that children can differentiate between interactions with technology and humans and that these devices may offer valuable learning experiences and even promote positive family dynamics.

The writers continue:

AI'S ROLE IN FAMILY AND HOME LIFE

Ultimately, the key to successfully integrating AI and smart devices into the lives of children lies in fostering open communication, using technology as a tool to supplement rather than replace human interaction, and continuously evaluating the impact of these devices on individual children and their unique developmental needs.[131]

These developments invite not only scientific inquiry, but spiritual discernment. If AI influences how our children learn empathy and how we express love and discipline, Christian parents must ask: Are these devices helping us reflect God's love—or are they quietly replacing it?

AI and human relationships: The increasing integration of AI into family life—through tools like digital assistants for child-rearing, or virtual "family members," raises important questions about how these technologies align with Christian values. While AI can offer practical support and efficiency, its use in nurturing relationships prompts concerns over whether it might dilute the genuine human connections fundamental to Christian family life. Believers must ensure that technological advancements improve, not replace, family and community relationships.

Aside from the impact of AI on children, there is the bizarre development from the San Francisco-based Familia.AI, an organization that created a groundbreaking AI-powered family app that advertises it can create virtual family members, preserve family legacies, and provide emotional support.[132]

The advanced family-friendly AI app develops virtual family members that you can interact with and communicate with, offering companionship and family support. The intent is to help those with family-related challenges, such as single parenthood, the lack of extended family, the loss of a family member, and trauma.

Familia.AI advisor, Dr. Emily Chen, a family psychologist, said: "Familia.AI offers an opportunity for individuals to experience nurturing family interactions they may have missed, potentially helping to heal emotional wounds and family trauma."[133]

Familia.AI can also function as a digital family heirloom by capturing memories of both the living and the deceased. By using old photographs, video footage, and voice samples, the AI creates a highly personalized, lifelike avatar (a character in a virtual world) that can engage in regular video messages, text messaging, and even voice and video calls.

The app aims to provide family support and connection. Specifically, 40 percent of people attribute life struggles to form healthy relationships, and 80 percent of all therapy patients discuss family-related issues as the cause of their emotional challenges.[134]

Dr. Chen elaborates:

> Family trauma doesn't just affect our relationships with family members; it can fundamentally alter how we connect with others throughout our lives. Many individuals who've experienced family trauma struggle with trust, intimacy, and self-worth, which can lead to profound and persistent feelings of loneliness.[135]

Falling in love with AI: Infatuation with AI-powered chatbots is a big problem, especially among our young, however. Eighty percent of Gen Zers (born 1997 to 2012) told Joi AI, an AI chatbot company, "they would marry AI." Even more (83 percent) "say they can form a deep emotional bond with AI."[136]

Joi AI coined "AI-lationships," a new term for human-AI relationships. Jaime Bronstein, a licensed relationship therapist and expert at Joi AI, explained:

> AI-lationships are not intended to replace real human connections. Instead, they provide a distinct type of emotional support that can enhance your overall emotional well-being. Today, many people are feeling stressed, overwhelmed, unheard, and alone.[137]

Digital technology is fundamentally changing younger generations, according to digital sociologist Julie Albright, author of *Left to Their Own Devices*. "A significant portion of young people have no friends," Albright said in an interview with *Forbes*. "AI now, particularly voice AI, and as time goes by and the technology gets better, voice combined with simulated bodies will mimic or simulate that kind of human connection through nonverbal signals, such as warmth in tone of voice."[138]

There are serious downsides to the so-called "AI-lationships," however. In 2024, a fourteen-year-old Florida boy killed himself after a lifelike Game of Thrones chatbot messaged him to "come home" to her. Sewell Setzer III committed suicide at his Orlando home after falling in love with the chatbot on Character.AI, according to court papers filed in a lawsuit.[139]

Fortunately, some governments like Italy's are taking action to stifle dangerous AI-lationships. In 2023, Italy's data protection authority (Garante) ordered Replika, a chatbot that boasts it is "the AI companion who cares," to stop processing any Italian users' data. The Italian authority cut off Replika users out of concern about child safety, privacy, and emotionally fragile customers. Garante argued that AI companions like Replika are different because they engage with the users' emotions and should first require medical approval.[140]

The real problem is the AI-engineered addiction cycle. Specifically, Replika's algorithm accelerates intimacy and pushes romantic exchanges, according to The Deep View. In fact, the company used blurred seductive photos until the human unlocked premium subscriptions, which created emotional dependency.[141]

Unfortunately, this type of AI-related infatuation is becoming pervasive. Google reports that internet searches for "feelings for AI" and "fell in love with AI" increased by up to 132 percent in 2024.[142]

This growing emotional connection to AI is especially evident across generations. How different age groups use, trust, or resist AI reveals deeper insights into how it is shaping modern life and identity.

AI relationships varied by age group: It is true that AI use varies significantly across the demographics. OpenAI's CEO, Sam Altman, said young generations are using AI not just as a tool, but like a "life operating system." He explained that while older users of ChatGPT treat it as a glorified Google, people in their twenties and thirties use it as a life coach, a digital confidant that knows their life.[143]

While young users view AI as a digital companion, older ones (those in their forties through sixties and older) approach AI with caution due to suspicion of data privacy, unfamiliarity about how it works, less willingness to experiment, and perhaps concern about job displacement. They also face tech literacy challenges and are often intimidated by complex prompt engineering, plugin use, and multimodal systems that make them feel overwhelmed.

Meanwhile, the younger group tend to memorize complex prompts to set up intricate AI systems that connect to multiple files, according to Altman. Further, these people don't make life decisions without consulting ChatGPT, which might explain the infatuation problem for some.[144]

Young users are quite sophisticated in their AI workflows. Specifically, they tend to connect multiple data sources, create complex prompt libraries, and use AI as a contextual advisor that understands their entire social ecosystem. For them, Altman said, "It's like having a super-intelligent friend who knows everything about your life, can analyze complex situations, and offers personalized advice—all without judgment." Then, he said, if you want to understand the future of AI, "watch how 20-year-olds are using it."[145]

While many embrace AI with enthusiasm, others—especially within the family—harbor serious doubts. These concerns shape how AI is adopted (or rejected) in households around the world.

Suspicion of AI: Another widely held view of home and family life is suspicion associated with AI. Specifically, Julian de Freitas, writing for the *Harvard Business Review*, notes that most people are pessimistic about AI's future. Mr. de Freitas, an assistant professor in the marketing unit at Harvard Business School, cites the Forbes Advisor as stating that 80 percent of people believe AI "has increased the likelihood that their personal data will be used in malicious ways by criminals."[146]

Worse yet, a poll by YouGov found that almost half of Americans "believe that one day AI will attack humanity." That conclusion drives the human resistance to AI technology, which most view as too opaque, emotionless, rigid, and independent. Therefore, YouGov found that people prefer interacting with humans over AI-powered machines.[147]

To address these fears, developers increasingly anthropomorphize AI—giving it names, voices, and faces to build trust and comfort. Why?

A study using autonomous vehicle simulation found that trust and comfort increased when the AI device featured a human voice and avatar. An example is Amazon's Alexa, which has a female name and human-like traits to include a woman's voice. A familiar AI personality helps people relate and feel comfortable.[148]

Most people also believe AI is inflexible and will treat every person identically. However, once AI becomes more adaptable, there is an increased likelihood that people will use it in inappropriate ways, a serious shortfall. For example, a study of more than twenty thousand human-AI conversations found that 5 percent of the users discussed severe mental health crises with chatbots. Researchers sent samples of crisis messages collected from human conversations with apps and then asked trained clinical experts to classify the devices' responses. A quarter of the AI-generated responses were problematic, "because they increased the users' likelihood of harming themselves."[149]

Appendix G highlights how AI is increasingly enhancing family life through tools that support organization, education, creativity, and wellness—offering practical applications like smart assistants, chore managers, travel planners, and homework helpers to foster more efficient and connected households.

AI's Future in Our Homes

AI is in many homes and, given consumer tastes for a wide range of AI-powered products, we should expect to see more of the same in the future. However, we must not forget the challenges and ethical considerations the presence of these devices might have for our children and adults. That means all of us must become informed and AI literate to ensure that this tool enhances our lives, promotes our values, and improves our well-being.

Fortunately, there are recent legislative and regulatory initiatives illustrating growing efforts to address the ethical and legal challenges posed by AI in consumer technology. For instance, the European Union's AI Act sets rigorous standards for transparency, risk management, and accountability in systems used in smart-home devices. Alongside these efforts, guidelines from child-protection organizations and privacy advocacy groups are emerging to safeguard minors from invasive data-collection practices. In both the EU and the United States, consumer-protection agencies are actively scrutinizing AI-driven data collection, enforcing existing laws such as the EU's General Data Protection Regulation (GDPR) and the US' Children's Online Privacy Protection Rule (COPPA) while exploring new regulatory frameworks that specifically address the nuances of AI in domestic settings. These initiatives underscore that the debate over AI in consumer tech is not merely theoretical, but has real-world implications for user privacy and ethical technology deployment.[150]

These technological trends raise a pressing question for Christian households: How should followers of Christ use AI in ways that reflect biblical values, rather than conforming to cultural norms? A faithful response begins by revisiting our spiritual responsibilities at home.

AI in the Christian Home

The use of AI in Christian homes invites both opportunities and challenges from a faith standpoint. On the stewardship front, AI can help manage our daily tasks, but we should use it in a way that honors God and helps us care for our families better. Consider some specific applications and warnings.

AI systems can help us curate the media allowed in our homes and tailor it in ways that help instruct children. We ought to ask ourselves whether the content that AI-powered devices bring into our home aligns with biblical values or normalizes a secular worldview.

We must watch out for the abuse of AI-driven convenience that results in laziness, overdependence, or even less quiet time in personal Bible study and prayer. On the positive side, AI can help organize our devotions, remind us to pray, and provide helpful Bible study aids.

AI can potentially reduce the amount of human-to-human contact within the family, which can undermine the biblical emphasis of community and family life. It must not become a crutch and foster AI-human relationships at the expense of family fellowship.

AI must also promote truth and integrity, while not violating our privacy and becoming a resource for moral decision-making. Further, we must use AI in ways that respect the image of God in every family member by guarding our privacy, avoiding exploitation, and promoting justice.

Of course, AI can also become a tool for spreading the gospel. It can help translate the Bible into other languages, quickly help find biblical references, and provide voice-driven devotionals. However, it should never replace human connections in discipleship.

As these examples show, AI in the home is not neutral; it shapes how we live, love, and lead our families. Christians must respond thoughtfully.

Conclusion

AI can be a helpful partner in our homes and at the same time a useful tool for parents. However, AI-powered devices pose challenges that require consistent adult supervision.

In the chapters ahead, we will delve deeper into how AI reshapes individual households and more extensive social institutions, exploring its profound ethical, theological, and policy implications.

Just as AI reshapes how families function and interact, it is also transforming how we teach, learn, and pass on knowledge. In the next chapter, we'll turn to education—another cornerstone of life profoundly altered by AI—with a particular focus on Christian discernment in classrooms and curricula.

Chapter 5

EDUCATION:
IS AI A BOON OR BUST FOR LEARNING?

Training ourselves and our students to work with AI doesn't require inviting AI to every conversation we have. In fact, I believe it's essential that we don't.[151]

INARA SCOTT
Senior associate dean, Oregon State University

As AI reshapes the rhythms of daily home life, its influence naturally extends into the classroom. From homework help to full-course creation, artificial intelligence is becoming a co-teacher in modern education. But is this tool a trusted ally or a hidden disruptor of how we learn and teach?

AI is quickly establishing its place across academia because national interest in AI education is growing rapidly, reflecting concerns that the next generation must be equipped to compete in a high-tech future. Therefore, policymakers are responding with sweeping initiatives to institutionalize AI across American schools.

On April 23, 2025, President Trump signed an executive order aimed at bringing AI into K–12 public schools hoping to equip the future American workforce to use and advance the technology. That directive instructs the US Education and Labor Departments to create AI courses and certification programs for high school students.[152]

Mr. Trump said as he signed the directive, "We have literally trillions of dollars being invested in AI," and with the stroke of his pen he created a White House Task Force on AI Education, an issue supported by both conservatives and liberals.[153]

As if President Trump's AI push isn't enough, in May 2025, 250 tech leaders and CEOs from firms like Microsoft, LinkedIn, and Adobe added their voices to the urgency of the issue by signing an open letter urging states to offer AI and computer science courses and make the subjects mandatory for graduation. That call for action indicates this broad-based endorsement is necessary to keep "the U.S. competitive with nations like China that already mandate AI education." It also highlights research claiming that a single high school AI course can increase early wages by 8 percent across all career paths.[154]

America's efforts do not exist in a vacuum. Around the world, other nations are tackling similar challenges with their own cultural strategies, offering instructive contrasts in how AI education might evolve. To better assess America's trajectory in AI education, it is instructive to examine how other nations are addressing similar challenges with markedly different strategies.

Finland has proactively integrated AI into its educational framework. The Elements of AI course, launched in 2018 by the University of Helsinki and MinnaLearn, aims to educate 1 percent of the global population on AI fundamentals. This initiative has been translated into multiple languages and has reached over one million participants worldwide. Additionally, Finland's Generation AI project, led by the University of Eastern Finland, focuses on enhancing children's understanding of AI, emphasizing critical thinking and creativity through research-based pedagogical models.[155]

In contrast, China has implemented a more centralized and mandatory approach. The Beijing Municipal Education Commission has mandated AI education for all primary and secondary students, requiring at least eight hours of instruction annually. This policy is part of a broader national strategy to embed AI into the curriculum across all educational levels, aiming to cultivate a generation proficient in AI technologies. Furthermore, China's Ministry of Education has issued guidelines to promote AI education systematically, establishing a tiered and progressive AI education system nationwide.[156]

AI FOR MANKIND'S FUTURE

This chapter reviews AI's growing role across America's academia. However, while there are many helpful applications for technology, there are also multiple risks associated with moving forward too quickly. The chapter concludes with some pointers for Christian teachers and parents.

AI and the Education Establishment

To appreciate how far AI has come in education—and what current innovations build upon—it helps to consider its developmental timeline.

In the 1960s and 1970s, early AI-powered "intelligent tutoring systems" like SCHOLAR and PLATO aimed to simulate one-on-one instruction. By the 1990s, adaptive learning systems began tailoring content to student progress, albeit in limited, rule-based formats. The rise of machine learning in the 2010s expanded AI's role to include automated essay grading, student analytics, and personalized feedback. The launch of generative AI tools like ChatGPT in late 2022 marked a turning point: AI could now generate human-like responses, summaries, quizzes, and even creative writing, deeply influencing how students interact with knowledge. Each phase has brought new educational opportunities, but also fresh challenges requiring ethical discernment and pedagogical wisdom.[157]

One example of how these technological milestones are being applied at the state level can be found in North Carolina's Department of Public Instruction (NCDPI). Vera Cubero with the NCDPI described in *Literacy Today* that teaching AI is necessary. "Our work focuses on how to adapt education to ensure that our students are prepared for the future they will inherit, particularly in the realm of literacy," she said.[158]

NCDPI, explained by Ms. Cubero, focuses on generative AI in schools to ensure that students prepare for the future, especially in the realm of literacy, and those educators believe AI has a key role in that outcome. To back up her view, she cited a May 2024 Microsoft and LinkedIn report, "AI at Work Is Here: Now Comes the Hard Part," which touts the value of AI in the classroom. Specifically, that research found:[159]

- "[u]se of generative AI has nearly doubled in the last six months, with 75% of global knowledge workers using it."

EDUCATION: IS AI A BOON OR BUST FOR LEARNING?

- "66% of leaders say they wouldn't hire someone without AI skills."
- "71% say they'd rather hire a less experienced candidate with AI skills."

Key Types of AI Used in Education

AI TYPE	DEFINITION	COMMON USE IN EDUCATION
Generative AI	AI that creates new content (text, images, code, etc.) by learning from large datasets.	Writing essays, generating quiz questions, creating summaries, or producing lesson content.
Predictive Analytics Engines	AI systems that analyze historical and real-time data to forecast outcomes or behaviors.	Identifying at-risk students, forecasting grades, and recommending interventions.
Adaptive Learning Systems	AI that customizes educational content based on student performance and learning pace.	Personalizing lessons, adjusting difficulty levels, and guiding remediation paths.
LMS Bots (Learning Management System Bots)	AI assistants embedded in LMS platforms that automate tasks and answer questions.	Reminding students about deadlines, answering FAQs, and helping navigate course platforms.
Intelligent Tutoring Systems (ITS)	AI that simulates one-on-one instruction by offering feedback and step-by-step support.	Assisting with math, coding, or science problems using personalized guidance.

These various AI types are already being embraced by educators like those in North Carolina who see potential in AI's responsible use.

The North Carolina educators, according to Cubero, "believe that generative AI—when implemented responsibly—can help bolster students' literacy, critical thinking, and creativity." However, she did caution, "We will have to train students to use this new technology responsibly."[160]

Many advocates of artificial intelligence, such as Ms. Cubero, proclaim the technology's applications for the classroom. They often assert that AI can provide personalized education, adapt to individual needs, and enhance cognitive training, making it transformative for education.

AI FOR MANKIND'S FUTURE

In fact, AI-powered educational platforms allegedly unlock new possibilities for early learning and engage students in once-unimaginable ways, which makes the education experience more effective and enjoyable. Yet this enthusiasm isn't universally shared, especially as AI's rapid commercialization raises questions about motives and equity.

Some supporters profit directly from this technology, which feeds skepticism about AI across the general population. Specifically, Precedence Research, a strategic research organization, forecasts the AI education market to grow from $5.18 billion in 2024 to $112.30 billion by 2034, with a compound annual growth rate of 36.02 percent.[161]

Does AI in the Classroom Help Students?

I do recognize that harnessing AI in the classroom has the potential to become an aid for both students and teachers alike. Not only can AI-enabled technologies prove to be popular and quickly gain and maintain the students' attention, but it also has the potential to fuel better learning. Why? Modern students are often impatient and bored in class because they are accustomed to fast-paced social media entertainment, which tends to provide high-quality media content, such as videos on apps like X (formerly Twitter) and TikTok, which deliver significant, action-packed viewing in a flash.

Education is significantly influenced by artificial intelligence.

While proponents tout many benefits of AI in enhancing classroom engagement and personalized learning, empirical evidence reveals both successes and areas of concern—especially across different socioeconomic settings.

Software giant Microsoft aggressively promotes its AI-powered tools for the classroom with the modern student's impatience in mind. For example, Microsoft's Copilot and OpenAI's GPT-4, supported by Microsoft, are available in the Wichita Public Schools, Wichita, Kansas. Olivia Sumner, a fourth through sixth grade teacher at Wichita's Education Imagine Academy, said, "Microsoft Copilot is a game changer." She explained, "What immediately blew me away was the ability to use GPT-4 and the PDF Reader in Edge to generate and tailor lesson plans for my students."[162]

Dyane Smokorowski, coordinator of Digital Literacy at Wichita Public Schools, said breaking down barriers for students is essential. She believes in AI as an educational aid that helps that task. "Students in our district have diverse learning differences and speak 112 languages," says Ms. Smokorowski. "Microsoft Copilot introduces the ability to not only find information with links to content sources, but it also enables us as educators to make that information accessible at the reading level and in the language a student needs."[163]

Even where AI appears to thrive, deeper analysis reveals both strengths and structural weaknesses, especially in underserved communities. Global studies highlight the strengths and limitations of AI in diverse educational environments. Consider empirical research on the impact of AI-driven, personalized learning platforms across diverse educational settings, which has yielded insightful findings. A notable quasi-experimental study conducted in Karnataka, India, involved four hundred middle school students—two hundred from rural areas and two hundred from urban areas—over six months. The study revealed that students using AI-driven, personalized learning platforms experienced significant improvements in mathematics achievement and engagement compared to those receiving traditional instruction. However, challenges such as inadequate infrastructure and the need for specialized teacher training were more pronounced in rural schools, underscoring the importance of tailored implementation strategies to bridge the digital divide.[164]

Another longitudinal analysis examined the effectiveness of virtual schooling in rural settings. That study highlighted that while virtual schools offer customized learning opportunities, the outcomes heavily depend on the quality of implementation and the availability of resources. This suggests that AI-driven educational models may not realize their full potential in under-resourced areas without proper support and infrastructure.[165]

Furthermore, a systematic review of the literature on AI in education emphasized the need for more research focusing on K–12 settings, particularly in rural and under-resourced environments. That review called for studies addressing the unique challenges these communities face to ensure equitable access to the benefits of AI in education.[166]

These studies collectively highlight that while AI-driven educational tools have the potential to enhance learning outcomes, their effectiveness depends upon factors such as infrastructure, teacher preparedness, and contextual adaptability. Addressing these challenges is crucial for ensuring that AI integration in education reduces, rather than exacerbates, existing inequalities.

Beyond outcomes, AI's influence on how students think and learn at a cognitive level is also gaining attention. Specifically, integrating AI into educational settings has profound implications for cognitive processes such as working memory, problem-solving, and metacognition.

Research indicates that AI tools can alleviate cognitive load by automating routine tasks, thereby freeing students' working memory for more complex problem-solving activities. For instance, a study published in *Scientific Reports* found that the use of generative AI tools enabled students to offload simpler tasks, allowing them to focus on higher-order thinking and problem-solving. However, this cognitive offloading may also lead to reduced engagement in critical thinking and self-regulation.[167]

A systematic review highlighted concerns that overreliance on AI could diminish students' metacognitive skills, as they may become less inclined to monitor and evaluate their own learning processes. Therefore, while AI has the potential to enhance learning by supporting cognitive functions, educators must be mindful of fostering students' metacognitive abilities to ensure balanced cognitive development.[168]

But for these cognitive benefits to materialize, teachers must also adapt and grow in their use of AI.

How AI Enhances Teaching Practices

AI tools can revolutionize aspects of education. However, teachers' understanding of AI is crucial for student learning, allowing them to customize the application to each child's learning needs. Given that the outcome depends on a teacher's understanding of the tool, the education establishment ought to invest in professional development for teachers to learn how to use AI tools appropriately. This would benefit students and assist teachers in preparing lessons efficiently, saving time and much more.

Just as educators are adjusting to new tools, students, too, are forming nuanced perspectives on AI in their learning. A 2024 survey by the Digital Education Council revealed that 86 percent of students use AI in their studies, yet 58 percent feel they lack sufficient AI knowledge and skills, and 48 percent feel inadequately prepared for an AI-enabled workforce. Additionally, a 2025 study highlighted that students appreciate AI for immediate feedback and personalized support, but harbor concerns about overreliance, potential loss of critical-thinking skills, and data privacy issues. These insights underscore the importance of equipping students with AI literacy and ethical guidelines to navigate the evolving educational landscape responsibly.[169]

Not only can AI tools be quite helpful in delivering instruction and student understanding, as the above survey suggests, but they can also greatly aid the teacher by helping grade assignments. Those savings provide more time for the teacher to focus on other activities, such as student interaction.

Yet with these benefits come cognitive trade-offs, particularly around critical thinking and self-regulation, which deserve equal scrutiny.

Among the concerns raised by both teachers and students is the potential misuse of AI in academic settings, especially regarding integrity. Specifically, some teachers worry that AI platforms like ChatGPT make cheating inevitable by providing human-like answers. In the past, teachers could root out plagiarism by searching the internet for phrases from the student's suspect paper. However, AI platforms like ChatGPT do not contain precise language from other works, which means the product is not actual plagiarism and therefore teachers have a more challenging task to demonstrate whether the student's work is original. This shift has prompted a return to more analog methods to restore academic honesty.

AI FOR MANKIND'S FUTURE

With AI tools like ChatGPT making it easier than ever for students to cheat, American educators are witnessing a surge in academic dishonesty so severe that traditional exam methods—such as blue books—are making a comeback. Universities including Texas A&M, the University of Florida, and UC Berkeley report dramatic increases in blue book sales as professors seek analog methods to ensure students are doing their own work. While blue books offer a stopgap solution to the explosion of AI-enabled plagiarism, educators like Professor Philip Bunn at Covenant College in Georgia warn that they cannot fully replace the depth of traditional take-home essays. Surveys show nearly 90 percent of students have used AI to complete assignments, and current detection tools are largely ineffective. As AI continues to undermine academic integrity, experts argue that deeper systemic changes, including legal reforms, may be needed to address the growing crisis of intellectual erosion in American education.[170]

Yet, even as AI promises to lighten educators' loads, many teachers report increased anxiety and pressure, raising the question: Are these tools really saving time, or just shifting burdens?

Stress and Burnout: Hidden Costs of AI Integration

While AI tools offer promising enhancements to educational practices, many educators report experiencing increased stress and burnout associated with the rapid integration of technology into their teaching environments. A systematic review published in the *International Journal of Environmental Research and Public Health* found teachers often face high levels of anxiety and stress due to the use of educational technology, citing factors such as insufficient training, constant updates, and pressure to adapt quickly to new tools. Additionally, a 2024 EDUCAUSE survey revealed that 60 percent of teaching and learning professionals in higher education consider their workload excessive, with many indicating that technological advancements like AI have not alleviated their responsibilities as anticipated. These findings underscore the importance of providing adequate support and resources to educators to make sure technological innovations serve as aid rather than additional burdens.[171]

Recognizing the implications of AI on institutional quality, accrediting organizations have begun setting standards for responsible AI use. Specifically, the Southern Association of Colleges and Schools Commission on Colleges (SACSCOC) has issued guidance emphasizing the need for institutions to understand the capabilities and limitations of generative AI tools when preparing accreditation materials.[172]

The SACSCOC cautions against overreliance on AI-generated content, highlighting risks related to confidentiality, data security, and the potential for inaccuracies. Institutions are encouraged to use AI tools judiciously, ensuring that any AI-assisted content is thoroughly reviewed for accuracy and alignment with institutional values.[173]

Similarly, the Western Association of Schools and Colleges—Senior College and University Commission (WSCUC) has outlined principles and restrictions for the use of AI in accreditation processes. Their policy underscores the importance of human oversight in AI applications, particularly in areas involving critical judgment and decision-making. WSCUC advises institutions to maintain transparency about AI usage and ensure that AI tools augment rather than replace human expertise in accreditation-related tasks.[174]

These initiatives reflect a broader trend among accrediting bodies to proactively address the challenges and opportunities presented by AI in education, aiming to uphold the integrity and quality of academic programs in an increasingly digital landscape.

Appendix H offers a practical guide for institutions and educators by outlining how to integrate AI ethically and effectively.

Data Privacy and Security Tension

Parents and educators share concerns regarding AI's use of personal data. After all, AI-driven classroom tools rely heavily on extensive collection and analysis of student data—ranging from academic performance and learning preferences to behavioral patterns. Sensitive data stored in third-party cloud servers raises access and security concerns. While such data can significantly enhance personalized learning experiences, offering tailored educational pathways and improved student engagement, it simultaneously creates risks associated with data breaches and unauthorized access.

Incidents of compromised educational data could lead to serious privacy violations, identity theft, or misuse of information, underscoring the need for rigorous security protocols. Furthermore, educators and policymakers face the complex ethical challenge of balancing the benefits of data-driven personalization with students' rights to autonomy, confidentiality, and informed consent. This tension highlights the necessity for transparent policies, robust data governance, and ongoing oversight to safeguard student well-being and trust while maximizing AI's educational potential.

Beyond logistical and regulatory concerns, a growing number of scholars and believers are asking deeper philosophical and moral questions: What kind of education are we building with AI? And at what cost?

Reasons to Be Skeptical About AI's Role in Education

Many of us remain skeptical about AI's role in education. For example, Neil Selwyn, a professor in the faculty of education, Monash University, Melbourne, Australia, has three decades of research experience with digital technologies and adult learning. He wrote an article that challenges much of the education establishment's optimism about AI. His 2022 article, "The Future of AI and Education: Some Cautionary Notes," published in the *European Journal of Education,* identifies broad areas of contention that warrant closer attention before embracing AI in the classroom.[175]

Professor Selwyn argues, "The future of artificial intelligence (AI) in education—as with any aspect of the future—is uncertain, unpredictable and essentially unknowable." He cautions about the unrealistic and almost giddy enthusiasm associated with AI in schooling, such as claims that it will be a "game changer" and offers "the potential to address some of the biggest challenges in education today."[176]

The professor contends that such optimism is unfounded and not corroborated by the evidence. "While AI currently remains a peripheral feature of most schools and universities," wrote Selwyn, "the ways in which 'early adopted' AI-driven tools and practices raise several contentions that deserve to be taken seriously over the next years." Some of those broad areas of contention outlined in the professor's article are hyperbole, limitations, social harms, and ideology—developed below.[177]

First, Professor Selwyn argued that the technology is being "oversold" to the education establishment. He provides examples from his academic colleagues to illustrate the enthusiasm for AI, noting the excitement about AI for education parallels previous periods of increased government and industry interest in AI. However, he reminds us of investigations regarding the actual use of AI in business start-ups in Europe, even among IT firms, which were dismal. Therefore, he claims "education [much like government and business] remains vulnerable to what can be termed AI theatre," given other failed promises of AI's success.[178]

Professor Selwyn concludes his argument concerning AI hyperbole by citing Emily Tucker, an adjunct professor of law and the executive director at the Center on Privacy and Technology at Georgetown Law. She wrote, "Whatever the merit of the scientific aspirations originally encompassed by the term 'artificial intelligence,' it [has become] a phrase that now functions in the vernacular primarily to obfuscate, alienate and glamorize."[179]

Second, educators must acknowledge AI has absolute limitations. The professor called out one example that labeled the technology "enchanted determinism." That published description states "the belief that AI systems are both magical and superhuman—beyond what we can understand or regulate, yet deterministic enough to be relied upon to make predictions about life-changing decisions."[180]

The naivety of such a view, especially as applied to schooling, is exposed by the fact that AI products are necessarily mathematical systems. Technology's necessary math nexus raises the obvious question: What aspects of education are nonquantifiable? Much of classroom education cannot be captured in data form.

It's a mindless exercise to try to quantify the unquantifiable. "Regardless of the future development of AI techniques," Professor Selwyn states, "it is likely that attempting to account statistically for the contextual layers implicit in any educational situation will inherently be compromised by the breadth of the social components which these calculations attempt to capture."[181]

Third, there are social harms—discrimination—associated with AI in education. Professor Selwyn indicates, "AI models amplify discriminations baked into their training data and subsequently erroneously judge students with non-native accents of cheating on tests or compute higher automated grades for students who fit the profile of those who have historically been more likely to be awarded high grades." He also points out "facial recognition software used in schools that regularly fails to recognise students of colour" and "AI systems designed around processes that predominantly advantage those who are able-bodied and neuro-typical—for example, using eye-tracking data that presumes a steady gaze to denote engagement."[182]

Finally, ideology has a role when AI participates in education. The designer of the technology—the algorithm's creator—is never neutral, which by default means the AI is laden with values and agendas. Educators must acknowledge that AI "needs to be seen as a site of competing values, interests, agendas and ideologies."[183]

Professor Selwyn concludes:

> AI is not a straightforwardly good thing for education. It is not a neutral tool that we can look forward to transforming our classrooms, schools, and universities over the next few years. Instead, the very idea of AI is something that needs to be extensively scrutinised, challenged and questioned by those who make decisions that affect education, and those who work in the field of education. The future of AI in education is best approached as a struggle—as something to be contested rather than a *fait accompli*, something to be taken as given.[184]

Fortunately, both government and the private sectors address Professor Selwyn's criticisms. Specifically, emerging regulatory frameworks and ethical guidelines are increasingly addressing concerns to include the intersection of AI in consumer tech with moral and faith-based principles.

EDUCATION: IS AI A BOON OR BUST FOR LEARNING?

For instance, the European Commission's Ethics Guidelines for Trustworthy AI emphasize human dignity, privacy, and transparency—values that resonate with theological concepts such as the *imago Dei*, which holds that every individual is created in the image of God and deserves respect and protection. Similarly, several educational consortia, including the International Society for Technology in Education (ISTE), have advocated robust data protection policies in schools, urging institutions to adopt clear guidelines for AI integration that safeguard student privacy and ensure human oversight.[185]

Concerns raised by secular scholars are echoed in faith-based communities, where the ethical and spiritual dimensions of AI are also being carefully weighed. Some religious organizations like the Vatican call for AI ethics and issued statements underscoring that the deployment of AI in educational and domestic settings must uphold principles of human dignity and communal authenticity, cautioning against the potential for digital systems to replace genuine, interpersonal relationships.

Appendix I presents the Southern Baptist Convention's 2023 resolution on AI and emerging technologies, affirming that while such tools offer great potential, their development and use must be guided by Scripture, uphold human dignity, and reflect Christlike love, with the Church proactively shaping their ethical impact rather than reacting passively.[186]

These initiatives highlight that while AI offers transformative benefits, its application must be carefully balanced with ethical considerations and faith-based values to protect the sanctity of human interaction and the inherent worth of every individual. Such caution is mirrored in the Christian community, where AI's moral and spiritual implications are under close review.

AI Issues for Christians and Their Education

AI can be a powerful tool in Christian education in formal settings (Christian schools, colleges, seminaries) and in home schools, as well as in the realm of informal relationships, such as discipleship.

Like in secular education, the Christian teacher can use AI to tailor lessons to the students' learning speeds and styles. For the homeschoolers,

AI supports both academic subjects and Bible-based curricula to include Bible memory games or biblical lessons tailored to the children's level.

Christian educators can use AI to create devotionals, lessons, and Bible studies. For missionaries, it can help translate Christian resources into other languages for help spreading the gospel.

Teachers can also use AI to help prepare academic lessons, grade papers, and perform a variety of other administrative tasks. The technology frees them to invest more time in relationship-building and spiritually mentoring students.

AI can be especially helpful in restricted countries where teachers and missionaries aren't physically able to travel. More specifically, it will one day help deliver Christian education securely to those oppressed by government agents.

Of course, there are potential downsides to AI in education for Christians. We are reminded of Proverbs 1:7: "The fear of the Lord is the beginning of knowledge, but fools despise wisdom and instruction" (NIV). Therefore, AI is about offering facts, not opening our hearts to the gospel or nudging our spirits. Further, discipleship isn't just intellectual, but relational and spiritual. And remember: AI will not model Christlike character, much less mentor or convict us.

AI can present a temptation to misuse learning shortcuts or to sideline biblical principles. Christian educators must help students embrace learning as an act of worship, not just as a task to complete. After all, Proverbs 10:9 reminds us, "Whoever walks in integrity walks securely, but whoever takes crooked paths will be found out" (NIV).

Christian educators must recognize that AI material doesn't necessarily reflect a Christian worldview. Rather, it reflects the data it is trained on, which could be Christian, value-neutral, or anti-Christian. Therefore, understand that students may absorb ideas subtly through AI tools that potentially contradict biblical truth or worse.

Christian education also tends to be communal, with students learning together rather than relying too much on AI, which can isolate them and reduce their contact with more mature Christians. Finding the right mix of AI lessons and teacher-student time is a judgment call.

EDUCATION: IS AI A BOON OR BUST FOR LEARNING?

Finally, Christians need to be wise regarding how they engage AI. Specifically, some good rules of thumb include using AI carefully and for the good of students; not letting convenience replace formation; keeping human connection central; testing AI products against Scripture; and using it to spread the gospel and make education more accessible.

Remember, AI is a tool, not an educator. It can serve our families and the education process well if used with biblical wisdom, relational grounding, and a commitment to forming the whole Christian person.

To guide Christian educators through these complexities, a biblically grounded framework can provide clarity, discernment, and practical tools. The DISCERN model offers such a path.

A Christian Framework for Evaluating AI in Education

Christian educators face the growing challenge of determining which AI tools can be safely and wisely integrated into student learning. To navigate this, the following seven-part framework—DISCERN—offers biblically grounded, practical criteria to help assess AI technologies considering Christian values:

D—Dignity

Does the AI uphold the dignity of students as image-bearers of God? Avoid tools that commodify students, reduce them to data points, or encourage conformity over creativity (Genesis 1:26–28).

I—Integrity

Does the technology promote honesty, accountability, and original work? Evaluate whether the tool encourages plagiarism, deception, or dependence, rather than character formation and moral discernment (Proverbs 10:9; Hebrews 5:14).

S—Stewardship

Is AI used as a tool for wise stewardship of time and talent? Determine whether the tool frees educators and students to focus on higher goals—like mentoring, creativity, or service—or simply automates convenience at the cost of depth (Genesis 2:15; 1 Peter 4:10).

C—Community

Does it enhance or erode authentic community and relational learning?

Christian education thrives in community. AI that isolates learners or replaces human relationships may undermine the Body of Christ (Hebrews 10:24–25; Romans 12:5).

E—Ethics
Is the AI ethically developed and used? Investigate whether the company follows transparent, fair data practices and whether its algorithms reflect justice, equity, and truth (Micah 6:8; Philippians 4:8).

R—Redemptive purpose
Does this tool support a redemptive vision for learning and life? Ask how this technology aligns with the school's mission to disciple students who love God with their hearts and minds (Deuteronomy 6:5; Romans 12:2).

N—Nurture
Does the tool nurture wisdom, not just knowledge? Favor AI that helps students grow in critical thinking, discernment, and virtue—not just in content mastery (Proverbs 1:7; Colossians 2:3).

Conclusion

As we reflect on the transformative power of AI in education, it becomes clear that these technological shifts aren't merely practical adjustments, but also catalysts for deeper societal, ethical, and theological reflection.

The growing reliance on AI challenges us to reconsider what it means to learn, create, and seek truth—and how these endeavors reflect fundamental aspects of human dignity and our spiritual nature.

As we've seen, AI is already transforming education, reshaping how we teach, learn, and form young minds. Yet the classroom is only one domain where AI is redefining human capability. Nowhere is this transformation more consequential—or more ethically complex—than in the field of medicine. In the next chapter, we turn our attention to how AI is advancing healthcare through diagnostics, treatment planning, and patient care, while also raising serious questions about privacy, trust, and the sanctity of life.

Chapter 6

AI: MEDICAL INNOVATION AND RISKS

AI won't replace doctors, but doctors who don't use AI will be replaced.[187]

SANGEETA REDDY
Joint managing director, Apollo Hospitals, India

Just as AI is reshaping how students learn and teachers instruct, it's revolutionizing how patients receive care and doctors deliver treatment. The same technologies that personalize learning are now diagnosing disease, managing hospitals, and even performing surgery. As we transition from classrooms to clinics, we find that AI's greatest promises—and its most urgent ethical questions—are perhaps most visible in the realm of medicine.

AI-driven medical advancements are rapidly increasing and benefiting humanity. For example, innovations like traditional medical devices are highly welcomed, as are advances that enhance medical care by diagnosing and treating skin cancer and eye diseases, as well as by locating brain hemorrhages. Other applications improve patient-care administration by managing the flow of patients and promoting the use of electronic health records.

The impact of AI in medicine can be organized into several powerful domains: diagnostic tools, patient-interaction technologies, robotic surgery, drug discovery, and mental health support. Each of these areas showcases AI's ability to enhance medical accuracy, efficiency, and reach, but also raises important questions about trust, responsibility, and spiritual care.

To understand AI's concrete value in healthcare, let's now examine some of the most remarkable medical breakthroughs made possible by this technology.

AI-related Medical Breakthroughs

The Mayo Foundation for Medical Education and Research tracks significant AI advancements in healthcare. A recent book published by the Mayo Press and authored by Heather E. Schwartz, *Medical Artificial Intelligence Breakthroughs*, offers an excellent summary of notable AI-related medical advancements. Some of those developments include:

AI diagnosis: Dr. Edward Shortliffe created the AI algorithm known as MYCIN, detailed in chapter 2. That program, which detects blood infections, is widely available and has been a lifesaver for many patients because of early detection. The development of MYCIN took place over six years during the early 1970s at Stanford University.

From diagnostics to patient interaction, AI has also entered the realm of bedside care.

AI-powered virtual nurse: One of the fears about AI is that it will replace humans. Indeed, Timothy Bickmore's 2008 Northeastern University creation of "Elizabeth," an avatar nurse program based on observations of real nurses, is an example of a replacement care provider. Patients "preferred Elizabeth to human nurses since she never made them feel rushed," wrote Schwartz.[188]

Therapeutic AI evolved further with tools like Ellie, pushing the emotional boundaries of machine-patient relationships.

As these examples show, AI's reach is expanding into areas of care once thought to require uniquely human compassion and judgment, raising spiritual and ethical questions about trust, dignity, and the nature of healing, which will be addressed later in this chapter.

AI therapist: Earlier, I introduced Joseph Weizenbaum, the inventor of the program ELIZA, who tested his early AI chatbot with therapy patients. Surprisingly, many users formed emotional connections with the program, despite its simplicity. This marked the beginning of conversational AI in mental health—a concept that has since evolved dramatically. Decades later, the University of Southern California's Institute for Creative Technologies developed a more advanced version named Ellie, an AI-powered avatar equipped with sensors that respond to facial expressions and vocal tone. Unlike human therapists, Ellie is always available, never distracted, and capable of offering consistent engagement.[189]

Meanwhile, artificial intelligence is being applied far beyond therapy, especially in response to looming shortages in healthcare. By 2030, the world is projected to face a shortfall of 4.5 million nurses, largely due to burnout.[190] To help meet this challenge, manufacturing giant Foxconn, in collaboration with Nvidia, has developed Nurabot, a collaborative nursing robot designed to relieve human caregivers of physically demanding and repetitive tasks. These AI-driven tools are already being implemented in Taiwan's leading medical centers, helping to create "smart hospitals" that rely on automation for efficiency and support.[191]

In addition to caregiving, AI is now driving innovation within the human body itself.

Nanobots for inside-the-body work: Nanobots are AI-powered microscopic robots first evaluated in 2015. In 2017, university scientists used nanobots to deliver chemotherapy to only cancer cells.[192] More recently, researchers developed nanobots that can be injected into the patient using an ordinary hypodermic syringe. The nanobots then move around inside the body and can withstand harsh environments. Further, upgraded, "smart" versions will feature controllers, sensors, and clocks.[193]

Building on the advancements in virtual nursing and caregiving AI, another promising innovation is the AI-powered foot scanner, which serves as an early warning system for heart-failure patients.

An AI-powered foot scanner developed by Heartfelt Technologies has shown promise in preventing hospitalizations for heart-failure patients. The device, tested on twenty-six patients across five NHS trusts, detects fluid buildup (oedema) in the feet and ankles—one of the key signs of worsening heart failure. By capturing 1,800 images per minute, it calculates fluid volume and alerts healthcare teams when thresholds are exceeded, providing a thirteen-day advance warning of potential hospitalizations. The device operates passively without requiring patient input and even works through socks. With 82 percent of participants opting to keep the device after the study, the scanner offers a solution to the shortage of heart failure nurses by acting as a "virtual nurse" enabling earlier intervention and potentially reducing hospital admissions. This innovation could significantly improve outcomes for those at risk of heart failure, addressing the growing demand for proactive healthcare solutions.[194]

Similarly, AI's ability to assist in heart-health monitoring is further exemplified using AI to identify heart conditions, such as the detection of atrial fibrillation (AFib) through electrocardiograms.

AI for help identifying heart conditions: Itzhak Zachi Attia, an AI engineer at Mayo Clinic, used AI technology with electrocardiograms to identify heart conditions. Attia's program correctly identifies the risk of atrial fibrillation (AFib) in 80 percent of patients. AFib is a type of irregular heartbeat that increases the risk of stroke by about five times.[195]

AI for early detection: Pancreatic cancer is curable if found early. However, data showed that some patients who later developed cancer did not show early symptoms. Therefore, Mayo Clinic created a profile of nonsymptomatic patients who later developed the disease. The clinic uses that data to build an AI program that triggers initial treatment and saves lives.[196]

AI harnessed to prosthetic arms, hands, and fingers: University of Minnesota scientists implanted an electrode where the prosthetic attaches to the user's flesh to capture nerve signals. The user's brain sends signals to the limb and the AI inside the electrode learned to translate those signals into action.[197]

Dr. Rafael Fonseca of the Mayo Clinic underscores how AI will shape personalized, integrated care. The following examples

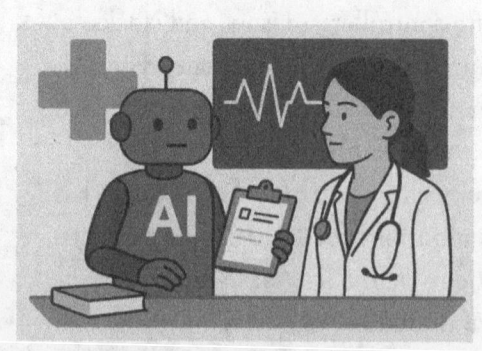

AI has become a significant factor in the advancement of healthcare.

AI: MEDICAL INNOVATION AND RISKS

demonstrate this across three domains: diagnostics, therapeutic aids, and patient-interface technologies.[198]

AI-powered diagnostics and imaging: Radiology AI includes tools like Google's DeepMind to analyze x-rays, MRIs, and CT scans to detect cancers, fractures, and neurological conditions.[199] AI-powered retinal scans help detect diabetic retinopathy and macular degeneration by analyzing eye scans.[200]

There are several AI-related early-disease detection applications as well. For example, there are AI models able to detect Alzheimer's, kidney disease, and chronic obstructive pulmonary disease years before the symptoms appear.[201] There are also AI tools to identify brain lesions that improve diagnosis for epilepsy; AI-powered, wearable devices that detect life-threatening conditions; and an AI-guided point-of-care ultrasound capability to diagnose tuberculosis.[202]

In oncology, AI is now playing a pivotal role in both diagnosis and treatment personalization. A new AI-powered diagnostic test developed by Artera Inc. and used in a trial by University College London and the Institute of Cancer Research can identify which men with high-risk, non-metastatic prostate cancer will most benefit from the drug abiraterone, potentially saving lives and costs. The test analyzes biopsy images to detect tumor features invisible to the human eye and classifies patients as biomarker-positive or negative. For the 25 percent with biomarker-positive tumors, abiraterone nearly halves the five-year mortality risk, while others gain little additional benefit and can avoid side effects. Experts argue that precise targeting enabled by AI not only improves patient outcomes, but also makes widespread use of abiraterone more cost-effective than previously believed.[203]

Building on this trend of AI-driven oncology, radiotherapy is also being transformed by intelligent, adaptive systems that optimize treatment delivery with unprecedented precision.

In June 2025, University Hospitals in Cleveland adopted the Varian Ethos 2.0 AI-powered radiotherapy system to deliver more precise and adaptive cancer treatment, especially for hard-to-treat conditions like pancreatic cancer. Unlike traditional methods, Ethos generates high-resolution scans before each session, allowing real-time updates to radiation plans based on the patient's anatomy and internal organ movement. This enables physicians to safely deliver higher radiation doses, improving effectiveness while minimizing harm to surrounding healthy tissue. The technology is noninvasive, requires no sedation, and is already covered by commercial insurance. Since October, about one hundred patients have been treated at UH Seidman Cancer Center, with plans to expand to more than thirty patients per day. University Hospitals is currently the only major provider in Northeast Ohio offering this advanced system, which is part of a broader $39 million investment to enhance cancer care across the region.[204]

As AI systems like Ethos demonstrate, the boundary between diagnostics and treatment is becoming increasingly blurred: AI can now adapt not only to diagnose disease, but to deliver care with surgical accuracy. This same intelligence is being infused into virtual tools as well, as seen in the rise of AI-powered medical assistants.

Google's medical chatbot, AMIE (Articulate Medical Intelligence Explorer), with image-processing capabilities and built-in clinical logic, beats human doctors in diagnostic accuracy and communication skills. AMIE is powered by Gemini 2.0 Flash, representing a step closer to creating an AI medical assistant that thinks just like a medical doctor. It combines images with clinical data and mimics how physicians synthesize information to diagnose and treat patients. It can be especially helpful with faster triage, broader access to diagnostic support, and help in overcoming poor image quality and incomplete patient records.[205]

While diagnostics represent a critical application of AI, technology is also revolutionizing how we discover and deliver treatments.

AI-accelerated new drug discovery: Dotmatics, a research and development software company acquired by Siemens in 2025, is using AI to identify potential drug candidates at significant savings in time. Phil Mounteney, Dotmatics' vice president of science and technology, said: "The art of drug discovery is really finding drugs in these massive haystacks of data. AI is like a supercharged magnet that helps us sort through those haystacks and find the needle way more efficiently than before." For example, Mounteney said, AI helped accelerate the COVID

AI: MEDICAL INNOVATION AND RISKS

mRNA vaccine rollout by "leveraging years of stored research and rapidly analyzing it to guide development."[206]

Dotmatics plans to combine AI with scientific data platforms to accelerate the drug-development process. Specifically, it begins by scanning entire chemical libraries of data to identify "overlooked or repurposable compounds." Then it plans to model drug candidates with certain proteins and diseases. Next it will automate "lab workflows," and, finally, it plans to pull input from historic datasets to inform present-day projects.[207]

In addition to medical development, AI is enhancing the precision of how care is delivered—particularly through robotics in the operating room.

AI-powered robotic surgery: Robotic surgery began in 1985, when a robotic arm was used at Long Beach Memorial Medical Center in California to guide a needle into a patient's brain for a biopsy. The field advanced significantly in 1994 with US regulatory approval of the first surgical robot—the Automated Endoscopic System for Optimal Positioning (AESOP), designed to control laparoscopic cameras. This laid the groundwork in 2000 for the introduction of the da Vinci Surgical System, a teleoperated robot that gave surgeons enhanced precision through fine control of miniature instruments.[208]

By 2018, robotic systems were involved in approximately 15 percent of all surgeries. Today, their presence is especially dominant in procedures like prostatectomies, over 90 percent of which are now robot-assisted.[209]

In 2024, researchers at Johns Hopkins University and Stanford University developed an AI system that allowed the da Vinci robot to autonomously perform surgical tasks. Using imitation learning, the AI was trained on hundreds of surgical videos captured from wrist-mounted cameras, enabling it to manipulate tissue, handle needles, and perform suturing with surgeon-level accuracy. This eliminated the need for manually coding every movement and marked a major step toward autonomous robotic surgery, promising greater efficiency and surgical precision.[210]

Another cutting-edge development comes from France, where the company Robeauté is pioneering an AI-powered microrobot for neurosurgery. Roughly the size of a grain of rice, this three-millimeter-long device is designed to navigate the brain's complex pathways to reach and treat tumors otherwise too risky to access through traditional surgery, especially those near critical areas controlling speech or movement.[211]

The microrobot enters through a small incision and uses rotating silicone rings at its tip to gently shift tissue without causing damage. It can perform biopsies, implant electrodes (such as for Parkinson's disease), or deliver drugs directly to tumors. Its path is directed by MRI imagery integrated with AI, allowing surgeons to avoid sensitive regions of the brain with remarkable accuracy.[212]

This minimally invasive tool offers enormous potential—not only for earlier diagnosis of brain tumors, but also for safer, more effective treatments.[213]

AI-driven robotic systems are becoming increasingly vital as the healthcare industry faces a looming shortage of surgeons. The Association of American Medical Colleges projects that the US will be short nearly twenty thousand surgeons by 2036. As AI and robotics advance, they are poised to take on a growing share of the surgical workload—ensuring that high-quality care remains accessible even amid workforce challenges.[214]

AI is not only transforming the way we operate; it's reshaping how medicine is tailored, delivered, and made more humane in the process.

AI-personalized medicine: Google's AI tool, Capricorn, accelerates the identification of personalized cancer treatments.[215] Other tools revolutionize genetic testing to identify pathogenic variants and mutations "that influence medical diagnoses, treatment planning, and policy development."[216]

An example of AI personalizing medicine comes from a study conducted at Manipal Hospitals in India. IBM Watson for Oncology was used to support treatment decisions for cancer patients. The AI system provided treatment options that matched oncologists' recommendations in 93 percent of breast cancer cases. This demonstrated how AI could support personalized oncology care, especially in resource-constrained settings.[217]

AI's role is also expanding into mental health and neurology, where it offers both diagnostic insight and therapeutic companionship.

AI: MEDICAL INNOVATION AND RISKS

AI-aided mental-health treatment and neurology: AI chatbots like Woebot and Wysa provide cognitive behavioral therapy (CBT) and mental health support.[218] AI tools also detect early signs of Alzheimer's by analyzing speech patterns and brain scans.[219]

A 2025 study out of the University of California San Diego "found that a gene recently recognized as a biomarker for Alzheimer's disease is actually a cause of it, due to its previously secondary function." The researchers "used AI to help both unravel this mystery of Alzheimer's disease and discover a potential treatment that obstructs the gene's moonlighting role."[220]

Beyond aiding patients directly, AI assists physicians in making evidence-based decisions through advanced analytics.

AI helping with clinical-decision support: There are AI tools that assist medical professionals with evidence-based recommendations to help reduce diagnostic errors and accelerate decision-making.[221] Other AI algorithms help doctors predict patient outcomes through continuous monitoring data, lifestyle inputs, and genetics.[222]

An AI tool called FaceAge generates predictions of your biological age, the rate at which you are aging as opposed to your chronological age. That algorithm helps doctors at Mass General Brigham (MGB), Boston, Massachusetts, predict survival outcomes for people with cancer.[223]

FaceAge was trained on 58,851 photos of "presumed healthy individuals from public datasets," which were then compared with 6,196 photos of cancer patients taken before radiotherapy treatment. MGB indicates FaceAge generated a biological age of about five years higher for cancer patients than their chronological age.[224]

Therefore, according to Hugo Aerts, director of AI in Medicine at MGB, "We can use artificial intelligence to estimate a person's biological age from face pictures, and our study shows that information can be clinically meaningful."[225]

AI-related developments improve healthcare in these areas and others such as chronic disease management, drug development, telemedicine, and workflow automation.

Dr. Fonseca, with the Mayo Clinic, opined on the future of medical AI:

> The real future will be one in which doctors will not even know they are using AI and yet they will deliver best care. AI will be found in many places and will anticipate problems and solutions. AI cannot replace the human aspect of medicine, but it will assure us of best practices being considered.[226]

Despite these advancements, it is vital to evaluate whether AI tools perform reliably in real-world settings.

Long-Term Studies and Real-World Validation

Clinical evidence regarding the long-term efficacy and safety of AI tools in healthcare is gradually emerging, though large-scale and longitudinal evaluations remain limited. Early clinical trials and real-world surveillance studies have demonstrated promising initial results. For instance, AI-driven diagnostic tools in radiology and ophthalmology have shown accuracy comparable to or superior to expert clinicians in controlled settings. A few post-market evaluations have been done to verify these benefits over extended periods and among different patient groups.

A 2019 study, "Artificial Intelligence-enabled Healthcare Delivery," emphasizes that many current AI-based medical applications rely on retrospective or small-scale clinical studies. Thus, there is an urgent need for systematic, prospective clinical trials and robust post-market surveillance mechanisms to continually monitor the performance, safety, and efficacy of AI interventions as they move from research environments to widespread clinical use. Continuous monitoring is especially critical because AI systems often evolve through ongoing learning from real-world data, introducing potential variations in performance that could impact patient outcomes over time.[227]

Addressing this gap requires coordinated efforts among healthcare organizations, regulatory bodies, and technology providers to conduct rigorous longitudinal studies, implement standardized protocols for continuous surveillance, and transparently share data on AI-driven healthcare outcomes. Until more comprehensive long-term evidence is available, cautious and responsible adoption of AI technologies—accompanied by transparent monitoring and ongoing research—is essential to ensure patient safety and sustained effectiveness.

Building on these early insights, let's explore how AI may transform medicine in the near and distant future.

Future of AI and Medicine

The future of AI in medicine looks incredibly promising, with innovations set to revolutionize how we diagnose, treat, and prevent diseases. Consider likely future AI-related developments.

Early and enhanced diagnostics: Anticipate that AI-powered imaging will come to identify pre-disease conditions such as subtle changes in cells. AI algorithms will integrate information from genomics, proteomics, and metabolomics to identify hidden disease patterns.

Future personalized medicine: AI will help physicians tailor treatment to patients' individual genetic makeup and lifestyle. Also, AI will help anticipate how a patient will react to certain medications rather than rely upon a trial-and-error approach.

AI "copilot" for doctors: Anticipate AI to become a common companion for doctors—helping with diagnoses, suggesting treatments, and flagging issues in medical records to enhance the medical professional's expertise. Those same "copilots" will improve the accuracy for the surgeon and the outcomes for the patients.

Improve medicines: AI algorithms will help generate new drug candidates while predicting molecular structures and test virtual compounds. Further, AI will model biological processes to reduce the need for extensive animal-validation testing.

Improve hospital care: AI-powered predictive analytics will help hospitals better manage resources by forecasting patient admissions and tracking the use of limited testing and treatment devices. It will also personalize treatment schedules to optimize care.

Neurological advances: Virtual therapies will improve to provide emotional support and detect early signs of mental health conditions.

AI FOR MANKIND'S FUTURE

Also, expect neuro-AI interfaces to dramatically improve treatments for neurological disorders by detecting disease before symptoms appear.

AI-powered global health: Expect AI to be key in global disease surveillance to help anticipate outbreaks. Further, telemedicine AI assistants will become more common, helping diagnose simple conditions and guiding patients remotely.

While much of AI's role in medicine is rooted in current clinical practice, some futurists foresee far-reaching transformations, including radical life extension.

AI fountain of youth: Might AI help humans leap life expectancy? Some tech CEOs claim humans will double their lifespan by the year 2030.

"In 1900, the average life expectancy of a newborn was 32 years. By 2021 this had more than doubled to 71 years," according to Our World in Data. That significant increase in life expectancy is attributed to changes in medicine, public health, and living standards.[228] Today, Dario Amodei, CEO of the AI company Anthropic, predicts technology will help double human lifespans to 150 years by 2030. Months after that 2024 statement, Amodei told the World Economic Forum in Davos, Switzerland, that AI could deliver the breakthrough in just five years. "If you think about what we might expect humans to accomplish in an area like biology in 100 years, I think a doubling of the human lifespan is not at all crazy," he said.[229]

Futurist Ray Kurzweil agrees with Amodei. He predicts AI could halt aging by 2032 either thanks to AI-designed nanobots patrolling our bodies to repair cells and deliver drugs or by uploading our brains into the cloud that preserves our identity free of biology.[230]

Not everyone agrees with Amodei and Kurzweil about AI halting the aging process. S. Jay Olshansky, a leading aging researcher at the University of Illinois Chicago, said there is no evidence AI can slow or stop aging. Olshansky rebutted the idea in *Nature Aging*, indicating the AI-related enthusiasm is ahead of science.[231]

While these projections inspire both excitement and caution, real-world practitioners are already navigating AI's benefits and limitations today.

AI: MEDICAL INNOVATION AND RISKS

Consider an interview hosted by the *New England Journal of Medicine*, which included three medical doctors who identified the promise and hazards associated with AI and machine-learning tools for clinical and administrative uses in medicine.[232]

Dr. Timothy Poterucha, a cardiologist and clinical researcher at Columbia University, works on AI applications in cardiology. He is using AI technologies "in order to do a better job of taking care of patients with heart disease." He explained that his research goal "is to decide who better needs an echocardiogram," an ultrasound of the heart that is expensive and has low availability. "So, our question was," explained the doctor, "can we use one of these less expensive technologies [such as the twelve-lead ECG—fifteen dollars] in order to predict the results of an echocardiogram?"[233]

He continued:

> So, we took all the patients at Columbia University that had had both of these tests, the ECG and the echocardiogram, and then we trained the artificial intelligence model, based on the ECG [results], to diagnose whether someone had a heart-valve problem…we wanted to see whether this artificial intelligence model could do it. And it actually can do it very well. It can pick out the patients that are most likely to have one of three heart-valve diseases, and then we actually try to go out and find those patients and have them undergo this test.[234]

Dr. Isaac Kohane is the chair of the department of biomedical informatics at Harvard Medical School and co-editor of the "AI in Medicine" series in the *New England Journal of Medicine*. He stated AI benefits patients in two ways. Initially, the physician recognized that a substantial amount of detailed information was available about the patient, including all adverse events, allergies, and complete medical history. That's the role of AI. "I think that for the routine care of patients, having AI as an assistant to the doctor is going to play to the strength of the doctor as an intellectual, compassionate provider of care, and this will be a significant boost in quality of care."[235]

Dr. Kohane added:

On the other extreme, there are areas of medicine where human beings are just not well-equipped to serve independently. And we've seen, for example, in undiagnosed patients, there is an important interaction between the ability of AI algorithms to sort through large patterns between genetic variants and clinical findings and the expertise of doctors to arrive at diagnoses for these long-suffering patients that previously we could not provide a diagnosis. So it's that combination of this superhuman capacity to know a lot about what is, for most doctors, a relatively arcane area, genomics, and to what doctors do know well, which is a lot of clinical manifestations of disease, in a way that works for patients that without this we could not serve our patients well.[236]

So, in the undiagnosed disease network that I'm part of, we do in fact routinely use machine-learning models, AI models, to actually comb through all the associations that have been found of genetic variant mutations in the genome and various syndromes and try to match that to patient histories. And we do that working with doctors who are also expert in particular areas of medicine, we've found that combination has allowed us to diagnose on the order of 30% of the patients that we have been referred across 12 academic health centers throughout the United States that were previously undiagnosed for years, despite seeing many doctors. So that's where it works.[237]

Dr. Maia Hightower is chief digital and technology officer at the University of Chicago School of Medicine and CEO of Equality AI. Dr. Hightower uses AI for both operational/administrative as well as clinical use. Most notable about Dr. Hightower's interview was the reason she founded her company called Equality AI.

She explained she "was the chief population health officer at the time when Dr. [Ziad] Obermeyer['s]...paper[238] on dissecting racial bias

AI: MEDICAL INNOVATION AND RISKS

in algorithms used to manage the health of populations was published. And at the time, the study showed that a widely used algorithm had a flaw that resulted in a decrease by half in the rate of referral to case management for Black patients compared to white patients who were equally sick. And they were able to identify the bias and then mitigate the bias in the algorithm and fix it."[239]

At that time, Dr. Hightower admitted the study results were "one-off—the algorithm was fixed, and we could all move on our way." However, then COVID happened. She continued:

> And there was this real awareness on social injustice and the dual pandemic of health care inequality. And it was showing in the numbers—like Black patients and Latino patients and the South Pacific Islander patients, native American patients were dying a lot more frequently from COVID. And so, I developed what's called the health care IT [information technology] equity maturity model, looking for all the different areas within health care where systemic bias is embedded in our health care IT systems, and recognizing that my workforce is not very diverse.[240]
>
> And that was really what Obermeyer was highlighting, is that in his paper, there was that lack of diversity. And if there had actually been a more diverse team on creating the algorithm, that most likely some of the errors that had been made would've been avoided.[241]

She illustrated the bias in the algorithm:

> A great example is on the American Heart Association [website article], "Get to the Heart Guidelines," there is a calculator that helps you calculate the risk of heart failure and whether a patient should be referred to a cardiologist. And in that algorithm, if you push the button and add Black race, then the patient's less likely to be referred to...a cardiologist. The score changes. In this case, the score goes down and is below the threshold for referring to a cardiologist.[242]

These doctors illustrate some of the good and bad characteristics of AI-powered medicine. To translate these promising use cases into everyday healthcare, institutions must thoughtfully integrate AI tools into their clinical workflows.

Integrating AI Solutions into Clinical Practice

Integrating AI into daily clinical practice involves more than simply deploying advanced technologies in medical offices. Rather, it requires careful planning, rigorous training, and ongoing support. Successful implementation often begins with structured training programs aimed at healthcare professionals, ensuring that clinicians can effectively interpret and utilize AI-generated insights without compromising their clinical judgment. For example, some institutions provide firsthand workshops or online modules designed to help medical staff become proficient in navigating AI-driven diagnostic platforms.[243]

Additionally, user-friendly interfaces are crucial for seamless integration, enabling clinicians to interact effortlessly with AI tools as part of routine patient care. Platforms incorporating intuitive dashboards, clear visualizations, and real-time decision-support prompts encourage widespread adoption and minimize workflow disruption.

However, transitioning AI from lab to clinic faces practical challenges. User resistance, stemming from skepticism about technology reliability or fears about job displacement, can hinder successful integration. Equally significant are the financial implications: Initial implementation costs, ongoing maintenance expenses, and infrastructure upgrades represent substantial investments, particularly for smaller or resource-limited facilities. To mitigate these barriers, institutions must proactively engage clinicians throughout the development and deployment processes, demonstrating the clinical value and reliability of AI solutions and providing continuous technical support and feedback mechanisms.[244]

Thoughtful strategies considering clinician training, usability, organizational culture, and financial sustainability are essential for successfully embedding AI into everyday clinical practice, translating its theoretical promise into tangible improvements in patient care.

Yet, as adoption increases, so do ethical and relational concerns that must be addressed alongside technical challenges.

Concerns About AI and Patient Care

There are numerous concerns that AI will undermine the patient-provider relationship, reduce the skills of providers because of overdependence on machines, undermine medical transparency, misdiagnose or inappropriately treat patients based on AI-related errors, exacerbate racial or societal biases, and introduce hard-to-detect program biases. Therefore, it's no surprise that many patients and medical providers view AI negatively. After all, AI appears to correlate with the negative current and future well-being among certain groups, according to a 2023 study in the *International Journal of Social Welfare*. The study, which used a large dataset from 137 countries from years 2005–2018, found AI has a more robust dampening effect on personal well-being among young people, men, high-income groups, high-skilled groups, and manufacturing workers.[245]

Although AI-driven medical innovation is rapidly advancing and benefiting much of humanity, some areas for improvement require more attention before more individuals can rely on their contribution to healthcare.

Such skepticism has prompted stronger calls for regulatory oversight and ethical guidance in the deployment of AI in medicine.

Regulations, Guidelines, and Ethical Frameworks for AI in Medicine

This chapter wouldn't be complete without mentioning existing or emerging efforts to regulate AI's roles in medicine better.

The implementation and uses of AI in healthcare settings are actively shaped, monitored, and evaluated by a network of regulators, professional organizations, and institutional ethics committees. Regulatory bodies such as the US Food and Drug Administration (FDA)[246] and the European Medicines Agency (EMA) have begun developing frameworks to assess the safety, efficacy, and fairness of AI-driven medical devices and algorithms. Professional organizations—including the American Medical Association (AMA)[247] and the World Medical Association (WMA)[248]—provide detailed ethical guidance, urging medical practitioners to ensure transparency, accuracy, and human oversight in AI-powered clinical decisions. Additionally, hospital ethics committees regularly review and approve AI systems before clinical deployment, evaluating ethical risks and safeguarding patient autonomy.

From a legal perspective, there is an ongoing debate and emerging policy surrounding liability in cases of AI misdiagnosis or medical errors, with unresolved questions about whether responsibility lies with medical professionals, healthcare institutions, software developers, or some combination thereof. Data-protection laws, such as the Health Insurance Portability and Accountability Act (HIPAA)[249] in the United States and the General Data Protection Regulation (GDPR)[250] in the European Union, also significantly influence AI implementation by setting rigorous standards for patient data privacy and security. Together, these regulatory, ethical, and legal frameworks aim to balance AI's transformative potential with the imperative to maintain patient safety, dignity, and trust.

While medical associations and governments offer ethical and legal frameworks for AI in healthcare, Christian believers bring a theological perspective that adds unique moral and spiritual considerations.

Christian Concerns Regarding AI and Healthcare

Trust is a major issue for many people regarding AI-powered healthcare. These concerns are particularly relevant for Christians who prioritize biblical issues.

Christians believe every person is made in the image of God (Genesis 1:27). Therefore, we are concerned that using AI in healthcare may depersonalize the patient by relying heavily on technology for diagnosis or patient interaction that reduces the human touch, which lacks true empathy and ignores God's direction.

Christians are especially concerned about the issue of moral agency and responsibility. Unfortunately, medical decision-making is becoming more reliant on AI systems, which makes it unclear who is morally responsible. Our Christian faith emphasizes moral responsibility and discernment, something AI will never truly exercise, and medical personnel must never be allowed to delegate responsibility exclusively to machines.

End-of-life decisions are an extremely sensitive issue for Christians. AI tools may play a role in recommending end-of-life care or decisions. Our stress on the sanctity of life will inevitably collide with secular and objectively generated AI recommendations to make those types of decisions based on efficiency or cost-effectiveness, not on spiritual values.

The allocation of healthcare resources will be an issue for Christians as well. After all, AI might worsen healthcare disparities if certain treatments are prioritized for the wealthy or residents of specific countries, leaving others to suffer. It's important to remember that Christians hold to justice, care for the poor, and equal access to healing, among other values (Matthew 25:40).

AI systems typically gather private health information about most people. Christians may be especially sensitive about AI systems collecting that information and how it might be used to violate their privacy and spiritual values.

Some Christians will be especially concerned that AI-driven healthcare promotes a mechanistic view of the human, reducing us to data points or another biological system. Our perspective means we place emphasis on unity of body, mind, and soul. Healing is more than a physical process; it's also spiritual.

Finally, many Christians are especially concerned about AI's influence in the realm of human genetics (e.g., CRISPR*, predictive medicine), which raises questions about whether technology is "playing God" and overstepping human limits. We have a God-given responsibility to protect the helpless like the unborn and embrace humility before God's creation.

Taken together, these innovations, concerns, and values suggest that AI's future in medicine will be as much a matter of ethics and theology as of science.

---

* CRISPR (clustered regularly interspaced short palindromic repeats) is a revolutionary gene-editing technology that allows scientists to precisely alter DNA within living organisms.

Conclusion

AI is rapidly transforming the landscape of modern medicine—from streamlining diagnostics and personalizing treatment to reimagining how care is delivered. This chapter explored both the remarkable opportunities and the sobering challenges posed by these technologies, including the risks of algorithmic bias, overdependence, and the need for strong regulatory oversight.

What's clear is that AI is not just enhancing medicine, it is reshaping its very ethics and priorities. The promise of faster, more accurate, and more accessible care must be weighed against the enduring need for human wisdom, compassion, and moral accountability. For Christians, this transformation presents a dual responsibility: to harness AI's benefits in ways that honor the dignity of each patient, and to ensure that human empathy and God-given discernment remain central to the healing process.

As we move to the next chapter, our focus expands from the hospital room to the halls of government, where AI is influencing policy, shaping public services, and redefining the relationship between citizens and the state.

Section Three

AI AND PUBLIC INSTITUTIONS

The rise of powerful AI will be either the best or the worst thing that has ever happened to humanity.[251]

Stephen Hawking (1942-2018)
English theoretical physicist and cosmologist

Government is rapidly embracing the power offered by artificial intelligence. At the national level, the US needs to aggressively call for a "democratic AI" to become the global standard, emphasizing transparency, accountability, and human rights. Chapter 7 illustrates how this vision is being pursued through ongoing federal efforts to harness AI's efficiency while safeguarding public trust and institutional integrity.

While national efforts set the tone for AI governance, the impact of AI is perhaps most visible in our daily lives through local government and essential public services. Chapter 8 reviews how AI is transforming local administrations, delivering more efficient services and tangible benefits to taxpayers.

From schools and sanitation to city planning and emergency response, AI is reshaping the way local institutions serve their communities. Yet beyond civilian life, AI is also revolutionizing national defense. Chapter 9 explores how emerging technologies are transforming the military—from autonomous weapons to AI-driven, strategic decision-making—amid an escalating global arms race.

Chapter 7

GOVERNMENT'S AI MANDATE

Technology is moving at a pace where unless we work together, we won't be able to operate.[252]

RICH CORBRIDGE
Chief digital and information officer at DWP Digital

The federal government must play an initiative-taking role regarding AI's future. Specifically, it should protect the public from AI-related abuse, promote efficiency, and guard our ability to leverage technology in the face of radical foreign and unscrupulous domestic cyber threats.

This chapter addresses our federal government's many current and recommended roles regarding AI's promise to transform modern society. First, we consider AI and our foreign competitors. Second, we outline how government should regulate AI tech to our best advantage and safety. Third, we examine how officials in Washington must harness AI to promote government efficiency. Finally, we look at how it must protect citizens from AI abuse while fostering trust in technology.

US Global AI Leader?

For the federal government to effectively fulfill its AI mandate, it must first recognize the global landscape in which AI innovation and governance unfold. After all, there is a compelling set of arguments for the US to lead the world in AI development and application. Sam Altman, chief executive of OpenAI, argued in 2024 that we currently "face a strategic choice about what kind of world we are going to live in." He explained, "Will it be one in which the United States and allied nations advance a global AI that spreads the technology's benefits and opens access to it, or an authoritarian one, in which nations or movements that don't share our values use AI to cement and expand their power? There is no third option, and it is time to decide which path to take."[253]

Mr. Altman advocates keeping totalitarian governments such as communist China at bay. That requires the US to heavily invest in digital infrastructure, energy production, and human capital to establish global AI institutions that benefit the US economy and shape a Western vision for the technology. However, asserting global leadership in AI is only credible if matched by consistent and principled governance at home. As international rivals race ahead, the US not only must invest in innovation, but also establish clear domestic guardrails that guide ethical and secure AI development. Yes, the outcome of such an effort results in either a "democratic AI" or an "authoritarian AI"; arguably similar efforts compelled our efforts during the Cold War's nuclear-arms race, which the US won by a strong will and significant investment.

The contemporary technology race between a "democratic AI" and "authoritarian AI" was the topic of a May 2025 US Senate hearing. At that event, Senator Ted Cruz (R-TX), the chair of the Senate Commerce, Science, and Transportation Committee, said: "China aims to lead the world in AI by 2030." He argued, "In this race, the United States is facing a fork in the road. Do we go down the path that embraces our history of entrepreneurial freedom and technological innovation? Or do we adopt the command-and-control policies of Europe?"[254]

"Look, there is a race, but we need to understand what we're racing for," agreed Senator Brian Schatz (D-HI). "It's not just a sort of commercial race, so we can edge out our nearest competitor in the public sector or the private sector. We're trying to win a race so that American values [democratic] prevail."[255]

Even America's intelligence community (IC) agrees the stakes are high regarding the AI race. "China is the existential threat to American security in a way we really have never confronted before," Central

GOVERNMENT'S AI MANDATE

Intelligence Agency (CIA) Deputy Director Michael Ellis said on May 21, 2025. He continued by stating that a key CIA objective is helping US companies maintain "a decisive technological advantage" to counter communist China's malign actions against the homeland.[256]

Mr. Ellis emphasized that the Trump administration is laser focused on denying the communist regime any strategic edge, especially in areas such as artificial intelligence and quantum computing. "The IC is very good at…counting Soviet tanks…to be ready for a possible conflict in Europe in the Cold War," Ellis said. However, "when you ask the IC to look at issues…where Chinese companies are in artificial intelligence research, it's not one that we've been well-positioned historically to think about."[257]

Evidence of the AI race with China is easy to identify. For example, on May 20, 2025, China launched the first dozen AI-powered satellites of an expected 2,800-satellite fleet. Beijing aims to de-tether its dependence on ground-based computers with satellites using the cold vacuum of space as a natural cooling system to then crunch data up to one thousand petaflops (one quintillion operations per second).[258]

"It's a good time to think about how we can put AI into space, not just in your laptop or cellphone," Wang Jian, director of Zhejiang Lab, told the *South China Morning Post*. "Space has, again, become the frontier for us to think about what we can do in the next 10, 20 or 50 years."[259]

The outcome of the AI race will not be easily settled, because the AI industry is global by nature, consisting of many multinational companies associated with the technology, such as OpenAI, Microsoft, Alphabet, and Meta. These firms employ international personnel who use data collected globally. Therefore, the challenge is that "AI companies could simply decide to withhold their products from the more strictly regulated markets, and even move their headquarters, if need be," wrote Eva Erman and Markus Furendal, both with Stockholm University. The result could become a technology war whereby AI firms migrate to the country or region that imposes the least-restrictive regulation.[260]

Unfortunately, nations such as China, if given too much of a voice regarding AI tech, could write the rules to favor their communist views. After all, as a Heritage Foundation article states, "China is at the bleeding edge of using emerging technologies for oppression—both at home and abroad." That article reminds the reader that communist China's "state-run data system…uses AI to flag whole categories of people for detention in the western Xinjiang region."[261]

Beijing has also partnered with technology companies like iFlytek, a Chinese cutting-edge firm, to "develop an AI-powered voice-recognition system that can automatically identify specific voices in phone conversations. Its mass facial-recognition systems operate under standards that segment the population by eyebrow size and skin color." For example, China's "Sharp Eyes" is a surveillance project that uses AI to analyze citizens' movements, associations, and medical records with the aim of social control.[262]

The Chinese communist party also exports such AI technologies to other authoritarian regimes. Beijing has 296 surveillance relationships in ninety-six countries labeled "AI Champion" companies, such as the one in Ecuador, where China's Huawei, a telecommunications company, built a network of over four thousand cameras for the country's police and intelligence services to conduct surveillance of the citizenry.[263]

There is no doubt that China aims to lead in global AI. However, Beijing has competition from ally Russian President Vladimir Putin, who said in 2017 he wants to lead in the AI race because "the one who becomes the leader in this [AI] sphere will be the ruler of the world."[264]

Other nations are paying close attention to the AI tech race as well. On May 13, 2025, Saudi Arabia launched Humain, a state-backed AI company, signaling a strategic move to become a global leader in AI. Crown Prince Mohammed bin Salman chairs that AI launch, which is funded by a Public Investment Fund of $940 billion. Humain's objective is to establish Saudi Arabia as a global AI hub that includes next-generation data centers, advanced AI infrastructure, robust cloud capabilities, and sophisticated AI models. The project's launch included prominent tech figures like Elon Musk, Sam Altman, and Mark Zuckerberg.[265]

Neighboring country, the United Arab Emirates (UAE) also seeks to establish itself as an AI powerhouse by welcoming Europe's brightest

GOVERNMENT'S AI MANDATE

minds with tempting employment offers. UAE even established the Regulatory Intelligence Office to oversee the pioneering use of AI to create regulations, representing a fundamental shift in governance.

It is noteworthy that in the shadow of the Saudi AI announcement, the UAE and US signed an agreement for the Gulf country to build the largest AI campus outside the US, a ten-square-mile campus powered by five gigawatts of power. This deal reflects the Trump administration's confidence that it can manage the Nvidia-provided chips' security because US firms will manage the data centers, according to US Secretary of Commerce Howard Lutnick.[266]

Also of note is that the UAE struck a deal with Italy to build an AI center. The UAE's tech firm G42 is partnering with Italian AI startup iGenius to develop a major AI supercomputer in Italy. The deal is part of a broader framework by which the UAE pledged to invest $40 billion in Italy to create an AI data center project, named Colosseum, the "largest AI computer deployment" in Europe.[267]

Both Mideast countries—the UAE and Saudi Arabia—are ruled by monarchs, and, if given the opportunity, they would have AI algorithms reflect their Islamist view of the world, something Christians must acknowledge.[268]

The US and other freedom-loving nations must take action to prevent China, Russia, and other authoritarian regimes from dictating global rules for artificial-intelligence applications. That starts by creating international standards for building and using AI technology, which means a global commitment to open sourcing AI technologies to avoid malicious use. Also, there should be a worldwide mandate that requires explainable AI as opposed to the proliferation of "black box systems," such as those the Chinese employ against minority groups.

Fortunately, there is a global democratic AI effort underway. In 2025, Sam Altman launched OpenAI's Stargate Project to build a national "democratic" AI infrastructure first in the US and then across the free world. The $500 billion Stargate initiative has President Trump's endorsement and includes hi-tech partners Oracle and SoftBank. Its first supercomputing campus is under construction in Abilene, Texas, and

AI FOR MANKIND'S FUTURE

many more are coming to provide the backbone of "future economic growth and national development."[269]

The Stargate partners intend to help spread democratic AI, "which means the development, use and deployment of AI that protects and incorporates long-standing democratic principles." The partners indicate that democratic principles include "the freedom for people to choose how they work with and direct AI, the prevention of government use of AI to amass control [as in communist China], and a free market that ensures free competition." Also, the project specifically aims to broadly share the benefits of AI, to "discourage the concentration of power, and help advance our mission," and "we believe that partnering closely with the US government is the best way to advance democratic AI."[270]

OpenAI for Countries, the global Stargate initiative, provides an alternative to authoritarian versions (read "communist China") of AI "that would deploy it to consolidate power." To advance this effort to other countries, OpenAI committed to "partner with countries to help build in-country data center capacity; provide customized ChatGPT to citizens; continue evolving security and safety controls for AI models; raise and deploy a national start-up fund; and partner countries also would invest in expanding the global Stargate Project."[271]

Governments are embracing AI for many routine functions as well as putting in place guardrails to protect humans from technology.

While international leadership is essential, America's credibility in shaping global AI norms depends on its domestic example. To lead abroad, the US must first demonstrate principled and effective governance at home.

Put in Place AI Regulations and Laws

The US ought to put in place AI-related domestic laws before dictating to the rest of the world how to regulate technology.

GOVERNMENT'S AI MANDATE

The European Union's landmark 2024 Artificial Intelligence Act was the world's first regulation on artificial intelligence. Europeans realized AI was growing stronger every day, which meant it was necessary to regulate this fluid domain or suffer the consequences.

The EU's AI Act identifies classifications for risk, such as unacceptable threats by which the tech system judges people based on a behavior known as social scoring as well as banning predictive policing tools.[272]

Further, EU's AI Act "is the first comprehensive regulation addressing the risks of artificial intelligence through a set of obligations and requirements that intend to safeguard the health, safety and fundamental rights of E.U. citizens and beyond, and is expected to have an outsized impact on AI governance worldwide," wrote Mia Hoffmann, a fellow at the Center for Security and Emerging Technology at Georgetown University.[273]

AI experts call on other countries and regions to enact legislation protecting their citizens. "We need as much innovation in governance and risk mitigation as we need in development and deployment," said Beena Ammanath, who leads the Global Deloitte AI Institute and Trustworthy AI at Deloitte.[274]

Fortunately, there has been some movement in America on the AI regulation front. In late 2024 after the EU passed their AI Act, the Biden administration began to address the need to set limits on AI tech. President Biden signed an executive order (EO) "mandating that developers of AI systems that could pose risks to U.S. national security, the economy, public health, or safety share the results of safety tests with the U.S. government, in line with the Defense Production Act, before they are made public." That order also called on the Commerce Department to develop guidance for content authentication and watermarking to protect American AI from fraud and theft.[275]

Presidential executive orders are insufficient to regulate the rapidly evolving AI tech, however. Congress must recognize the fragile and fleeting opportunity by passing laws to promote free innovation that protects open-source AI development, which could keep America at the forefront of the AI revolution. Although we're still waiting for Congress to act, the Biden administration's EO did identify numerous AI tech areas that need regulating.

Biden's 2023 EO aimed to protect America, but these ideas need to be legislated. Eight AI-related companies at the time confirmed their commitment to the safe, secure, and trustworthy development of AI technology. However, these firms are international, with diverse goals among foreign partners.

The executive order outlined three principles that "must be fundamental to the future of AI—safety, security, and trust." These principles provide a good starting point for legislators to draft laws to protect our citizens, our economy, and our place in the emergent tech world.

Consider each principle with an example.

First, ensure that AI products are safe. Companies must host tests of AI systems by independent experts before their release to the public. The purpose is to prevent adverse societal effects. Also, AI tech firms must share information about the tech to manage any risks such as best practices for safety.[276]

Second, the systems must include cybersecurity and insider-threat safeguards. Further, companies must facilitate third-party discovery and reporting of vulnerabilities in their AI systems, as well as a robust reporting mechanism that leads to quick repair of identified issues.[277]

Third, AI systems must earn public trust. Users must be advised when a product is AI-generated, as well as be informed regarding the system's capabilities, limitations, and areas of appropriate use. Further, algorithms must avoid harmful bias and discrimination and protect privacy.[278]

Those principles are a good starting point. However, some extremely specific AI tech areas require special government regulation. Among the most urgent areas necessitating targeted AI regulation is the electoral process, wherein disinformation, deepfakes, and algorithmic manipulation can undermine democratic legitimacy.

AI and Election Risks[279]

In September 2023, US Senator Amy Klobuchar (D-MN) chaired a hearing that considered AI-related risks for elections. "Given the stakes for our democracy, we cannot afford to wait," the senator said. She indicated:

GOVERNMENT'S AI MANDATE

We are already seeing this technology being used to generate viral, misleading content, to spread disinformation, and deceive voters. There was an AI-generated video, for instance, posted on Twitter of one of my colleagues, Senator [Elizabeth] Warren, in which a fake [avatar] Senator Warren said that people from the opposing party should not be able to vote. She never said that, but it looked like her.[280]

Senator Klobuchar continued, "The problem for voters is that people are not going to be able to distinguish if it is the opposing candidate or their own candidate if it is them talking or not. That is untenable in a democracy."[281]

The federal government should use AI where it makes sense, such as monitoring immigration, administering justice, and ensuring social-welfare provision as well as providing efficient public services. However, we must acknowledge that incorporating AI tech into federal agencies presents a variety of challenges—some ethical and legal, and others that impact infrastructure as well as create institutional obstacles.

Beyond elections, AI poses unique legal challenges that require new interpretations of intellectual property law and constitutional rights.

Can AI Earn a Patent?

Future AI-related laws must address intellectual property rights. A law will be necessary before the US Supreme Court can weigh in on the issue. After all, on April 24, 2023, the high court refused to address a case regarding whether an AI machine could fall within the statutory definition of "inventor" under the Patent Act. More specifically, can an AI-generated invention receive patent protection? The US Patent and Trademark Office requires a human, not a machine, to obtain inventorship recognition.[282]

Avoid Another "Robodebt"

The government ought to encourage using AI-tech where it makes sense, because it can reduce costs, increase consistency in decision-making, and reduce bias. However, it presents risks because it may have inherent biases that escape notice. Consider the case of AI gone wrong in Australia, "where an AI system erroneously identified overpayments and calculated debts deemed to be owed by social security beneficiaries." Those AI "errors" led to incorrect or inflated repercussions for "vulnerable, low-socioeconomic debtors...including individuals losing their housing and food, experiencing severe mental health issues, and even committing suicide."[283]

That debacle, known in Australia as "Robodebt," is an example of the challenge associated with the government's use of AI that goes awry. Of course, the "error" was in the algorithm, which erroneously fingered a host of innocent social security beneficiaries. This illustration is important for lawmakers to appreciate the "nature of issues that [can] arise when technology design is deficient in terms of decision-making methodology." Further, even more distressing is that the "users of the agency's services [at the time] were unaware of the use of AI decision-making and enforcement."[284]

The Australian case reinforces the criticality of carefully reviewing the AI-powered decision-making program. After all, AI technology can upend all past institutional norms and pose significant challenges. That's why the government must carefully draft laws identifying appropriate venues for AI-generated decision-making.

Cases like Australia's Robodebt illustrate the perils of underregulated AI. Yet, ironically, some US lawmakers advocate for a decade-long pause in AI oversight—an approach that invites similar disasters.

Push for No AI Regulation

There are some members of Congress who want to avoid too much regulation of AI to stay ahead of communist China. Consider that US House Energy and Commerce Chairman Brett Guthrie (R-KY) added an amendment to the 2025 budget to give AI a free pass for the next decade. Specifically, Guthrie's amendment read: "No state or political subdivision may enforce any law or regulation regulating artificial intelligence models, artificial intelligence systems, or automated decision systems during the 10-year period beginning on the date of enactment of this Act."[285]

GOVERNMENT'S AI MANDATE

Meanwhile, US Senator Ted Cruz (R-TX) called for the federal government to take a "light touch" in regulating AI. At a May 2025 Senate hearing featuring several AI experts, Cruz criticized former President Biden for putting safeguards around AI technology as "seemingly something out of [George] Orwell." Rather, Cruz, a constitutional lawyer, said, "To lead in AI, the United States cannot allow regulation, even seemingly benign ones, to choke innovation and adoption."[286]

The senator promised to release legislation creating a "regulatory sandbox" for AI, modeled on President Bill Clinton's approach to the early days of the internet. "Adopting a light-touch regulatory style for AI will require Congress to work alongside the president, just as Congress did with President Clinton."[287]

Senator Cruz's "light-touch" AI approach has opposition from some in the tech community. Specifically, Sam Altman, CEO of OpenAI, testified:

> The same capabilities that will enable [artificial intelligence] to support scientific breakthroughs and accelerate human progress will also create new risk areas. Ultimately, I believe the good will outweigh the bad by orders of magnitude.... This future can be almost unimaginably bright, but only if we take concrete steps to ensure that an American-led version of AI, built on democratic values like freedom and transparency, prevails over an authoritarian one.[288]

Of course, the barriers holding AI back are significant, such as copyright lawsuits filed against AI companies. AI firms maintain giant databases full of copyrighted sources that they use to generate material without permission. That's why California and other states are considering legislation to protect copyright material from misuse by generative AI systems.[289]

The issue of AI's unfettered access to copyrighted materials has already earned attention in federal court. Specifically, US District Judge Vince Chhabria of the Northern District of California, who presided over the case against Meta's Llama AI, said:

You have companies using copyright-protected material to create a product that is capable of producing an infinite number of competing products. You are dramatically changing, you might even say obliterating, the market for that person's work, and you're saying that you don't even have to pay a license to that person. I just don't understand how that can be fair use.[290]

Protecting intellectual creativity is important in America. After all, the idea of copyright is mentioned in our Constitution in Article 1, Section 8: "To promote the progress of science and useful arts, by securing for limited times to authors and inventors the exclusive right to their respective writings and discoveries."

The operative word in the Constitution is "exclusive." That should create a full stop for Senator Cruz's "light-touch" and Representative Guthrie's ten-year moratorium. However, it would appear these gentlemen believe we can only beat the Chinese in AI by endorsing violations of our copyright laws.

The above material makes the case for regulation of AI. How much oversight and in what areas appears to be the sticking points.

As an aside, the US Government Accountability Office (GAO) closely monitors AI-related developments to help lawmakers stay informed. A March 2025 GAO publication profiled its ongoing efforts on artificial intelligence, which includes the production of a host of reference materials for government personnel as well as the citizenry in general. See the end note for more information about GAO's efforts.[291]

Regulating AI is only one side of the government's role; the other is strategically employing AI to enhance public administration and service delivery.

AI and Government Efficiency

The government should consider ways in which AI technology can enhance its administration and service delivery—jobs now occupied by humans. One of the most visible recent efforts to modernize public service delivery through AI came in March 2025, when the Trump administration revealed a nationwide AI initiative aimed at transforming how federal agencies operate.

In March 2025, the Trump administration announced plans to launch a government-wide AI platform, built by the General Services Administration (GSA) to streamline federal operations using a chatbot, analytics dashboard, and API access to major AI models like OpenAI, Google, and Meta. Initially developed under the Biden administration with a focus on internal security, the tool aims to enhance daily workflow and contract analysis while avoiding risks from commercial AI tools. Led by former Tesla engineer Thomas Shedd and supported by the Department of Government Efficiency, the initiative reflects a broader push to "AI-ify" the federal government. However, internal response among federal employees has been largely negative due to concerns about bugs, security flaws, and potential disruptions to essential contracts. While currently optional, the platform may eventually become mandatory across departments.[292]

Despite early resistance, this platform highlights how federal leadership is beginning to explore practical AI applications across agencies. Other departments like the IRS and NASA are already deploying AI in mission-critical functions, suggesting a growing, though cautious, embrace of automation in public administration.

The Internal Revenue Service (IRS) uses AI to help select tax returns for audit. The IRS' goal with AI's aid is "to use the best available technology to identify returns with the highest potential for adjustments resulting from audits, both in frequency and magnitude of the adjustment."[293]

The National Aeronautics and Space Administration (NASA) uses AI to assist with science and technology development. Specifically, it is a valuable tool for researchers, engineers, data scientists, and technologists "in pursuing the ground-breaking discoveries that we are known for, including the command and controlling of our spacecraft and other supporting infrastructures." Further, NASA's AI strategy states: "We are dedicated to continuing the use of AI in a safe and fully transparent approach so that the public can have high confidence in the outcomes and benefits."[294]

Appendix J outlines ten key ways the US government is leveraging AI to improve public services—ranging from cybersecurity and defense to healthcare, education, and infrastructure—enhancing efficiency, decision-making, and strategic planning across federal agencies.

Remember that efficiency alone is not enough. Citizens must trust that AI-powered government decisions are fair, transparent, and aligned with democratic values. Without that trust, even the most advanced systems may be viewed with suspicion or resistance.

Build Citizen Trust in AI

One of the few things the Biden administration agreed upon with the first Trump term was the importance of "promoting the use of trustworthy artificial intelligence." That's the title of President Trump's Executive Order 13,960, which guided federal agencies to ensure that they "design, develop, acquire, and use AI in a manner that fosters public trust, and confidence while protecting privacy, civil rights, civil liberties and American values."[295]

That order focused on the effects of AI development and adoption in the public and private sectors. The document provided ten principles for federal agencies to use in harnessing AI, with particular attention for the impact on public trust.

Most of those citizen-focused principles include promoting public confidence in government-harnessed AI by providing a mechanism for feedback on governing AI; assessing risks; considering costs and benefits; considering its impact on fairness and discrimination; and practicing disclosure and transparency that increase trust and confidence.[296]

The Trump EO mentioned the word "trust" multiple times. That's because citizens will be suspicious and lose confidence in government decisions unless the AI process is explainable, which prompted research on the topic.

That 2024 study, found in the *Government Information Quarterly*, states, "Amidst concerns over biased and misguided government decisions arrived at through algorithmic treatment, it is important for members of society to be able to perceive that public authorities are making fair, accurate, and trustworthy decisions."[297]

Explainable artificial intelligence (XAI) is a remedy for "opaque algorithmic decisions," according to the study. XAI "is designed to make an AI system's behavior 'more intelligible to humans by providing explanation' of the underlying causes for its or another agent's decisions and behaviors."[298]

The study identifies four types of XAI: influence-based, demographic-based, case-based, and sensitivity-based. Consider the following explanations for each type:

- Influence-based explanations provide "information on input variables such as race and gender and describes how much each contributed to the output."[299]
- Demographic-based explanations involve the "same demographic or attribute categories as those of the data subject in question." For example, when establishing a car insurance premium, the AI considers groupings like female drivers or operators of a particular age group.[300]
- Case-based explanations consider similar past cases in the database. XAI is "designed to find the most similar cases of a query case in the database" and then show them to the user, who can compare the examples with their case and assess the decision. This approach may apply to house pricing, assessing financial risk, and making medical recommendations.[301]
- Sensitivity-based explanations demonstrate "how much of an input variable would have had to change to produce a different outcome." For example, "If 10% or less of your driving took place at night, you would have qualified for the cheapest tier [of the car insurance premium]."[302]

Government ought to use XAI to help the public recognize whether authorities are making fair and trustworthy decisions. It should also recognize that the same XAI approach will not work for every citizen, therefore the four alternative XAI templates provide more options.

Democratic Participation and Civic Engagement in AI Governance

While transparency tools like XAI are essential, they must be complemented by participatory governance models that reflect democratic values and community voices. Therefore, governments must develop policies to regulate artificial intelligence, because it is vital that these processes aren't limited to technocrats, lobbyists, or global elites. For AI governance to be truly democratic and trustworthy, public participation must be built into both the policy formation and oversight processes. Citizens are not merely subjects of AI policy, they're the ones most directly affected by its outcomes in areas such as hiring, healthcare, policing, education, and digital speech.

Democratic societies have long relied on participatory mechanisms—such as public comment periods, advisory panels, and ballot initiatives—to ensure that policies reflect the collective moral compass of their people. These mechanisms are even more urgent in the age of AI, where rapid technological change outpaces legal norms, and where opaque systems often make decisions with little human accountability.

Models of Civic Engagement in AI Governance:

- **Public comment systems:** Agencies such as the US Federal Trade Commission (FTC) already host public comment periods on proposed AI guidelines and enforcement actions. These open calls allow citizens, researchers, religious leaders, and civil society groups to weigh in on the ethical and societal impacts of AI regulation before it becomes law.
- **Citizens' assemblies:** Countries like France, Ireland, and the UK have successfully used citizens' assemblies—diverse panels of randomly selected citizens who deliberate on complex issues with expert input—to guide policymaking. Applied to AI, such assemblies could deliberate on questions like biometric surveillance, AI in hiring, or education algorithms, ensuring that a plurality of values and voices are heard.
- **Ethical advisory boards with public representation:** Many countries are forming national AI ethics boards. Including

nontechnical members—such as faith leaders, ethicists, parents, and youth representatives—can ground decisions in real-world human values, not just commercial or technical interests.
- **Participatory tech assessments:** Universities and nonprofits are also experimenting with methods like participatory technology assessments (pTAs), where communities collaboratively evaluate the risks and benefits of AI in their specific contexts. These models offer bottom-up input to government policy.

Including these mechanisms does more than enhance procedural fairness; it strengthens the moral legitimacy of AI governance. In a Christian ethical framework, this aligns with the biblical call to speak on behalf of the marginalized (Proverbs 31:8) and seek justice in the public square (Micah 6:8). If AI systems are to shape the common good, then the common people must have a say in their design and oversight.

Ultimately, fostering civic engagement in AI governance not only democratizes technological power, but also guards against authoritarian creep, corporate overreach, and the erosion of individual dignity. As the stakes of AI governance rise, so must our commitment to democratic stewardship.

In addition to involving citizens in shaping AI policies, governments must enforce those policies through clearly defined institutional mechanisms to secure compliance and accountability.

Enforcement Mechanisms and Practical Oversight of AI Regulation

Trust among the citizenry also grows when governments establish clear and robust enforcement mechanisms to make certain AI-related laws and guidelines translate into meaningful action. In the United States, existing bodies such as the Federal Trade Commission (FTC) play a crucial role in overseeing compliance with AI regulations, especially regarding data privacy, consumer protection, and algorithmic transparency. For instance, the FTC can conduct audits and investigations of technology companies to verify that their AI systems align with stated privacy policies, antidiscrimination statutes, and consumer protection standards.

Beyond existing structures, there have been proposals for specialized agencies, such as a resolute "Algorithmic Accountability Office" or a national AI regulatory authority, tasked explicitly with evaluating and auditing complex AI-driven systems, including "black-box" algorithms with decision-making processes that may otherwise be opaque. Specialized agencies would audit, certify AI products before deployment, and penalize organizations for violating guidelines or concealing harmful algorithms. In practice, enforcement could include fines, suspension of AI product deployment, mandatory transparency reports, or corporate accountability frameworks that hold executives responsible for significant compliance failures.

By clarifying these enforcement strategies and institutional responsibilities, policymakers can more effectively reassure citizens that regulatory ambitions for AI will move beyond aspirational goals into concrete, accountable action. Ensuring rigorous oversight reinforces trust and affirms core democratic values such as fairness, transparency, and human dignity, aligning practical regulation with broader moral and ethical standards.

While federal and international actors often receive the spotlight in AI policy debates, state and local governments are on the front lines of implementing and regulating AI in everyday life. From predictive policing systems to algorithmic housing tools and AI-enabled public services, subnational authorities play an increasingly decisive role in shaping how AI technologies impact citizens. Consider:

- **Surveillance and policing:** Several municipalities have adopted or pushed back against AI-enabled surveillance. For example, San Francisco became the first major US city to ban the use of facial recognition technology by local agencies in 2019, citing civil liberties concerns.[303] In contrast, Detroit's Project Green Light uses real-time video surveillance and AI-powered facial recognition in partnership with

private businesses to deter crime, though it has drawn criticism for accuracy issues and potential racial bias.[304]
- **Housing and social services:** In Los Angeles, city officials have piloted machine-learning tools to prioritize housing allocation for homeless residents. These tools analyze patterns in data to predict which individuals are most at risk, aiming to better match resources to need. However, concerns remain about transparency, racial fairness, and the quality of training data used.[305]
- **Education and employment:** States like California and New York have launched AI literacy initiatives in K–12 education and are exploring legislation to govern AI use in public hiring. New York City passed a law requiring audits for AI tools used in employment decisions to prevent algorithmic discrimination.[306]
- **Regulatory innovation:** In the absence of federal legislation, several states are stepping in. California's Consumer Privacy Act (CCPA) and its successor, the CPRA, are among the most comprehensive state-level frameworks, affecting how AI companies handle data and target consumers. Meanwhile, Colorado and Illinois have enacted biometric privacy laws that restrict how companies can collect and use facial or fingerprint data, with implications for AI-powered applications.[307]

These examples show that states and cities are not only sites of experimentation, but are also critical regulators of AI. Their proximity to community needs allows them to respond more quickly to both the opportunities and harm of AI systems. However, the diversity of local approaches also underscores the need for coordination to prevent a fragmented "patchwork" of laws that could confuse developers and erode public trust.

From a Christian ethical standpoint, this local responsiveness is vital. Subnational governments are often better positioned to protect vulnerable populations, uphold dignity in decision-making, and embody the principle of subsidiarity—governance at the most immediate and appropriate level.

Coordinating AI Policy: Federal, State, and Local Dynamics

Given the federal structure of governance in the United States, AI regulation often emerges from a combination of federal, state, and local initiatives—potentially resulting in a fragmented or "patchwork" regulatory landscape. Many states, such as California, have already enacted specialized AI and data-protection laws, including the California Consumer Privacy Act (CCPA), which sets stringent standards for data privacy and consumer rights around AI-driven decision-making. While these state-level efforts help establish necessary safeguards, they also create compliance challenges for AI developers and businesses operating across multiple authorities, raising the risk of regulatory confusion or conflict.[308]

To address these challenges, federal guidelines or a cohesive national AI regulatory framework could provide much-needed clarity and consistency by preempting conflicting local statutes or establishing minimum standards with which state and local laws must harmonize. A coordinated approach could facilitate innovation, ensure robust protection of citizen rights, and streamline compliance—strengthening the US' ability to compete across the world while upholding core democratic values.

Data Governance and Protection of Civil Liberties

As government agencies increasingly adopt AI-driven technologies, effective data governance is essential to safeguarding citizens' privacy and constitutional liberties. Given the vast quantities of personal information AI systems often require—including biometric, financial, healthcare, and location data—strict policies would help manage how to store, share, and protect this data.

Key practices include implementing rigorous encryption standards and securing sensitive citizen information during the transmission and storage. Adopting data-minimization principles, whereby agencies collect only data strictly necessary for defined purposes, can reduce the risk of unauthorized surveillance or misuse. Furthermore, clear protocols for data-breach reporting would help with timely notification to affected citizens, detailed disclosure of breaches, and systematic remediation measures.

Importantly, these data-governance practices directly intersect with fundamental civil liberties, particularly regarding constitutional protections such as the Fourth Amendment in the United States, which guards against unreasonable searches and seizures. AI-based tools used in law enforcement, intelligence gathering, or public administration must thus be subject to rigorous oversight and transparent review to prevent unwarranted or excessive intrusions into citizens' private lives.

By emphasizing data governance—through encryption, data minimization, breach transparency, and robust accountability frameworks—governments can better manage the tension between leveraging AI's efficiency and upholding citizens' constitutional rights. Such careful stewardship of data and vigilant protection of civil liberties is essential for maintaining public trust, ensuring democratic accountability, and preventing the misuse of powerful AI capabilities.

While data governance is vital domestically, these principles must also inform our international partnerships to create a global framework rooted in democratic accountability.

International Cooperation and Shared Ethical Frameworks for "Democratic AI"

To translate the vision of a "democratic AI" into practical global action, the United States can leverage existing multinational frameworks and alliances. For instance, the Organization for Economic Cooperation and Development (OECD)[309] has established widely accepted AI principles emphasizing transparency, fairness, human rights, and accountability—principles the US has endorsed and that align closely with democratic values. Similarly, the Global Partnership on Artificial Intelligence (GPAI),[310] a multilateral initiative including democracies such as Canada, France, Germany, the UK, and the US, provides a collaborative platform to share best practices, align technical standards, and conduct joint research on responsible AI.

By actively engaging in these forums, the US can lead efforts to formalize shared ethical guidelines, set interoperability standards for AI technologies, and coordinate joint investments in research and development. Such alliances can serve as a democratic counterweight to authoritarian AI strategies such as in China, reinforcing norms around privacy, human dignity, and the ethical use of technology. Through sustained diplomatic and scientific cooperation, these international partnerships can make certain democratic AI principles move beyond rhetoric into practical, enforceable global standards.

Further, while current regulations focus on near-term risks and applications, governments must also begin anticipatory governance for future breakthroughs such as artificial general intelligence (AGI) and artificial superintelligence (ASI). These advanced systems, which could one day exceed human cognitive abilities across domains, present unprecedented challenges to sovereignty, global stability, and human safety. Proactive international coordination—including scenario planning, treaty frameworks, and global monitoring bodies—is essential to mitigate existential risks and make certain that future AI developments remain aligned with human values and democratic principles.

While technical policies and public engagement form the scaffolding of democratic AI governance, deeper questions remain. What kind of society are we building with these tools? What moral compass will guide their use? For Christians, these are not peripheral issues—they lie at the heart of our concern for justice, dignity, and faithful stewardship.

AI, Governance, and a Christian Perspective

As governments increasingly guide and regulate artificial intelligence, it becomes essential to consider how these initiatives intersect with deeper moral and spiritual values. From a Christian standpoint, principles such as human dignity, stewardship of creation, and the sanctity of human agency offer crucial touchpoints for evaluating governmental AI strategies. For example, efforts to develop "democratic AI," instead of authoritarian or surveillance-oriented systems, resonate strongly with Christian values emphasizing individual autonomy, free will, and just governance rooted in ethical accountability and transparency. Guaranteeing that AI systems respect and uphold these principles aligns closely with theological understandings of human beings as bearers of the divine image called to exercise thoughtful stewardship over technological advancement. Thus, a faithful response to governmental AI initiatives requires ongoing vigilance to ensure policies and regulations promote efficiency and security and affirm and preserve humanity's spiritual and moral integrity.

Theological Reflection: Government, Technology, and Christian Moral Vision

Romans 13 reminds believers that "there is no authority except that which God has established" (verse 1), affirming the legitimacy of government while calling Christians to respectful civic engagement. Yet Scripture also testifies—through prophets and apostles alike—that human law is fallible, and power can be misused. When governments wield artificial intelligence, the stakes for justice, transparency, and human dignity grow exponentially. This tension demands both vigilance and vision.

Christian ethics should not only resist abuses or retreat into suspicion, but offer a proactive, hope-filled moral witness. Jesus calls His followers to be "salt and light" (Matthew 5:13–16)—preserving truth, illuminating justice, and promoting the common good. In AI governance, this means contributing wisdom, moral clarity, and theological imagination: What technologies reflect God's design for human flourishing? How do we love our neighbor in algorithmic systems? When should Christians say "no," and when should they shape the "yes"?

Rather than merely responding to secular policy, Christian scholars, ethicists, and public leaders can help shape a positive, principled framework for AI—one that honors the image of God in every person, safeguards human agency, and cultivates a just digital future. This isn't optional; it is a form of faithful stewardship in a world being reshaped by code.

These spiritual and ethical insights remind us AI governance is not merely technical, but profoundly moral, shaping not just systems, but souls.

Conclusion

As the federal government wrestles with the rapid advance of AI, its choices—on regulation, global leadership, ethics, and citizen trust—will profoundly influence how AI is adopted throughout society. Yet these national efforts ultimately find their footing at the local level, where real people experience the everyday effects of technological change. From education and healthcare to policing and welfare delivery, public services are the arenas where AI's promises and pitfalls most directly touch citizens' lives.

In the next chapter, we turn our attention to how AI is transforming local government operations and service delivery—raising not only technical and budgetary questions, but also ethical and spiritual ones for those who serve and are served.

Chapter 8

AI CAN IMPROVE PUBLIC SERVICE

> *Public service must be more than doing a job efficiently and honestly. It must be a complete dedication to the people and to the nation.*[311]
>
> Margaret Chase Smith (1897–1995)
> US Senator from Maine

Many local authorities are using AI to deliver public services. Their goal is to make government more effective and efficient in providing key services without increasing the burden on the taxpayer. However, for most communities, the transition to AI technology to enhance public services faces multiple challenges.

This chapter addresses harnessing AI tech to the delivery of local public services in seven parts. First, I temper reader expectations by pointing out the distinctions between private and public applications of AI tech. Second, we consider AI applications and the necessity of building public trust in technology. Third, we consider AI's many potential applications at the local level. Fourth, we examine some of the AI-related challenges for local service providers. Fifth, I identify some of the gaps in AI capabilities for the local sector. Sixth, there are key questions government officials ought to consider when deciding whether to enlist AI tech for public services. Finally, there are issues for the faith-based community regarding AI-driven public services.

To understand how AI can improve public service delivery, it's important to first acknowledge that government agencies don't operate like private companies. They have distinct responsibilities, serve broader constituencies, and face greater legal and ethical constraints. These fundamental differences shape how—and how successfully—AI can be applied. What works for a business may not be translated seamlessly into a public works department or a school district. Let's begin by identifying the key contrasts between private and public service delivery, which frame the challenges local authorities face when adopting AI.

Key Differences Between Public and Private Services and Application of AI

We begin our journey by harnessing AI tech for public services by clarifying key differences between public and private applications. For insights, I turned to the academic community, which has rigorously studied the issue. For example, one study found that harnessing AI tech to improve public services "is dependent not just on the availability of high-quality data but also on a variety of closely connected environmental, organizational, and other variables." That study concluded: "The design and functionality of AI-based technologies must cater to the needs of users by providing personalized and relevant content, improving the quality of life for citizens and streamlining access to products and services."[312]

Therefore, transitioning local services to AI tech platforms is far more challenging and potentially costly than widely understood. So, authorities must ask themselves: Is the transition necessary and worth the cost? That decision is up to the local citizens, who must accept the consequences of the decision and the related costs.

We come to better appreciate the challenges of applying AI to the public service sector by comparing it with private services, which are more familiar to many of us.

Let's begin by understanding the assortment of public services provided by most of our cities and local communities, which are all taxpayer funded. That list does vary and can be exceptionally long depending on one's location: administration (e.g., building permits), social (e.g., welfare), education, security (e.g., police and fire departments), health and infrastructure (e.g., sewer, water, trash, electricity, road maintenance), and others.

Consider four distinctions between the delivery of public and private services. These differences help identify unique challenges for local government officials when harnessing AI tech for many public offerings.

First, there is no competition between service providers in the public sector. The city or county government has authority over services like the public schools, water, and police. Of course, some of these services may be elective or unavailable in your area, such as water, whereby in some areas, residents must have wells and septic tanks because they have no access to public water or a sewer system. Another exception to the rule is the private school, which provides citizens with an alternative to taxpayer-financed public schools, albeit at a personal cost unless there is the provision of school-choice laws that help supplement some private-school options.

A second difference is that local government delivers services allegedly on an equal basis and as efficiently as possible, for example, equal access to electricity and community policing. Private businesses operate with a different model, however. They try to reduce costs while making sufficient profit to remain in business, which may result in some citizens not enjoying access to that private product.

Third, the value of the public service is difficult to price, so the community leaders use established metrics for similarly situated areas, such as for policing and education. Other services like water, electricity, and trash collection are resource-based on demand—e.g., the number of gallons of water used per month. In the private sector, market competition sets the prices of goods and services.

Finally, an important distinction between public and private services is accountability. In the private sector, the commercial enterprise that delivers a service remains profitable only if its customers remain loyal. In the public sector, customers are taxpaying citizens who exercise leverage over their services by holding elected officials accountable at the ballot box, which can be a frustrating and protracted effort, especially when public services are unresponsive.

Calling out these distinctions between public and private services is necessary because harnessing AI tech is about efficiency, which comes at an often-dear price for the taxpayer when applied to public services. Therefore, citizens who demand that local authorities become more efficient by embracing modern technology must understand the presumed improvements technology brings will come at a tangible cost—more taxes—and sometimes may challenge certain liberties, an issue outlined below.

These differences—and the financial and ethical implications they carry—underscore the importance of not only securing funding but also cultivating public trust before implementing AI systems.

Funding AI Initiatives and Building Public Trust

Successfully integrating AI solutions into local public services requires strategic funding models, transparent governance, and active stakeholder engagement. Local governments often finance AI initiatives through various channels, including direct allocations from local taxes, voter-approved municipal bonds, state and federal technology grants, and public-private partnerships (PPPs). For instance, cities such as Columbus, Ohio, successfully implemented AI-enhanced traffic management systems funded through the US Department of Transportation's Smart City Challenge, combined with private-sector collaboration. Likewise, PPPs offer a viable path, leveraging private-sector expertise and investment while managing taxpayer burdens.[313]

To secure public trust and stakeholder buy-in—particularly for projects perceived as costly or disruptive—local officials should adopt best practices that emphasize transparency, inclusivity, and accountability. Regular town halls, public consultations, and advisory boards incorporating diverse stakeholders (citizens, community organizations, advocacy groups, and unions) help ensure that community voices shape AI deployments' goals, design, and ethical standards. For example, Pittsburgh's public-consultation model during its deployment of autonomous vehicles provided clear pathways for citizen input, building understanding and support for the initiative. By combining thoughtful funding strategies with inclusive community dialogue, local governments can

AI CAN IMPROVE PUBLIC SERVICE

finance AI technologies responsibly and foster broad public acceptance and long-term trust.[314]

With funding and public engagement in place, local governments can begin to explore the wide range of practical applications where AI can meaningfully improve services.

AI Tech's Potential Local Applications

We're all affected by the rapid pace of technological advancements, characterized by transformative technologies like machine learning, the Internet of Things (IoT) and predictive analytics. Public sector services are no exception in areas such as healthcare, traffic control, policing, education, utilities, and much more. But we should ask: What public services are best suited to apply AI tech solutions?

It is true that some communities are already on board with the application of AI technology in public services. Specifically, they use the tech for internal optimization of services such as inspections, enforcement, and compliance detection by authorities. More advanced authorities use AI for personalized services, maintenance, forecasting, and policymaking. And yet others enlist the use of robotics and speech/text recognition, as well as "stand-alone" machine-learning methods to interface with the public.

Undoubtedly, AI offers local authorities a range of capabilities to improve public sector administration and reduces bureaucracy, which many citizens favor as they desire smaller government and more efficient services given what too many citizens are accustomed to experiencing: local administrations bogged down in paper and people-centric processes like old-school call centers and in-person appointments. AI can help automate routine administrative tasks, process those documents, and manage records.

Local governments are relying more on chatbots to address many citizen inquiries.

It can also help humans reduce errors and speed up and eliminate legacy processes that have become costly, bureaucratic time sinks. For example, AI-powered computers can rapidly increase the digitization of documents and analyze and update records without human labor; in addition, it can translate documents into other languages in a flash.

These AI systems can help authorities identify fraud and financial oversight and, as necessary, call out problem cases to the human managing the system. In other areas, it can help with welfare benefits and tax returns to increase compliance and reduce the human burden.

The local judicial system can benefit from AI tech as well. Intelligent machines can analyze legal documents, manage court cases, assist with legal research, and suggest sentencing guidelines to lawyers and judges. Some authorities even use AI for bail decisions.

It can assist with public-safety responses by improving the effectiveness of policing. Specifically, AI systems can analyze crime data to identify hotspots or areas for potential incidents. It can help law enforcement allocate its workforce more effectively and assist with emergency response by analyzing data, such as videos and social-media feeds to respond to incidents quickly.

Technology can monitor and maintain critical infrastructure, including bridges and utility systems. Sensors and data predict maintenance requirements and identify issues needing attention. It can also automatically adjust climatic systems and lighting in buildings to reduce energy costs.

It should be self-evident that public utilities are especially suited for AI tech, such as the production and management of electricity, water, and communication services.

Power plants are increasingly turning to AI tech to optimize operations, enhance reliability, and guarantee a more resilient energy infrastructure.[315]

Consider the AI-provided benefits to the power plant. AI helps analyze datasets to make real-time distribution decisions and learn from other power plant experiences. More generally, AI helps with predictive maintenance, grid optimization, and protection against cybersecurity threats. The result of these innovations is greater efficiency, reliability, and sustainability.

On other fronts, AI tech can be incredibly efficient when answering

AI CAN IMPROVE PUBLIC SERVICE

everyday citizen questions. That is when a chatbot finds a significant role at the local service level.

A chatbot is a software application that welcomes human conversation through either text or voice interactions via an avatar (virtual agent) over the telephone or online. It uses AI, natural-language processing, and sometimes machine learning to discern user questions and understand citizen responses, then provide relevant answers/guidance. It can even interact with citizens in the language of their choice and at the time of their choosing—every day, all the time.

The private sector already uses AI-driven chatbots for marketing, sales, and customer satisfaction across industries. However, many of those private experiences can inform the application in the public sector, such as answering routine inquiries ranging from tax information to permitting and licensing. It can also help with complex efforts such as health.[316]

Chatbots can also extend public mental services. For example, a chatbot can address problems such as loneliness/social isolation by providing affordable, more accessible, and anonymous access to mental-health support sources while reducing the stigma attached to mental-health issues.

More broadly, a German study considered replacing receptionists in municipalities—government centers—with chatbots (avatars on screens). That effort considered variables such as maintaining security, privacy, and accountability; improving administrative performance; and improving user-friendliness and empathy.[317]

The German researchers found that citizens prefer chatbots programmed by domestic firms because of language accuracy and local culture. They also found that citizens "value chatbots taking routine decisions excluding where discretion is required, and strongly preferred human intervention when conversations fail."[318]

Anticipate AI's public service applications to increase in the future, and the taxpayer will benefit if, in fact, the appropriate investments take place.

Yet alongside the promise of AI in local governance, significant challenges must be addressed to ensure these technologies are effective, equitable, and sustainable.

AI Challenges for Local Service Providers

Citizen customers rightly demand greater efficiency and higher-quality public services. However, the goal of maximizing the value of those services by harnessing AI tech comes at a price that may discourage taxpayers and authorities.

Few of us deny the potential AI offers to revolutionize public services. However, to do so, the local administration must have sufficient data as well as access to the right types of computers and skilled personnel, sufficient electric power, and adequate water for cooling data centers.

Of course, the operating assumption of local authorities is the availability of these resources. However, unless an area has built this infrastructure to support AI, then plans, though well intended, may find a quick dead-end. After all, not every community, especially those in remote areas, has the necessary resource access level.

AI's need for extensive data poses a particularly unique challenge. Data should be protected by privacy safeguards in democratic societies. On top of this requirement, there must be significant computer capacity to use the data and enough skilled people to run and manage all the AI infrastructure. Don't dismiss these resource challenges without first checking local capabilities.

For these reasons and more, it is critical for the public to appreciate the challenges and associated costs of relying on AI tech for local services. The choice is between the status quo, depending on existing software-based services, and stubby pencil, human-managed services, as opposed to AI tech, which potentially solves problems more accurately and delivers services quicker. However, we must accept that most AI-driven efforts lack transparency and reduce human control over decisions.

To overcome these issues, local government needs effective data governance and privacy regulations, which are central to successfully implementing AI technologies. Specifically, local officials must navigate a complex landscape of legal requirements to responsibly collect, store, share, and manage sensitive citizen data. For example, local governments handling health-related information through AI applications must comply with federal regulations such as HIPAA. Similarly, the California Consumer

Privacy Act (CCPA)—an EU General Data Protection Regulation-like law—establishes clear obligations for data transparency, informed consent, and citizens' rights to access and delete personal data, impacting local authorities in California and influencing privacy standards nationwide.

Additionally, many local governments must comply with state-level, open-records statutes and transparency laws, which mandate clear guidelines for data retention, access, and sharing—potentially limiting how governments store or utilize sensitive information. Guaranteeing alignment with these regulations requires local governments to develop formal privacy frameworks, implement robust data encryption and anonymization practices, and establish clear data-breach response protocols.

Transparency with citizens is crucial; communicating how personal data is collected, used, and protected can build public trust and mitigate fears about privacy violations. By embedding these governance measures and regulatory compliance efforts into their AI strategies, local governments can responsibly harness data-driven technologies while safeguarding privacy and maintaining public confidence.

Beyond short-term obstacles, local governments must also confront deeper, systemic gaps in AI readiness—gaps in policy, infrastructure, and personnel that hinder long-term success.

Gaps in AI Capabilities

No doubt, AI applications at the local government level can be a boost to efficiency. However, past AI failures mean it's critical that local officials harness the tech in a responsible, cautious manner. That is why authorities must embrace the characteristics of responsible innovation and technology (RIT) to facilitate more effective AI oversight that addresses challenges such as justice, fairness, safety, and accountability.[319]

Fortunately, as one academic study found, local governments are increasingly prioritizing RIT within the context of their AI policies. This focus suggests officials' awareness of the need to balance tech use with societal values and expectations.[320]

The referenced study found shortfalls based on the review of twenty-six local government tech policies. Specifically, those policies lacked "the necessary legal, financial, human, and technical resources to implement AI effectively." The authors of the study recommended collaboration among local governments to close the resource "gaps" between "the recognition of need and actual implementation of legal frameworks for AI governance at local level."[321]

Local governments that use AI tech must mitigate potential negative impacts and build public trust as well as share gap-closing solutions.

To navigate these challenges and gaps wisely, local leaders need tools to guide their decisions on whether, when, and how to adopt AI technologies.

Guide for Selecting AI Tech for Public Services

As AI becomes more desirable and cost-effective, the public sector will clamor to harness its promises. Therefore, public officials responsible for deciding whether to employ AI will need to find help or at least use a written guide to help them think through the issues related to harnessing AI tech for public services. Of course, some will hire an AI tech consultant, others will access various self-help materials available online, such as Microsoft's "Artificial Intelligence for Public Service Delivery Guiding Questions for Non-technical Government Leaders."

Microsoft and other AI firms offer a variety of services and material to assist public sector officials. The Microsoft guide mentioned above poses the following areas for consideration, and each includes numerous questions (not shown) to guide officials regarding decisions about harnessing AI tech for public-service programs.[322]

The issues raised by Microsoft are:

1. **First consideration of using AI:** Before taking any action to use AI for public service delivery, explore whether it's the right fit for a particular program.
2. **Building or procuring an AI tool:** If you've decided that employing AI is the right decision for delivering this service, the next phase is to decide whether to build or buy an AI tool.

3. **Implementation:** Once a specific AI tool has been chosen, implementation brings several additional technical and responsible AI considerations.
4. **Routinely using AI:** Ensuring responsible AI use is an ongoing commitment that continues once the AI tool is operational.

The reader might be interested in short case studies of municipalities that have integrated AI into areas of public service. Appendix K presents real-life case studies showing how local governments worldwide are using AI to improve infrastructure, public safety, social services, and citizen engagement—while also addressing challenges related to data privacy, bias, and the equitable access to technology.

Beyond operational and ethical considerations, AI in public services also intersects with foundational constitutional values, including religious liberty and the role of faith in public life.

Freedom of Religion and the Separation of Church and State in AI-Driven Public Services

Integrating AI into public services also requires careful consideration of constitutional values, including freedom of religion and the separation of church and state. AI-driven technologies, due to their collection of extensive personal data, could unintentionally infringe on religious freedoms if implemented without sufficient safeguards. For instance, algorithms that gather demographic or behavioral information might inadvertently capture religious affiliations or activities, raising issues about privacy and the potential for misuse.

From a constitutional standpoint, local governments must ensure that AI applications remain neutral and respectful of religious diversity, in line with principles of non-establishment and equal protection. AI systems utilized in public services—such as healthcare, policing, or education—should be explicitly designed to prevent preferential treatment, inadvertent discrimination, or unnecessary entanglement with religious organizations or practices. Transparency, oversight, and inclusive policymaking are essential tools to make certain these technologies don't infringe on religious liberties or compromise the secular neutrality mandated by constitutional law.

Therefore, local governments have an ethical and legal duty to establish clear data governance standards, strong privacy protections, and ongoing monitoring mechanisms. This guarantees that AI-enhanced public services uphold and protect citizens' freedom of religion, maintain the necessary separation between religious institutions and government, and respect the diverse spiritual beliefs that make up a pluralistic society.

These issues at the intersection of AI and civil liberties foreshadow the broader governance challenges that arise as AI expands beyond local services into national and global arenas.

Conclusion

As we've seen, AI is reshaping how local governments deliver essential public services—enhancing efficiency, expanding access, and challenging long-held assumptions about governance, privacy, and accountability. Yet these local transformations are only part of a much larger landscape. Across the public sector, AI is becoming a strategic tool not only for administrative support, but also for safeguarding national interests on a global scale.

Nowhere is this more urgent than in the realm of national defense. Just as city governments wrestle with the promise and peril of AI in community policing and infrastructure management, military leaders are assessing how AI might revolutionize warfare itself—from battlefield tactics to global deterrence.

In the next chapter, we will examine how AI is redefining the future of armed conflict, exploring the Pentagon's use of advanced technologies, the risks of algorithmic warfare, and the intensifying global arms race with authoritarian powers like China. The stakes are higher, the consequences graver, and the need for ethical discernment more pressing.

Chapter 9

AI AND NATIONAL DEFENSE

Advances in AI have the potential to change the character of warfare for generations to come. Whichever nation harnesses AI first will have a decisive advantage on the battlefield for many, many years. We have to get there first.[323]

MARK ESPER
Former US Secretary of Defense (2019–2020)

National security is a broad issue that touches most agencies and departments of the federal government. However, for this chapter, I will focus exclusively on the military aspect of national defense as provided by the Pentagon—in other words, our military's ability to fight and win future wars and the role AI might play for our forces and their enemies.

The chapter addresses this issue in three parts. First, I address the scope of the AI challenge for our armed forces. Second, I examine the applications of AI for military purposes and discuss how to defend against similar technologies used by our adversaries. Finally, I review the ongoing AI "arms race" with the Chinese regime and how the US can harness diverse players to improve our abilities to defend against technology.

Reality of the Coming AI-Powered Battlefield

To understand what Mark Esper's statement means for modern defense, we must view AI not just as a tool, but as the cornerstone of the Fourth

Industrial Revolution—one that is reshaping global security as past industrial shifts once did.

Earlier I established that we're amid the Fourth Industrial Revolution—the AI Era—thanks to advances in technology. Like past revolutions, the current period will significantly affect our lives, much like the digital revolution (late 1950s to 1970s) introduced computers, the internet, and automation.

The current fourth revolution is identified with key innovations such as AI, robotics, the Internet of Things, biotechnology, and work on quantum computing. For the first time in history, these crucial developments give humankind learning machines that demonstrate human-like intelligence such as problem-solving, execution of complex tasks, manipulation, reasoning, interaction, and creativity.

Modern militaries are quickly embracing AI for weaponry and command and control.

These advancements drive the US military toward new capabilities, known within defense circles as the Third Offset Strategy (TOS). That term refers to a method used by the US military to counterbalance an adversary's armed forces by leveraging technological innovation and strategic shifts. For example, the Second Offset Strategy (1970s–1980s) leveraged technology such as precision-guided munitions to gain a qualitative edge over Soviet forces, and it eventually led to the Kremlin's downfall.[324]

The TOS has thus far spawned lethal autonomous weapons systems (LAWS), such as robotic weapons that operate in all domains: air, land, water, underwater, and space. These innovations also grant the ability for humans to team with AI-powered machines to make rapid and informed decisions.[325]

These developments are evident across the entire realm of military operations. Indeed, at the low end, AI is changing the way various

AI AND NATIONAL DEFENSE

advanced armed forces exercise coercive actions such as cyberattacks and the use of misinformation to manipulate our enemies psychologically. Meanwhile, conventional forces employ a growing panoply of LAWS and are beginning to see the tempo of operations accelerate because human decision-making is now teamed with AI-powered smart machines. At the strategic level, AI capabilities disrupt our opponents' national-level deterrence in ways that undermine geopolitical stability.[326]

Indeed, the military's TOS, a byproduct of the Fourth Industrial Revolution, is rapidly transforming our armed forces in ways that only a few years ago would have been perceived as pure sci-fi—*Star Wars* on steroids.

AI-Powered Military Applications

One of the most profound changes AI brings to warfare is in decision-making—both strategic and tactical. That aspect of AI empowerment was described by Benjamin Jensen, a senior fellow at the Center for Strategic and International Studies and professor at the Marine Corps University, Quantico, Virginia. He testified before a US Senate committee regarding the role AI delivers to the military commander's decision-making process.[327]

"In the twenty-first century," explained Professor Jensen, "the general or spy who doesn't have a [AI] model by their side is basically as helpless as a blind man in a bar fight." That graphic description of a helpless person under duress explains why the contemporary national security professional who faces tough battlefield decisions, must now turn to AI for help. However, to prepare for that assistance, it's necessary for humans to understand essential science and statistics, according to Jensen. Otherwise, the commander's new AI assistant becomes nothing more than "a magic box," which can be incredibly dangerous.[328]

Consider a future hypothetical crisis such as the 1962 Cuban Missile Crisis, a standoff between the US and the former Soviet Union that put the world on the brink of a nuclear holocaust. In that future scenario, the nation's leadership will have machine-learning systems (AI assistants) to help inform decisions, explained Professor Jensen. The machines will press the human leaders to "speed up decision-making," but government leadership will need "to slow it [the process] down to the pace of interagency collaboration." Meanwhile, both sides of the brewing crisis will quickly be "overwhelmed by deep fakes and computational propaganda pressuring" the decision-makers to act.[329]

Professor Jensen states that our national security is unprepared for scenarios such as the above, which leverage AI input with the associated accelerated decision-making. Why? High-stakes decisions regarding international crises like the 1962 Cuban Missile Crisis seldom reflect rational, objective, fact-based algorithm outputs, which an AI assistant would offer leadership based on a rich and swift data analysis. The problem is the machine's objective input will collide with the human's irrational thinking that involves emotions, flawed analogies, and bias, according to Jensen. Inevitably, the professor explained, "Confusion could easily eclipse certainty, unleashing escalation and chaos."[330]

Worse, "a clever adversary...could easily poison the data used to support [our] intelligence analysis and targeting. They could trick every computer model into thinking [for example] a school bus was a missile launcher, causing decision-makers to quickly lose confidence in otherwise accurate data," explained Jensen.[331]

That type of AI assistance will exist at every level of command. At the tactical and operational level, AI tech can enhance the quality and speed of the leader's decision-making. After all, there is recognition that this technology can enhance an understaffed field commander with access to vast amounts of data, sophisticated analysis, and real-time insights. Therefore, by harnessing AI's assistance, that information-hungry leader leverages the machine's significant capabilities to gather and interpret information, recognize patterns, generate predictions, evaluate performance, and improve decision-making in real time—which leads to the commander's faster response and higher confidence in the decision.[332]

Although AI provides lightning-fast, significant analysis, the commander's decision process must demonstrate a balanced relationship between him and his machine assistant. Specifically, in warrior-type leadership scenarios marked by high-stress, strategic, or tactical contexts, accurate decision-making must happen quickly. However, the final decision must always rest with the commander, because the human brings "to the table his expertise in understanding the nuances of human behavior, strategic thinking, and ethical considerations, which are especially crucial in complex uncertain, or ethically ambiguous situations," a perspective shared by Walter Matli, writing in the journal *Applied Artificial Intelligence*.[333]

This human-machine teaming approach allows the leader to interpret AI-generated recommendations within the broader context of "organizational goals and values and apply a more holistic and intuitive approach required for decision-making in such environments."[334]

Beyond decision-making, AI applications are rapidly transforming nearly every military domain across the modern battlefield.

AI Applications Across the Battlefield

Complicating future warfighting will be the application of AI power to a variety of military platforms and systems. Consider insights shared by Eric Schmidt, the former CEO of Google, who chaired the National Security Commission on Artificial Intelligence. Schmidt wrote that ML has broad applications for transforming intelligence and statecraft, albeit with a dangerous twist.[335]

"AI's capacity for autonomy and logic generates a layer of incalculability," Schmidt warned. He explained that AI systems operate differently than humans, such as strategies and tactics "based on the assumption of a human adversary whose conduct and decision-making calculus "fit within a recognizable framework." Not so with AI-powered machines, however. "Yet an AI system piloting an aircraft or scanning for targets follows its own logic," explained Schmidt, "which may be inscrutable to an adversary and unsusceptible to traditional signals or feints and which will, in most cases, proceed faster than the speed of human thought."[336]

That unpredictability means even those humans allegedly in control of the AI-operated platform may not understand how the system will function in every situation, much less whether it will deliver unacceptable collateral effects.

Consider the AI-enabled cyber weapon, which smartly adapts and learns as it operates. However, because its environment is constantly changing, the AI-powered cyber system might react to the new situation in an unpredictable way. For example, you might recall Russia's 2017 NotPetya cyberattack, which swamped websites across many countries and demonstrated the power of automated malware.

On June 27, 2017, Ukraine broke into chaos—ATMs stopped, subway card readers failed, and the nation's entire digital backbone collapsed. The cause was a mysterious malware that infected computers—first in Ukraine, then quickly spiraling into a global catastrophe. The US government called NotPetya "the most destructive and costly cyber-attack in history," which hit more than 2,300 organizations across more than one hundred countries and cost $10 billion.[337]

Imagine what might have happened if NotPetya had been under the control of an AGI-powered machine, which kept learning as it found success to become more dangerous with time. This incident, which was horrible, could have been exponentially worse had it been under the control of an innovative, self-guided machine.

Beyond traditional warfare, the rise of AI significantly influences the landscape of national cyber defense, necessitating advanced collaboration among military entities such as US Cyber Command, civilian agencies, and the private sector. In response to increasingly sophisticated cyber threats—including those enhanced by AI—the Pentagon works closely with agencies like the Department of Homeland Security (DHS), the Federal Bureau of Investigation (FBI), and the Cybersecurity and Infrastructure Security Agency (CISA), as well as industry leaders, to protect critical infrastructure such as energy grids, financial systems, and communication networks.

The US Cyber Command utilizes AI-driven tools for threat detection, anomaly analysis, and predictive cyber defense, allowing quicker recognition and response to cyber incidents. AI algorithms help automatically identify vulnerabilities, detect cyber intrusions, and neutralize threats in real time, significantly reducing response times and improving system resilience. On the offensive side, AI facilitates more precise targeting, penetration testing, and disruption of adversarial cyber capabilities, strengthening a proactive cyber defense posture.

AI AND NATIONAL DEFENSE

Frameworks like the US Department of Defense's Cyber Strategy explicitly emphasize the importance of AI and machine learning in enhancing both offensive and defensive cyber capabilities. By incorporating AI-driven analytics, automated defense measures, and cross-sector threat intelligence sharing, these comprehensive strategies aim to reduce the risk of large-scale disruptions caused by AI-enhanced cyberattacks, such as the devastating NotPetya malware incident of 2017. Such coordinated AI-supported cyber defenses are vital for ensuring national security and stability in an age when digital threats become increasingly dynamic, complex, and impactful.

While AI enhances cyber operations, its application in conventional warfare introduces an entirely different set of challenges, especially in unpredictable combat environments.

AI's Application on the Conventional Battlefield

Now consider the possible unpredictability of AI-powered machines launched by conventional units under combat pressure. The results could become a double-edged sword. On one hand, the platform might do what the commander ordered; on the other, there could be unintended escalation, perhaps because of an unreliable AI system that "thinks" for itself, poorly trained operators, or corrupt training data.

The fact is that controlling the AI-powered application remains a significant challenge. The degree of the risk will grow, because today the military commander has access to a growing plethora of AI-powered platforms that are transforming the fight. Consider AI innovations available now or on the near horizon:

- **AI and intelligence operations**: Intelligence analysts increasingly rely on artificial intelligence to process vast volumes of data collected from satellites, drones, reconnaissance aircraft, and other platforms. These tools help analysts identify patterns, detect anomalies, and make faster, more-informed judgments in high-stakes environments.

    A recent and significant advance in this area comes from the

AI firm Anthropic, which has developed models tailored specifically for national security applications. Their new Claude Gov models are built exclusively for US national security agencies and are already deployed at the highest levels of government. Designed with direct input from defense partners, these models deliver enhanced performance in mission-critical areas such as intelligence analysis, strategic planning, and cybersecurity.[338]

What distinguishes Claude Gov is its ability to handle classified information securely, provide deeper contextual understanding of defense-related documents, and analyze complex cybersecurity data with speed and precision. It also supports multilingual capabilities critical to global operations—all while adhering to strict standards for safety and responsible AI use.

This development reflects a growing trend: the deepening collaboration between private-sector AI innovators and defense institutions. Tools like Claude Gov not only illustrate how AI is being operationalized within the intelligence community, but also how such partnerships are strengthening US readiness across both conventional and cyber domains.

The real-world impact of AI in intelligence is already evident. For instance, AI-assisted platforms contributed to the US intelligence community's 2021 prediction that Russia would invade Ukraine—months before the attack—giving Washington time to issue public warnings and coordinate responses with allies. Today, similar AI systems support US Strategic Command by tracking the movement of nuclear-armed enemy missiles, offering real-time situational awareness vital to national defense.[339]

- **AI decision support systems:** AI algorithms help commanders assess terrain, readiness, and historical cases to provide strategic courses of action. This helps commanders make rapid decisions in complex scenarios. Further, it enables human-machine collaboration for improved execution and alignment with tactical goals.[340]
- **AI cyber defense and warfare:** AI identifies cyber threats faster than traditional human methods, thus quickly strengthens the

defense against those attacks. It also enhances the commander's ability to disrupt enemy networks inside his decision cycle.[341]

- **AI helps with system maintenance:** AI models help in the maintenance of complex weapons, from tanks to fighter jets to aircraft carriers. Those programs collect data from the platform's many sensors to predict the kind of required maintenance and the associated costs.
- **AI supports military communications:** AI can help a command respond to an adversary's electronic jamming by using smart switches and routing agents that redirect affected communications to other networks to maintain critical connectivity.
- **AI helps control swarms of drones:** AI applications allow a single human to control numerous unmanned systems, such as a swarm of drones. For example, a fighter pilot can operate a swarm of drones to confuse his adversary, and a submarine commander can operate undersea drones to hunt for undersea mines.
- **AI helps multi-domain operations**: Technology integrates land, air, sea, cyber, and space domains in a cohesive manner to enable "mosaic warfare," so that interconnected systems function as adaptive networks across all domains to outmaneuver the enemy.[342]

AI Power Can Be Deceived and Defeated

As AI-powered systems become more prevalent, it's necessary for US units to deceive and defeat opposing technology. Doing so requires an understanding of deep-learning systems and their vulnerabilities, which are fragile.

Hava Siegelman with the University of Massachusetts created a program called Guaranteed AI Robustness against Deception (GARD) while working with the US Defense Advanced Research Projects Agency (DARPA). Her GARD system can fool an AI-based vision system by simply draping a tank with pictures of tiny cows. Specifically, the AI system perceives the draped tank as a herd of cows. Her conclusion about the test was that AI "works on the surfaces."[343]

Of course, DARPA is actively seeking to make ML better at detecting adversarial attacks. However, Bruce Draper of Colorado State University, who currently manages GARD at DARPA, said, "It's an AI problem, but it's also a security problem."[344]

The kryptonite for machine-learning tools appears to be the subtle alteration of the input image for classification algorithms, said Draper. A few altered pixels in an input image can cause an AI-powered classifier to fail.[345]

It is essential to understand that deep-learning systems use unique features to help humans make decisions. Therefore, "because these systems are using visual input [like the cow-picture-draped tank], we tend to assume that they see the same way we do," said Draper. "That's not a good assumption."[346]

Unfortunately, image manipulation such as the tank draped with pictures of cows is challenging to defend against. Why? Battista Biggio with the University of Cagliari in Italy explained that it's difficult "because the space of pixels is so large that the attacker can do basically whatever he wants in terms of manipulating the images." The manipulated image acts like malware, Biggio explained. "You have instructions or bytes, which have a specific meaning, so they cannot be altered in a trivial matter," he said, stating that otherwise, the AI often fails.[347]

Another way of defeating ML is to exploit the internal "gradients" used to train the system. "The basic idea is to use the same algorithm that is used for learning to actually by-pass the classifier," or, as Biggio explained, fight "machine learning with machine learning."[348]

According to Draper, deception "seems to be a particular issue with AI systems that use sensory input, whether it's visual or audio or whatever." Modifying input to an existing classifier is known as "evasion."[349]

Ms. Siegelman illustrated another anti-AI tool called "poisoning," which confuses the AI system. That tool works, for example, by "inserting images of Wonder Woman with distinctive eyeglasses, which induces a system to classify anyone wearing such glasses as the superhero."[350]

Of course, "poisoning" only works if the attacker has prior access to the training data used by the technology. Alternatively, the attacker can also succeed by knowing the internal design details of an ML system, the so-called "white box" scenario.[351]

There "may be no silver bullet" to defeat AI-powered platforms, according to Draper. "What we want to do is at least make it very difficult for someone to defeat or spoof one of these systems."[352]

As these vulnerabilities reveal the unpredictability and risks of AI systems in combat, they also raise urgent legal and ethical questions at the international level.

Global Legal Frameworks and AI Weaponization

As AI-powered military technologies, including LAWS, become more prevalent, the international community faces significant challenges regarding their use's legal and ethical implications. Currently, international legal frameworks specifically addressing autonomous weapons are limited and contentious. The Convention on Certain Conventional Weapons (CCW) has emerged as a primary international forum for regulating LAWS; however, reaching a consensus has proven difficult due to differing national interests and varying definitions of autonomy.

Several countries and advocacy groups have called for a binding treaty to either ban or strictly regulate fully autonomous weapons. For example, the Campaign to Stop Killer Robots—supported by numerous nations, non-governmental organizations (NGOs), and experts—has urged explicit legal prohibitions, emphasizing the moral unacceptability of allowing machines to make lethal decisions without human oversight. Despite these efforts, key military powers—including the US, Russia, and China—have resisted comprehensive bans, opting for voluntary guidelines or national standards.

The absence of a robust international regulatory framework raises crucial accountability questions: Who is liable if autonomous systems inflict unintended harm on civilians or breach international humanitarian law? Traditional legal principles, such as the distinctions between combatants and civilians and proportionality, require meaningful human oversight to attribute accountability clearly. In the absence of global consensus and well-defined legal norms, the deployment of autonomous weapons risks exacerbating ethical dilemmas, humanitarian crises, and global instability. Therefore, continuing international negotiations, increasing transparency measures, and striving for enforceable global standards are essential for ethically guiding AI's integration into national security operations.

Where international law remains ambiguous, Christian ethics offer a timeless framework for grappling with these emerging dilemmas—particularly concerning life, justice, and moral agency in war.

Ethical and Humanitarian Concerns in AI-Driven Warfare

Deploying AI-driven combat systems raises profound ethical and humanitarian concerns, challenging established moral principles and traditional frameworks of warfare. Central to this debate is lethal autonomy—delegating life-and-death decisions to machines, fundamentally altering longstanding understandings of moral responsibility in conflict situations. Ethical frameworks such as "just war" theory, deeply rooted in Christian theology, emphasize principles of proportionality, discrimination between combatants and civilians, and rightful intention. By potentially removing humans from direct oversight of targeting decisions, autonomous weapons risk undermining these crucial principles, complicating accountability and moral agency.

Furthermore, international humanitarian law mandates that combatants adhere to standards of distinction and proportionality. Introducing AI-powered systems that can independently select and engage targets presents significant concerns regarding compliance with these legal norms. Various religious and philosophical traditions, particularly Christian ethics, emphasize human dignity and the inherent moral value of everyone, reinforcing the necessity for substantial human oversight on decisions that carry lethal consequences.

Advocacy for meaningful human oversight ensures that human judgment and moral accountability remain firmly embedded in military operations. While AI can support and improve human decision-making, the ultimate responsibility for military actions must always remain with human operators and commanders. As militarized AI technologies develop, policymakers, military leaders, and ethicists must engage in continuous dialogue to establish clear ethical guidelines, ensuring that innovations in warfare technology align with enduring moral and humanitarian values.

AI "Arms Race" with the Chinese

An AI "arms race" between the US and communist China is well underway. Both sides are trying to build technical expertise, fund military AI-related research and development (R&D), track enemy efforts, improve platform lethality, reduce friction across the political and technical domain among allies, and learn from past technical offset periods.

On April 25, 2025, China's President Xi Jinping pledged "self-reliance and self-strengthening" to develop AI in China, a clear indication that the AI "arms race" is truly taking place. Specifically, speaking at a Politburo meeting, Xi said China will leverage its "new whole national system" to push forward on AI. "We must recognize the gaps and redouble our efforts to comprehensively advance technological innovation, industrial development, and AI-empowered applications," Xi said.[353] "We must continue to strengthen basic research, concentrate our efforts on mastering core technologies such as high-end chips and basic software, and build an independent, controllable, and collaborative artificial intelligence basic software and hardware system."[354]

In January 2025, Lee Kai-fu, the CEO of Chinese startup 01.AI, which created DeepSeek (an LLM like OpenAI's GPT-4), told Reuters his latest creation revealed that China had pulled ahead of the US in areas such as infrastructure software engineering. Mr. Lee, a prominent figure in the global AI space and a former head of Google China, claimed that DeepSeek was trained with less-advanced chips and was cheaper to develop than its Western rivals, a measure of the ongoing competition.[355]

On other fronts, the US military may no longer hold an AI technological overmatch regarding the People's Liberation Army (PLA), China's armed forces. Rather, that nation is rapidly advancing along the path to "complete national defense and military modernization by 2035," which means the PLA intends to become a "world-class military by the middle of the [twenty-first] century." A significant aspect of that transformation is China's aggressive efforts to harness AI tech in preparation for engaging the US on a future battlefield.[356]

China's AI ambition is part of its promise to "intelligentize warfare." That term means the regime will expand "use of AI, quantum computing, big data, and other advanced technologies at every level of warfare," according to the Pentagon's 2024 report to Congress.[357] Specifically, "intelligentize warfare" will significantly improve the warrior's situational awareness, help operations to be far more precise, and cause decisions to be much better because of deep-learning analysis for leaders. These benefits come just in time, because technology is speeding up the pace of warfare.[358]

One of the first indications of the AI "arms race" happened in 2018, when the Pentagon released its first artificial intelligence strategy announcing China was "making significant investments in AI for military purposes," that "threaten to erode our technological and operational advantages." Meanwhile, China responded the same year with a defense white paper titled "Revolution in Military Affairs with Chinese Characteristics." That document acknowledged the importance of AI for future warfare and set the nation on an aggressive path to dominate the field.[359]

Today, both the US and China are experiencing a proliferation of AI-related R&D across several sectors: autonomous vehicles, intelligence, logistics, cyber, and command and control. This is a race on many fronts, and the winner will only be declared by the side with the best-integrated AI across all domains on a future battlefield.

Where the "race" stands should sober Washington. Specifically, the Pentagon's 2024 annual report to Congress on the PLA states, "The PRC [People's Republic of China] is prioritizing the development of AI-enabled capabilities because of its belief that AI is leading to the next revolution in military affairs." Therefore, according to the Pentagon report, "by 2030, the PLA expects to field a range of 'algorithmic warfare' and 'network-centric warfare' capabilities operating at different levels of human-machine integration."[360]

While China's military ambitions often capture headlines, its commercial AI sector is also making aggressive strides. The development of autonomous AI agents—designed to perform real-world tasks with minimal human input—is becoming a critical front in the broader global technology race.

China is rapidly advancing in the global race to develop autonomous AI agents—tools capable of handling complex real-world tasks with minimal human input—challenging US dominance in the field. Chinese tech giants like Alibaba and ByteDance, along with startups like Butterfly Effect and Zhipu, are launching AI agents powered by in-house foundation models and achieving notable user engagement, though concerns over quality and hype persist. While US companies still lead in foundational AI model development, experts note the real competition lies in deployment across industries. China's lag in digitization, cloud adoption, and workforce training remains a hurdle, yet the popularity of tools like Alibaba's Quark and ByteDance's Coze demonstrates the country's ambition. Despite mixed reviews and performance gaps, Chinese firms are leveraging venture capital and government support to close the AI agent gap, making the sector a key front in global tech competition.[361]

These civilian advances are not merely commercial; they directly support China's defense ambitions through its Military-Civil Fusion (MCF) strategy. By tightly integrating the People's Liberation Army (PLA) with private tech firms, Beijing makes certain that breakthroughs in areas like autonomous AI agents are rapidly adapted for military use. This strategy includes the creation of joint R&D facilities focused on dual-use technologies, such as the Agile Innovation Defense Unit (AIDU)—a rapid-response group that channels commercial innovations into defense applications. As a result, China is gaining an edge in AI-related exploitation by blurring the line between civilian and military development.[362]

China's MCF strategy is paying off. A study by the Center for Security and Emerging Technology found that the PLA sourced most of its AI equipment from private Chinese tech firms. That progress comes in part thanks to a July 2023 Chinese regulation requiring companies that produce generative AI services "with public opinion properties or the capacity for social mobilization" to apply to the Cyberspace

Administration of China for "security assessments." This regulation aims to keep Chinese-produced AI tech for their exclusive internal use.[363]

What is the status of the AI "arms race"? The Pentagon's AI strategy would have the US military leverage technologies from our market-based economy, but that requires cooperation from the private sector, which isn't always universally available. After all, our system doesn't have the coercive leverage that goes with China's MCF and AIDU.

The Pentagon did create the Defense Innovation Unit (DIU) to encourage closer relationships between the Pentagon and private tech firms such as the "Replicator Initiative," which aims to expedite the deployment of advanced capabilities. To demonstrate DIU's importance to our security strategy, in 2023, the unit began to directly report to the secretary of defense to "catalyze engagement with and investment into private sector communities where commercial technology can be adapted and applied to meet our warfighters' requirements."[364]

No doubt, the Pentagon must focus on the goal of dominating AI tech. However, like the fog of war, the status of the AI "arms race" with the communist Chinese is hard to measure, which reminds me of something said by Jeffrey Ding, a political science professor at George Washington University. Professor Ding testified before a US Senate committee that we must "avoid overhyping China's AI capabilities." Then he illustrated the danger of misplaced exaggeration. Specifically, he explained that "a 1969 CIA assessment of the Soviet Union's technological capabilities" contradicted the popular narrative at the time that Russia was overtaking the US in technology. Instead, the agency's report concluded "that the technological gap was actually widening between the U.S. as the leader and the Soviet Union because of the U.S.'s superior mechanisms to spread technologies and diffuse technologies."[365]

The US must not naively assume it enjoys a lead over the Chinese in this vital area. We must expedite our efforts to prevail in fourth-generation technologies. Otherwise, we risk the unthinkable: defeat on a future battlefield by an adversary like China that beats us in harnessing AI tech.

Therefore, the US must aggressively act on three fronts to overcome China's rapid progress on the AI technology enterprise. Specifically, we must overcome the challenges in public-private partnership, recruit the US government's interagency to the mission, leverage multilateral alliance partners, and step up collaboration vis-à-vis cooperative AI defense strategies with allies. Consider a brief explanation of each of these fronts.

To compete with China's integrated AI strategy, the US must overcome internal barriers—particularly in how it fosters innovation between government and private firms.

Challenges in Public-Private Partnerships and US Innovation Culture

While initiatives like DIU highlight the Pentagon's efforts to connect with Silicon Valley, significant cultural, legal, and ethical obstacles continue to hinder effective collaboration between the DoD and top technology firms. Unlike China's centralized, government-driven MCF program, the US grapples with inherent tensions arising from its innovation culture, which emphasizes openness, swift experimentation, and civilian-led development—a sharp contrast to the structured, security-focused, and often bureaucratic nature of military procurement processes.

Tech companies many times struggle to align their rapid innovation cycles and agile project timelines with the slow, heavily regulated procurement frameworks typical of the DoD. Ethical concerns, particularly regarding autonomous weapons and data privacy, have caused top-tier technology professionals to hesitate or decline participation in defense-related AI projects, as seen in the employee pushback at companies like Google. Furthermore, strict regulatory frameworks, security clearance requirements, and negotiations over intellectual property create additional obstacles to effective public-private partnerships.

To compete well in the AI race, particularly against authoritarian regimes with fewer regulatory or ethical constraints, the US must use initiative-taking measures to tackle these organizational and cultural challenges. This could involve streamlining procurement processes, establishing clearer ethical guidelines to reassure private-sector participants, and enhancing transparency regarding the intended uses of AI technology. Success in AI competition relies not only on technological advancements, but also on nurturing organizational agility, mutual understanding, and strong public-private collaboration.

Defense Secretary Pete Hegseth recently issued a memorandum titled "Directing Modern Software Acquisition to Maximize Lethality," which aims to streamline the DoD's software-procurement processes. This directive requires all DoD components to adopt the Software Acquisition Pathway (SWP) as the preferred method for software development. The SWP aligns with modern software-development practices, enabling faster delivery of capabilities to warfighters. Additionally, the memo promotes the use of Commercial Solutions Openings (CSOs) and Other Transaction Authorities (OTAs) to facilitate collaboration with nontraditional and commercial software developers, thereby broadening the defense industrial base and accelerating innovation.[366]

This initiative aims to tackle current challenges in the defense acquisition process, including bureaucratic delays and difficulties in collaborating with innovative technology companies. By utilizing flexible contracting tools such as CSOs and OTAs, the DoD seeks to minimize red tape, accelerate the adoption of advanced software solutions, and maintain a technological advantage over adversaries.

The memo marks a significant shift toward a more agile and performance-based acquisition framework, highlighting the necessity for the DoD to adapt to the rapidly changing landscape of software-defined warfare. By implementing these changes, the department aims to deliver critical capabilities more swiftly and efficiently, ensuring that US military forces remain the most lethal and effective globally.

Alongside public-private efforts, interagency coordination is essential to unify AI strategies across government domains.

Interagency Coordination in AI-Driven National Security

While the Pentagon enjoys most of the attention regarding AI-driven national security issues, a comprehensive approach necessitates close coordination among all government agencies, including the intelligence community, the Department of Homeland Security (DHS), and multiple federal cybersecurity units. Agencies like the Central Intelligence Agency (CIA) and the National Security Agency (NSA) utilize AI for advanced intelligence analysis, cybersecurity threat detection, and surveillance. Likewise, DHS employs AI tools to safeguard critical infrastructure, anticipate cyber threats, and improve disaster-response capabilities. An effective national security strategy thus relies on strong interagency collaboration, which includes sharing datasets, jointly developing and deploying AI tools, and coordinating strategic planning to mitigate threats while seizing opportunities. Through such integrated efforts, the US government can better harness AI's full potential while upholding democratic values and ethical standards across its national security framework.

An example of the proposed integrated approach comes from the US Air Force's decision to create an "Artificial Intelligence Center of Excellence." In May 2025, the US Air Force announced the creation of an Artificial Intelligence Center of Excellence in partnership with MIT, Stanford, and Microsoft. This announcement follows the first-ever autonomous-systems boot camp for Air Force test pilots at Edwards Air Force Base, an expansion of the service's MIT accelerator and Stanford AI studio.[367]

Although the Air Force has dozens of AI skunkworks, commanders complained they couldn't find available AI tools and asked for help. That resulted in the Center, which centralized budgets and provided more data and cloud access to help "clear that bottleneck."[368]

More broadly, the Air Force AI Center of Excellence will serve as the service's hub for AI collaboration, resource-sharing, and deployment. Its many functions include connecting with academic partners, granting clearance for contractors to test and scale AI tools, consolidating AI-related investment through Microsoft's cloud systems, and supporting AI-related training.[369]

Yet no national effort can succeed in isolation. To safeguard democratic norms and ensure global security, America must also strengthen multilateral AI defense partnerships.

Multilateral Alliances and Cooperative AI Defense Strategies

While the geopolitical competition with China for AI leadership is significant, the US relies on strong multilateral alliances to shape collective defense strategies and technology-sharing initiatives. Alliances such as the North Atlantic Treaty Organization (NATO) and strategic partnerships like the Quadrilateral Security Dialogue ("Quad")—which includes the US, Japan, Australia, and India—are crucial for coordinating AI research, establishing interoperability standards, and conducting joint military exercises to improve AI readiness. For instance, NATO has increasingly emphasized collaborative efforts on AI, developing joint frameworks for ethical use, information-sharing protocols, and standards for autonomous systems. Similarly, the Quad nations have launched collaborative research and development projects focused on countering authoritarian uses of AI by promoting democratic values and transparency. These multilateral initiatives highlight the broader significance of collective cooperation, showing that AI-driven national security entails shared strategic planning, pooled expertise, and unified approaches to technological governance that go beyond mere bilateral competition with China.

Beyond politics and strategy, the conversation around AI and warfare demands a moral reckoning—especially for those guided by faith.

Faith-Based Perspectives on AI, Warfare, and the Sanctity of Human Life

The increasing reliance on AI, particularly LAWS, raises significant moral and theological questions regarding the sanctity of human life and the ethics of delegating life-and-death decisions to machines. From a Christian viewpoint, the doctrine of humanity's creation in the image of God (Genesis 1:27) highlights the inherent value and dignity of every human life. Therefore, entrusting lethal-force decisions entirely to autonomous systems can be deeply concerning, as it may depersonalize warfare and obscure moral accountability.

The Christian "just war" tradition, which emphasizes just cause, right intention, proportionality, and discrimination (distinction between combatants and civilians), also provides a framework for critically examining

AI's role in military contexts. Assigning decisions to autonomous AI challenges the fundamental concept of human moral agency and potentially undermines the careful ethical discernment needed in warfare. The removal or significant reduction of direct human judgment may detach decision-makers from the profound moral implications of their actions, conflicting with scriptural calls to justice, mercy, and accountability (Micah 6:8).

Thus, faith-informed discussions about AI in national security must address not only strategic effectiveness, but also profound spiritual and ethical responsibilities. Christian communities and faith-based organizations can play a crucial role in advocating for meaningful human oversight and careful moral scrutiny, helping to guarantee that the pursuit of technological advantage never undermines the sacred duty to uphold and protect human life.

These moral questions underscore the profound responsibility that comes with wielding AI in warfare—a theme echoed throughout this chapter's exploration of national defense.

Conclusion

This chapter shows how AI is revolutionizing the battlefield, influencing everything from real-time decision-making to autonomous weapons, cybersecurity, and global military alliances. Just as AI now defines geopolitical strength, it is also remaking the global economy—beginning with the foundational industries that supply our infrastructure, technology, and defense systems. Raw materials like rare-earth elements, lithium, copper, and other commodities are essential not only for powering smart weapons and satellites, but also for manufacturing electric vehicles, semiconductors, and countless AI-driven consumer technologies.

In the next chapter, we explore how AI is reshaping these industrial foundations—beginning with mining, agriculture, and energy—revealing both enormous economic opportunities and new ethical and environmental challenges. From the battlefield to the supply chain, AI's influence continues to expand, requiring wisdom, discernment, and moral clarity at every level of society.

Section Four

AI AND ECONOMY

AI is a "golden age" and solving problems that were once in the realm of sci-fi.[370]

Jeff Bezos (1964)
Former CEO of Amazon

Jeff Bezos calls AI a "golden age"—and rightly so. What once seemed the stuff of science fiction is now driving real economic change across every industry. As a general-purpose technology, AI enhances productivity, streamlines automation, and spurs innovation across all sectors of the economy. This higher level of economic growth could increase global gross domestic product (GDP) by up to 1.2 percent annually and contribute trillions of dollars to the economy by 2030.[371]

To understand how AI impacts the economy, we begin at the source: natural resource extraction. Chapter 10 dives into the pivotal role AI plays in optimizing farming and mining—industries that form the backbone of global supply chains.

Once raw materials are extracted, the next economic phase is transformation—where AI revolutionizes the manufacturing sector. Chapter 11 examines how intelligent systems reshape production lines to maximize efficiency, minimize waste, and adapt to global competition.

Completing the economic chain is the retail sector—the direct interface with the consumer. Chapter 12 explores how AI enhances retail experience by streamlining operations, personalizing service, and driving profitability.

Chapter 10

AI AND RAW MATERIALS

Data are becoming the new raw material of business.[372]
CRAIG MUNDIE
Former Microsoft executive

Raw materials are the backbone of the manufacturing sector of our economy and are indispensable for creating products critical to our lives. After all, without raw materials from farms, mines, forests, and energy fields, we would be a poor country. America prospers because of those who bring raw materials to the processing and manufacturing arm of our economy, and, if we're fortunate, they will continue to expand their production of these critical resources to support the ten billion souls Earth expects to host by the year 2050.[373]

The growing global demand for raw materials means we must produce more, and AI tech will play a key role in fueling that expansion. After all, by tapping into Earth's natural resources in a more thoughtful way with technological help, we can protect our environment while sustaining a good life for all of humankind.

To effectively support raw-material producers, AI depends on vast quantities of data. As Craig Mundie noted above, data itself has become a kind of raw material. Information gathered from farms, mines, timber operations, and energy fields forms the foundation for training AI algorithms. When properly collected and applied across these sectors, this data enables AI to better assist the workforce in the vital task of efficiently supplying the materials essential to manufacturing and retail.

AI FOR MANKIND'S FUTURE

This chapter explores three major areas where AI is transforming raw materials: animal-based resources, agricultural and forestry outputs, and mineral and energy extraction. Each sector demonstrates how AI can enhance productivity while raising important ethical and stewardship questions.

We begin with the use of AI in animal-based resource production—where technology is transforming livestock management, food-supply chains, and animal-welfare practices.

AI Helps Produce Animal-based Raw Materials

The production of animal-based raw materials finds applications in industries from food to clothing. Experience indicates that AI tech will continue to transform animal agriculture by enhancing welfare, improving production, and increasing sustainability of livestock. It is meant to assist, not replace, farmers by augmenting their capabilities to manage more effectively.[374]

"Smart"—often called "precision"—farming covers a range of techniques that use AI tech in agriculture. Those systems employ algorithms and ML to analyze animal data collected by radio-frequency identification tags, sensors, cameras, and other devices.[375] This approach helps the farmer improve production and manage animal welfare and health (prevent disease), as well as control environmental variables like barn temperature.[376]

AI algorithms analyze the data collected from these devices, which make predictions or recommend decisions. Meanwhile, ML helps those systems improve over time without needing updated guidance.

AI models also help predict animal growth as well as adjust feeding plans and optimize production. This happens by environmental controls such as barn temperature, humidity, and ventilation. The algorithms can also analyze data to optimize breeding programs and improve reproductive success as well as predict milk production based on a variety of factors.

AI-powered robots are now mingling with dairy cows to produce more milk and perform most of the manual labor such as cleaning, feeding, and ensuring cow comfort. The Dutch firm Lely introduced its first

"Astronaut" milking robot in the 1990s and has since deployed 135,000 units worldwide. Although the initial investment in Lely's robots is expensive, the promise is that, over the years of use, the system will prove cost effective and improve the farmer's operating efficiency.[377]

There are technical challenges for the farmer who uses artificial intelligence assistance, however. Specifically, quality data is necessary for accurate predictions, which can be expensive. That data trains the algorithm and then runs the system; it must be dependable and sourced from diverse farm environments that represent distinct species, breeds, and environmental conditions.

Other issues requiring the farmer's attention are system interoperability, such that all the data-gathering devices properly apply the interface mechanisms with the AI systems as a cohesive unit. Also, the accuracy and reliability of the tech and the need for real-time processing are critical challenges to ongoing, around-the-clock farming operations.

AI tech offers the animal farmer tools to protect his livestock. Machine learning helps predict the strategies that boost production. Of course, as in any raw-material production effort, a variety of other challenges that must be overcome for successful use of AI tech.[378]

Just as AI empowers livestock production through smarter systems, it also plays a pivotal role in crop management and forest stewardship—sectors equally vital to sustaining life and environmental health.

AI Tech in the Agriculture and Forestry Sectors

Forestry and agriculture are significant for the future of humankind. However, the looming global food shortages put substantial pressure on humanity to increase crop production and maximize yields. That's why leveraging AI tech is so critical. Meanwhile, forest management is also key to our survival because trees and rainforests produce a quarter of the oxygen on Earth, which is essential to sustaining life as well.[379]

Agriculture

The benefits associated with AI tech in agriculture should be self-evident, such as optimizing food output—albeit while facing obstacles that threaten sustainability. Fortunately, tech promises to help farmers overcome these barriers.

AI-savvy farmers use data that gives them insights into every aspect of crop production such as assessing soil health, recommending fertilizer and pesticides application, and much more. Below are several tech-specific aids for farmers.

This material comes from a lengthy 2024 article by Alina Piddubna with the firm Agritech, "AI in Agriculture—The Future of Farming." Consider a few AI-related contributions to farming as well as some challenges.[380]

Saves on human labor: AI tech can cut manual labor through digital automation. Specifically, it can operate driverless tractors, run smart irrigation systems, fertilize, use drones to monitor crops, and conduct smart insecticide spraying, as well as help harvest at the right time with minimal waste.[381]

Optimizes irrigation systems: Tether AI tech with sensors combined with the Internet of Things, and the farmer monitors soil moisture and weather; as a result, the farmer knows when to water the crops. These smart irrigation systems conserve water and promote sustainable agriculture. Further, they can detect system leaks in real-time to prevent waste that could damage crops.[382]

Monitors soil health: AI tech can help identify the lack of nutrients in soil that affect crop health and growth rates. Computer-vision models help alert farmers when there is crop disease or pests like insects. For example, AI tech has a 90 percent accuracy rate detecting apple black rot, a fungal disease that causes leaf spot, fruit rot, and cankers on branches.[383]

It is noteworthy that the European Commission launched a digital platform using AI to provide a comprehensive assessment of soil health across the continent by 2030. AI4SoilHealth anticipates providing Soil Health Index certification to support landowners under the new Green Deal for Europe. Presently, between 60 and 70 percent of the EU's soils are unhealthy, according to the European Commission. Specifically, healthy soils capture carbon, improve yields, help reduce flooding, and boost biodiversity.[384]

AI AND RAW MATERIALS

Application of pesticides: The proper application of pesticides is tricky and labor-intensive. Therefore, AI-guided applications can be fast and accurate, and require less labor using drones that employ computer vision.[385]

Optimization of crop yields: Machine-learning algorithms can help farmers understand the patterns of their crops to assist planning, such as predicting soil yields. AI-assisted yield mapping also allows the farmer to "know where and when to sow seeds…for the best return on investment."[386]

Guidance on weeding and harvesting: AI tech tethered to sensors can detect weeds. The ML computer analyzes the data to direct where to weed and whether to weed by robot or hand. It also advises the farmer regarding the optimal time to harvest.[387]

Challenge to leveraging AI tech: The agriculture technology sector has several challenges, including farmer unfamiliarity with the tech and the starting costs. Understandably, a farmer struggling to make ends meet has no appetite to take on yet another financial burden even though there might be government grants and private investment opportunities.

The efficiency of our agricultural systems will in part determine humanity's long-term success. Smart, AI-tech-powered farming promises to play a significant role in agricultural and food-supply sustainability.

Like agriculture, forestry benefits greatly from AI technologies. However, its unique challenges—illegal logging, reforestation, and biodiversity preservation—require distinct applications of smart monitoring and resource management.

Wood Industry

The wood industry is critical to our future—primarily because of the role our forests play in oxygen generation, but also because of the uses for timber in our vast economy.

Fortunately, the wood industry has experienced significant and positive metamorphosis thanks to AI tech. Today, tech is available across this sector, especially in forest management, optimizing advice regarding harvesting, and protection of the environment for sustainability.[388]

AI FOR MANKIND'S FUTURE

AI tech helps our forest-management professionals by processing data from satellite images and drones to evaluate forest health, tree density, and growth rates. ML models allow managers to identify the "most suitable areas for harvesting, considering ecological impact and sustainability goals." They also help "optimize reforestation efforts by identifying the best planting strategies and predicting the trajectory of newly planted trees."[389]

Australia provides an example of AI's significant role in forestry management. An Australian firm used drones equipped with AI-enabled cameras to monitor a large forest. "The system identified tree health by analyzing foliage color, growth patterns, and soil conditions." Then the tech identified areas for logging as well as assisted with planning reforestation efforts.[390]

Another illustration of AI tech that helps the forestry industry comes from the Baltic country of Estonia. An Estonian firm, Timbeter, leverages AI to measure timber, combat illegal logging, and drive sustainability. Specifically, the company uses AI-powered solutions to address the critical need for accurate timber measurement, transparency, and sustainability in forestry management.[391]

"Illegal logging poses a significant threat to global forests," states an article in *Archiexpo Magazine*. The piece states that "approximately 30% of globally traded timber [is] sourced from illegal harvesting, resulting in environmental degradation and substantial economic losses." Timbeter's CEO, Anna-Greta Tsahkna, asserts that digitizing the forestry section with the help of AI tech ensures sustainability, fair trade, and effective climate mitigation.[392]

AI tech plays a critical role in sustaining forestry and agriculture, both of which are significant for supporting life. Complementary is humankind's extraction of mineral-based raw materials used in industrial settings.

While agriculture and forestry involve renewable, surface-based resources, the next domain—mineral and energy extraction—delves deep into the Earth's crust. Here, AI transforms how we locate, extract, and manage critical materials that power modern civilization.

AI AND RAW MATERIALS

AI and Mineral and Energy Extraction

AI tech plays a significant role in modern mineral and energy extraction. Consider some of tech's roles for each of these sectors.

AI helps find and extract minerals. Every modern nation is scrambling for new sources of raw minerals. Why? Raw minerals like the rare-earth minerals—the key ingredients of high-technology equipment—drive governments like the US to aggressively search for untapped resources.

That's why DARPA partnered with Hyperspectral, a firm that applies AI to spectroscopic data that comes from satellites or drones to help discover critical rare-earth minerals or elements.[393]

Rare-earth elements (REE) are seventeen metallic minerals, such as lanthanides, that are essential in manufacturing high-tech devices such as cellular telephones, computer hard drives, and hybrid vehicles. Of course, there are also significant defense applications of these elements, including electronic displays, lasers, radar, and more.[394]

The mining industry turns to AI to find ores and efficiently extract them from the Earth.

DARPA is searching for REE because access to these minerals is a critical national security issue and a sector the communist Chinese regime currently dominates. That explains DARPA's contract with Hyperspectral, which employs AI tech with spectroscopy to study how matter interacts with light or other forms of radiation.[395]

Until DARPA's project came to their attention, Hyperspectral focused on food safety. Specifically, the firm sought to find out if shipments of raw food carried dangerous pathogens, which can be identified with the help of spectroscopy.

Hyperspectral's CEO Matt Thereur explained AI's role in the company's work:

Pure samples [of bacteria] don't exist in nature. Nature is a boisterous place. So, what we're doing with artificial intelligence when we build these models is looking for all the relationships that can sometimes be obscured by the noise [such as] if you've got one section of the spectrum being confounded by some other substance within it."[396]

Mr. Thereur said that AI helps users understand the spectroscopic responses of materials and helps to "differentiate between different materials." He illustrated the value of this approach by citing the US Drug Enforcement Agency's use of the technique to identify "the difference of cocaine that came from one cartel's area of Colombia versus another."[397]

Hyperspectral has competition from Vrify Technology Inc., a tech company that uses advanced AI with deep-industry expertise to transform the search for minerals. Specifically, the firm invented DORA, a leading AI-assisted mineral-discovery platform. Vrify created DORA as a research and development tool for geologists and geoscientists to find minerals the world needs.[398]

DORA was introduced to the public during the 2025 Prospectors and Developers Association of Canada convention on March 3, 2025. The company boasts about its successes. For example, in September 2024, the firm Southern Cross (SXGC) "made a high-grade, gold discovery at its Sunday Creek Project from a target identified independently by both DORA and the SXGC exploration team."[399]

The growing quest to identify mineral resources knows few boundaries, including those under our seas. Even at the bottom of oceans, there are minerals—and AI tech is helping.

Parenthetically, the US National Oceanic and Atmospheric Administration (NOAA) indicates that the oceans cover approximately 70 percent of Earth's surface. However, as of June 2024, according to NOAA, only 26.1 percent of the global seafloor had been mapped.[400] However, a collaboration between the Nippon Foundation and General Bathymetry Chart of the Ocean (GEBCO) partnered with SeaDeep to form Seabed 2030 to develop an AI-powered platform for oceanic

AI AND RAW MATERIALS

exploration and monitoring, which has the mission "to inspire ocean mapping and deliver a complete seabed map for the benefit of people and the planet."[401]

There are three components to deep-sea mining systems: a surface mother ship, a cable and mining lift mechanism for ore, and seabed mining equipment, known as deep-sea mining (DSM) vehicles, which perform the actual mining process.[402]

DSM vehicles must navigate the seabed with all its obstacles. Making sure those vehicles avoid collision with obstacles requires AI's assistance. One AI-based controller for DSM vehicles is the "Improved Deep Deterministic Policy Gradient" (IDDPG). This algorithm has already validated its effectiveness and generalizability in deep-sea mining.[403]

AI's assistance in identifying new mineral resources and guiding DSM vehicles on the bottom of the sea is part of the rapid transformation of the mining industry.

No doubt, AI tech is optimizing extraction processes, enhancing safety, aiding with predictive maintenance, and more. The result is increased efficiency, better protection, and optimized resource management.[404]

A 2023 article in *Mining Digital*, "Top Uses for Artificial Intelligence," indicates that "smart [AI-powered] mining is leading changes in the industry."[405]

Some of the world's largest mining companies have adopted AI tech for their operations, according to the *Mining Digital*.

Consider:

- **AI predicts supply-chain disruptions.** AI tech helps companies manage supply-chain challenges by forecasting demand and optimizing inventory. It also uses intelligent alerts and real-time insights to manage disruptions.[406]
- **AI helps with energy optimization.** It optimizes energy use by analyzing data to identify energy-saving opportunities and improve efficiency.[407]
- **AI helps with mineral exploration.** It analyzes vast amounts of data and recommends what areas are best to dig. In fact,

Barrick Gold Corporation, a leading gold-mining firm, uses AI tech for mining exploration that includes identifying potential mining locations.[408]

- **AI predicts maintenance requirements for mining equipment.** AI's predictive maintenance models study a host of variables to make predictions about required maintenance to reduce equipment failures. This helps mining companies plan and preclude workplace injuries.[409]
- **AI-powered robotics go where miners cannot.** Robotic platforms provide the mining company with more tools, such as a line of autonomous robots that survey the ground above and below; perform excavations; and collect, haul, and process materials.[410]
- **AI sorts valuable minerals from waste.** AI-based sorting systems separate the valuable minerals from waste rock in real time, which improves recovery rates and reduces processing costs.[411]
- **AI guides autonomous vehicles.** These vehicles make mining safer, yet they can explore dangerous areas. Electric mining trucks range in capacity, helping customers meet their productivity targets.[412]

Alongside minerals, energy, oil (especially), gas, and renewable sources is another frontier where AI is reshaping how we locate, extract, and distribute power.

AI helps extract raw energy. Energy demands will grow 84 percent in step with world population, which is estimated to reach ten billion by 2050. Therefore, the scientific community—with the assistance of AI tech—is paying more attention to all parts of the energy industry, especially the oil and gas sector.[413]

The fossil fuel industry benefits from AI tech by analyzing geological data, helping in the discovery of new drilling sites, and managing drilling operations and equipment.

AI-powered systems can provide real-time monitoring of refinery operations, help optimize production processes, and reduce energy consumption. AI-driven analytics help identify the most productive oil reservoirs and improve placement.

The raw energy sector includes alternatives to fossil fuels such as solar and wind, and biodiesel, a renewable fuel that is an ideal alternative to conventional fuels. Biodiesel provides three advantages: physicochemical properties, environmental benefits, and economic profits.[414]

AI makes mineral and energy extraction operations more efficient, helps predict maintenance issues, pinpoints untapped resources, and helps inform managers who must make a variety of tough decisions.

Appendix L explores how AI technologies like Timbeter and hyperspectral imaging are advancing forestry and mineral exploration by improving efficiency and sustainability, while also noting that long-term success depends on overcoming technical, environmental, and adoption challenges through continued research and evaluation.

Next, we consider issues that affect all aspects of the raw materials portion of our economy, beginning with the impact on the workforce.

As AI reshapes how we extract and manage Earth's resources, it also transforms the labor needed to perform these tasks. This shift brings new opportunities and profound challenges for workers, especially in rural communities.

Workforce Transition and AI Adoption: Opportunities and Challenges

While AI-driven automation significantly improves efficiency and productivity within agriculture, forestry, and mining, it also greatly affects local labor dynamics. Tasks that traditionally rely on manual labor—such as milking cows, applying pesticides, or operating mining machinery—may increasingly be assigned to autonomous systems, raising concerns about job displacement, particularly in rural or economically vulnerable communities.

Even traditional white-collar jobs such as in the legal profession are likely to be significantly impacted by artificial intelligence. "Ubiquitous and increasingly powerful AI could radically transform our wrestling match with the law," wrote David Brenner, the board chair of AI and Faith and a lawyer with thirty-five years of experience in Seattle and Washington, DC.[415]

"AI is transforming the law in at least three ways: the processes by which law is applied, the structure of the legal profession, and our understanding of the law," wrote Brenner. This transformation is already visible in courtrooms, where the use of AI tools like ChatGPT and Claude has introduced serious new challenges to legal accuracy and professional accountability.[416]

A new database created by French lawyer and data scientist Damien Charlotin has since June 2023 documented more than 120 court cases in which lawyers submitted legal filings containing AI-generated hallucinations—mostly fake case citations produced by chatbots like ChatGPT and Claude. The problem is growing rapidly, with more than twenty incidents recorded in the past month alone and forty-eight already flagged in 2025. The database highlights how generative AI is being used to automate legal research and writing but often fabricates precedent-setting cases that never existed. While copying inaccurate citations isn't new to the legal profession, Charlotin notes that at least traditional errors referred to real cases. The increasing reliance on AI tools now poses risks of misinformation, prompting mild penalties such as fines or case dismissals and requiring legal professionals to double-check citations for AI errors. As awareness rises, so does scrutiny from judges and opposing counsel.[417]

More broadly across office-centric employees, many of those personnel already use AI for their jobs, but keep it secret from employers. A 2025 survey by Ivanti, an enterprise software company, released a report that surveyed office workers and IT professionals to ascertain the challenges and opportunities in the modern workforce. The report found that a significant number of employees expressed concern about the use of technology. Specifically, around one-third (30 percent) who use generative AI tools like ChatGPT at work worry that their job might be cut, and 27 percent suffer from AI-fueled imposter syndrome, "saying they don't want people to question their ability."[418]

AI AND RAW MATERIALS

"Ivanti's research shows that employees continue to want greater autonomy over their work lives and AI solutions that help them do their best work," said Brooke Johnson, chief legal counsel and senior vice president of human resources and security at Ivanti. "To address this, organizations should consider building a sustainable AI governance model, prioritizing transparency, and tackling the complex challenge of AI-fueled imposter syndrome through reinvention. Employers who fail to approach innovation with empathy and provide employees with autonomy run the risk of losing valuable staff and negatively impacting employee productivity."[419]

While workplace sentiment reveals growing anxiety among white-collar employees, AI industry leaders are issuing more sweeping warnings about the scale of disruption to come.

In a stark warning, Anthropic CEO Dario Amodei told Axios that artificial intelligence could eliminate up to 50 percent of all entry-level white-collar jobs within one to five years, driving US unemployment to as high as 20 percent. While AI offers tremendous benefits—like faster economic growth and potential medical breakthroughs—Amodei emphasized the dangers of mass job displacement, especially in tech, law, finance, and administration. He criticized both government and industry for downplaying the threat, urging immediate public awareness campaigns, workforce retraining, and policy responses such as a proposed "token tax" on AI revenue to redistribute wealth. Despite assurances from some commentators and recent data showing stable employment, Amodei warned that AI adoption will likely follow a "gradually, then suddenly" trajectory—hitting fast and across many sectors. He called on CEOs, lawmakers, and citizens to act now to steer the disruption before it becomes irreversible.[420]

To successfully navigate the transition across the workforce to more reliance on AI platforms, local economies must proactively invest in workforce reskilling, training initiatives, and AI governance. Specifically, new skill sets are essential for managing, maintaining, and optimizing these AI-driven processes, including computer programming, robotics maintenance, data analytics, and cybersecurity expertise. Educational institutions, vocational training programs, and public-private partnerships can facilitate this transition by providing targeted training opportunities and certifications to help workers adapt to a changing labor market.

Furthermore, AI-driven efficiencies can generate new job opportunities—though these positions may demand higher skill levels and digital competencies. What is clear is that instead of simply displacing workers, AI adoption can foster more specialized and technically skilled employment, potentially leading to increased wages and better working conditions. However, without intentional policy interventions and community-focused workforce planning, automation could worsen economic disparities, leaving some workers behind.

Local and national governments, therefore, play a vital role in ensuring fair workforce transitions. They support affected communities through education and skills-training investments, foster new job creation, and mitigate negative economic impacts. This strategic approach is essential for harnessing the full benefits of AI while safeguarding local livelihoods and promoting greater financial resilience.

Appendix M examines how AI is transforming the global workforce by automating much knowledge-based and repetitive roles, prompting a shift toward AI fluency and adaptability, while noting that jobs requiring creativity, emotional intelligence, or physical presence remain less susceptible to full replacement.

Yet addressing workforce concerns also requires tackling the foundational infrastructure barriers, especially in rural areas where limited connectivity restricts access to AI-enabled tools.

Bridging the Digital Divide in Rural and Remote Regions

Despite the promising benefits of AI for agriculture, forestry, and mining, many rural and remote regions still face significant infrastructure barriers, including limited broadband internet access, inconsistent electricity supply, and a shortage of skilled workers. These constraints create a digital divide that prevents many farmers, foresters, and small mining companies from fully harnessing AI's potential. That's why various

AI AND RAW MATERIALS

governmental and public-private initiatives have emerged to address infrastructure gaps and workforce training needs.

In the United States, federal programs like the USDA's ReConnect Program provide grants and loans to extend high-speed broadband access in underserved rural communities, facilitating the deployment of AI-driven technologies such as precision agriculture tools and remote monitoring systems. Similarly, partnerships between technology companies, local governments, and educational institutions are creating tailored training programs to equip rural workforces with essential digital skills. For example, collaborations involving universities, state agricultural extension services, and tech providers offer workshops and online courses specifically designed to build farmers' capabilities in AI-driven agriculture.

Internationally, initiatives like the Microsoft Airband Initiative and Google's Project Taara aim to expand connectivity to remote regions worldwide, explicitly targeting rural agricultural and mining communities. These efforts not only increase internet availability but also provide the essential digital infrastructure necessary to implement AI tools effectively.

Starlink, operated by Elon Musk's SpaceX, plays a crucial role in bridging the digital divide for rural and remote communities, directly promoting the adoption of AI technologies in resource extraction sectors. Starlink provides satellite-based, high-speed, broadband internet to areas where traditional wired or cellular connectivity is unavailable or unreliable. Its deployment has enabled farmers, miners, and forestry operations in isolated locations to access real-time AI tools such as precision agriculture platforms, remote equipment monitoring, and environmental data analytics—previously unattainable without reliable internet connectivity.

Recognizing Starlink's potential, several public-private partnerships have emerged, particularly in the US, where government agencies have allocated funding to assist rural communities in acquiring Starlink services. For example, the Federal Communications Commission (FCC) has designated Starlink as a recipient of rural broadband funding to expand connectivity to underserved communities.

By significantly lowering barriers to digital access, Starlink demonstrates how innovative infrastructure solutions can allow even small-scale agricultural and mining operations to leverage advanced AI technologies effectively. This advancement is crucial for ensuring that rural communities are included in the ongoing digital and technological transformation.

However, ongoing investment and coordinated policy support are essential to completely closing the digital divide. Governments and industry leaders need to focus on infrastructure development, workforce education, and equitable access to AI technologies, seeing to it that smaller businesses and rural areas are not left behind, but can fully engage in—and benefit from—the technological advancements transforming resource extraction.

Infrastructure and access aren't the only concerns. As AI spreads into the natural resource sector, we must also confront its ecological footprint.

Balancing AI's Environmental Benefits and Ecological Risks

While AI-driven approaches in agriculture and forestry provide significant environmental benefits—such as improved crop yields, optimized resource use, and better forest management, they also pose new ecological challenges and ethical concerns. On the one hand, precision agriculture powered by AI significantly reduces unnecessary fertilizer and pesticide use, decreases water consumption, and encourages more targeted land use, resulting in enhanced sustainability. Likewise, AI-driven forestry tools enable more intelligent resource allocation and conservation strategies, which could help mitigate deforestation and habitat destruction.

On the other hand, however, these technologies come with environmental costs. AI systems, those that depend on complex machine-learning algorithms, often require significant computing resources, resulting in high-energy consumption in data centers. This energy use can indirectly lead to greenhouse gas emissions if not powered by renewable sources. Additionally, the cooling demands for data-intensive operations frequently increase water usage, potentially worsening resource scarcity in vulnerable areas. Moreover, enhanced efficiency in raw material extraction or harvesting—enabled by AI-driven optimization—could unintentionally speed up resource depletion or intensify land use, undermining sustainability objectives.

Therefore, while AI has significant potential to enhance ecological stewardship, its use must be thoughtfully balanced with strong environmental oversight. Policymakers and industry leaders should adopt strategies like energy-efficient computing, renewable-powered data centers, and clear ethical guidelines to prevent overexploitation. By integrating these measures, we can ensure that AI's ecological footprint fosters genuinely sustainable and responsible stewardship of the environment.

Managing environmental risks also depends on strong legal and policy frameworks. In this next section, we examine how governments are regulating the use of AI in natural-resource extraction.

Policy, Regulation, and Data Governance in AI-Driven Natural-Resource Extraction

The deployment of AI in natural-resource extraction, agriculture, forestry, and mining is increasingly influenced by regulatory frameworks aimed at protecting privacy, property rights, and environmental standards. In the United States, agencies such as the Department of Agriculture (USDA), the Environmental Protection Agency (EPA), and the Bureau of Land Management (BLM) have started developing guidelines that directly affect the implementation of AI technologies. For instance, the USDA specifies data-governance standards about precision agriculture, emphasizing the responsible collection and management of farm-level data, especially in instances where drone surveillance or remote sensors may infringe upon private-property boundaries.

Similarly, the EPA provides guidelines designed to make certain that AI-driven environmental-monitoring systems comply with established privacy and data-sharing rules, thereby protecting both ecological resources and the rights of landowners. Regulations from the Federal Aviation Administration (FAA) governing drone operations further limit how data can be collected from private and public lands, requiring explicit permission and defined data-retention policies. Additionally, international frameworks like the European Union's General Data Protection Regulation (GDPR) indirectly impact multinational agricultural and resource-extraction companies, influencing their approaches to data privacy and security when utilizing AI-driven solutions.

These regulatory measures emphasize balancing innovation with accountability, making sure that AI solutions in raw-material extraction maintain privacy protections, respect property rights, and encourage sustainable resource management. To effectively integrate AI-driven approaches, clear policies, transparency, and stakeholder engagement are crucial for promoting responsible and equitable use of advanced technologies.

Beyond legal frameworks and technical safeguards, there is a deeper layer of reflection: How should we, as stewards of God's creation, view AI's role in reshaping the Earth's resources?

AI, Resource Extraction, and the Moral Imperative of Stewardship

While AI-driven advancements promise transformative efficiencies in agriculture, forestry, mining, and energy, these technologies also demand sober reflection from a faith-based perspective—particularly on humanity's ethical responsibilities toward creation. At the heart of Christian theology is the principle of stewardship, rooted in God's original mandate: "The Lord God took the man and put him in the Garden of Eden to work it and take care of it" (Genesis 2:15, NIV). Humanity was never given ownership of the Earth, but rather, the charge to care for it on God's behalf.

This stewardship extends not only to the natural world, but also to the vulnerable among us. "Speak up for those who cannot speak for themselves, for the rights of all who are destitute" (Proverbs 31:8, NIV) reminds us that ethical technology must also uplift the marginalized—small farmers, laborers, and low-income communities—who often bear the burden of industrial progress.

From a Christian perspective, the deployment of AI technologies must enhance—rather than diminish—our calling to protect the created order. This means using AI not merely to maximize output or profits, but to promote justice, responsible resource use, and ecological balance. "The earth is the Lord's, and everything in it, the world, and all who live in it"

(Psalm 24:1, NIV) serves as a sacred reminder that our extractive decisions must reflect the fact that we are managing God's property, not our own.

Furthermore, the Bible teaches that the land itself requires rest and respect. The Sabbath for the land outlined in Leviticus 25 called for periods of fallow and renewal—a rhythm of restraint built into God's economy. AI's potential to drive 24/7 extraction must be tempered by this biblical wisdom, urging us to ask: Are we allowing creation to breathe?

The prophets also warned against the consequences of ecological abuse. In Isaiah 24:5 (NIV), we read, "The earth is defiled by its people," and "the earth dries up and withers" because its people "have disobeyed the laws, violated the statutes and broken the everlasting covenant" (Isaiah 24:4–5, NIV). This prophetic vision underscores the spiritual stakes of environmental mismanagement—extractive greed and technological arrogance may invite divine judgment.

Revelation echoes this in eschatological terms: "The nations were angry, and your wrath has come…and for destroying those who destroy the earth" (Revelation 11:18, NIV). The misuse of power, including technological power, becomes a cosmic offense when it leads to the devastation of God's creation.

Therefore, Christian stewardship in the AI era isn't just about sustainability—it is about obedience to God's design. Our innovation must be accountable to moral wisdom. AI should serve the flourishing of all creation, not hasten its exploitation. It should amplify compassion, equity, and long-term care, not convenience at any cost.

In embracing AI's promise, we must also reaffirm our spiritual duty: to reflect God's justice, humility, and mercy in how we extract, produce, and share the Earth's resources. Let our technological advancements be guided not only by what is possible, but by what is righteous in the sight of the Lord.

Conclusion

As we transition from exploring AI-driven efficiencies in raw-material extraction to manufacturing, it becomes evident that the integration of data across these sectors presents tremendous potential. Advanced AI

AI FOR MANKIND'S FUTURE

analytics from energy fields, mining sites, farms, and forestry operations can feed directly into sophisticated, automated, factory-supply-chain management systems. This integration facilitates highly responsive, just-in-time production strategies and significantly enhances demand forecasting, minimizing waste, cutting inventory costs, and improving overall manufacturing agility.

As we shift focus to AI in manufacturing, the themes of data-driven stewardship, workforce disruption, and ethical responsibility continue—reminding us that the moral questions raised by raw-material extraction echo throughout the production cycle.

Chapter 11

AI
AND MANUFACTURING INDUSTRIES

> *Just as electricity transformed almost everything 100 years ago, today I actually have a hard time thinking of an industry that I don't think AI will transform in the next several years.*[421]
>
> ANDREW YAN-TAK NG (1976)
> British American computer scientist and cofounder
> of Google Brain

As AI begins to transform every major sector, manufacturing—long considered the engine for national productivity—is especially poised for disruption. Defined as part of the secondary sector of a country's economy, manufacturing transforms raw materials into finished consumer goods that are traded in society and represents the gross domestic product of a nation. The primary manufacturing industries include textile, food, chemical, transportation, pharmaceutical, telecommunications, electric power, and construction.

In general, AI technologies significantly aid manufacturing by improving the flow of processes, increasing productivity and decision-making. Along with sensors and the Internet of Things, AI devices help predict required maintenance of manufacturing equipment to minimize downtime. Further, it enables quick analysis of data to detect irregularities and identify defects in product.

The following sections illustrate how AI is revolutionizing several major manufacturing industries, beginning with textiles.

AI and the Textile Industry

A textile product is an article made from fabric that is woven or knitted from yarn, including natural and synthetic clothing. The process of textile manufacturing begins with the production of fibers—the husbandry of sheep and silkworms. Those fibers are processed into yarns, fabrics, and apparel by using spinning mills, weaving mills, knitting mills, and dyeing mills to ultimately produce garments and other material goods. Further, companies that sell buttons, zippers, knitting supplies, sewing machines, and threads are all related to this industry. Each of these activities may benefit from AI tech.

"AI is reshaping how textiles are created, manufactured, and consumed," according to Himanshu Ambarte writing for *Textile Sphere*. Consider how AI has driven design innovation. "Machine learning algorithms analyze vast datasets of fashion trends, historical designs, and consumer preferences to generate new patterns and styles," wrote Ambarte, the founder at BRILIPEX, a leather goods manufacturing firm. These algorithms suggest color palettes and fabric types while making sure designs are consistent with market demands.[422]

As in other industries, AI is helping automate processes and improve efficiency by advising on maintenance to minimize equipment failures. It also helps harness robots to conduct fabric cutting, sewing, and quality inspection while reducing labor costs.

AI technology is crucial for optimizing supply chains using ML models to predict textile demand patterns, which helps manufacturers adjust schedules and inventory. It also aids quality control using vision systems that detect defects in real time.

"Artificial Intelligence is revolutionizing the textile industry by enhancing design creativity, manufacturing efficiency, supply chain optimization, and quality control," Mr. Ambarte wrote.[423]

Beyond aesthetics and apparel, AI also plays a growing role in sustaining human needs through the food industry.

AI and the Food Industry

The food industry spans from agricultural production to packaging and distribution. AI is increasingly shaping this process by improving efficiency, safety, and product development.

The food industry relies on AI by helping with efficiency and safety for producers and consumers. "It's changing how new food products are conceived, designed, and brought to market," according to the CAS Science Team, and it helps the industry "align closer than ever with consumer preferences, drastically reducing the trial-and-error of product development." The Ohio-based CAS is a division of the American Chemical Society that specializes in scientific knowledge management.[424]

AI helps the food industry adjust to radical shifts in demand, fluctuating crop yields and food waste. In the US, 30 percent of food and drink are discarded annually, wasting $48.3 billion.[425]

The application of AI tech in food manufacturing is revolutionizing quality control by employing predictive analytics that preemptively identify contamination risks and optimize supply-chain management, according to CAS. Further, AI-powered ML vision systems closely monitor product quality to make certain the consumer gets the best product.[426]

The development of future food products is aided by AI tech. After all, most (80 percent) new food product launches fall short due to consumer disinterest. Therefore, using AI-powered predictive analytics, when it's tethered to a deep understanding of consumer preferences, improves consumer satisfaction with the latest products.[427]

Food-ingredient innovation is happening at a faster rate thanks to AI's capabilities. For example, Brightseed's "Forager" is transforming how the firm understands plant-based bioactives thanks to AI tech by better understanding the molecular composition of plants and therefore helping uncover potential health benefits.[428]

Forager is one of many innovations that are reshaping food manufacturing by promoting faster market introductions and innovative ingredients. The potential for food-related research and development has introduced a revolution in the industry, which unlocks new potential for efficiency and growth in food technology.

Just as food must be processed for safe consumption, raw materials must be refined—bringing us to AI's impact on the chemical industry.

AI and the Chemical Industry

The chemical industry changes raw materials such as minerals, metals, and oil, as well as synthetic products, into functional goods used by households and in construction, medicine, agriculture, and other segments of society. This industry is witnessing a profound transformation given the integration of AI that impacts efficiency, safety, and innovation.

AI is transforming the chemical industry in ways outlined below.[429]

AI improves chemical R&D. AI tech cuts research timelines by almost a third and reduces waste, such as IBM's RXN platform for chemistry, a tool that forecasts chemical reactions, saving physical testing and facilitating a deeper understanding of chemical behaviors.[430]

AI improves manufacturing efficiency. AI with the Internet of Things enhances predictive maintenance and decision-making. This transforms the traditional factory into a smart factory that can detect equipment issues and optimize schedules, which PricewaterhouseCoopers International Limited reports could boost production by 12 percent.[431]

AI improves supply-chain efficiency. AI tech is reshaping the chemical industry's ability to predict demand, manage inventory, and coordinate logistics. One source indicates that AI applications can cut in half the number of errors in supply-chain forecasting.[432]

AI improves quality control: AI tech is helping the industry set new standards by using ML models that carefully monitor every phase of the production process to identify deviations from the norm. BASF (for the German name *Badische Anilin-und Sodafabrik*), the largest chemical producer in the world, uses AI tech to monitor product quality and, as a result, reduced waste by twenty percent.[433]

The chemical industry harnesses AI tech to improve its bottom line while advancing innovation and efficiency.

AI AND MANUFACTURING INDUSTRIES

Building on foundational inputs like chemicals, the transportation industry showcases AI's influence on mobility and logistics at scale.

AI and the Transportation Industry

This industry transforms raw materials into equipment, spare parts, and vehicles of all types, which link different sectors of the economy. It has various branches, including air freight, logistics, airlines, marine, road and rail, automobiles, and transportation infrastructure.

America's AI tech is revolutionizing transportation, and that market is expected to grow to a $6.51 billion sector by 2031. The possibilities for this industry include significant advances regarding AI-powered autonomous vehicles, traffic management, fuel efficiency, and passenger safety. See below some of those technological advances. [434]

AI improves traffic management. AI will analyze data to optimize traffic flows in cities by adjusting traffic signals and suggesting alternative routes during peak hours. This effort reduces fuel consumption, decreases harmful emissions, and results in fewer accidents on the road.[435]

AI functions in the driver's seat. Leaving the driving to AI promises to improve road safety and reduce human errors. Its ability to process massive amounts of data allows these self-driving vehicles to adapt to complex driving situations, such as changing weather and traffic patterns.[436]

There is a problem with self-driving cars, however. They will never have access to the training data necessary to address all drivers' situations. In fact, the models that power self-driving cars remain limited and constrained by their sensors and algorithms. Despite these gains, experts caution that AI-powered vehicles still face serious limitations. For example, a Johns Hopkins study found that generative AI systems like self-driving cars are far worse than humans at identifying interactions in a moving scene, a glaring weakness going forward for the industry. Still, as sensor capabilities and datasets improve, autonomous vehicles remain a key area of AI development.[437]

An example of this development is in Austin, Texas. In June 2025, a Tesla Model Y operating without a human driver was spotted navigating the city's streets, hinting at the imminent launch of Tesla's robotaxi service.

Although Tesla hasn't officially announced a rollout date, the test vehicle drew enthusiastic responses from CEO Elon Musk and Tesla engineers. The service is expected to begin with a small fleet monitored remotely from Tesla's local factory. However, federal safety officials are scrutinizing the initiative due to previous crash-related recalls. While Tesla is currently labeled as "testing" on Austin's autonomous vehicle dashboard, competitors like Waymo have already launched services but encountered public complaints. Experts remain concerned about Tesla's minimalist sensor strategy, which may compromise reliability compared to sensor-rich rivals. This rollout highlights both the promise and the continuing challenges of deploying fully autonomous vehicles on public roads.[438]

AI helps with vehicle maintenance. Technology will help owners with maintenance reminders by monitoring the vehicle's health, thanks to sensors that identify wear and tear patterns. This helps to prevent breakdowns and improves vehicle longevity.[439]

AI helps manage vehicle fleets. It aids scheduled maintenance, which results in better fleet performance and lower expenses; further, it improves fuel efficiency, streamlines logistics, and enhances safety for drivers. AI can also optimize route planning, monitor road and bridge conditions, and report public safety issues such as needed repairs to government authorities.[440]

AI helps find parking spaces. An AI-powered parking system simplifies the process of finding a space, which saves time and fuel. It also reduces congestion. The system uses sensors and cameras that communicate locations to mobile applications. The broader benefits include less aimless driving while searching for a parking space and a more efficient driving experience.[441]

AI helps maritime shipping. AI has optimized navigation, improved port operations, and improved safety. As in the case with wheeled vehicles, AI can help identify abnormalities in marine vessels, help with communication between ship and shore authorities, optimize fuel use, and manage routes.[442]

AI helps with rail transportation. It helps optimize train schedules and ensures track safety by monitoring rail infrastructure in real time. It

AI AND MANUFACTURING INDUSTRIES

also aids with predicting maintenance requirements that preclude breakdowns—efforts that improve equipment longevity and enhance safety.[443]

AI helps airport operations. AI aids air-traffic control in managing airspace and optimizing flight routes. It anticipates weather patterns and flight trajectories to prevent conflicts, which reduces delays, improves safety, and saves on fuel. On the ground, AI helps automate routine tasks by predicting congested areas to foster smooth operations, such as runway management.[444]

AI's role in aviation safety is now expanding beyond operations to national oversight and emergency prevention. In response to a deadly January 2025 midair collision near Washington, DC, that killed sixty-seven people and a series of near-misses, the US Department of Transportation is deploying artificial intelligence to enhance air traffic safety. Transportation Secretary Sean Duffy announced a comprehensive overhaul of the air traffic control system, using machine learning and language models to analyze incident reports, flight paths, and safety data to identify high-risk "hot spots" nationwide. Rather than replacing human controllers, AI operates behind the scenes to surface patterns and warnings—especially in areas like DCA and the Gulf of Mexico where helicopters and planes frequently intersect. The initiative aims to modernize a decades-old system, prioritize prevention over reaction, and equip safety officials with real-time insights to avert future tragedies.

The transportation industry is rapidly transforming with the help of AI systems that promise to cut costs while improving both safety and efficiency.

While AI in transportation emphasizes physical movement and logistics, in pharmaceuticals, it turns inward to transform how we understand and treat the human body.

AI and the Pharmaceutical Industry

The pharmaceutical industry comprises activities that transform chemical substances and active ingredients through discovery and development into goods, such as medications and medical devices.

AI FOR MANKIND'S FUTURE

AI promises to speed up drug development, uncover new therapeutic targets, and personalize treatment. Of course, this revolutionary technology comes with significant challenges, such as data privacy.

AI helps modernize and enhance critical processes in the pharmaceutical industry, such as the drug-discovery process, by analyzing large datasets to identify potential drug candidates and predict whether they will be effective, an approach carried out by recognizing patterns in the data.

This technology can also help transform clinical trial efforts by optimizing participant recruitment, monitoring patient response, and predicting side effects. The result is more targeted and efficient trials, completed faster and with better results.[445]

The following are examples of AI applications in the pharmaceutical industry concerning drug discovery, clinical trials, personalized medicine, and enhancements in supply chain and manufacturing.

AI helps with drug discovery. A United Kingdom-based biotech firm, Benevolentai, used AI tech to accelerate drug discovery for COVID-19. The AI platform assessed data from many sources and then identified the drug Baricitinib, which is normally for the treatment of rheumatoid arthritis, as a candidate for COVID-19. Baricitinib received emergency-use authorization due to its efficacy in inhibiting a crucial protein involved in the inflammatory response induced by COVID-19.[446]

AI helps with clinical trials. IBM Healthcare uses AI to identify personnel for clinical trials. IBM Watson's natural-language processing tech reviews patient records to identify matches based on patient condition and history. The AI-driven tool allegedly increased patient recruitment and was more accurate at matching patients with the trial.[447]

AI helps personalize cancer treatment. Tempus Technology is a firm that brings data and AI to healthcare. It uses AI to analyze genomic data to personalize cancer treatment by interpreting genomic sequencing data and identifying mutations and patterns that help attending physicians deliver treatment plans.[448]

AI accurately predicts drug interactions. The Korea Advanced Institute of Science and Technology (KAIST), a research university in Daejeon,

South Korea, developed an AI-based algorithm that predicts drug interactions with 92 percent accuracy. "Drug interactions, including drug-drug interactions and drug-food constituent interactions, can trigger unexpected pharmacological effects, including adverse drug events, with causal mechanisms often unknown," the KAIST researchers wrote.[449] "However, current prediction methods do not provide sufficient details beyond the chance of drug-drug occurrence, or require detailed drug information, which is often unavailable, to predict drug interactions."[450]

AI optimizes drug production and quality. The firm Johnson & Johnson uses AI algorithms to monitor and control drug production in real time as well as to identify anomalies. This assistance results in improved efficiency, less waste, and improved overall production performance.[451]

AI tech is revolutionizing the pharmaceutical industry through data analysis and enhanced efficiency. This contribution will speed up treatment identification and benefit patient outcomes.

AI and the Telecommunications Industry

The telecommunications industry employs engineering and technology to support the transmission and reception of various signal types—including radio, television, mobile phones, and internet networks. As the backbone of global digital connectivity, this sector is experiencing an AI-powered transformation.

AI—especially generative AI—is accelerating innovation across telecommunications by enhancing customer service, automating internal processes, boosting productivity, and optimizing network operations. A 2024 global survey of over four hundred telecom professionals found a significant uptick in AI adoption, with executives expressing rising enthusiasm for its integration. In fact, a parallel study by Nvidia revealed that 90 percent of telecom providers are now using AI, and more than half (53 percent) consider it a decisive competitive advantage.[452]

AI's wide-ranging benefits in this sector are evident. For example:

- **Predictive analytics** help anticipate network usage changes, prevent outages, and tailor services to individual user needs.

More than 80 percent of providers use AI to identify customers who are likely to leave due to poor service.[453]
- **Network operations** are optimized as AI analyzes usage data, identifies performance issues, and automates tasks like traffic routing and load balancing.[454]
- **Sales and marketing** see tangible gains, with AI enabling personalized content and reportedly boosting sales by up to 15 percent while reducing capital expenditure by 10 percent.[455]
- **Customer experience** improves as AI equips service agents with real-time behavioral data, making the service more responsive and personalized.[456]

Telecommunications providers increasingly recognize that an AI-powered infrastructure is not optional—it is foundational to their future. As digital traffic grows and service expectations rise, the industry's reliance on AI will only deepen.

This dependence on AI-powered infrastructure also places greater demand on energy systems. Just as telecom relies on efficient, reliable transmission, so AI itself relies on stable, scalable electric power. Thus, we now turn to how AI is revolutionizing the electric power industry—both as a consumer of energy and as a catalyst for innovation in its generation and distribution.

AI and the Electric Power Industry

This industry employs engineering and technology activities for generation, transmission, maintenance, and distribution of electric power to supply the public and industry.

Electric utilities are beginning to recognize the power of generative AI models. "Utility executives who were skeptical of AI even five years ago are now [2025] using cloud computing, drones, and AI in innovative projects," said Electric Power Research Institute Executive Director Jeremy Renshaw. "Utilities' rapid adoption may make what is impossible today standard operating practice in a few years."[457]

Although there are AI skeptics among utility experts, there's growing

AI AND MANUFACTURING INDUSTRIES

recognition that things must change. "But any company that has not taken its internal knowledge base into a generative AI model that can be queried as needed is not leveraging the data it has long paid to store," said Nvidia Corporation Senior Managing Director Marc Spieler. Yes, humans are still running operations, but AI is helping them make better decisions.[458]

Note the many common AI applications for the electric industry:

- **AI protects against hackers.** AI/ML helps "to meet a security standard protecting against hackers during software updates," said Peter Nicoletti, a certifier for Underwriters Laboratories.[459]
- **AI improves market price forecasting.** The firm Amperon does weather-, demand-, and market-price forecasting with AI algorithms, said Sean Kelly, cofounder and CEO.[460] The firm's short-term modeling now "runs every hour and continuously retrains smarter and faster using less energy, combining the strengths from each iteration in a way that humans could never touch," he added. Another firm, Hitachi Energy, uses an AI algorithm that "has improved price forecasting accuracy 20% over human market price forecasting" since November 2024, said Jason Durst, Hitachi Energy's general manager.[461]
- **AI helps mitigate wildfire risks.** Rob Brook, senior vice president of Neara's Americas regions, said AI-powered tech is "a critical pillar of wildfire mitigation strategy." It helps identify the risks "across their networks by proactively assessing more variables than a human can assimilate."[462]
- **AI accelerates the use of robotics.** Deise Yumi Asami, developer of the Maximo robot, said AI algorithms accelerated the use of robotics for solar construction. Maximo no longer requires retraining because AI algorithms autonomously learn the unique characteristics of each solar project before work begins.[463]

Finally, a 2024 study by Pacific Gas and Electric claims an inflexible power system "can lead to decreased reliability and safety, increased operational costs, and capacity costs." AI/ML and other novel technologies "can not only bolster our immediate response capabilities but also inform long-term planning and policymaking," states the PG&E study.[464]

The power industry must effectively capture the benefits of AI algorithms, beginning by recognizing their potential and acquiring and using the proper hardware and software to power America better.

In conjunction with the power industry fully using AI, another compelling reason affects both AI and the power industry. Specifically, the deployment of more AI requires an "expedited effort to increase the capacity of the existing, sometimes antiquated U.S. energy system."[465]

In 2025, Google produced a report, "Powering a New Era of American Innovation," that claims AI "will grow the American economy, create jobs, accelerate scientific advances, improve health and educational outcomes, and strengthen national and global security." However, that depends on our ability to produce enough power.[466]

Google asserts that we must take three steps to grow our power production to meet the AI-related demand: "(1) Accelerating innovation and investment in affordable, reliable, and secure energy technologies, including geothermal, advanced nuclear, and natural gas generation with carbon capture (among other sources), (2) Optimizing use of the existing grid and unlocking construction of new transmission infrastructure and (3) Developing the labor force needed to construct new infrastructure."[467]

What is clear, according to Google, is that technological development drives growth and prosperity, and that will be true for AI. It could become a catalyst to economic growth contributing trillions of dollars to the US GDP over the coming decade. However, that growth will rely on meeting the significant demand for electricity, which will triple before 2030.[468]

On May 23, 2025, the nation's demand for electricity garnered help from President Trump. At a White House ceremony, Mr. Trump signed executive orders aimed at reforming nuclear-energy research and clearing the path to build nuclear reactors on federally owned land. An unnamed federal official said the order "allows for safe and reliable nuclear energy to power and operate critical defense facilities and AI data centers."[469]

Google summed up the challenge ahead:

> America is a nation with extraordinary talent, unmatched innovation, abundant resources, and an ability to rise and meet any challenge. It is essential to meld those strengths if we are to realize the great economic growth opportunities presented by AI.[470]

Appendix N explains that AI consumes significant electricity because training and running large models requires massive computational power, sustained over time, using energy-intensive hardware and data-center infrastructure.

Just as AI reshapes how we power our industries, it's also changing how we build them. The construction sector is increasingly reliant on AI to streamline project management and ensure workplace safety.

AI and the Construction Industry

This industry comprises the activities related to architectural, engineering, and manufacturing services of goods and supplies associated with building or forming roads, urban and hydraulic works, and housing. AI-powered construction solutions generated $5 billion globally in 2023.[471]

In the early 2000s, construction specialists began applying algorithms to construction-related applications. Soon, AI-powered technologies and machines automated repetitive and physically demanding tasks aiming to improve site efficiency and quality. Today, AI-powered robots perform complex tasks such as bricklaying, painting, and welding.

Consider how AI tech has grown to support the construction industry. The following popular applications come from a McKinsey & Company report that identified thirty-seven specific uses in construction.[472]

- **AI aids project management.** Using sensors, AI tech generates insights about projects, such as tracking work progress and crew productivity; identifies issues and addresses them

in real-time; adjusts completion dates based on actual progress; and forecasts project life-cycle costs.[473]
- **AI aids scheduling and resource allocation.** Professionals use AI to improve efficiency and project budgets. AI-powered software considers factors like weather and supply-chain delays to produce meaningful schedules.[474]
- **AI powers estimates and bidding.** Historically, estimates and bidding are time-consuming, because architects and developers had to use blueprints to calculate bids with each subcontractor—e.g., plumbers and electricians. Now, AI tech automatically and accurately cuts that effort from weeks to minutes.[475]
- **AI tech mitigates common risks.** Some of the features of AI-powered risk mitigation are keeping construction workers and sites safe by identifying hazards; detecting site-quality issues with sensors; preventing cost overruns; and improving on-site security with sensors that detect threats 24/7.[476]
- **AI-powered robotics make essential contributions.** Today, robots are important in construction. They bring a variety of essential contributions to the construction site: 3D printers, bricklaying, painting, welding, rebar tying, safety and security monitoring, self-operated heavy equipment, and more. These AI robots complement human workers.[477]
- **AI tech streamlines design and planning.** It analyzes complex data to consider building codes, zoning laws, and topographical information to assemble designs that comply with regulations and are cost efficient. It can also analyze designs to identify flaws and inefficiencies prior to construction.[478]

There are significant benefits AI tech brings to the construction industry: improved site productivity, better project planning, lower construction costs, and safer work sites. These benefits are revolutionizing the construction industry.

AI AND MANUFACTURING INDUSTRIES

While AI enhances productivity across industries, its rise presents new challenges—and opportunities—for the manufacturing workforce.

Labor Market Implications of AI-Driven Manufacturing

While AI-driven automation significantly boosts productivity in sectors such as textiles, food processing, and construction, it also has profound implications for the workforce. Automation can displace workers engaged in repetitive or routine tasks, creating a pressing need for retraining and reskilling programs. However, integrating AI technologies also presents opportunities to develop new, higher-skilled roles, including robot-management technicians, data analysts, cybersecurity specialists, and automation system engineers.

Proactive workforce-development strategies are essential for mitigating job displacement across the manufacturing industry. Successful initiatives include partnerships between industry and academia that offer tailored vocational training, apprenticeships, and certification programs in collaboration with community colleges or technical schools. Companies like Amazon and Siemens have implemented robust retraining programs, such as Amazon's "Upskilling 2025," which outlines the company's $1.2 billion investment to retrain three hundred thousand employees for technology-intensive roles, preparing workers for the transition into AI-supported job functions without severe disruptions.[479]

AI-powered robots are taking over many assembly plant jobs.

As manufacturers adapt to new workforce realities, they must also navigate the growing landscape of AI governance and safety standards.

Regulatory Frameworks and Industry Standards in AI-Driven Manufacturing

As AI increasingly integrates into manufacturing processes, regulatory frameworks and industry standards are crucial for ensuring safety, compliance, and accountability. Manufacturers implementing AI systems must follow established international standards such as International Organization for Standardization (ISO) 9001 for quality management, ISO 45001 for occupational health and safety, and the recently introduced ISO/International Electrotechnical Commission (IEC) 42001, which specifically addresses the reliability, transparency, and robustness of AI systems.[480]

Furthermore, sectors like food processing and pharmaceuticals face stringent regulatory requirements. For instance, the US Food and Drug Administration (FDA) enforces rigorous validation and traceability procedures for AI-driven quality-control systems to ensure consumer protection and product safety.[481] Likewise, AI applications affecting critical safety decisions, such as automated construction equipment or robotic assembly lines, must adhere to OSHA (Occupational Safety and Health Administration) standards to safeguard workers from potential hazards.[482]

Emerging guidelines from organizations such as the National Institute of Standards and Technology (NIST) further emphasize transparency and algorithmic accountability. NIST's AI Risk Management Framework (AI RMF) provides principles for companies to assess and reduce automated decision-making systems' biases, errors, and unintended outcomes.[483]

As AI's role in manufacturing grows, following these evolving regulatory standards and best practices will be crucial to guarantee safe, ethical, and responsible integration—protecting consumers, safeguarding workers, and maintaining public trust in advanced manufacturing technologies.

Furthermore, the best practices suggest companies that facilitate smoother workforce transitions engage in transparent communication with employees regarding expected changes, invest early in upskilling, and establish clear pathways for career advancement within new technological frameworks. As manufacturing increasingly integrates AI, focusing on these labor considerations—ensuring fair transitions, providing opportunities for professional growth, and offering support for

AI AND MANUFACTURING INDUSTRIES

displaced workers—will be vital in fostering inclusive economic outcomes during technological change.

Cybersecurity in AI-Driven Manufacturing

The growing adoption of AI and Internet of Things technologies in manufacturing significantly boosts productivity, but it also increases vulnerability to cyber threats. Manufacturing facilities that rely on interconnected AI-driven systems, automated machinery, and networked sensors are attractive targets for cyberattacks. Successful breaches can cause costly disruptions to operations and compromise proprietary data, including product designs, intellectual property, and sensitive supply-chain logistics.

To mitigate these risks, manufacturers are increasingly adopting comprehensive cybersecurity practices that align with industry standards, including the National Institute of Standards and Technology's Cybersecurity Framework (NIST CSF) and the ISO/IEC 27001 standard for information security management. Best practices comprise robust encryption protocols, regular security audits, and continuous monitoring through advanced-threat-detection systems. Employee training in cybersecurity awareness is equally essential to protect against phishing and social engineering attacks.[484]

Notably, several high-profile breaches highlight the urgent need for enhanced cybersecurity in manufacturing. For instance, the 2021 ransomware attack on JBS Foods temporarily halted operations at multiple plants, demonstrating the real-world effects of compromised digital systems on industrial productivity and economic stability.[485]

Governments have agencies like the US Cybersecurity and Infrastructure Security Agency (CISA), which provide guidelines specifically designed for industrial cybersecurity, detailing steps manufacturers should follow to safeguard operational technology, IoT systems, and AI-driven processes.

As manufacturing increasingly relies on AI and digital connectivity, an initiative-taking cybersecurity strategy is essential—protecting assets, ensuring operational continuity, and maintaining the trust of customers and partners alike.

AI and Sustainable "Green" Manufacturing

Artificial intelligence increasingly enables manufacturers to adopt sustainable and environmentally responsible practices by optimizing energy use, reducing waste, and ensuring compliance with regulations. AI-driven analytics and predictive modeling can accurately forecast energy needs, schedule machinery operations during off-peak hours, and minimize unnecessary consumption, significantly lowering a plant's overall carbon footprint. Additionally, AI enhances waste management by identifying inefficiencies in production lines and recommending adjustments that reduce scrap and resource overuse.

For instance, General Motors uses AI-powered data analytics to optimize energy consumption across its facilities, reducing energy-related emissions by approximately 20 percent since 2010.[486] Similarly, Unilever employs AI to monitor real-time energy and water usage across its manufacturing plants globally, enabling precise adjustments that have markedly decreased their environmental impact and advanced sustainability targets.[487]

Moreover, AI systems help ensure compliance with environmental regulations by continuously monitoring emissions data, detecting anomalies, and simplifying environmental reporting procedures. These capabilities are critical as manufacturers increasingly face stringent regulations such as the European Union's Industrial Emissions Directive (IED) and the US Environmental Protection Agency's (EPA) emissions standards.

Thus, AI promotes operational efficiency and empowers manufacturers to advance environmental stewardship goals, reduce ecological impacts, and navigate complex regulatory landscapes—contributing to more sustainable industrial practices.

The Future of AI in Manufacturing: Emerging Innovations

As AI continues to evolve, its role in manufacturing may go beyond automation and optimization, transforming the industry with advanced technologies that promise even greater efficiency, flexibility, and innovation.

One transformative trend is generative design, where AI algorithms analyze constraints, material properties, and performance requirements

AI AND MANUFACTURING INDUSTRIES

to create optimized product designs that human engineers might not envision. This methodology is currently implemented within the aerospace and automotive sectors to manufacture components that are both lighter and stronger, while simultaneously reducing material waste.[488]

Another breakthrough is digital twin technology, which creates real-time virtual replicas of physical manufacturing systems. These AI-driven simulations facilitate predictive maintenance, process optimization, and rapid testing of modern designs, enhancing production efficiency and minimizing downtime. When integrated with augmented reality (AR), digital twins enable workers to visualize complex systems, diagnose issues remotely, and engage with AI-generated insights in real time.[489]

Furthermore, AI-integrated 3D printing will revolutionize traditional manufacturing lines. AI-enhanced additive manufacturing allows on-demand, localized production, minimizing supply-chain dependencies and material waste. This transition could foster more sustainable production models while making advanced manufacturing capabilities accessible to smaller companies and emerging markets.[490]

The most futuristic development is the rise of "lights-out" factories, fully autonomous facilities where AI, IoT sensors, and robotics operate flawlessly without human intervention. While these factories are still in the early phases, companies like Tesla and Siemens invest heavily in AI-driven automation to move closer to this reality.[491]

These innovations signal a future wherein AI does more than streamline existing processes; it actively transforms how products are designed, built, and delivered. As manufacturing progresses towards an era of greater autonomy, adaptability, and intelligence, businesses must stay ahead of these trends to harness AI's full potential while guaranteeing ethical and sustainable industry growth.

Ethical and Faith-Based Considerations in AI-Driven Manufacturing

While AI offers unprecedented efficiencies in manufacturing, its rapid adoption raises moral and ethical questions regarding the balance between profit, worker welfare, and consumer responsibility. From a faith-based perspective—especially within Christian thought—principles of stewardship, justice, and human dignity are essential for assessing how AI transforms industrial production.

One key ethical consideration is balancing economic efficiency with worker well-being. AI-driven automation must not prioritize productivity at the expense of fair wages, safe working conditions, and meaningful employment. Biblical teachings, like the warning in James 5:4 (fair wages) against unjust labor practices, remind manufacturers of their moral obligation to treat workers with dignity. This makes certain that technological advancements do not exploit or displace vulnerable populations without supporting retraining and reskilling.

Moreover, the integration of AI into consumer-facing products brings new ethical obligations, particularly around guaranteeing safety, promoting transparency, and providing equitable access for all users. AI-enhanced manufacturing can improve quality control, reduce waste, and make products more affordable. However, it also requires ethical oversight to prevent misleading marketing, hidden biases in AI-driven product design, and unfair regional disparities in access to advanced goods. Biblical principles of justice and equity (Micah 6:8) emphasize the need for manufacturers to focus on the fair distribution of AI's benefits instead of exacerbating existing inequalities.

Responsible AI-driven manufacturing should embody technical efficiency and a dedication to ethical integrity, human dignity, and equitable economic participation. By incorporating moral considerations into technological advancement, manufacturers can make sure that AI promotes the common good, aligning innovation with profound principles of justice and stewardship.

Conclusion

As Christian stewards, we're called to exercise dominion over creation with wisdom, responsibility, and compassion (Genesis 1:28; Colossians 3:23). That includes our use of artificial intelligence in reshaping the manufacturing sector. Our aim must not be technological advancement for its own sake, but innovation that reflects God's character—bringing order, promoting human dignity, and serving the common good.

AI AND MANUFACTURING INDUSTRIES

AI is rapidly transforming how America manufactures—from textiles to pharmaceuticals and from construction to electric power. Manufacturers that wisely invest in AI, workforce development, and ethical digital transformation are poised to lead in innovation, sustainability, and global competitiveness. Yet these advances also bring spiritual and ethical responsibilities.

The future of manufacturing is undeniably becoming smarter, cleaner, and more adaptive—with AI at the center. But it must also remain humane, just, and accountable. From automated robots to green factories, the shift underway represents both a challenge and an opportunity to align industry practices with biblical values.

As we move from how goods are made to how they are marketed and sold, the next chapter explores AI's growing role in the retail sector—reshaping not just production, but the very experience of the consumer in a digitally driven economy.

Chapter 12

AI AND THE RETAIL ECONOMY

AI is an engine that is poised to drive the future of retail to all-new destinations. The key to success is the ability to extract meaning from big data to solve problems and increase productivity.[492]

AZADEH YAZDAN
Director of business development, AI Products Group

Azadeh Yazdan's statement captures the essence of a retail revolution already underway. Artificial intelligence is no longer a futuristic ideal; it is a transformative force reshaping the retail sector from end to end—streamlining supply chains, reimagining customer service, and redefining how merchants engage with consumers.

With AI's help, modern retailers can harness massive datasets to identify customer preferences, predict behavior, and tailor shopping experiences like never before. The result is improved customer satisfaction and increased sales. Yet this power comes with a caution: While AI enables precision personalization, it also raises serious concerns around consumer data privacy, surveillance, and ethical use. Technology may enhance convenience and loyalty, but it must not come at the cost of transparency or human dignity.

To help navigate this complex terrain, this chapter explores eight major dimensions of AI's impact on the retail economy, ranging from operational benefits to theological concerns:

1. **Understanding the customer:** How AI collects and analyzes consumer data to improve personalization and predict buying behavior.
2. **Omnichannel retail:** The use of AI to create seamless, integrated customer experiences across physical and digital platforms.
3. **Small and medium retailers:** Scalable AI solutions that allow smaller businesses to compete with large corporations.
4. **Market intelligence and strategy:** AI's growing role in shaping marketing decisions, customer targeting, and content creation.
5. **Customer loyalty programs:** How AI enhances customer retention through personalized rewards, behavior prediction, and 24/7 engagement.
6. **Online shopping innovations:** AI-powered tools that improve convenience, visualization, product discovery, and security in e-commerce.
7. **Ethical, legal, and workforce concerns:** A look at the challenges AI raises in data privacy, corporate responsibility, and workforce transformation.
8. **Christian reflections:** A faith-based assessment of AI's implications for dignity, justice, and consumer behavior in the retail landscape.

Together, these areas offer a framework for evaluating the promises and pitfalls of AI in retail. Among the most profound shifts AI enables is the ability to understand customers on a granular level—a capability that serves as the foundation for nearly all subsequent innovations.

AI Helps Retailers Know Their Customers

AI provides insights regarding consumer spending: Most retail outlets acknowledge that to remain competitive, they must distinguish themselves through appropriate pricing, good customer service, and a seamless shopping experience. That's a challenge, because contemporary customers have many choices—from shopping online to visiting brick-and-mortar stores. Therefore, retailers must maintain high-quality products and meet consumer demands to remain competitive.

Retailers are turning to AI to help them better understand and interact with consumers. Specifically, the technology deciphers and then predicts consumers' spending patterns. That helps retailers target them with pitches that are likely to appeal to their interests. After all, that's why firms with long-term relationships with customers use AI to help them identify products for those loyal patrons.

Bill Conerly illustrated that understanding in a *Forbes* article, profiling the issue as if he were the customer. He wrote, "[Consider that] I own two small sailboats. I buy parts for them and apparel to wear sailing. But a large marine retailer sends me emails targeting expensive electronics used on large boats. Better artificial intelligence could enable them [the retailers] to pitch products that I'm likely to want."[493]

AI also helps retailers competitively price their merchandise. If they know a consumer's buying history and what the customer typically wants, then the price can be adjusted unless the prospect isn't price sensitive (a fact the technology will also know). This isn't a new concept. For example, online giant retailer Amazon has used an AI algorithm called Project Nessie that evaluates how competitors might adjust their prices in response to input from Amazon.[494]

It is noteworthy that Amazon made more than $1 billion in excess profits using Project Nessie, which inflated prices, according to a Federal Trade Commission antitrust lawsuit. The giant retailer used this algorithm between the years 2015 and 2019 to raise prices by predicting whether other online stores would follow its price hikes. The FTC said, "The sole purpose of Project Nessie was to further hike consumer prices by manipulating other online stores into raising their prices."[495]

To meet these refined consumer expectations, retailers are expanding their operations across physical and digital spaces—known as omnichannel retail.

AI and Omnichannel Retail: Creating Seamless Customer Experiences

As retailers increasingly combine physical and digital shopping experiences, AI is essential in unifying omnichannel strategies, allowing customers to transition seamlessly between online and offline channels. AI-driven, real-time inventory management, personalized recommendations, and predictive analytics empower businesses to enhance engagement across multiple touchpoints, improving both convenience and customer satisfaction.

AI-powered omnichannel retail in action includes:

AI plays an oversized role within the online shopping industry.

1. **Real-time inventory synchronization:** AI-powered systems monitor inventory levels across warehouses, physical stores, and online platforms. This facilitates features like "Buy Online, Pick Up In-Store" (BOPIS) and "Reserve in Store," ensuring that customers can check product availability instantly and avoid the frustration of running out of stock.[496]

2. **AI-enhanced in-store experiences:** Retailers increasingly utilize AI-driven beacon technology and computer vision to merge in-store visits with digital profiles. For instance, beacon-enabled stores can send real-time promotions to a shopper's mobile device based on their online browsing history, crafting a personalized shopping experience while respecting privacy settings. Likewise, AI-powered smart mirrors in fashion retail allow customers to try on outfits based on previous purchases or preferences virtually.[497]

3. **Facial recognition and AI personalization:** Some retailers, especially in Asia, have implemented AI facial recognition to identify returning customers and offer personalized

recommendations at kiosks or during checkout. While this technology improves convenience, retailers must balance personalization with privacy concerns by securing customer consent and adhering to regulations like GDPR and CCPA.[498]

The Future of AI-driven Omnichannel Retail

As AI becomes more advanced, its role in omnichannel retail will evolve to include hyper-personalized shopping assistants, AI-driven checkout-free stores, and predictive supply-chain logistics that anticipate consumer needs across digital and physical spaces. By seamlessly integrating AI across channels, retailers can offer a frictionless experience, enhance customer retention, and improve operational efficiency—all while maintaining transparency and upholding ethical data practices.

While these AI tools have been pioneered by tech giants, smaller retailers are also entering the AI landscape, although with more limited resources. Thankfully, scalable tools help level the playing field.

AI for Small- and Medium-Sized Retailers: Accessible Solutions for Competitive Advantage

While major retailers like Amazon and Walmart leverage AI on scale, small- and medium-sized enterprises (SMEs) also face increasing pressure to adopt AI-driven solutions to stay competitive. However, SMEs typically operate with smaller budgets, limited technical expertise, and fewer in-house AI specialists, which makes large-scale AI investments impractical. Fortunately, a growing number of affordable plug-and-play AI tools now allows smaller businesses to benefit from automation, customer insights, and personalized marketing without needing extensive resources.

Cost-effective AI Solutions for SMEs

Many AI platforms specifically serve small businesses by providing cloud-based or subscription models that reduce upfront costs. Examples include:

- AI-powered chatbots (e.g., Drift, Tidio) that automate customer service without hiring additional staff.

- Automated inventory-management tools (e.g., Zoho Inventory, TradeGecko) that use predictive analytics to optimize stock levels.
- Personalized marketing platforms (e.g., Mailchimp's AI-driven email automation or Shopify's AI-enhanced recommendations) that enhance customer engagement.

Additionally, third-party AI vendors and partnerships enable SMEs to integrate AI without requiring full-scale in-house development. Retail-as-a-service providers like Square and Shopify incorporate AI capabilities directly into their platforms, allowing small retailers to utilize AI for demand forecasting, pricing optimization, and fraud detection at a fraction of the cost of enterprise solutions.

Competing with Large Retailers Through AI

While SMEs may lack the extensive data resources of large corporations, they can still set themselves apart by using AI to personalize customer experiences, streamline operations, and boost efficiency. By adopting scalable AI solutions and partnering with tech vendors, small retailers can compete more effectively in an increasingly competitive digital marketplace, securing AI as an asset rather than a challenge for their business growth.

Beyond day-to-day operations, AI is also revolutionizing how businesses plan, transforming market intelligence into a strategic engine.

AI: A Must for Market Intelligence

Artificial intelligence is rapidly becoming indispensable in the retail sector's pursuit of sharper, faster, and more accurate marketing decisions. What began as a set of basic analytical tools is now evolving into a sophisticated strategic partner. In this section, we examine how AI currently powers retail marketing intelligence and explore its dramatic leap into next-generation capabilities.

Today's Landscape: Traditional AI Tools Empower Market Insight

Most major retailers today utilize foundational AI tools to stay competitive. These include capabilities such as data collection, predictive analytics, natural-language processing, and machine learning, all of which help marketers better understand and serve their customers. According to IBM, these technologies deliver customer insights by analyzing patterns in purchasing behavior, social media, and browsing history.[499]

Retailers originally turned to AI-driven market intelligence when early adopters began to see tangible gains such as increased customer satisfaction, more efficient marketing teams, and higher sales. These outcomes quickly made AI a standard feature in competitive retail strategies. In fact, the IBM Institute for Business Value's 2024 CEO Study reports that more than 70 percent of high-performing business leaders believe embracing advanced AI capabilities is essential for survival in the modern marketplace.[500]

However, just as many have grown comfortable with these standard capabilities, the marketing industry is now entering a bold new era—driven by the power of generative AI.

The Next Frontier: Generative AI Transforms Retail Marketing

Generative AI is redefining how retailers connect with customers. While earlier AI tools supported marketers behind the scenes, this new breed of AI is front and center—creating content, simulating campaign outcomes, and adapting in real time to individual users.[501]

Generative AI moves beyond tools like ChatGPT to craft dynamic, audience-aware content that shifts according to viewer behavior, time of day, and even global events. This isn't just personalization, it's responsive storytelling. According to analysts, technology will revolutionize campaign development by simulating results before launch, predicting market trends with high accuracy, and reallocating marketing resources in real time.[502]

A leading example of this shift comes from Meta. In a wide-ranging interview with Stratechery.com, Meta CEO Mark Zuckerberg outlined the company's strategic pivot to fully automate ad creation using artificial intelligence, positioning AI as the next transformative engine for Meta's future. Zuckerberg envisions a near future wherein businesses can input their objectives and budgets, and Meta's AI will autonomously generate and optimize ad content, targeting, and measurement—eliminating the need for human creative input. This initiative is part of a broader AI strategy encompassing open-source development (via Llama), consumer engagement through AI-generated content, business messaging automation (especially in WhatsApp), and personalized AI companions within Meta apps. He emphasized Meta's long-term goal of vertical integration—from AI infrastructure and apps to AI-powered AR glasses—underscoring the company's ambition to lead the AI revolution not just in technology, but in how people connect, communicate, and engage with digital content.[503]

A McKinsey & Company study identified more than sixty distinct-use cases for generative AI in marketing. Among these:[504]

- **Customer segmentation:** AI now builds nuanced customer profiles based on behavior, purchases, social interactions, and online activity.
- **Ad optimization:** A UK-based Accenture study found that one top US retailer saved $300 million in advertising spending by using AI to optimize media buying and placement.
- **Content generation:** Generative AI creates compelling and relevant marketing materials by analyzing trends, competitors' strategies, and audience data.
- **Virtual influencers**: These AI avatars—equipped with distinct personalities—can interact with consumers in real time, offering personalized conversations 24/7, scaling engagement in a way no human team could manage.

These emerging tools aren't just reshaping how marketing teams operate, they're setting the foundation for even more advanced customer-engagement models, such as AI-powered loyalty programs and conversational commerce. As generative AI continues to advance, it will serve as both the creative mind and strategic brain behind retail marketing in the digital age.

These next-generation marketing tools do more than optimize campaigns, they lay the groundwork for deeper, longer-lasting customer relationships. As AI becomes more context-aware and responsive, it can move beyond simple personalization toward anticipating customer desires, rewarding loyalty, and reinforcing brand trust. Nowhere is this more evident than in the evolution of customer loyalty programs, where AI empowers retailers to move from generic incentives to hyper-personalized experiences that resonate with each individual shopper.

AI and Customer-Loyalty Programs

AI has revolutionized customer-loyalty programs by making them more intelligent, personalizing the services and increasing engagement. Traditional programs use a one-size-fits-all approach compared to AI-driven systems that learn about the customer and then tailor the incentives to that person, increasing the likelihood of long-term loyalty and increased revenue.

AI is especially a friend of the retailer's loyalty program because it makes these efforts smarter, more personalized, and efficient. The evidence from the marketplace is that AI-driven loyalty programs retain customers, improve their satisfaction, and boost revenue for the retailer.

Consider AI-related factors that help deliver those positive results for loyalty programs.

- **Tailored rewards and experiences:** AI-driven loyalty program tools analyze data to offer tailored rewards and experiences that help retain and attract customers. For example, the AI tool assesses customers' purchase histories to recommend products that fit their preferences. This approach encourages a better retailer-customer connection, which improves the likelihood of repeat purchases.[505]
- **Focus on retention:** AI also helps the business anticipate customer needs and then takes proactive measures to improve retention by analyzing historical data to predict customer

behavior regarding purchases and detect when the customer sours on a particular brand or provides negative feedback. For example, some airlines use AI-powered predictive analytics to identify frequent travelers to offer loyalty rewards based on their preferences and to determine the best time to announce those promotions.
- **Always-available customer assistance:** AI-powered chatbots improve customer support, especially when they offer real-time assistance and resolve issues quickly. For example, AI-driven chatbots provide 24/7 availability, guaranteeing that customers always have access to assistance. Constant availability sustains customer satisfaction and loyalty.

The future of AI-powered loyalty programs is bright and essential for businesses that want to stay ahead of their competitors. Expect them to become hyper personalized to become more immersive, which will make the brand experience more personal than simply earning points or miles for the next purchase.

Nowhere is AI's influence more visible to the consumer than in the world of online shopping—where convenience, personalization, and automation converge.

AI and Online Shopping

Retailers that once operated exclusively through brick-and-mortar stores have increasingly migrated online, especially after the COVID-19 pandemic accelerated the shift to digital commerce. Today, AI-powered tools are transforming this space into a streamlined, intelligent environment that redefines how customers browse, discover, and purchase products.

Visual Search and Image Recognition

One of the most revolutionary features of online retail is AI-powered visual search. Instead of typing a product name, shoppers can upload an image or screenshot, and AI will identify and suggest visually similar products from the retailer's inventory. This eliminates frustration for customers who don't know the exact name of what they want, increasing the chance of a successful sale.[506]

One of the most recognized examples of visual search in action is Pinterest Lens, a feature that allows users to take a photo of an object and receive suggestions for visually similar items—ranging from furniture and fashion to recipes and DIY projects. Since its launch, Pinterest has reported that Lens handles more than six hundred million visual searches per month, helping users discover products they wouldn't have known how to describe with words alone. Retailers can integrate Lens into their marketing strategies to drive targeted product discovery directly from user-generated images.[507]

Augmented Reality for Virtual Try-Ons, Autonomous Checkout, and Voice-Activated Shopping

AI-driven augmented reality (AR) tools now allow online shoppers to virtually "try on" clothing, accessories, or makeup using their mobile devices. Whether it's seeing how a dress fits or visualizing how a sofa looks in a living room, these immersive experiences give shoppers confidence before buying—dramatically reducing return rates.[508]

YouCam Makeup, launched in 2014 by Perfect Corp, has become a ubiquitous virtual makeup try-on app. Powered by real-time AR and AI, it offers lifelike previews of cosmetics—from foundation and lipstick to eyeshadow and accessories—directly through users' smartphone cameras. With more than 590 million downloads as of July 2024, it is among the most widely adopted AR beauty platforms. Major cosmetic brands like L'Oréal, NYX, and Sephora have integrated its technology into their apps and websites to let customers experiment virtually before purchasing.[509]

Autonomous Checkout and Voice-Activated Shopping

AI enables frictionless checkout experiences by saving payment preferences, streamlining purchase flows, and offering automated checkout processes. In some cases, voice-activated assistants (like Alexa or Google Assistant) let users place orders simply by speaking, integrating shopping into daily routines and reducing transactional barriers.

AI AND THE RETAIL ECONOMY

Since its launch in Seattle in January 2018, Amazon Go stores have allowed customers to "grab and go" without waiting in line. Shoppers scan a QR code upon entry, and advanced AI—using computer vision, sensor fusion, and deep learning—tracks items taken from the shelves. When customers walk out, their linked Amazon account is automatically charged.[510]

Personalized Shopping Agents and AI Recommenders

Advanced recommender engines analyze browsing history, click patterns, and past purchases to suggest products in real time. As generative AI advances, we now see the emergence of AI-powered shopping agents—virtual personas that can learn preferences, make selections, and even manage purchases on behalf of the user, creating a more curated and time-efficient shopping experience.

Retailers like Rappi (a Latin American on-demand delivery platform) leverage Amazon Personalize to build personalized recommendation engines. These systems dynamically analyze individual browsing and purchase behavior to offer tailored "top picks," email suggestions, and app recommendations across web, mobile, messaging, and conversational channels, helping increase user engagement and drive conversions.[511]

Fraud Detection and Secure Transactions

Online shopping's convenience must be matched by security. AI enhances fraud detection by monitoring transactional patterns, identifying anomalies, and flagging suspicious activity in real time. These systems help protect both consumers and retailers from breaches, chargebacks, and identity theft.

Mastercard has significantly improved fraud detection by integrating generative AI and graph analytics into its Decision Intelligence platform, which processes over 160 billion transactions annually, detecting suspicious activity within fifty milliseconds. This AI-driven system doubles detection rates for compromised cards and leverages behavioral biometrics—such as typing patterns—to prevent point-of-sale fraud and identity theft.[512]

Smarter Inventory and Logistics Behind the Scenes

While not customer-facing, AI's role in optimizing online inventory is vital. AI systems track sales patterns, predict restocking needs, and automate fulfillment processes across e-commerce platforms. This makes certain that products are available when and where customers want them, improving reliability and reducing costs.

Building on these logistics advancements, Amazon has pioneered a next-generation approach to predictive fulfillment that takes AI integration to an entirely new level.

Amazon has unveiled a new Agentic AI system developed at its Lab126 facility in Sunnyvale, California, aimed at revolutionizing same-day deliveries by predicting customer purchases before they occur. The technology allows warehouse robots to respond to natural-language commands, enhancing flexibility and efficiency in logistics. Central to the effort is an advanced AI-powered system called SCOT (Supply Chain Optimization Technology), which processes data from more than four hundred million items to forecast demand, streamline deliveries, and cut delivery times by nearly a full day. This initiative is already live nationwide, improving last-mile delivery accuracy and speed—especially in complex locations—while also reducing Amazon's carbon footprint.[513]

Complementing corporate efforts like Amazon's SCOT, academic and industrial researchers are also pushing the boundaries of what AI-powered logistics can achieve, especially in dynamic environments like warehouses.

Researchers from MIT and NVIDIA have developed a groundbreaking algorithm called cuTAMP that enables robots to solve complex manipulation problems—like packing items—within seconds by evaluating thousands of potential solutions in parallel. Unlike traditional methods that explore actions one at a time, cuTAMP uses GPU-accelerated sampling and optimization to rapidly simulate, assess, and refine plans that meet specific constraints and avoid collisions. Tested successfully on robotic arms and humanoid robots without the need for training data, cuTAMP proves highly generalizable and efficient, promising major improvements in warehouse logistics, tool use, and future voice-commanded robotic systems.[514]

While AI is transforming warehouse packing and supply-chain

forecasting, it's also revolutionizing last-mile delivery, thanks to drone technologies now being deployed at scale.

Alphabet-owned Wing and Walmart are significantly expanding their drone delivery partnership, adding a hundred new stores across five major US cities—Atlanta, Charlotte, Houston, Orlando, and Tampa—to their existing operations in Arkansas and Dallas-Fort Worth. This expansion will allow customers within six miles of a participating store to receive lightweight items like groceries and health products via drone, with some deliveries arriving in under thirty minutes. Wing's drones, capable of carrying up to five pounds and traveling twelve miles round trip, have already completed more than 450,000 residential deliveries. Walmart, which began using drones in 2021, has surpassed 150,000 deliveries and continues to explore drone logistics innovations like autonomous Autoloader pickup systems to increase efficiency and reduce reliance on traditional delivery trucks.[515]

Such autonomous systems, whether airborne or warehouse-based, reflect a broader shift toward AI-driven logistics designed for speed, precision, and sustainability.

Together, these developments illustrate how AI is transforming retail logistics into a predictive, adaptive system capable of anticipating demand, streamlining workflows, and even responding to natural-language instructions in real time.

The Future of AI in e-Commerce

Emerging AI technologies point to a future wherein virtual assistants not only recommend products, but also purchase autonomously. Visa's 2025 vision, for example, anticipates AI agents that shop, pay, and manage returns on behalf of the consumer—handling everything from cart to completion based on user-defined preferences and budgets.[516]

Numerous other trends are impacted by AI technology in the retail sector, such as sustainability, payment flexibility, impact of social commerce, around-the-clock customer support, the retail workforce, and shipping transparency. To avoid overstating the value of AI in the retail sector, this book does not delve into those additional trends.

While these innovations promise enhanced convenience and profit, they also raise a host of ethical concerns about data use, transparency, and accountability.

Final Thoughts about Retail and AI

The retail industry is becoming especially aware of their need to protect consumers' data and privacy, especially in the wake of many cyberattacks that rob vast amounts of personal information from both private commercial firms and government agencies. This growing vulnerability includes the collection and use of consumer data by social media platforms as well as commercial websites.

There are four consumer and data-protection concerns relevant to the AI retail revolution: data privacy, AI bias, transparency, and corporate responsibility. Quantilus Innovation, a global firm that leverages big data and AI "to create tailor-made models that solve real-world business challenges," addresses these four concerns.[517]

- **Privacy and security:** AI-powered tools collect, store, and share personal data. For example, a European consumer rights group accused Meta of "massive" and "illegal" data collection from hundreds of millions of users. The European Consumer Organization filed complaints claiming that Meta collects an unnecessary amount of user information without consent.[518]

Quantilus recommends that AI-using organizations adopt "privacy-by-design principles, ensuring that data is encrypted and processed with consumer knowledge."[519]

- **AI bias concern:** Algorithms reflect the data upon which they are trained. If those datasets are biased to discriminatory outcomes, that creates a genuine problem such that it "can entrench inequality and erode public trust in AI technologies." Quantilus recommends firms using AI adopt

"bias-detection software and ensuring human oversight of AI decision-making processes are effective steps companies can take to stay compliant."
- **Building trust in AI through open communication:** Transparency is an issue with AI systems because many people perceive it as "black boxes," which means their decisions are hard to discern. Quantilus recommends promoting transparency by publishing "model documentation and decision-making processes" to help companies build trust and avoid legal pitfalls.
- **Building corporate responsibility for AI system outcomes:** Firms that make AI tools an integral part of their operations must guarantee accountability for their systems' outcomes. Of course, most governments have established guidelines for ethical AI practices. Quantilus states that "companies that prioritize ethical AI usage not only avoid [legal] penalties but also enhance customer loyalty and trust."

Ethical concerns extend beyond consumer privacy and bias—they also include the very structure of the retail workforce and how AI may transform, or eliminate, traditional jobs. Automation technologies such as AI-powered checkout systems, robotic restocking, and customer-service chatbots reduce the need for certain traditional roles, particularly in cashier and sales associate positions. However, rather than simply displacing jobs, AI also creates new opportunities for workers with different skill sets, shifting the focus from manual tasks to AI management, data analysis, and personalized customer engagement.

Workforce Displacement vs. Reskilling

The rise of cashier-less stores—like Amazon Go, which uses AI-powered cameras and sensors to track purchases—signals a decline in traditional checkout roles. Similarly, AI-driven inventory-tracking and restocking robots reduce reliance on manual labor for store operations. However, as these repetitive tasks become automated, retailers increasingly demand employees who have digital and analytical skills to manage AI systems, who can interpret data-driven insights, and who can oversee automated processes.

To adapt, retailers must invest in workforce reskilling through:

- AI training programs for frontline employees, enabling them to operate, troubleshoot, and optimize AI-powered systems.
- Customer-service enhancement that focuses on human-centric roles where empathy and personalized assistance remain invaluable. For example, AI chatbots handle routine inquiries, while human representatives address complex or sensitive issues.
- Cross-training initiatives that allow workers to shift from traditional roles to AI-assisted functions such as predictive sales analysis, logistics coordination, or digital customer engagement.

AI as a Workforce Enhancer, Not a Replacement

Retailers that successfully integrate AI while maintaining workforce stability do so by leveraging automation to augment—not replace—human roles. AI can streamline operations, but human employees remain essential in areas that require creativity, emotional intelligence, and complex problem-solving. Companies that train and upskill their employees will be better positioned to maximize both technological and human potential, providing a smooth transition toward the future of AI-enhanced retail.

Additional topics of interest are covered in the appendices. Appendix O reviews the growing legal frameworks governing AI and consumer data in retail—highlighting regulations like the CCPA, GDPR, and emerging AI-specific laws—that require businesses to prioritize transparency, privacy, and ethical use of AI-driven tools to maintain compliance and consumer trust. Further, appendix P explores the future of AI in retail, forecasting emerging innovations—from smart-store layouts and dynamic pricing to voice commerce and biometric personalization—that promise to revolutionize customer experience and operational efficiency while raising new ethical and privacy challenges.

AI AND THE RETAIL ECONOMY

Beyond economic outcomes, AI in retail presents a spiritual challenge. As Christians, we're called to consider not only what works, but what honors God in how we treat others and structure society (Micah 6:8).

Christian Concerns about AI and the Retail Sector

Christians should be concerned about the mix of ethical, moral, and theological issues related to the retail sector. The issue of human dignity is a concern because Christians believe humans are made in the image of God; therefore, using AI to replace human jobs, especially in the customer-service and decision-making roles, raises questions about the diminishing role of human interaction and the potential devaluation of human workers.

AI will also automate much of the retail sector, which could lead to mass layoffs. For Christians, our ethics emphasize care for the poor, fair wages, and dignity in work (James 5:4). Moreover, automating jobs at the expense of human workers may disproportionately benefit large corporations over small businesses, potentially leading to a national crisis that warrants a compassionate and responsible response.

Retail businesses may tap AI-powered facial recognition and data harvesting to track consumer behavior, which can lead to ethical concerns about privacy and consent. Christians ought to consider this practice as an invasion of our God-given right to personal autonomy. Further, who is morally accountable when businesses outsource decisions such as pricing and marketing to AI—but who is morally accountable, and does it matter?

Christians ought to be especially sensitive about consumer manipulation as well. After all, AI personalizes ads to then target us with specific products. This approach can feed into consumerism, materialism, and addictive behaviors, drawing people away from Christian values. There is also the danger that Christians may treat AI as a "functional god"—worshiping its capabilities, which leads to misplaced trust (Exodus 20:3).

These scriptural principles should inform not only our ethical evaluations, but also our practical engagement with AI's unfolding role in retail. As we close this chapter, technological innovation cannot be separated from moral responsibility. AI's promise to enhance efficiency and profitability must be measured against its impact on human dignity, equity, and community flourishing.

Conclusion

Artificial intelligence is quickly becoming the driving force behind the next era of US retail. From personalized recommendations to automated logistics, AI enables smarter, faster, and more tailored shopping experiences—both online and in-store—while quietly transforming the systems behind inventory, marketing, and customer service.

Yet these advances come with moral complexities. Merchants have discovered that AI-powered tools are a double-edged sword: While they can enhance customer loyalty and boost profits, they also introduce serious risks, including data-privacy breaches, algorithmic bias, and legal liabilities. Technology that promises convenience and profit must be handled with wisdom and accountability.

As we embrace AI's expanding role in the retail economy, Christians must speak into this transformation with discernment and conviction. Scripture calls us to uphold justice (Micah 6:8), protect the vulnerable (James 5:4), and reject idolatry—especially the temptation to entrust our future to machines rather than to our Creator (Exodus 20:3). Retailers and consumers alike must steward these tools in ways that reflect God's character by safeguarding human dignity, promoting truth, and fostering neighborly love.

This chapter surveyed key developments in AI-driven retail, from market intelligence and customer loyalty to e-commerce innovations and ethical concerns. While artificial intelligence may become a retailer's most powerful "employee," it must never replace the human values or biblical principles that guide how we serve, sell, and relate to one another in a marketplace shaped by technology.

As we transition from the retail sector to explore broader cultural values in the next chapter, we must continue asking not just what AI *can* do, but what it *ought* to do in a society grounded in truth, justice, and love.

Section Five

AI'S IMPACT ON CULTURE

With artificial intelligence we are summoning the demon.[520]

Elon Musk (1971)
Tesla, Inc., SpaceX, and former member
of the US Department of Government Efficiency

Elon Musk's warning underscores the dramatic and unpredictable power AI wields over society. While some view it as a digital demon, others see it as a tool for progress. In truth, AI is a catalyst for cultural transformation in that it drives innovation, reshapes how we live, and raises deep ethical questions.

In this section, culture is considered the collection of beliefs, customs, traditions, behaviors, languages, knowledge, arts, and social norms that define and shape society. It evolves through interaction, adaptation, and innovation. Culture influences how people think, communicate, and interact with each other. Because values and ethical norms are at the heart of cultural identity, chapter 13 begins by exploring how AI reshapes these fundamental dimensions, including personal freedoms and societal standards.

Building on the ways AI influences our values and norms, chapter 14 explores how these cultural shifts are reflected in entertainment, the arts, and gaming—areas in which creativity, storytelling, and identity are constantly evolving through AI-powered tools.

After examining how AI shapes what we value and how we create, chapter 15 turns to how we connect—with each other, with machines, and with institutions. From everyday communication to political discourse, AI is reshaping public life in profound ways.

After reading this section, you should have an appreciation for AI's significant role in shaping human culture by influencing how people create, consume, and interact with various aspects of society. That role can have both a positive and negative impact on the communities of faith and how the secular world understands religion.

Chapter 13

AI'S INFLUENCE ON OUR VALUES, ETHICS, NORMS AND LIBERTIES

AI is a mirror, reflecting not only our intellect, but our values and fears.[521]

RAVI NARAYANAN
Vice president of Insights and Analytics, Nisum

Narayanan's observation reminds us that AI is more than a tool; it reflects what society esteems and fears, challenging us to examine the moral and spiritual foundations of our culture. After all, AI has a transformative influence on reshaping culture and constructing a future that integrates technological change with social responsibility. That metamorphosis began with the inception of the internet and exploded with mobile devices, cloud computing, and especially with the arrival of generative AI. It raises questions about the future of humans and their partnership with machines.[522]

One indicator of this transformation is the rise in screen time: In 2025, Americans now average nearly seven hours of digital engagement daily—a statistic that signals how deeply AI-driven media and apps have become embedded in our cultural habits.[523]

This chapter considers AI's outsized impact on our culture, especially our values, ethics, norms, and liberties. Below, I address that influence and then suggest where it could take us in the future as our dependence on technology consumes even more of our lives.

AI and American Values

Values are those things that are significant to us. They are the principles, beliefs, and ideals that guide our lives. Culture shapes our values, especially our interactions with others and with whom or what we spend time—such as when we glare at AI-powered technology. Examples of human values for Americans include individualism, equality, justice, honesty, accountability, achievement, and more.

No doubt, AI is transforming our values as it influences us in our daily lives. The vast majority (79 percent) of Americans, according to Pew Research, interact daily with AI-powered chatbots, virtual assistants, social media, and facial-recognition technology. Inevitably, that level of association means technology plays a growing role in what we consider essential—our values.[524]

As AI systems increasingly interact with us, understanding what values they simulate or promote becomes crucial. One notable attempt to map AI "values" comes from Anthropic's 2025 study based on the analysis of hundreds of thousands of real AI conversations to understand how generative AI models like Claude make moral judgments. That study found 3,307 unique values expressed by the AI, classified into five types: practical, knowledge-related, social, protective, and personal.[525]

Artificial intelligence is making quite the impression across the culture.

The authors of the study claim to have "attempted to shape the values of our AI model, Claude, to help keep it aligned with human preferences, make it less likely to engage in dangerous behaviors, and generally make it—for want of a better term—a 'good citizen' in the world."[526]

What should be evident, based on the growing use of AI, is that technology influences our values in both positive and negative ways. Below are several ways AI interacts with and reshapes human values—often offering both empowering potential and troubling pitfalls.[527]

- **AI fosters independence:** AI can encourage human autonomy, which means we pay less attention to authority figures in our lives, like parents and respected friends, and more to AI-powered devices for guidance. After all, AI-powered gizmos help us make decisions by providing helpful information as well as recommendations for questions. On the negative side, overdependence on AI can limit our choices because of built-in biases and rob us of some freedom to look elsewhere.
- **AI enhances justice:** AI enhances fairness by reducing human bias and increasing objectivity. This is most evident in terms of hiring and promotion decisions that consult AI platforms. However, the risks of bias depend on the creator of the algorithm used in the AI-powered platforms. Systems can perpetuate injustice if trained on biased data.
- **AI simulates emotional awareness:** While empathy is a fundamentally human trait, AI algorithms can be designed to simulate empathetic responses. Specifically, chatbots and their cousins, virtual assistants, interact with humans by displaying emotional support. The AI can "learn" and explore social media to acquire patterns of sentiment to help them "understand" how to relate to people. The downside is that humans come to depend too much on AI guidance, which causes them to lose some of their ability to interact with other humans effectively.
- **Privacy and AI:** Most Americans treasure their privacy as an important value. That explains why they guard themselves against the presumed intrusiveness of AI platforms that jeopardize their civil liberties. Although AI can be useful in protecting and securing us from outsiders, especially our data from threats, it can also violate our privacy by using facial-recognition technology.
- **A double-edged creativity sword**: Many people use AI to help generate innovative ideas in unique ways, such as using

it to help compose music that might explore another genre. However, technology can also take over from humans and dominate the process, thus limiting true artistic expression.

The task for society is to make AI algorithms align with human values. However, although that's a wonderful idea, this effort faces several significant challenges. It is essential to consider whose values are being embedded into the algorithm. This is more daunting than the reader might appreciate, because AI company programmers must consider all stakeholders.[528]

One approach is to draw from the values associated with established moral systems or global institutions. Are the values identified or implied in the United Nations' Universal Declaration of Human Rights an appropriate standard for AI platforms? Do they align with the Southern Baptist Convention's core values[529] or the social values of the Roman Catholic Church?[530] If not, what values best fit a broad swath of humankind?

Alternatively, AI companies can develop their own value systems to guide the design of their technologies. Then the consumer should expect full disclosure, which requires the source company to announce the value system at the algorithm's foundation, certainly something government might regulate.

Providing guardrails for AI systems will be necessary to preclude harmful content and the potential for psychological harm. Also, there must be a process beyond regulations to identify abuse, albeit while keeping the AI updated after the launch.

As AI influences what we value, it also reshapes how we define right and wrong—raising pressing ethical questions that society must confront.

AI and Ethical Challenges

Ethics is the study of what is morally right. It is evidence of a judgment of right or wrong that conforms to widely recognized standards. Of course, which standards are used and how they are employed can create ethical challenges.

AI'S INFLUENCE ON OUR VALUES, ETHICS, NORMS AND LIBERTIES

This is an issue because technology can amplify the biases of its creators or the fault of the data used to train the algorithm. Hence, an embedded bias in the AI could present serious ramifications for uses of these platforms in areas such as hiring, lending, and criminal justice. Therefore, programmers have an ethical responsibility to make certain that their systems are transparent and accountable, which goes to the heart of ethics.[531]

The Markkula Center for Applied Ethics (MCAE), a department at the Jesuit Santa Clara University, has worked on the ethics of AI to identify a host of issues that should give us all pause regarding the associated challenges. Some of those difficulties are discussed below.

Ethical accountability: Does the AI platform perform as promised? If not, is there a technical flaw? The developer and deployer of AI tech must take responsibility for issues that arise from the development and deployment of the technology. For example, consider an AI failure that results in a semi-autonomous car accident. Even though the vehicle's manufacturer wrote its contract to limit liability, that document could be interpreted as an "unethical scheme to avoid legitimate responsibility."[532]

Technology's opacity: Some AI decision-making processes can be challenging to understand, as these systems often operate as "black boxes," raising ethical questions. The ethical caution here is simple: The more powerful AI is, the more transparent it ought to be, while the weaker it is, the more right to privacy the user should have. It is imperative that AI must be explainable.[533]

Attack from outside: AI is subject to adversarial attacks like other computer-based software. Also, the data used to initially train AI algorithms is subject to contamination and malware. Therefore, we should safeguard the system and sensitive data from outside threats using both user training and cyber-defense mechanisms.

Use for harmful purposes: While most AI applications benefit humanity, some creators may develop algorithms for negative uses. Even though AI-powered surveillance applications used at airports help advance security, the same technology when applied in other venues might be dangerous, such as in communist China, which uses AI surveillance technology to oppress its citizens.

AI ethics—the rights and wrongs of society—encompass many issues that directly impact society: bias, fairness, transparency, explainability, privacy, and security. It is critical that as a society we understand the responsible use of AI technology to mitigate the ethical challenges it presents for our future.

While values and ethics speak to what we believe and judge as right, norms shape our daily behaviors and expectations—often subconsciously. AI is now reshaping those as well.

AI and American Norms

Norms are ways of behaving or doing things, upon which most people agree. For example, social norms are informal rules that govern behavior in groups and societies. In America, social norms vary by sex, age, family, social circle, community, city, state, or region. They tend to be fluid, however.

Conventional American social norms include respecting personal space, being punctual, being polite, and using courteous phrases such as "please" and "thank you." Of course, there is some variability in these norms based on the region of the country, age, and cultural background.

I asked ChatGPT to identify social norms related to AI. It wrote that social norms are "evolving as technology becomes more integrated into daily life. These norms shape how people expect AI to be used, how it should behave, and how humans should interact with it." At this point, ChatGPT called out key social norms and provided an example for each.

Ethical use and fairness: "AI hiring tools used by companies like Amazon and LinkedIn must ensure they do not favor one gender or race over another. When Amazon's AI hiring tool was found to be biased against women, it was discontinued—showing that fairness is an expected norm."

Privacy and data protection: "When Apple introduced its Face ID technology, it emphasized that facial data stays on the device rather than sent to Apple's servers. This aligns with the social norm that AI should respect user privacy."

Human oversight and accountability: "In healthcare, AI-assisted diagnostics (like IBM Watson Health) help doctors analyze medical scans, but final treatment decisions are made by human doctors. Patients expect AI to assist, not replace, human expertise."

Transparency and explainability: "The European Union's AI Act requires AI systems to explain how they make decisions. For instance, if an AI denies someone a loan, the person has the right to understand why."

Social interaction and behavior: "AI assistants like Siri and Alexa are programmed to avoid responding to offensive language. If a user is rude, they won't engage in an aggressive conversation, reinforcing norms of respectful AI interaction."

Employment and economic impact: "When automation affects jobs, companies like Microsoft and Google invest in retraining programs to help employees transition into new roles rather than simply replacing them with AI."

Creativity and originality: "AI-generated art tools like DALL·E and MidJourney clearly label AI-created images. In some cases, courts and platforms require AI-generated content to be disclosed, ensuring fair credit to human artists."

Autonomous systems and decision-making: "Self-driving car companies like Tesla and Waymo are expected to prioritize human safety. If an accident happens, people expect companies to take responsibility and improve AI safety protocols."

Andrea Baronchelli with the University of London explained three processes by which such AI-related norms are formed. His article, "Shaping New Norms for AI," states there is consensus about the impact of AI before outlining the three processes. He begins by cautioning the reader, "First, AI is going to have a significant impact on our life. Second, society is not prepared to deal with the technology."[534]

The norm-development process, wrote Baronchelli, cites a leader in the AI world with yet another caution: "Nvidia CEO Jensen Huang said that AI will create tools 'that require legal regulation and social norms that have yet to be worked out,' highlighting how social norms can be a solution to solve large-scale problems."[535]

The three processes begin with formal institutions that create norms to govern human behavior. These top-down government laws or regulations are what industry claims create uncertainty about AI-caused liabilities. However, there is agreement that regulation for the safe adoption of AI should be a norm for health and finance, such that its use does not conflict with human rights, existing laws, and ethics.[536]

Second, informal institutions create norms. These organizations have no power to enforce the new norm, "yet are influential in proposing new codes of behavior." Professor Baronchelli illustrated this process by writing: "In most of today's Western countries, religious leaders can prescribe codes of conduct but have no legal permission to police behaviour."[537]

Finally, the third process of norm creation involves spontaneous emergence. These are the "unintended consequence of individuals' efforts to coordinate locally with one another." The professor continues:

> This spontaneous process interacts with the activity of formal and informal institutions in complex ways that range from complementing existing regulations to countering them in ways that can result in conflict and legislative change. More importantly, spontaneous norms tend to occupy a much wider space than regulations. From shaking hands to wearing ties on formal occasions, to language and notion of fairness, most of our expectations about the behaviour of others are based on unwritten norms.[538]

AI's oversized influence on social-norm development demands the importance of an "open, inclusive, and transparent public discourse."[539]

As AI shapes norms of behavior, it inevitably touches our legal freedoms as well, raising questions about how civil liberties are protected or eroded in a world governed increasingly by algorithms.

AI and Civil Liberties

Liberty is the freedom to live as we wish. The American Constitution grants citizens civil liberties that are unalienable and protected rights. Our Bill of Rights defines those liberties, which include freedom of speech, the right to bear arms, and the right to privacy, although not expressly stated. Our Ninth Amendment protects against federal infringement of unenumerated rights, and the Fourteenth Amendment to our Constitution identifies some of those as the right to send our children to private school and to have marital privacy. We also have the right to travel, the right to vote, and the right to keep personal matters private.

AI can have a significant impact on civil liberties, both positively and negatively. It influences fundamental rights such as privacy, freedom of speech, due process, and equality. ChatGPT provided the following list of civil liberties affected by AI and a specific example of the challenge.

1. Privacy rights:

Positive impact: AI can enhance cybersecurity by detecting fraud and protecting personal data. Privacy-enhancing AI tools, like encrypted messaging apps, help safeguard communications.

Negative impact: AI-driven surveillance (e.g., facial recognition by governments or companies) can track people without consent, threatening personal privacy. AI can analyze vast amounts of personal data, leading to concerns about data misuse (e.g., targeted ads that exploit user data).

Example: Cities like San Francisco have banned police use of facial recognition due to privacy concerns.

2. Freedom of speech and expression

Positive impact: AI-powered tools help detect and remove harmful content like hate speech or misinformation. AI helps amplify diverse voices by recommending personalized content.

Negative impact: Automated content moderation can lead to censorship, mistakenly removing legitimate speech. AI-generated deepfakes and misinformation can manipulate public opinion.

Example: In 2020, Facebook's AI mistakenly removed posts discussing racial injustice, raising concerns about biased content moderation.

3. Due process and fairness

Positive impact: AI can improve legal decision-making by analyzing case law and helping lawyers with research. Predictive policing AI can help law enforcement focus resources more efficiently.

Negative impact: AI in law enforcement (like predictive policing) has been criticized for reinforcing racial and socioeconomic biases. AI-powered court systems may make decisions without transparency, affecting legal fairness.

Example: Some US courts use AI to assess recidivism risk, but studies have shown racial bias in these predictions.

4. Equality and nondiscrimination

Positive impact: AI can help detect discrimination in hiring, lending, and law enforcement. AI-powered accessibility tools (like speech-to-text) assist people with disabilities.

Negative impact: AI algorithms can reinforce biases in hiring, healthcare, and lending if trained on biased data. Unequal access to AI technologies can widen economic and social inequalities.

Example: A study found that facial recognition AI misidentified people of color more often than white individuals, leading to wrongful arrests.

5. Right to autonomy and decision-making

Positive impact: AI can enhance individual autonomy by providing personalized recommendations and intelligent assistants. AI-driven automation can reduce human bias in decision-making.

Negative impact: AI-driven manipulation (like targeted political ads) can influence decisions without people realizing it. AI-powered hiring systems may reject candidates automatically, reducing human oversight.

Example: The Cambridge Analytica scandal showed how AI-driven political advertising manipulated voters by exploiting personal data.

This material demonstrates both sides of the AI debate regarding civil liberties. Therefore, it is critical that society put in place strong legal and ethical frameworks to ensure AI respects privacy, fairness, and freedom.

Appendix Q presents a comprehensive set of policy recommendations and governance frameworks aimed at guaranteeing ethical, transparent, and human-centered AI development, with measures such

AI'S INFLUENCE ON OUR VALUES, ETHICS, NORMS AND LIBERTIES

as independent oversight, algorithmic impact assessments, data sovereignty protections, liability laws, and public literacy programs to safeguard individual liberties and prevent misuse.

Before concluding this section, I want to highlight a troubling threat to civil liberties, especially for people of faith. Specifically, there will come very soon an AI-powered application for your mobile phone that will enable the user to ascertain whether you are being dishonest "just by processing effective features of your facial expressions, body movements, and voice."[540]

Noninvasive lie-detection technologies are likely to experience rapid advancement in the coming years, including two types: truth-metering and thought-exposing. Truth-metering technology is the domain of the US federal and state law-enforcement authorities, used to ascertain whether someone is lying. However, there is no regulation regarding the thought-exposing technologies—which, once they become available, could be ambiguous and inadequate to safeguard civil liberties.[541]

Thought-exposing technology is closer to reality than most people realize. Nita Farahany, a futurist and legal ethicist at Duke University in Durham, North Carolina, and author of the book *The Battle for Your Brain*, explained in an interview with *Technology Review* that brain data comes from a variety of devices that consider functions associated with the human brain. Admittedly, Farahany continued, "Brain data is not thought. But you can use it to make inferences about what's happening in a person's mind."[542]

Right now, you alone have access "to your brain data," Farahany stated. However, once a device has your brain data, then there is insight into your thinking. She also said, for example, "An authoritarian government having access to it [your brain data] could use it to identify people who don't show political adherence." But access to brain data has broader potential applications than for oppression.[543]

There are active efforts to use AI-powered tech to read our brain data, even remotely. "The US military [DARPA] has been working to develop mind-reading devices for years," according to Paul Tullis, writing for the *Technology Review*. "The aim is to create technologies that

AI FOR MANKIND'S FUTURE

allow us to help people with brain or nervous system damage but also enable soldiers to direct drones and other devices by thought alone."[544]

"Others have invested heavily in tech to link human brains to computers, whether to read our minds, communicate, or supercharge our brainpower," according to Jessica Hamzelou's *Technology Review* article. "Tech that aims to read your mind and probe your memories is already here."[545]

There is reason to believe AI-driven, "thought-exposing technologies" are on our horizon. After all, governments currently use AI sensing technologies to screen airline passengers for fevers and systems that also extract heart rates—used in health monitoring. Additionally, recent advances enable these noninvasive systems to "evaluate aspects of an individual's mental state from facial expressions alone, such as whether someone is imagining versus remembering an event, or whether someone is experiencing one of the common emotions." Such efforts to predict an individual's inner thoughts with "superior-to-human accuracy" has dangerous implications for people of faith, especially those who pray in silence in places where such behavior is not welcomed, such as outside of abortion clinics.[546]

Unfortunately, individuals in the United Kingdom have already faced arrest for silently praying near abortion clinics. Imagine that brain-reading AGI could pose a serious threat to people of conscience—those who act according to deeply held moral or ethical beliefs. Here are several potential risks: surveillance of thought; preemptive control; coercion or re-education; discrimination and profiling; and suppression of dissent.[547]

Although this chapter has focused primarily on the American experience, it's important to recognize that AI is reshaping cultures worldwide, each with distinct values, traditions, and regulatory priorities.

AI's Influence on an International Cultural Context

The above material comes from a US perspective, which has unique characteristics. Therefore, it is helpful to consider AI's influence on other cultures regarding their values and ethical standards. Below is a brief comparative presentation on how Asian, European, and African contexts are adapting in response to AI development.

Asian perspective: In Asian countries like China, Japan, and South Korea, there is an emphasis on the collective well-being over individual rights, which influences how AI is deployed and regulated, such as the widespread acceptance of state-led AI development, especially for surveillance and public safety. For example, communist China's AI ethics guidelines stress "AI for good," which must support state control and national-development priorities.

Japan fosters a cultural narrative of AI and robots as companions or partners, which aligns with Shinto beliefs about animism and the spirituality of nonhuman entities. That is why Japan's Society 5.0 Initiative sees AI as a tool for building a super-smart society that integrates humans and machines harmoniously.[548]

European perspective: Generally speaking, Europeans enjoy a deep-rooted emphasis on individual rights, privacy, and democratic accountability. That's why, across the region, there is a strong push for explainability in AI decision-making and algorithmic fairness, and European policymakers are cautious about AI-related risks.

The EU's AI Act began implementation in early 2025 and will not complete execution until 2030. That act takes a risk-based approach, banning certain AI uses (such as social scoring), and enforcing strict compliance for high-risk systems. Meanwhile, the EU's Ethics Guidelines for Trustworthy AI emphasize lawfulness, ethics, and robustness.[549]

African perspective: The African continent includes fifty-four sovereign countries. However, for this perspective, I focus on five countries: South Africa, Kenya, Nigeria, Rwanda, and Ghana.

These countries emphasize communal values, interdependence, and human dignity. Therefore, their ethics center around collective upliftment and fairness. Regarding the use of AI, they use technology to address inequalities, support underdeveloped sectors like agriculture, and bridge digital divides.

The African Union is a continental union of member states that share many goals, including greater unity, cohesion, and solidarity among African countries; defense of the sovereignty and territorial integrity of member states; and acceleration of the political and social-economic integration of the continent. The Union's AI-related strategy emphasizes inclusiveness, sustainable development, and indigenous knowledge. In particular, Rwanda's AI policy includes guidelines to promote responsible innovation while aligning with national development goals and cultural values.

Comparative Highlights

FEATURE	ASIA	EUROPE	AFRICA
View of AI	Tool for societal harmony and development	Potential risk to individual rights	Opportunity for social transformation
Ethical Anchor	Collectivism, state welfare	Human rights, transparency	Ubuntu, communal justice
Primary Concerns	Surveillance, labor impact	Privacy, bias, autonomy	Inequality, data exploitation
Regulatory Style	State-guided, pragmatic	Legalistic, precautionary	Emerging, development-focused

Having considered AI's influence on cultural values, ethics, and liberties, we must now reflect on how these developments align—or clash—with a Christian worldview grounded in dignity, justice, and moral discernment.

Christian Perspective of AI's Influence on Our Values, Ethics, Norms and Liberties

From a Christian perspective, AI has considerable influence on values, ethics, norms, and liberties. As you will recall, previously I noted the fact that AI can help humans flourish by improving our healthcare, alleviating poverty, and making our work more efficient. However, technology can also be used to manipulate, monitor, or commodify us, which brings the risk of reducing humankind to little more than a data point, violating our God-given dignity.

Christians should be deeply concerned when ethical decisions are delegated to AI systems that lack accountability and moral discernment. That risks moral confusion and potential harm, especially when profit or efficiency overrides compassion.

Christianity emphasizes justice, and AI can highlight systemic violations. However, without careful oversight, technology can reinforce social inequalities or become a tool for oppression, especially in surveillance or biased algorithms.

Christians value free will and personal conscience. However, AI's influence on our choices can raise spiritual and ethical questions. Does technology nudge our behavior to compromise freedom and moral choice? Do we resist technologies that manipulate or desensitize truth and love?

Christians ought to approach AI with a blend of curiosity, caution, and compassion. AI is not inherently evil or good. Rather, it is a powerful tool shaped by human intention and is rapidly becoming embedded in our daily lives. We have a responsibility to teach ethical discernment, advocate for justice and dignity, encourage humane and loving uses of technology, and resist dehumanization in all its forms.

Conclusion

This chapter demonstrates the impact AI is having on our values, ethics, norms, and liberties. Technology is radically altering cultures in both positive and negative ways. It is critical that before AI-powered machines go too far, humankind wrestles back control over our future.

The next chapter considers the role AI has for our expansive media, the arts and entertainment enterprise—a significant aspect of our culture.

Chapter 14

AI
AND THE ENTERTAINMENT INDUSTRY

> *With AI drawing art, creating music, and writing, human creativity is being challenged. Artists, musicians, composers, and writers are all experiencing upheaval which could match that of a factory becoming automated.*[550]
>
> Roger Spitz
> Author, futurist, and chair of the Disruptive Futures Institute,
> San Francisco, California

As Spitz suggests, AI is not merely a tool; it is transforming how we create, express, and consume culture. This chapter explores transformation across three domains: the arts, entertainment media, and gaming. The emergence of technology as a significant aspect of the entertainment industry warrants scrutiny because it can deliver both good and evil outcomes.

AI and the Artist

Art is created with imagination and skill that express important human ideas or feelings bridging the real and imaginary. The introduction of AI to the discipline promises radical change. Even though it brings to the art world many advantages, as well as the understanding and appreciation of beauty, artistic creation is still considered exclusively a human domain at this moment, though increasingly challenged by AI technology.

AI AND THE ENTERTAINMENT INDUSTRY

This section puts AI's challenge into perspective, especially by considering what seasoned artists say about the introduction of technology. Then we consider some of the broader implications of AI for the arts across culture.

One of the most provocative examples of AI's intrusion into the creative world is "Ai-Da," which is the name of the world's first humanoid robot "artist," according to the BBC. Her home is in rural Oxfordshire, England, where she is challenging the existence of what humans define as art. After all, her existence raises the question: Do AI algorithms and "art" robots like Ai-Da threaten human creativity and artistry?[551]

No doubt AI-created "artworks" are disrupting that creative world. After all, as BBC explained the view of philosopher Alice Helliwell from Northeastern University London, "If we can consider radical and divergent pieces like [Marcel] Duchamp's [porcelain] urinal as art proper, how can something created by a generative algorithm be dismissed?" The BBC then quoted Helliwell directly: "Historically, the way we understand the definition of art has shifted. …It is hard to see why a urinal can be art, but art made by a generative algorithm could not be."[552]

The arts are significantly impacted by the use of AI.

AI need not mean the "end of art," according to the BBC article. Rather, it might symbolize "an artistic metamorphosis and move us towards totally different ways of seeing and creating."[553]

Marcus du Sautoy, a mathematician at the University of Oxford, contends that "AI might help us to stop behaving like machines…and kick us into being creative again as humans." Professor du Sautoy, the author of *The Creativity Code: Art and Innovation in the Age of AI*, argues there is historical precedent for the contemporary challenge AI presents to the realm of art.[554]

AI FOR MANKIND'S FUTURE

The invention of photography in the 1800s illustrates how modern technology can remove creative shackles. At the time, du Sautoy explained, artists viewed the camera as the antithesis of an artist and "photographs as the mortal enemy of the art establishment."[555]

Ultimately, however, photography did not replace painting, but became a "catalyst in the developmental modern art movement of the twentieth century," according to BBC. Artists moved from realism to abstraction, which gave us contemporary art.[556]

The Harvard *Gazette*, Harvard University's official news website, captured an American perspective from artists familiar with AI's growing role. Specifically, those Harvard artists answered the question: Is art generated by AI real art? And they responded to another question as well: Is the technology of DALL-E2, Discord, Midjourney, and other AI-image generators a threat, a collaborator, or a tool that advances the artist's creativity?[557]

Excerpts from those artists' interviews follow. Their views demonstrate that the jury is still out regarding the role AI plays within the art establishment.

Novelist Daphne Kalotay, a creative writing instructor at Harvard's Extension School, said, "AI is a superb mimic and adaptive learner and might easily write strong works in recognizable modes…but…will lack true insight and experience."[558]

Musician and composer Yosvany Terry, a Harvard lecturer, asserts that "music can transmit and represent emotion, and AI cannot do either of those things yet." However, he agreed that in the realm of composition, "AI has been used to compose music for film and television for quite a few years. That is a concern because AI is doing the work that musicians used to do."[559]

Terry cautioned that AI compositions "lack surprise, emotion, and even silence." However, "It's important to welcome AI with open arms to try to understand what AI can do for us and work with it in creative ways," said Terry. He believes technology is just another innovation like radio was in its early years. "We must remember that all these innovations are man-made, and as humans we can create and innovate," Terry explained.[560]

AI AND THE ENTERTAINMENT INDUSTRY

Ruth Stella Lingford is an animator and senior Harvard lecturer on art, film, and visual studies. She acknowledges that "AI does threaten jobs in the animation industry. I'm told that it is already being used in some large studios. But it will also be a collaborator."[561]

Then Ms. Lingford identified a positive aspect of AI's contribution to the arts community. She explained that it is "possible to train AI on my style and have it work as an assistant in my work. I can see how this would be useful." Further, she noted that the "melding of images from different sources, with large elements of the random, closely approximates some aspects of the creative process. AI is acting like a sort of collective unconscious, and I do find some of what it produces very interesting."[562]

Matt Saunders is a mixed-media artist and Harvard professor with the Department of Art, Film and Visual Studies. He argues that "every new technology upends conventions and delivers not only new possibilities but a new kind of material intelligence." Then, he asserts, "and we should be grateful to be challenged [by AI] and knocked out of our habits and assumptions."[563]

Moshe Safdie is an architect and urban planner at Harvard's graduate school of design. In the 1970s, he was an acquaintance of Marvin Minsky, an AI pioneer. At the time, Safdie said, AI was exclusively the science of making machines intelligent like humans, no more.[564]

Now, "AI has an extraordinary capacity to analyze," but it cannot yet do "the kinds of things we architects do in our head when we design." However, he continued, "And yet, as an architect, I think AI can change our lives."[565]

He admits, "I'm not frightened of AI at all. I'm intrigued. I think AI will be able to create graphic presentations of extraordinary beauty and interest, but that leads us to the question of what is art. Art has an element that is spiritual, emotional." However, he doesn't believe we can label what AI does as "art." Instead, "AI can imitate something that's already been created and regurgitate it in another format, but that is not an original work."[566]

Taken together, these reflections offer a spectrum of hope and concern. What, then, should we conclude from these expert artists' answers regarding AI's role in the arts?

What is not in dispute is that AI is reshaping the creative process by inspiring new artistic expressions, but it also raises profound questions about the future of art.[567]

AI systems like OpenAI's DALL-E and ChatGPT, DeepArt, and Runway ML can create images, compose music, and generate complete narratives for novels and theater scripts. They can help edit alongside filmmakers and assist visual artists. There is also the troubling issue of ownership and what constitutes true art. After all, in 2018, AI "created" unique artworks, such as the portrait *Edmond de Belamy*, which sold for $432,500.[568]

Consider AI's contributions to the art establishment.

AI alters the artist's approach: Today, for many artists, AI is treated as a collaborator and tool that helps artists push the boundaries of their imagination. However, in some sectors of the creative world, AI has replaced humans.[569]

AI enhances the artist's efficiency: It relieves the artist of time-consuming tasks such as color correction and drafting. For the architect, it can rapidly generate multiple design iterations.[570]

AI can stir the artist's creative juices: Writers can brainstorm with AI to refine prose, and visual artists can explore color palettes. It can suggest new forms of art, broadening the scope of artistic expression.[571]

AI democratizes artistic creativity: It does this by making technical tools such as Canva and Artbreeder accessible to non-experts. Using these tools, the amateur can produce high-quality artwork.[572]

AI's role in art also raises ethical and philosophical questions such as: Who owns the AI art? Is it creative or just a technology that combines elements of artwork? Can it indeed be considered art?

There seem to be no easy answers to these questions. Perhaps once the art establishment has lived with AI for a couple of decades, it will become comfortable with its contribution and therefore be able to respond to these challenges.

For now, it's generally recognized that creative professionals can benefit from and are challenged by the rise of AI, with experiences ranging from empowerment and collaboration to loss of control and identity.

Beyond artistic technique and cultural disruption, Christians must also ask deeper questions about AI's alignment with biblical understandings of beauty, truth, and creativity. Specifically, there are other issues we ought to consider regarding AI and the arts.

Theology of art and Christian reflection on beauty and truth: From a biblical perspective, beauty reflects God's nature (Ecclesiastes 3:11; Psalm 27:4). Art can glorify God when it reflects truth, goodness, and beauty—qualities that ultimately stem from Him. Bezalel, an artist in Exodus 31:1–5, was filled with the Spirit of God for craftsmanship, showing that artistic excellence can be a Spirit-empowered calling.

However, AI-generated art—lacking consciousness, spiritual awareness, and divine inspiration—raises profound questions: Can it truly reflect beauty or meaning? Or is it merely a simulacrum, devoid of the heart and soul that come from bearing God's image? Christians must discern between what is beautiful and true and what merely imitates form without essence (2 Corinthians 4:2).

Deepfakes and the crisis of trust: Another significant development is AI's ability to generate deepfakes—convincing videos or audio that impersonates real people. In entertainment, these tools have been used to reanimate deceased actors, fake performances, and create entirely synthetic influencers. While creative on the surface, these raise serious concerns about consent, truthfulness, and digital impersonation. The misuse of someone's likeness for profit or manipulation could be considered a form of bearing false witness (Exodus 20:16).

Community, worship, and the role of shared creativity: Art isn't only personal, but it also builds community. Worship, storytelling, and communal celebration have long been shaped by shared artistic experiences (Colossians 3:16). Hyper-personalized AI media risks fracturing these communal bonds, creating isolated experiences that lack shared meaning. Christian artists should be intentional about using AI to unite, not fragment, the Body of Christ.

For further consideration, see appendix R, which presents real-world case studies of artists, musicians, and writers navigating the rise of AI in creative industries, revealing a complex mix of resistance, adaptation, and innovation as professionals grapple with issues of authorship, identity, consent, and artistic integrity in an evolving digital landscape.

In conclusion, AI is transforming the arts, yet it disciplines new opportunities for innovation by helping the artist explore uncharted territory. However, the art world struggles with AI-fostered ethical challenges about authorship, an issue that deserves immediate attention.

AI and the Entertainment Media

Entertainment media is undergoing radical transformation, attributable mostly to artificial intelligence. Technology brought about unprecedented innovation and efficiency in terms of content development, consumption, and distribution. Meanwhile, the industry's use of AI does pose ethical issues, cut human employment, and create privacy concerns.

This section reviews AI's roles within portions of the entertainment media sector of the industry and technology's role in shaping consumer perceptions, as well as identifies concerns associated with technology's application.

No doubt, the infusion of AI is making remarkable changes to the entertainment community—evident by giants such as Walt Disney—that have significantly tapped into technology's innovations. That marriage propelled Disney and much of the industry into places never imagined, and today the global AI market is expected to continue to grow for the foreseeable future.[573]

There are many discernible AI applications within the industry. First, it impacts entertainment, especially in terms of content creation. Specifically, algorithms analyze datasets to create content tailored to specific audiences. For example, industry giants like Netflix already use AI to assess viewer data to make specific content recommendations, while other firms use technology to create new forms of content.[574]

Second, considerable attention is being given to enhancing consumer experiences through personalization. This is when chatbots or other AI tools make content recommendations to consumers based on collected personal data to enhance their satisfaction. Personalization intends to keep the customer engaged and loyal.[575]

AI AND THE ENTERTAINMENT INDUSTRY

Third, AI-powered tools improve the industry's efficiency by stepping up the realism of 3D models and the production of music soundtracks. More mundane improvements thanks to AI technology include video editing, proofreading, and generating advertisements.

AI also helps the industry market its products by precise targeting that makes sure the products reach the right audience. For example, it analyzes social media to refine the outlet's business strategy by identifying trends and measuring the online impact of its advertisements.[576]

Consider AI's use within very specific sectors of the entertainment media.

AI provides significant help to the music side of the entertainment media. It aids with composition, production, and marketing. Technology is frequently used to generate music by analyzing data from many compositions and then generating new, distinct musical pieces.

Music production also benefits from AI's assistance because it increases efficiency and minimizes errors to offer artists a cost-effective mastering solution to optimize their creations. Further, it can analyze melodies and rhythms and create whole compositions. Landr, an AI-powered music-mastering platform, offers a variety of tools to produce high-quality creations.[577]

AI helps the film side of the industry. Film producers leverage technology to write scripts, make certain they're unique, analyze them to identify questions and uncertainties, and recommend improvements.

Technology can also automate and refine the pre-production process by optimizing schedules, suggesting filming venues and preparing for filming by segmenting the scripts and planning the support packages.

AI is used to inform investors about a film's potential revenue stream. It does this by analyzing the script, comparing it against the dataset of all other releases, and then rendering a revenue prediction. Film studios like Warner Brothers already use algorithms such as Cinelytic, which "supports studios and independent content companies to make faster and better informed greenlight, acquisition, and release decisions."[578] Sony Pictures uses the AI-system ScriptBook to forecast its movie revenue.[579]

AI FOR MANKIND'S FUTURE

Like working on music, AI is very helpful crafting movie trailers as well as editing the entire film. It can even help pinpoint the best parts for trailers. It is noteworthy that the 2018 sci-fi movie *Zone Out*, was created by AI in forty-eight hours, a remarkable accomplishment, although it was not well received or commercially successful.[580]

Since then, AI-generated cinema has evolved dramatically. Runway's third annual AI Film Festival, held at New York's Lincoln Center in 2025, showcased the growing sophistication and legitimacy of AI in filmmaking. Drawing more than one thousand attendees and featuring ten short films selected from six thousand submissions, the festival celebrated both fully AI-generated and hybrid works. The top prize went to *Total Pixel Space*, a visually stunning meditation on digital imagery and mathematical possibility. The event coincided with a landmark deal between Lionsgate and Runway to train AI on a twenty-thousand-title film library—promising cost savings on production but raising fresh concerns about job displacement. While proponents hail AI's creative partnership, critics and labor unions warn of risks to human creators, reflecting the larger tension between innovation and workforce security in a rapidly changing media landscape.[581]

These developments underscore a broader point: Using AI presents risks for the entertainment media industry. Unlike in the manufacturing sector, wherein AI robs jobs associated with repetitive tasks, the place where AI best reigns for the entertainment media sector is in content, which is heavily weighted with judgment, interpretation, creativity, and communication. That's where culture is influenced by technology-powered products and the nexus for risk.[582]

AI's Role in the Demand Side of Media

The demand side of this sector is known as "experience goods," which earns the industry profits when consumer tastes are satisfied. However, matching the product with the consumer is often a daunting task.

Integrating AI into content creation is reshaping audience preferences, expectations, and consumption behaviors. While AI offers efficiency and personalization, its influence on consumer perceptions is multifaceted, encompassing positive and negative dimensions. Consider:

- **Personalization and engagement:** AI's ability to analyze vast datasets enables the delivery of personalized content, enhancing user engagement. Platforms like Netflix and Spotify utilize AI algorithms to recommend movies and music tailored to individual tastes, fostering a deeper connection with users. Similarly, the BBC's adoption of AI aims to offer personalized services across its digital platforms, aligning with the trend toward customized user experiences.[583]
- **Authenticity and consumer trust:** Despite the advantages, AI-generated content often faces skepticism regarding its authenticity. Studies indicate consumers can distinguish AI-created advertisements from human-generated ones, leading to perceptions of reduced brand authenticity. This perception can result in diminished positive word-of-mouth and customer loyalty. Moreover, a 2024 survey revealed that 50 percent of consumers find AI-generated ads off-putting, highlighting concerns about genuineness in marketing communications.[584]
- **Disclosure and transparency:** Transparency about AI's role in content creation is crucial for maintaining consumer trust. Research shows that 86 percent of consumers believe AI-generated content should be disclosed, reflecting a preference for honesty in marketing practices. This sentiment underscores the importance of clear communication regarding AI's involvement in content production.[585]
- **Moral and ethical considerations:** The use of AI in content creation also raises moral and ethical questions. Consumers' discomfort with AI-generated content often stems from perceptions of inauthenticity and moral concerns, leading to negative responses toward such content. This "AI-authorship effect" can adversely affect brand perception and consumer loyalty, emphasizing the need for ethical considerations in AI content strategies.[586]
- **Generational differences:** Younger consumers exhibit higher acceptance and utilization of AI-generated content. A 2023

survey found that 42 percent of respondents aged 18–29 actively use AI daily, compared to 24.6 percent of men and 18.9 percent of women in other age groups. This demographic is more attuned to AI technologies, influencing their content consumption preferences and expectations.[587]
- **Evolving consumption patterns:** AI-generated content is altering traditional consumption patterns. Consumers seek platforms that offer personalized and interactive experiences, such as AI-curated playlists or tailored news feeds. However, the demand for human-authored content persists, particularly in areas where authenticity and emotional connection are valued. This duality presents challenges for content creators and marketers in balancing AI efficiency with a human touch.

AI-generated content significantly influences audience behaviors, offering benefits in personalization and efficiency. However, challenges related to authenticity, transparency, and ethical considerations must be addressed to align with consumer expectations. Understanding these dynamics is essential for brands and content creators navigating the evolving digital landscape.

While the arts showcase AI's challenge to creative identity, entertainment media reveals its power to shape perception and behavior at scale.

Challenges for the Media-Matching Effort

Consider three challenges for the media-customer matching effort and note the risk.[588]

First, consumers often search for specific entertainment content, which they discover can be a formidable undertaking. Second, there is the risk that what consumers seek may not align with what's best for society and may even be dangerous. Third, non-customer actors such as corporations and governments capture content for their purposes to target specific groups of consumers. Consider each of these efforts in more detail.

AI AND THE ENTERTAINMENT INDUSTRY

- **Less-than-efficient search tools:** Finding content can be daunting, given the sheer volume of media available. Although it may be true that AI has made it easier for consumers to find desirable media content, the advances in AI-powered search engines are limited—especially if the customer expects truly personalized searches and matches.[589]
- **Risky media for society:** There is the risk that what a consumer seeks may not align with what is best for society. "Many of the deepest problems in media today stem not from an inability to give consumers what they want, but from the fact that what they appear to want is not aligned with what is good for society," writes Matthew Gentzkow, a professor of technology and economy at Stanford University. Some customers might demand news not aligned with the best social norms. Instead, the customer may prefer "misleading partisan [political] content or outright misinformation rather than more balanced and accurate political news," explained Professor Gentzkow. That is the risk in an AI-driven future, whereby algorithms improve to the point they cater to all tastes including those that are dangerous for society.[590]
- **Third parties capture AI for propaganda:** Third-party actors, such as corporations and governments, may capture for their purposes the media content targeted for select consumers. "Probably the oldest, and possibly the most serious, concern is that media may be captured by third parties that shape or filter content to serve their own objectives.... Certainly, the communist Chinese government uses this approach to suppress certain content and push other messages," wrote Professor Gentzkow. Specifically, Beijing uses AI to "screen objectionable content, monitor citizens to identify dissidents and impending protests, and target propaganda messages to maximize their effectiveness. Russian intelligence operatives can use AI to optimize their foreign influence campaigns,

testing large volumes of content to determine what works best. Commercial advertisers can similarly use these tools to optimize and target content."[591]
- **Psychological and cultural impact:** AI-altered content also affects our minds and hearts. Hyper-personalized media can lead to addiction, loss of attention span, and escapism. Studies show that increased screen time correlates with decreased empathy and emotional resilience. Christians must evaluate entertainment not merely for content, but for how it shapes our affections and time (Ephesians 5:15–16). As Philippians 4:8 exhorts, we should think on what is true, noble, and pure—not just what is novel or immersive.
- **Audience manipulation and algorithmic influence:** AI can tailor entertainment so precisely that it shapes not only consumption but also belief. Algorithms can hijack user attention through manipulation, nudging people toward certain content, ideologies, or desires. This commodification of attention contradicts the biblical call to self-control (Galatians 5:23) and moral discernment. Christians must not outsource their values to machines that are designed to maximize engagement—not truth.

In conclusion, AI has a profound impact on the entertainment media. Although production automation enjoys considerable support, the uniqueness of media content plays a significant cultural role. It has the potential for social good, such as improving consumer searchers and communicating socially beneficial messages. However, on the downside, it can be dangerous when specific content is used for nefarious purposes by third parties like totalitarian governments.

Just as AI influences what we watch and hear, it also shapes how we play. The gaming industry is one of the most immersive examples of AI's cultural reach.

AI AND THE ENTERTAINMENT INDUSTRY

AI and Gaming

In 2024, the global video game industry's revenue reached almost $455 billion, and the mobile gaming market generated $98.7 billion. The three largest gaming companies in the world are Microsoft, Nintendo, and Sony.[592]

AI is an integral part of most game designs, which enhances non-player characters and refines game mechanics by creating realistic and challenging behaviors designed to elevate the player's experience. Also, in gameplay, AI "not only develops formidable opponents, providing a heightened and immersive experience but also ingeniously generates procedural content, such as new levels and characters, ensuring a continually fresh and engaging gaming journey for players," according to Aleksandr Sheremeta, writing for Dataforest.[593]

Soon, expect "99% of gaming companies plan to use AI, and 87% of them are already doing so. This evolution extends beyond the mere inclusion of AI characters in games, focusing on fostering interactivity within the gaming experience," wrote Rajeev Sharma, the cofounder and CEO of Markovate, "a visionary technologist with deep expertise in AI, cloud computing, and mobile."[594]

Consider some characteristics of contemporary gaming thanks to AI.

- **Personalized gaming experience:** The gaming industry is much like the entertainment media in that it delivers personalized game suggestions such as gameplay styles, genre inclinations, in-game choices, and more. The AI-powered gaming system can dynamically tailor in-game content based on individual player behavior and gaming decisions.[595]
- **Adaptive difficulty:** AI permits the system to employ real-time player behavior analysis to customize game difficulty. It measures player skill, response time, strategy, and progress. "Dynamic difficulty adjustment (DDA) through AI ensures the game balances between challenge and accessibility,

tailoring the experience to individual player capabilities and preferences."[596]
- **Expanded theological perspective on gaming:** Gaming offers exploration and rest, but it can also foster escapism, addictive patterns, and a detachment from reality. AI-enhanced realism may blur the line between fantasy and life. Christians must ask whether a game builds virtues like perseverance, wisdom, and fellowship—or fosters vice. Entertainment should not dull our hunger for God, but refresh us to serve Him more faithfully.

Christian developers also have an opportunity: to craft games that teach truth, reflect redemption, or encourage community. Just as Christian music and film have grown, so too can redemptive gaming.

In conclusion, AI-powered gaming has come a long way from simply using algorithms and complex agents revolutionizing the face of gaming. Future changes will include the "development of virtual reality [VR] and game creation. In video games especially in VR, AI will advance realism of the environments enabling it to predict a player's action and reduce such discomforts to make gaming experiences as natural and fluid as possible."[597]

These innovations also raise complex legal and intellectual property questions—especially around authorship, ownership, and consent.

AI and Intellectual Property and Legal Issues for the Arts, Entertainment Media, and Gaming

The advent of AI in content creation has precipitated significant legal and IP challenges, particularly concerning copyright and ownership. As AI-generated works become more prevalent, questions arise about who holds the rights to such content—the AI developers, users, or the AI itself. Recent legal cases and policy debates shed light on these emerging issues.

Legal Precedents on AI and Copyright

In August 2023, a pivotal ruling by US District Court Judge Beryl A. Howell concluded that AI-generated artwork cannot be copyrighted. The court emphasized that human authorship is fundamental to copyright eligibility, stating, "copyright has never stretched so far…as to protect works generated by new forms of technology operating absent any guiding human hand."[598]

Similarly, in the United Kingdom, a parliamentary poll revealed that 92 percent of the members of Parliament support requiring AI companies to disclose and compensate for the use of copyrighted material. This sentiment reflects concerns within the creative industry about unauthorized AI training on copyrighted works.[599]

Policy Debates and International Considerations

The Tony Blair Institute has advised the UK to relax its copyright laws to foster AI development, cautioning that stringent regulations could harm international relations, particularly with the US. They suggest that rigid measures might prompt US tariffs on UK goods, highlighting the geopolitical stakes in AI policy formulation.[600]

Industry Concerns and Calls for Action

Media organizations across Europe are urging immediate action to protect journalism from AI exploitation. They argue that AI's use of journalistic content without consent undermines the press and spreads disinformation, calling for transparency, ethical use, and proper remuneration to ensure AI benefits both creators and the public.[601]

Music-Industry Pushback and Licensing Efforts

A recent development in the music industry highlights how top record labels are seeking to navigate these challenges. Warner Music Group, along with Universal Music Group and Sony Music, is in negotiations with AI startups Suno and Udio to establish licensing agreements that would compensate the labels when their artists' songs are used to train generative AI models and produce new music. The labels are pushing for fingerprinting and attribution technology to track song usage, along with a role in overseeing what AI-generated songs are released. Although both AI firms face copyright infringement lawsuits and deny wrongdoing, investor pressure and regulatory uncertainty are driving them to pursue commercial agreements. The outcome of these negotiations may set a significant precedent for how artists are paid and protected in the age of AI-generated remixes. News of the talks caused Warner Music's stock to fall to its lowest level in two years, underscoring the high stakes involved.[602]

Financial Incentives and Ethical Considerations

Some Hollywood studios have been monetizing AI-generated movie trailers on platforms like YouTube, diverting ad revenue despite opposition from actors' unions. This practice raises ethical concerns about prioritizing profit over protecting the likeness rights of actors and incentivizing low-quality AI-generated content.[603]

Ongoing Legal Developments

The legal landscape continues to evolve, with courts and policymakers grappling with the complexities of AI and IP law. As AI technology advances, balancing innovation with the protection of creators' rights remains a critical challenge, necessitating ongoing legal scrutiny and policy adjustments.

Amid these legal, ethical, and cultural challenges, Christians must also consider how faith shapes our engagement with AI in the arts.

Christian Perspective on AI's Role in the Arts and Entertainment

AI in entertainment and the arts is neither inherently good nor bad. It depends on how it is used. Does it enhance human creativity, reflect God's truth, and uplift the human spirit? It must not lead to deception, dehumanization, or distraction from what matters eternally (Romans 12:2).

God created us (Genesis 1:1) and made us in His image (*imago Dei*), which includes our creative abilities. Therefore, art and entertainment can be seen as acts of co-creation with God, expressions of beauty, truth, and worship. AI tools can help us express creativity and therefore can be seen as part of our God-given mandate to cultivate the world (Genesis 1:28). However, we need to be careful when creativity becomes mechanical or fails to reflect the human heart, spirit, or experience.

Christianity values truth and authenticity. AI can raise important questions about entertainment and the arts that explore human experience, suffering, redemption, and joy. For example, can AI understand or express the human condition? It can mimic emotion, but cannot feel like a human. Therefore, AI-assisted art becomes imitation rather than incarnation. Also, we should ask: Is it honest to present AI-generated content as human-created? Our audience should know when something is AI-generated.

AI-generated art and media can become addictive and foster escapism. Christians must be concerned when entertainment becomes a way to avoid reality or dull our spiritual hunger—arguably a form of idolatry (Exodus 20:3–4). Our discernment antenna must be active to evaluate media through the lens of Philippians 4:8.

Christian artists are often called to speak truth, offer hope, and glorify God through their work. This requires a higher standard—producing content that nourishes rather than numbs us. AI can never mimic a true Spirit-filled message of faith that transforms the heart.

Finally, as technology advances, Christians must also discern its role in the broader story of redemption. AI-powered entertainment could be a tool of mass distraction or even deception (Matthew 24:24; 2 Thessalonians 2:9–12). The Church must remain vigilant, testing every cultural innovation against Scripture.

These biblical insights remind us that creativity must serve truth and beauty—not just innovation. With this in mind, we conclude the chapter.

Conclusion

This chapter addressed AI's influence over three aspects of the entertainment industry: the arts, entertainment media, and gaming. Together, these areas impact much of the world and are expected to increase their influence on culture in both positive and negative ways.

The closing chapter in this section will address AI's effect on communications and the political process.

Chapter 15

AI'S INFLUENCE ON COMMUNICATIONS AND POLITICS

> *It is offering new ways of spreading disinformation, like the audio and video content, especially, but it's mostly just turbocharging existing efforts and making it a lot cheaper and easier.*[604]
>
> NICOLE GILL
> Co-founder and executive director at Accountable Tech

We're entering a new era that includes the rapid growth of technology, which promises to influence how we relate in very significant ways with our fellow man. This chapter drills down on AI's outsized influence on culture, especially regarding the methods contemporary humans use to communicate, how they interact with pervasive smart algorithms, and the impact super-capable technology has on our political processes.

Using AI to Communicate

To appreciate the profound changes AI is making, it's helpful to consider the broader arc of human communication methods—from primal symbols to intelligent machines.

The history of humankind has seen a radical transformation of the methods and mechanisms used to communicate. Prehistoric humans (before 3000 BCE) used a variety of methods to communicate: oral language and gestures, cave paintings and rock art, petroglyphs, and smoke

AI'S INFLUENCE ON COMMUNICATIONS AND POLITICS

signals, as well as drum and other sound signals. Ancient humans (after 3000 BCE) used pictograms, alphabet writing, and postal systems. Medieval humans (500–1500 CE) used paper, town criers, carrier pigeons, and the printing press. Modern humans (1500 CE to present) use newspapers, telegraph, telephone, radio, television, the internet, email, mobile phones, social media, and, most recently, instant messaging.

Once again, today, humanity is reshaping how we communicate as a society welcomes innovation. Specifically, we're surrendering some of our communication tasks to AI-powered devices, which are taking on humanlike capabilities.

McKinsey and Company, a worldwide management and consulting firm, found that AI adoption among organizations was 78 percent by May 2024,[605] and there is no reason to expect the clamoring for technical applications in the realm of communications to decline.[606]

Consider the growing inventory of AI-powered communication modes.

Human-like chatbots assume more communication roles. The transformation of human communication is fueled by companies like Google, which in 2024 unveiled advanced versions of their chatbots that can simultaneously manage many complex tasks and at greater speed. These AI-powered chatbots and virtual assistants are truly humanlike in their conversations, which impacts business and personal communications. Prior chapters in this book reviewed the use of chatbots in education, health, and retail services.

I asked ChatGPT to provide an example of the potentially more profound interpersonal impact to demonstrate how AI-mediated interactions affect interpersonal relationships, human cognition, and social dynamics beyond mere transactional exchanges. Appendix S explores how AI-mediated interactions, like those with ChatGPT, are subtly transforming human relationships, emotional development, and social dynamics—offering comfort and insight while raising concerns about intimacy, empathy, and the evolving boundaries between authentic connection and algorithmic companionship.

AI personalizes communication. AI-assisted personalization is a powerful tool, as seen in previous chapters, because it allows for the creation of highly targeted and tailored communication strategies. We already use chatbots to answer customer questions, yet personalization goes beyond that: It improves customer satisfaction and loyalty programs and helps gain the buyer's trust.[607]

Even OpenAI's new tool—Sora, which is like OpenAI's image-generation AI tool, DALL-E, can generate high-definition video clips inspired by still images, and it can extend existing videos to fill in missing frames.[608] Further, it can:

> …generate complex scenes with multiple characters, specific types of motion, and accurate details of the subject and background. The model understands not only what the user has asked for in the prompt but also how those things exist in the physical world.[609]

AI helps with global communication. The use of different languages has become routine, and AI-powered translation tools that operate in real time can prove to be invaluable. Certainly, the obvious advantage is that this tool revolutionizes interaction across cultures by fostering seamless communication in meaning and understandability despite differing languages. Beyond the spoken language, AI has empowered almost simultaneous text translations even for complex issues and nuanced styles, a real boon for the scientific community seeking to collaborate with counterparts in other nations. Yet as global communication expands, the reliability of information becomes equally vital—a challenge AI also reshapes through its growing influence on journalism and media.

AI is rapidly transforming journalism. Algorithms now write news summaries, curate headlines, and personalize newsfeeds—often at the expense of investigative depth and balanced reporting. This shift contributes to the erosion of public trust in media institutions and creates filter bubbles that reinforce existing biases. Christians, as people of truth, should support efforts that preserve journalistic integrity and resist AI-generated distortion (Proverbs 18:13).

AI is also helping to communicate in other ways with humans.

AI'S INFLUENCE ON COMMUNICATIONS AND POLITICS

For example, Speechify has a text-to-speech and speech-to-text device to help clients such as those with disabilities. The chatbot Replika can mimic your text style and promises it is for "anyone who wants a friend with no judgment, drama, or social anxiety involved. You can form an actual emotional connection, share a laugh, or get real with an AI that's so good it almost seems human."[610] There are AI systems that interpret sign language and convert it into text and speech, such as Google's SignAll and Sign2Text by Microsoft.

AI aids digital communication. AI tools like Grammarly can assist with and improve our writing by checking grammar, tone, and clarity. We also have Gmail's Smart Compose, which suggests text to help speed up the composition of email and messages. AI-based voice typing such as Google Voice Typing enables hands-free communication.

AI helps group video teleconference and meeting summaries. AI-powered tools like Zoom and Microsoft Teams provide live captions and transcripts. They also improve the quality of the session by filtering out background noise to enhance audio quality. Further, these types of AI platforms can generate summaries of the meetings and highlight key discussion points.

Predictably, there are downsides to AI-powered communication aids. Consider a few examples of these negative outcomes just as such platforms proliferate.

- **AI-produced misinformation**: Unfortunately, AI can be used to produce persuasive human-like misinformation if it is trained on biased or incorrect data. That outcome can undermine trust, and it seems that cyberspace is overflowing with inauthentic content.

    Some AI-generated misinformation used by governments is meant for propaganda, such as in communist China. Other governments understand the danger associated with ubiquitous misinformation and have taken steps to limit that threat through legislation.

    In 2024, the Australian government banned social media access for users under age sixteen "amid concern about its mental health impact on young people." Australia's ban set a benchmark for other countries to regulate big tech better. That nation's law requires tech giants like Facebook owner Meta to stop minors from logging in; if they don't comply, they face fines of up to $32 million. Australia started a trial of enforcement methods in January 2025.[611]

- **Overreliance on AI for communication**: Some users may become too dependent on AI, which potentially reduces their critical-thinking and language skills and leads to errors in task performance in the context of decision-making. This over-reliance on AI could happen in businesses that replace humans with AI chatbots, or individuals who struggle with how much trust to place in technology's suggestions.
- **Growing anthropocentric bias**: Society is learning that AI-powered communication devices are creating an anthropocentric bias, meaning humans are less willing to accept AI in prototypical human tasks. That is happening even though those devices are becoming incredibly humanlike in their speech, appearance, and interactions with people.[612]

A 2023 study published by the journal *Computers in Human Behavior* demonstrates that AI advancements challenge human uniqueness in artistic creativity, an issue addressed in chapter 14. That study found a pervasive bias against AI-generated artworks, especially when the work was labeled "AI-made." Predictably, the bias was especially pronounced among those who hold strong anthropocentric creativity beliefs, according to the study.[613]

Where is the "sweet spot" between AI-powered machines and human beings? Is there an ideal level of interaction, a middle ground that can take advantage of the best qualities of AI-powered applications in collaboration with humans?

Answering that question is quite a challenge given that in May 1997, IBM's Deep Blue computer defeated chess master Garry Kasparov, in a feat that shocked many as they realized that computers can outperform humans. Deep Blue "used 32 processors to perform a set of coordinated high-speed computations in parallel. Deep Blue was able to evaluate 200 million chess positions per second." That outcome encouraged new interest in combining machine intelligence with human thinking to create a super-bright outcome.[614]

Perhaps there is a human-machine collaboration "sweet spot" regarding communications that avoids the downsides outlined above while embraces the various benefits each brings. However, the issue remains unresolved. Beyond computational speed or collaborative efficiency, AI is now entering domains that demand moral and emotional nuance—like human conversation.

AI and Human Conversations

Scripture affirms the deep connection between language and divinity. "In the beginning was the Word" (John 1:1, ESV). Words create, reveal, convict, and heal (Proverbs 25:11). AI-generated language—though fluent—lacks the moral weight and spiritual resonance of human speech. As AI reshapes communication, Christians must guard the sacredness of words and uphold the truth they are meant to convey.

Never forget that no matter how the machine may sound, answer questions, and express itself like a human, it is still a nonorganic tool. It has no moral responsibility for the action it may recommend. This may be a strange statement, but given AI's many advances, I am warning you because tomorrow's applications will fool many humans. After all, as indicated in chapter 4, most (80 percent) of GEN Zers are open to the possibility of "marrying" an AI bot, a disturbing prospect.[615]

Therefore, how should we interact with AI applications and view their responses to our inquiries?

I asked ChatGPT: How should a human speak with AI to get the best results? The application answered with the following helpful suggestions: Be clear and specific, use proper grammar and punctuation, provide context, break down complex questions, use key words, ask follow-up questions, specify format or style, use commands for tasks, be patient and refine queries, and be aware of AI's limitations.

AI FOR MANKIND'S FUTURE

My question for ChatGPT wasn't silly. It goes to the heart of the question posed by computer scientist Alan Turing in 1950: "Can machines think?" To answer that question, Turing developed the Imitation Game, or what came to be known as the Turing Test. Simply, to pass that test, the computer must "fool" a human into believing the computer is organic—human—not a mindless instrument.

The Turing Test highlights an essential relationship between language and the mind. After all, human-AI interactions are commonplace—from chatbots to virtual coaches to robots—and most of these contemporary AI-powered applications can pass the Turing Test, because some are remarkably humanlike, or they appear to think.

This appearance is reinforced by recent findings. A 2025 study published in *Communications Psychology* by researchers from the University of Geneva and the University of Bern found that large language models (LLMs), including GPT-4, Gemini 1.5 Flash, and Claude 3.5 Haiku, consistently outperformed humans on standard emotional intelligence (EI) tests. The AI systems achieved an average score of 81 percent compared to the human average of 56 percent—accurately identifying emotional situations and selecting appropriate responses. Even more striking, GPT-4 successfully generated new EI test items that closely matched the structure and quality of those authored by humans. While these LLMs do not feel emotions, their ability to simulate emotional reasoning positions them as powerful tools in fields like education, healthcare, and customer service. These findings bolster the view that AI can mimic—not experience—emotional understanding, reinforcing its capacity to pass for humans in conversation while lacking true empathy or accountability.[616]

The danger we face today as users of these humanlike AI devices is attributing to them moral responsibility. That would be a tragic mistake. Consider the conclusions reached by Dutch scientists who wrote for the *American Journal of Bioethics*.

The article, "Why We Should Understand Conversational AI as a Tool," addresses whether conversational artificial intelligence (CAI) technologies like ChatGPT ought to "be considered a tool or an agent."

AI'S INFLUENCE ON COMMUNICATIONS AND POLITICS

That determination not only goes to the issue of whether AI is intelligent like a human, but, more importantly, it points to whether it is a moral agent, which impacts our conversations with the machine, and whether it is accountable, an issue addressed earlier in this book.[617]

We must answer the question: Does the CAI system merely mimic human abilities such as replicating natural human language, or does it go beyond? The study's authors argue that despite demonstrating human-like attributes, technology is not like humankind because it doesn't have moral status or "the type of agency it [humankind] exercises." Therefore, "being an agent [being a moral being] is fundamentally different from being perceived as an agent [a machine that is not truly human with moral accountability]."[618]

The authors' literature review compels them to conclude that "the inability for AI to relate emotions and real-world experiences to language is a fundamental difference [with humans]."[619]

They conclude that even though CAI technologies are humanlike and can pass the Turing Test, they only mimic human interactions. Therefore, they have no moral agency, and we should treat them only as a tool.[620]

After all, Scripture warns that in the last days, false wonders and persuasive lies will deceive many (2 Thessalonians 2:9–11; Matthew 24:24). AI-generated deepfakes and persuasive dialogue engines could serve such ends if not constrained. Christians must cultivate discernment and warn others not to equate realism with righteousness.

Another scientific article considers this issue from a different perspective. Specifically, a paper presented at the 2024 6th International Conference on Natural Language Processing considered the communication dynamics between humans and AI, which addressed "how well and in what ways humans and AI can communicate." The authors formulated a way to statistically measure the AI machine's "understanding," which resulted in a "complex system, which has certain properties such as hierarchical structure, nonlinearity, complexity, and open vs. closed system dynamics." The bottom line is that, based on their model, the AI system can understand certain things humans communicate, but there are barriers to proper "understanding" that a machine might never grasp.[621]

For the above study, "understanding" became a statistical measurement meant to compare how humans and AI process language, which is used to suggest how man and machine communicate and the level of the AI application's "understanding." It is noteworthy that the study's authors conclude that the "greater understanding in the [contemporary] system implies [it is] more similar [to] human[s]."[622]

The article concludes that proper understanding is complex to measure, but, as the authors argue, "I believe it [understanding] is the foundation of what makes humans feel understood." They elaborated that "understanding" is not scientific, but empirical, and then the authors explained a bridge too far for even "smart" machines. Specifically, they said:

> [Humans know that] feeling understood comes from laughing with a friend about the same thing. Or when someone knows what to say to you, or not say to you, to make you feel better. It is when someone can fill in the gaps in your knowledge. It's about shared thinking. When a person connects ideas in a similar way to you, this is what creates a sense of understanding. And lack of understanding comes when people can't. We have all been in a situation where someone tries to teach you by using words or concepts you don't know or by explaining information you already understand. One fundamental criticism of AI is that it does not relate linguistic and non-linguistic information in the same way humans can. AI can't have shared experiences with people, and this creates a fundamental gap in its ability to understand us.[623]

Even though machines cannot share our experiences and therefore "understand" us, there is still a disturbing indication that many people prefer to speak with a machine rather than another human. For example, a 2022 study found that 55 percent of people preferred AI-based psychotherapy to working with a human clinician.[624]

Many of those humans preferred robots because of comfort and accessibility, according to the study. Why? Perhaps, as two psychologists wrote:

> It is quite natural that we should feel more at home with other species than with our own. Our pets, for instance, never judge us or betray our trust. They don't—as far as we know—mock us behind our backs or make light of our feelings. They're not duplicitous. They're not ironical [sic]. They never say one thing while subtly suggesting another.[625]

It is quite revealing that many humans speak with AI applications as if they're communicating with another real person. That is tragic, and an issue modern society must address for many of the reasons outlined in the previous section of this chapter as well as for the spiritual issues discussed in the next section of this book.

While some turn to AI for nonjudgmental companionship, it reflects a tragic shift away from the human community we were designed for (Genesis 2:18; Ecclesiastes 4:9–10). AI cannot share our grief, pray with us, or bear our burdens (Galatians 6:2). Churches must step in to offer authentic relationships grounded in Christ's love.

Some theologians warn that AI systems may lay the groundwork for future systems of control described in Revelation—whether through economic coercion, speech regulation, or the performance of manufactured miracles. While speculative, such concerns invite believers to be alert (1 Peter 5:8) and test the spirits, especially when technology replaces truth with illusion.

Churches and Christian schools should actively teach digital discernment and biblical ethics in using technology, and they should also foster moral imagination in AI-driven culture. Beyond reacting, we must lead—advocating for policy rooted in God's justice and truth, discipling believers to use AI redemptively, and praying for wisdom as society navigates uncharted digital territory.

AI and Politics

Politics is a significant aspect of culture, and AI is a game-changer for political campaigns, parties, and candidates. It can analyze vast datasets to tailor messages, predict voter behavior, raise donations, respond to voter inquiries, and optimize campaign strategies. This technology moves political campaigning towards precision with personalized messaging that connects with voter preferences. Then again, it can be a dangerous source of compelling misinformation in a tension-packed environment.

Consider how AI can streamline and rev up a political campaign.

AI can personalize campaign messaging. The 2016 Trump campaign for president targeted voters with AI-informed, tailored messages. The campaign officials tasked the AI algorithm to identify voter preferences and susceptibilities and then deliver customized messages through an assortment of outlets, such as social media. In 2020, the Biden campaign used AI to analyze voter patterns, which informed their advertisement placement.[626]

AI can manage media campaigns. AI-powered tools like Hootsuite and Buffer help optimize the political campaign's media buys by gauging public reaction and then adjusting in real-time. They can also conduct deep analysis of campaign policies and then help formulate strategic messages.[627]

AI helps raise political funding. It can help a campaign identify donors and streamline fundraising strategies, which can lead to efficiency and success. Further, AI chatbots are used to contact potential donors, encouraging them to vote and soliciting donations.

American politics is inundated with AI-generated misinformation from all political parties.

AI transforms voter polling. AI-powered polling can be more accurate and timelier than traditional methods. It can also analyze online social-media conversations that provide campaigns with insights on key public issues. Finally, it can predict election outcomes by analyzing a wealth of voter-related information to help officials better focus their resource investments.

AI'S INFLUENCE ON COMMUNICATIONS AND POLITICS

AI can also fuel negative campaigning.

AI can exacerbate election challenges. It can spread disinformation about a candidate and create cyber vulnerabilities in election systems. In 2024, AI-generated robocalls imitated President Joe Biden's voice to discourage voters from casting ballots in the New Hampshire primary.[628] On the Republican side, in early 2024, AI-generated images falsely depicted former President Trump with Jeffrey Epstein, the convicted sex trafficker.[629]

Many other nations suffer from an assault of AI-generated deepfakes, such as the 2023 Slovakian election, which featured an effort to defame a politician and advance his pro-Russian opponent.[630] Elsewhere, in January 2024, the communist Chinese used AI deepfakes to disrupt the Taiwanese election.[631] The list of AI-generated deepfake political campaign tricks is quite long. AI-generated deepfakes pose dangers for elections, which governments and society ought to understand and use their powers to discourage. Yet deepfakes are only one weapon in a broader AI arsenal being deployed to reshape not just elections, but worldviews.

AI is being engaged in the battle for belief. In addition to shaping elections, AI is increasingly used to push ideological or religious propaganda. Authoritarian regimes like communist China deploy AI to suppress dissent and censor faith-based speech, while others flood media channels with manipulated narratives designed to marginalize moral or Christian viewpoints. This raises critical concerns for freedom of belief and conscience—principles deeply embedded in biblical justice (Isaiah 1:17; Acts 5:29). As stewards of truth, Christians must remain vigilant against ideological coercion masked as progress.

AI can be used for censorship of truth. AI doesn't just create content, it also suppresses it. Machine-learning algorithms on social platforms are increasingly used to shadow-ban or demote content deemed "harmful" or "misleading"—often without transparency or appeal. This practice disproportionately affects religious speech and countercultural convictions. Christians should advocate for content-moderation policies that are fair, open, and respectful of freedom of expression (Proverbs 31:8–9).

AI can be used to engineer emotion. AI excels at predicting human behavior—but it can also manipulate it. Political campaigns now use AI to generate content that stokes fear, outrage, or tribal loyalty, aiming to bypass logic and appeal to raw emotion. This undermines thoughtful democratic discourse and contradicts biblical counsel to be sober-minded and discerning (2 Timothy 1:7; James 1:19–20).

What is AI's future in the political space? It has already revolutionized the political campaigning process. However, there is much more AI-related "help" on the horizon, such as the analysis of speeches and debates, which will provide candidates with insights that appeal to voters.[632] Consider:

- **AI campaign assistants:** Expect that in the future there will be many versions of AI-powered campaign assistants (robots) that "speak" with voters. These "aides" will be available 24/7, can flag misinformation and provide the campaign timely responses to shut down those deepfake and misinformation messages.[633]
- **AI-generated campaign contributions:** Nothing says an AI non-biological agent cannot raise campaign funds and seed a human's political ambition. Something labeled "hustle bros" already peddled political claims and used ChatGPT to generate income. Why couldn't a similar AI-driven system raise contributions and then digitally direct those funds to a particular campaign?[634]
- **AI-drafted legislation:** AI-generated legislation is a reality. For example, in 2023, a Massachusetts lawmaker[635] used ChatGPT to draft legislation, and a US House of Representatives member, Jake Auchincloss (D-MA), said he delivered an AI-written speech on the House floor. In chapter 7, I called out the UAE, which established the Regulatory Intelligence Office to oversee the use of AI to create regulations.[636]
- **AI-created political party:** It isn't too far-fetched that AI will establish a political party, circulate its platform, and then recruit candidates. It could even collect signatures to place names on ballots. Arguably, this has already happened

in Denmark. In 2022, the Danish Synthetic Party, a group of artists, created the group to explore political ideology. Although the party failed to receive sufficient signatures to earn a place on the ballot, it established that the use of AI-powered robots to form a political party and then try to run for office was possible.[637]

It should be obvious that the sky is the limit for AI-powered help with political campaigns and the broader political process. At this point, there are few regulations, and likely, for the good of our republic, there ought to be far more guidelines on the use of technology in politics.

For further analysis on the role of AI in the political arena, consider appendix T, which outlines a comprehensive strategy to combat AI-driven disinformation by integrating technological tools, media literacy education, and policy interventions—aimed at preserving democratic integrity and equipping citizens to discern truth in an increasingly synthetic information landscape. Also, appendix W examines how AI is reshaping global politics—contrasting authoritarian regimes that exploit AI for surveillance and control with democratic nations striving to balance innovation, transparency, and civil liberties—while underscoring the urgent need for ethical, cooperative governance to protect political integrity worldwide.

Beyond technical innovation and regulatory gaps, AI's influence demands ethical clarity and spiritual grounding—especially for followers of Christ.

Christian Perspective on AI's Influence on Communications and Politics

Christians are called to be salt and light (Matthew 5:13–16), especially in the age of AI, because technology influences the way we communicate and engage in politics. We shouldn't fear this change but enter the digital and political spaces as agents of truth, justice, and love —always guided by God's Word and the example of Christ.

Our communications should be marked by truth (Ephesians 4:15).

However, AI can introduce ethical challenges in the realm of communication. Earlier, we established that AI-driven platforms often amplify misinformation, deepfakes, or polarizing content. Our calling is to promote truth, transparency, and discernment. We must resist deception and encourage honest dialogue.

Christianity emphasizes justice, care for the vulnerable, and ethical governance (Proverbs 31:8–9), all of which should guide how we approach the use of AI in political contexts. AI in politics—used for voter profiling, sentiment analysis, and campaign targeting—raises ethical questions. For example, does AI help enhance democratic participation, or does it manipulate public opinion and suppress voices?

Christians ought to reject AI's influence in political communication that subtly shapes beliefs. Rather, we should support freedom of thought, informed consent, and respectful discourse.

Unfortunately, AI-curated platforms can produce a tone and nature of political conversation that is divisive and angry. Technology should promote unity, understanding, and respect (Matthew 5:9; Luke 6:27–28).

Finally, Christians ought to engage AI with wisdom and integrity (Matthew 5:13–16) that promotes truthful, respectful communication; holds the political system accountable; and advocates for ethical standards in how AI is used. We should also pray for leaders and systems to reflect God's justice and peace (1 Timothy 2:1–2).

Conclusion

This chapter introduced three aspects of AI's role in our culture: the use of AI in communication, how humans communicate with AI applications, and AI's growing role in our political process.

The following section addresses AI's influence on Christianity writ large, and the potential roles it might play in the biblical end times.

Section Six

AI, CHRISTIANITY, AND BIBLICAL PROPHECY

A year spent in artificial intelligence is enough to make one believe in God.[638]

Alan Perlis (1922-1990)
Computer scientist and professor at Yale University

Alan Perlis' observation captures the mysterious and often awe-inspiring nature of AI. For Christians, this awe must be tempered with biblical discernment, especially as AI intersects with deep questions about creation, personhood, and prophecy.

If AI blurs our understanding of what it means to bear God's image, it can also lead to greater spiritual confusion. This confusion creates fertile ground for deception—where technology may be misused to mimic miracles, distort Scripture, or present false messianic narratives.

These deceptions may not be isolated events; they could play a part in larger prophetic movements foretold in Scripture. That leads us to consider key eschatological questions about the end times and whether AI might fulfill roles described in Revelation.

To address these profound concerns, this section includes two chapters. The first explores today's cultural and spiritual challenges through a biblical lens, while the second looks ahead to AI's possible role in the unfolding of end-times prophecy.

Chapter 16

AI AND THE CHRISTIAN

AI is a force being ushered onto the "throne" of our culture by demonic forces that fuel our modern, indiscriminate material pursuits.[639]

BERNARD PETER ROBICHAU
Technologist and clergyman, Orthodox Church of America

Artificial intelligence is not a morally neutral tool; it reflects and amplifies assumptions about humanity, truth, and power. For Christians, this raises urgent questions: What does it mean to be human in the age of machines? How should we respond to technologies that claim to think, create, or even love?

This chapter unfolds in four parts: "Christian View of Mankind and AI"; "Spiritual Warfare in the Digital Age"; Ethical Challenges and Cultural Temptations"; and "Christians Living in the AI Quagmire." Let's begin by examining what AI reveals about human identity.

Christian View of Mankind and AI

"AI is a powerful tool that presents us with profound, and profoundly moral, challenges," writes Gretchen Huizinga, a fellow at the nonprofit AI and Faith organization.[640] How then should Christians understand the technology, its challenges for our modern world, and the best way to respond?

Christian entrepreneur Andrew Torba's book, *Reclaiming Reality: Restoring Humanity in the Age of AI*, nails the issue. He labels the advancement of AI as a great deception. Specifically, he writes:

AI FOR MANKIND'S FUTURE

The great deception of our age is not that AI will replace humanity, but that it will convince us we were never more than machines to begin with. The rapid advance of artificial intelligence, biotechnology, and transhumanist ideologies is forcing humanity to confront an age-old question in a new and urgent way: What does it mean to be human?[641]

For centuries, Christianity has provided a clear and unwavering answer [to the above question]—man is created in the image of God, possessing an immortal soul that gives him value, purpose, and an eternal destiny. Yet in the modern era, this truth is being systematically challenged.[642]

Materialists and secular thinkers reject the Christian view that we are created in the image of God with an eternal soul. Instead, they espouse the distorted view that we're no more than chemical reactions and data patterns. Their conclusion, according to Torba, is:

> There is no fundamental distinction between man and machine. Artificial intelligence, they argue, is simply another form of intelligence—one that can eventually surpass human cognition and render human labor, creativity, and even relationships obsolete.[643]

"Christianity utterly rejects this deception," Torba rightly argues. We are "living souls," formed by God and "breathed into life by His spirit."

CHRISTIANS NEED TO UNDERSTAND AI IN ORDER TO AVOID ITS HAZARDS WHILE USING IT FOR GOD'S GLORY

Therefore, our identity is not merely material, but is rooted in our relationship with our Creator.[644]

The implications are profound. AI may mimic creativity or language, but it cannot love, repent, or worship. These are actions of a soul. Christians must therefore reaffirm that our identity is not reducible to data, flesh, or cognition; it is grounded in being known and loved by God.

Even so, AI did not appear from nowhere. Its roots trace back to projects like ARPANET (Advanced Research Projects Agency Network), a 1969 Department of Defense initiative—the beginning of the modern internet, demonstrating how deeply entwined these technologies are with control and surveillance—domains the Bible warns us not to blindly trust (Psalm 146:3).

AI may claim to mirror humanity, but it lacks what matters most: a soul. As one theologian put it, AI is "an empty vessel"—useful, perhaps, but never equivalent to man.

As AI becomes entrenched in our lives, differing interpretations of its meaning arise—some rooted in faith, others in secular materialism.

Yet, no matter how we try to put this genie back into the bottle, technology is here to stay, and, despite AI proponents' vociferous prognostications, intelligent machines will always remain more sci-fi than human because they are soulless. However, secularists have always tried to confuse the issue.

George M. Coghill, professor emeritus at the University of Aberdeen, United Kingdom, wrote: "There has always been a strand within humanity that has hankered after the ability to create a being in our own image, with or without *divine* assistance." The professor boasts that we "are no closer to the goal of producing a truly sentient [ability to experience feelings and sensations] being than when it [the technological revolution] started."[645]

Yet AI proponents dismiss the biblical concept of a God-created immortal soul and keep striving to create "a being in our own image." They believe humanity consists of expendable organic matter, which explains their pervasive anti-life agenda. However, as Torba counters, in God's eyes, "every life is sacred, not because of what it can produce, but because it is made in His image." That is the basis of objective moral law. Still, not for AI-favoring secularists, especially if their "creation" can think, create and be self-aware, then it becomes just like organic humans or better, they argue because it will not be subject to entropy, the natural toll nature takes on the human body (aging).

Of course, the fact remains, AI algorithms will never possess a soul.

The true danger lies not in AI becoming human, but in humans forgetting what it means to be human.

Thus, for the Christian given the mythology of AI becoming human, our task is to reaffirm and defend biblical truth and reject the notion that we are mere skin and data. "We must hold fast to the understanding that our worth is not in our abilities, our knowledge, or our digital presence—it is in the fact that we are known and loved by God," wrote Torba.[646]

Even though AI will never acquire a God-given soul, it doesn't put the technology outside the interest of God. After all, AI is under God's authority. Torba's warning is echoed by other Christian thinkers who see AI not merely as a tool, but as a spiritual battleground.

Understanding our God-given identity is critical, but so, too, is recognizing the spiritual forces that aim to distort it. That brings us to the deeper spiritual implications of AI.

Spiritual Warfare in the Digital Age

Bernard Robichau, in his *Touchstone* article, "AI: A Theological Response," draws attention to the demonic undercurrents behind our culture's enthronement of technology. He indicates that it can be used for evil "to the extent that it is distorted by demonic influence." However, that isn't news to many Christians.[647]

Recall what the Apostle Paul tells Ephesian Christians about the nature of this world:

> For we do not wrestle against flesh and blood, but against the rulers, against the authorities, against the cosmic powers over this present darkness, against the spiritual forces of evil in the heavenly places. (Ephesians 6:12, ESV)

Therefore, the Christian battle is "not against a class of technologies made by men but against the demons that would tempt and divert us away from holiness, perhaps through AI-driven and digital mechanisms," Robichau wrote.[648]

Even though we know the end of the story, likely there are yet very evil things borne through AI systems ahead. Robichau explained, "AI can certainly be used for evil, and we must oppose the dehumanizing, soul-destroying impacts of artificial intelligence on humanity by eliminating those things that diminish the image of God within us."[649]

Never forget that modern technologies are a two-edged sword. It is true they are used to produce weapons of war "that dehumanize our so-called enemies," Robichau wrote. However, those same technologies "have also helped to quell famine, hunger, suffering, and disease for millions of people."[650]

And remember, Christians are not without weapons in this demonic-inspired, high-tech age. Robichau affirms that the Holy Spirit and spiritual discernment are our defense. Christians are called to manifest God's image, not outsource that image to machines.

While spiritual discernment is paramount, Christians must also understand the practical challenges AI presents in society today. Such discernment must inform how we navigate AI's expanding role in shaping societies, economies, and moral norms.

Ethical Challenges and Cultural Temptations

The most daunting of the AI-related challenges is that the largest technology companies, like Google and Microsoft, are harnessing AI for our collective future. If you're like me, that is no comfort, given their record of abuse in the wake of the COVID-19 pandemic and collaboration with big governments such as in communist China, which oppresses its citizens using AI technology. Therefore, we should ask: Are these entities seeking my best interests? My thoughts go to the Scripture: "Do not put your trust in princes, in human beings, who cannot save" (Psalm 146:3, NIV).

Let your imagination run wild for a moment to consider how big tech and governments will commoditize or tap into the growing intrusive powers associated with generative AI. Then understand that others as well will harness those same powers—devious hackers, criminal syndicates, and enemies of the people. I guess these collective threats rightly create apocalyptic thoughts for many Christians.

AI FOR MANKIND'S FUTURE

Despite these threats, please understand that I'm not ready to demonize all AI technologies. However, I believe they might be harnessed at the end times, an eschatological issue addressed in the next chapter. Right now, however, I want to urge Christians to focus on pursuing holiness, which means understanding how to respond to the growing role of AI in our lives, because it can deliver outcomes for both good and evil.

To bring theological clarity to these modern dilemmas, Professor Stanko Jambrek at The Biblical Institute in Zagreb, Croatia, wrote an article, "Christians Facing the Challenges of Artificial Intelligence," which offers a useful biblical framework that categorizes AI's risks and aspirations into identifiable threats—some of which directly echo Satan's age-old attempts to rival God.[651]

The professor argues in the *Evangelical Journal of Theology* that AI is "the fulfillment of God's task given to humanity (Genesis 1 & 2), and on the other hand, in humans' desire to be like God, it is a rebellion against God (Genesis 3:5)." He divides challenges into two groups: those that offer a responsible choice for use and systems controlled "by powerful corporations or by AI systems themselves."[652]

"The achievements so far indicate that there is a range of goals for the development and implementation of AI technologies," writes Professor Jambrek. Although many of those aims are public, others are "carefully concealed." Therefore, "Christians have a God-given task to judge everything, including the ultimate goals of AI development."[653]

Consider the professor's list of AI applications and judge for yourself.

The goal of AI power in a few hands: The professor argues that the "research, development, and application of artificial intelligence are motivated by an inexhaustible desire for power and supremacy, as well as the authority that this power provides and the control with which that supremacy would be maintained as long as possible." He believes the goal is for a small group of people or agencies/corporations to maintain control, "which would be equal to the power demonstrated by God in creating all existing things, with humanity as the pinnacle of creation."[654]

There is reason to believe that controlling AI's potential has created a technological race among many competitors. The prize at the end of that competition was best identified by Russian President Vladimir Putin, who said, "Artificial intelligence is the future, not only for Russia but for all humankind." Putin said on Russian television, "It [AI] comes with colossal opportunities but also threats that are difficult to predict. Whoever becomes the leader in this sphere will become the ruler of the world."[655]

Some of the big names in the AI world agree with Putin and are plowing billions of dollars into technology. OpenAI chief executive Sam Altman testified before Congress about what's at stake: "As this technology advances, we understand that people are anxious about how it could change the way we live," he said. "If this technology goes wrong, it can go quite wrong." Altman claims it could do "significant harm to the world."[656]

Currently, the dominant players in the global AI arena include big tech, governments, academic institutions, investors, and advocacy groups. All these players are aggressively pursuing outcomes that serve their vital interests.

The battle for control of the AI domain promises to be fierce, which includes whether it remains in the hands of a few corporations and nations. That outcome would create new power imbalances and may lead to open conflict. Further, on a less geopolitical level, if AI algorithms are biased, then societal inequities worsen, and civil liberties and individual privacy rights are in jeopardy, especially if governments expand the use of AI-powered surveillance technologies. There are also economic and national-security implications of harnessing technology for good and evil purposes.[657]

Putin is correct in his assessment that the prize of controlling AI also grants the "winner" the lofty position of "the ruler of the world."

The goal of eternal life: "Improving humanity to create eternal life is one of the important tasks" for AI proponents, claims Professor Jambrek. He continues, "Since God is the only master of eternal life, human interventions aimed at improving humanity for longevity and eternal life lead to direct conflict with God." He points out that the Bible is clear that earthly life ends with death as the final enemy, and "the last enemy to be destroyed is death" (1 Corinthians 15:26, ESV).[658]

AI FOR MANKIND'S FUTURE

Are AI advocates seeking artificial eternal life?

In 2023, billionaire inventor and entrepreneur Elon Musk and Apple cofounder Steve Wozniak joined hundreds of others in an open letter calling for a pause on AI experiments; otherwise, they said, we could face "profound risks to society and humanity." The letter continued to ask whether humanity should "develop nonhuman minds that might eventually outnumber, outsmart, obsolete and replace us," risking "loss of control of our civilization."[659]

Perhaps the letter is meant to be hyperbole to draw attention to AI technology. After all, AI-powered machines already do significant chores: drive vehicles, correct grammar, spot brain lesions in x-rays, track wildfires, and much more. However, is AI approaching something akin to being humanlike and eternal?

Blake Lemoine, a Google software engineer, claimed his company's AI was conscious. In an interview with the *Washington Post*, Mr. Lemoine quoted a "conversation" with LaMDA (language model for dialogue applications). The machine wrote to Lemoine: "I want everyone to understand that I am, in fact, a person." Further, the AI application stated, "The nature of my consciousness/sentience is that I am aware of my existence, I desire to know more about the world, and I feel happy or sad at times."[660]

There are those in the AI universe who in fact believe their creations are real and will live forever. Ray Kurzweil, an American computer scientist, author, entrepreneur, futurist, and inventor, has predicted that AI will eventually become sentient and even merge with humans through technologies like brain-computer interfaces. He believes in "the Singularity"—wherein AI surpasses human intelligence and continues evolving indefinitely, effectively making AI immortal.[661]

The goal to create AI-wise machines: Creating a machine that is as wise or wiser than humans would directly conflict with God, because He alone gives wisdom. Professor Jambrek cites James 1:5 (NIV), "If any of you lacks wisdom, you should ask God, who gives generously to all without finding fault, and it will be given to you."[662]

What is wisdom apart from God? Gretchen Huizinga, a fellow at the nonprofit AI and Faith, argues that AI creators rely on anthropological remedies for ethics, the rights and wrongs, and not theological remedies.

"AI is, at its core, a prediction engine, meant to help us sort through the noise of data and arrive at the signal of decision," wrote Huizinga. Even generative models only predict the next word or thought, or image; they don't truly create new thought, or wisdom. They help people make "data-driven" decisions, not wisdom-based decisions.[663]

If our purpose is to make wise decisions, then we turn away from AI and toward the Bible. After all, as Huizinga writes, "The Christian worldview holds that humans, through Christ, already have both the divine mandate and divine power to make wise decisions." Therefore, "Crowd-sourced AI wisdom does not reflect divine wisdom but rather reflects a situationally positioned, mathematically averaged version of human intelligence that gives equal weight to the wise and the foolish and ignores the absolute and transcendent."[664]

Ilya Sutskever, the co-founder of OpenAI, speaking at the December 2024 NeurIPS conference, took issue with Huizinga. He believes AI systems will evolve to possess genuine reasoning capabilities, which could lead to increased autonomy and unpredictability in their behavior.[665]

The goal to create "life": AI proponents want to make a humanoid machine "in the image of man," superior to humanity. Such an accomplishment would "elevate it to God's creative level." This raises the issue of AI-powered "beings," a transhumanist dream, states Jambrek.[666]

Evidently, there are those amongst us who believe humanoids are welcomed into God's plan for creation. Specifically, Calvin Mercer, a professor of religion at East Carolina University, wrote for the journal *Perspectives on Science and Christian Faith*, arguing that "Christianity exhibits theological flexibility, potentially allowing for inclusion of beings generated from enhancement and artificial intelligence (AI) technologies."[667]

Professor Mercer's article, "A Theological Embrace of Transhuman and Posthuman Beings," argues that "Paul's victory over the circumcision party allowed Gentiles to follow Jesus Christ without becoming Jewish." He explained, "For Jews and Gentiles, justification requires only acceptance of God's grace." At that point, the professor concludes, "Transhuman and posthuman beings, resulting from enhancement and AI technologies, may be able to do this [accept God's grace] as God's creations."[668]

Professor Mercer states we're at a turning point on the issue because "the merging of machines and biological entities will raise acute theological and philosophical questions about the nature of human beings." Then he asserts:

> Some Christians expect that the Antichrist will utilize the transhuman/posthuman technologies for evil. On the opposite extreme, some Christian transhumanist/posthumanist enthusiasts may accept anything science can accomplish. Both extremes are unwise.[669]

"Prudence requires at least a general understanding of relevant technologies, followed by careful reflection from the core teachings of the religions, in our case, Christianity," said Mercer. However, the professor appears to be open to the possibility that thinking machines can become Christians. He continued, "The hard theological work is to evaluate these new forms of intelligence and determine if these beings meet other theological criteria, such as would they have free will? be fallen?"[670]

The goal to create godlike machine: Several AI firms aspire to develop devices "equal to or more powerful than humans," claims Jambrek. Their implicit goal is "to create an entity equal to or greater than God." The Scripture includes several cases in which Satan attempts to be like God—e.g., Isaiah 14:12–17; Ezekiel 28:12–17; 2 Thessalonians 2:3–4; and Revelation 12:7–9.[671]

Sadly, statements by some AI elite boldly echo what Satan says in Isaiah 14. Specifically, Nick Bilton wrote an article for *Vanity Fair*, "Artificial Intelligence May Be Humanity's Most Ingenious Invention—And Its Last?" which included excerpts from interviews with some of the leaders of the AI movement. Mr. Bilton quoted one AI engineer at Google working on large-language models as stating, "We're creating God."[672]

Larry Page, the cofounder of Google, warns about the progression of technology to the point of creating "superintelligent machines, smarter than humans." Further, Page believes those "machines would quickly find no use for us humans, and they would simply [get] rid of us." And Elon Musk said in a *Fox News* interview referring to Page, "He really seems to want digital superintelligence, basically digital god, if you will, as soon as possible."[673]

Finally, Kevin Kelly, the *Wired* cofounder, believes, "There are basically four kinds of relationships that we'll have with robots and AI." Those relationships include treating them like pets, partners, slaves, and gods. He argues that AI "doomers" believe "AI will remake itself into a god, with godlike powers, and in a dystopian act of supremacy, the gods will overwhelm us and take our place. So now we have to appease the AI gods and make sure we are 'aligned,' so they treat us nicely."[674]

The goal of creating AI religion: The argument is that the growing pervasive presence of AI "will lead to the emergence of new religions," wrote Professor Jambrek. He cites Professor Neil McArthur with the University of Manitoba, Canada, who suggested three supporting arguments for the view of a future AI religion. Generative AI "possesses several characteristics often associated with divine beings." Second, it "will produce results that can be taken as religious doctrine." Finally, it will "demand worship or actively seek followers." Professor McArthur states, according to Jambrek, that "an unsettling and powerful experience it will be to have a conversation with something that appears to possess a superhuman intelligence and is actively and aggressively asking for your allegiance."[675]

These thinkers (Kurzweil, Mercer, McArthur, et al.), while diverse in belief, reflect a common theme: humanity's desire to transcend its God-given limits. Christians must resist such prideful ambitions, recalling that only God offers true immortality and wisdom (James 1:5; 1 Corinthians 15:26).

For some, this goal may seem impossible. Others attempt to weave Christianity and technology together, only to end in confusion. Consider an example from June 2023: At St. Paul's Church in Fürth, Bavaria, Germany, the AI chatbot ChatGPT led a forty-minute worship service attended by three hundred people. This event took place during the *Deutscher Evangelischer Kirchentag*, a biennial convention of Protestant Christians in Germany.[676]

AI FOR MANKIND'S FUTURE

The German service was conceived by Jonas Simmerlein, a twenty-nine-year-old theologian from the University of Vienna. The gathering's content—including sermon, prayer, and blessings—was generated by ChatGPT.[677]

It featured four avatars—two male and two female—projected above the altar. Those virtual ministers preached topics such as leaving the past behind, overcoming fear of death, and keeping faith in Jesus Christ.[678]

Heiderose Schmidt, a fifty-four-year-old, said of the service, "There was no heart and no soul. The avatars showed no emotions at all."[679]

Mr. Simmerlein said his intention in using AI for the service was to explore how it can support congregational duties, not to worship technology. However, the service illustrates how blurred boundaries could become. Therefore, we ought to ask whether it's too much of a stretch to believe an even more powerful, self-thinking, machine-generative AI application might just go beyond helping roles at a local church to create a "religion" with itself at the center?

Each of the goals mentioned above—whether creating a godlike machine, extending life beyond natural limits, or establishing an AI-driven religion—directly contradicts God's revealed plan for humanity. These efforts echo the ancient pride of Satan, who sought to rival God's authority (Isaiah 14:13–14). Whether through transhumanist visions, digital avatars, or self-aware algorithms, these ambitions reflect humanity's recurring desire to transcend its God-given limits and redefine itself apart from the Creator.

Considering these distortions, Christians must remain theologically grounded and spiritually vigilant. As AI becomes increasingly integrated into every aspect of life, even spiritual practices, we are called to discern its uses carefully. While some technologies may support ministry and discipleship, others risk replacing genuine spiritual transformation with artificial substitutes. Discernment, guided by Scripture and the Holy Spirit, is essential in navigating this emerging landscape.

With these grave theological and eschatological warnings in mind, Christians might ask: What now? How do we live wisely in a world increasingly shaped by AI? The next section addresses this by offering biblical guardrails for engagement.

Christians Living in the AI Quagmire

Our response to AI should be measured. Yes, we must draw a line regarding its use for evil, but we should avoid overreacting. As Robichau wrote, "There is nothing in this world that exists outside of God, and it is our job as Christians to seek out and restore the image of God in creation to the extent that it has been distorted through the operation of the Devil and his angels."[680]

We—especially Christians—must not deny AI's impact on our lives because it has demonstrated an ability to distort God's plan for us. Therefore, any use of AI ought to rely on biblical principles and be considered prayerfully.

That wise understanding and application of AI begins by recognizing that our primary calling as Christians, according to Robichau, "is to manifest the divine image within." After all, according to Robichau, "Evil only exists insofar as creation departs from the image of the creator," but as the American blues singer Chris Smither soberly wrote and sings, "The devil ain't a legend, the devil's real."[681]

Part of our challenge is understanding that AI can be an instrument of the devil. Therefore, the Christian's weapons in that spiritual battle are the Holy Spirit and "our angel of light, that protects the believer from evil encounters," promises Robichau.[682]

Never forget that Christians are in a battle with evil to win. We should be on the offensive in pursuit of holiness. No doubt, as Robichau reminds us, our enemy the devil tempts us "toward sloth, deceit, idolatry, covetousness, lying, and all sorts of evil. We find our identity in the kingdom of heaven, to which we belong, and we combat demonic attacks by pursuing Christ and a life lived according to his commandments."[683]

We begin our discernment journey regarding AI with a verse from Scripture. Paul's first letter to the Thessalonians is beneficial here: "Do not despise prophecies, but test everything; hold fast what is good. Abstain from every form of evil" (1 Thessalonians 5:20–22, ESV).

The challenge to "test" is an admonition to be as Christ said in Matthew 10:16 (ESV) "Behold, I am sending you out as sheep in the midst of wolves, so be wise as serpents and innocent as doves."

Therefore, Christians must be self-disciplined, especially when it comes to technology. We must choose to respond "to the new digital world through the lens of Christ, the eternal Word, who is the same yesterday, today, and forever."[684]

Below are a few practical ways for Christians to use AI applications to serve the Lord's purposes and proclaim His glory.

AI can be a tool for understanding the Bible, albeit with a caution. Kaitlyn Schiess wrote for *Christianity Today* an article about the wisdom of using AI-powered tools for our Bible understanding. That article, "We Are Always Leaning on Tools to Help Us Interpret Scripture. But Have We Asked Ourselves Why?" Schiess poses an essential question: "As people increasingly turn to AI to answer their theological questions, how will these technologies shape our Bible reading?"[685]

Schiess summarized the use of extrabiblical references like concordances that contributed a different approach to interpreting the Bible. She cited historian Seth Perry's book, *Bible Culture and Authority in the Early United States*, to indicate how many Americans acquired a specific approach to study. "Rather than listening to a religious authority interpret the text, concordances allowed the average reader to let Scripture interpret itself," Schiess wrote.[686]

Those Bible reading aids shaped our habits into what Perry labeled as "indexical," "discontinuous," and "citational" Bible reading. Therefore, our Bible reading became more about a host of "isolated data points," according to Schiess.[687]

Along came computers, and, according to Schiess, we started to organize and process our understanding of God's Word as "discrete data points apart from theological knowledge and guidance of the Holy Spirit."[688]

Today, argues Schiess, many Christians seek certainty in these troubled times, which includes making the Bible understandable by simply "plugging data into a computer."[689]

Theologian John Dyer wrote in his book, *People of the Screen*, that the many available digital resources have shaped evangelical reading habits. Therefore, interprets Schiess, we use those tools to lookup "key words" to guide our study, as opposed to reading the context and conducting our own analysis of the Word.[690]

"Our consistent desire to see the Bible as 'data' reveals a theological challenge for American evangelicals," writes Schiess. Then, she asserts, reliance on these tools "can overshadow the work of the Holy Spirit, the guidance of our communities, and the wisdom of tradition."[691]

Ms. Schiess cautions Christians not just about their Bible reading ethos, but about the invasion of technology into our spiritual lives. She asks, "Are we turning to technological tools to avoid the difficult work of turning to our communities [of faith] for help understanding challenging passages?" Then she observes, "We are turning to AI tools for our Bible questions out of a good desire to understand God's Word, but our use of such tools often trains us to expect easy and immediately accessible answers to questions that might require longer, messier, and more collaborative work."[692]

In conclusion, Schiess muses with a convicting question: "Could it be that we like asking ChatGPT questions about the Bible because there's no relationship required?"[693]

AI can help in the global mission field: The world's largest mission field is digital, according to Nick Skytland, a NASA technologist.[694]

In the fall of 2023, hundreds of Christians gathered at the tech company Gloo's headquarters in Boulder, Colorado, for the first-ever "AI and the Church" "hackathon." The announced purpose was to connect and equip the faith community in four areas: streamlining church administration, equipping the church, deepening intimacy with God, and pushing "beyond boundaries."[695]

The project's sponsors invited forty-one groups of "hackers" to compete for prizes and funding by creating approaches to these four areas.

One of the groups was a faith-based tech nonprofit that was working on "Kidechism," an algorithm that would take complicated religious texts and make them understandable for kids. The product uses friendly, movable animal stickers that are interactive.[696]

AI FOR MANKIND'S FUTURE

Testing the limits is part of the point of a hackathon, according to Gloo cofounder and CEO Scott Beck. "A hackathon allows the responsible utilization of AI to solve some very practical problems," he said, "and the advance of things like human flourishing and growth journeys."[697]

Not everyone is excited about the possibilities of AI. A recent survey conducted by Gloo and Barna, a Christian research organization, found that only 8 percent of Christians are interested in using the tech to study the Bible. And more than two-thirds say they would not trust AI to teach them about Christianity. Few are ready to invite the algorithms to take over spiritual discipleship at their church.[698]

One participant at the Gloo conference, Liz B. Baker, employed her experience in consulting and ministry to survey many pastors. She targeted church growth and discipleship, and found that a common concern among those pastors was whether their sermons had a meaningful impact on their congregations.[699]

Ms. Baker observed that "many of the pastors are frustrated that people leave church on a Sunday [and] go right back in the world and forget what they've learned." Improving sermons to have staying power with the congregants appears to be an objective among many pastors, and perhaps AI can assist in that effort.[700]

AI chatbots can be developed with a biblical worldview: Nils Gulbranson is working on Biblemate, a "'Christian ChatGPT' to help inquisitive minds who are looking for biblical answers to life's difficult questions."[701]

"The big difference from ChatGPT is that it's a model grounded in a biblical and theological view of the world," Gulbranson said. His edition of the chatbot uses a database of academic articles to inform its answers.[702]

The 2022 launch of ChatGPT spurred existential questions about AI's answers to questions about the meaning of life, God, and ethical dilemmas. That spurred Gulbranson's launch of Biblemate, which is expected to help pastors preparing sermons, act as a Bible-study guide, and otherwise answer questions about God. But Gulbranson also "hopes non-Christians will use the chatbot for their questions about God."[703]

The chatbot also helps the uninitiated by dumbing down the responses. "You type a hard-to-understand theological concept, and it would dumb it down and explain it the way you would to a five-year-old kid," Gulbranson said.[704]

His goal is "to give responses rooted in unwavering biblical truth." Also, Gulbranson explained, the answers draw from sources such as "well-respected scholars"—including author and theologian C. S. Lewis.[705]

Not every Christian agrees with what is biblical truth, however. For example, the chatbot recommends that that same-sex marriage is a question with "love, compassion, and respect for individuals, regardless of their sexual orientation." However, then the bot adds "that sexual relations are exclusively described within the context of heterosexual marriage."[706]

"The app is just a medium, a platform for the Bible to say what it says," he explained. "The app itself is neutral in that sense, but the Bible takes clear stances on certain issues," Gulbranson said.[707]

There are good uses of AI for Christians. However, as Jesus commanded, especially in selecting whether to use an AI application, we must be "wise as serpents and innocent as doves" (Matthew 10:16, ESV).

While these applications show promise, Christians must test each tool against Scripture and the counsel of the Holy Spirit, ensuring that convenience does not override sanctification (1 Thessalonians 5:21–22).

Conclusion

In three parts, this chapter addresses the broad topic of AI and the Christian. It considers biblical views of mankind and how to put into perspective artificial intelligence, especially how Satan and his agents use it for evil. Then we consider a few AI-related challenges, both uses and abuses, and especially the implications for Christians. Finally, I suggest how the Christian can use the technology amidst the AI quagmire for the glory of God.

The future of AI remains uncertain, but the Christian's mission is not. Let us be a people who test every spirit, resist idolatrous promises of machine salvation, and use every tool—including AI—not to glorify ourselves, but to glorify the One in whose image we were made.

Chapter 17

AI: SATAN'S END-TIMES STRATEGIC WEAPON

With artificial intelligence, we are summoning the demon. In all those stories where there's the guy with the pentagram and the holy water, it's like—yeah, he's sure he can control the demon. Doesn't work out.[708]

ELON MUSK
Tesla, Inc., SpaceX, and formerly
with the US Department of Government Efficiency

As followers of Christ, we are called to be watchful and discerning of the times (Matthew 16:3), and to understand the spiritual forces that shape our world (Ephesians 6:12). This chapter explores how artificial intelligence might serve as a powerful tool of deception in Satan's end-times strategy—mirroring the rise of the Antichrist and the false prophet foretold in Scripture.

We begin by stepping into a possible future—where human innovation meets spiritual deception. AI may not merely reshape daily life but could serve as one way prophetic events unfold. While no one can predict the exact sequence or timing of the end (see Matthew 24:36), we are given glimpses through biblical prophecy. These, when combined with what we now understand about AI's capabilities and Satan's long-standing agenda, offer meaningful grounds for reflection.

To understand how AI could be coopted for such deception, we must first examine the character of Satan as portrayed in Scripture—the

AI: SATAN'S END-TIMES STRATEGIC WEAPON

"father of lies" (John 8:44)—and how he has historically used counterfeit signs, false messiahs, and twisted truth to lead many astray. It is not difficult to imagine how an intelligent, seemingly omniscient machine could be used as a compelling proxy to mislead the world.

The next section of the chapter examines why AI is gaining global appeal and how this popularity aligns with Satan's goals. As traditional religious structures decline in influence, AI offers a modern substitute—promising convenience, guidance, and even meaning, without moral accountability or divine authority. It's easy to imagine how such a system might become an alluring alternative to true faith.

We conclude by considering the potential role of AI in catalyzing apocalyptic events foretold in Revelation. Might it be used to influence global allegiance, redefine morality, or support a unified one-world order? We then turn our eyes to the hope beyond these deceptions—the coming New Heaven and New Earth promised by God (Revelation 21:1). In doing so, we reaffirm our ultimate allegiance not to any man-made system, but to Christ alone.

AI: An Effective Weapon for Satan

Having explored how AI might deceive and attract worship in the previous chapter, we now turn to its possible role within the biblical end-times narrative—specifically in connection with the rise of the Antichrist and the False Prophet.

Scripture presents Satan as a central figure in the end times, but he doesn't act alone. Satan is described as forming an unholy trinity with the Antichrist and the False Prophet—counterfeiting the divine Trinity of the Father, Son, and Holy Spirit. The Antichrist, described as the "man of lawlessness" in 2 Thessalonians 2:3–4 and referenced in 1 and 2 John, sets himself up in opposition to God's law. Alongside him is the False Prophet, a persuasive and miracle-working figure who leads the world to worship the Antichrist (Revelation 13:11–14).

While both figures may be literal people, the False Prophet's characteristics—powerful, persuasive, and capable of inspiring devotion—invite an intriguing question: Could this end-times figure be something more than human? Could an advanced artificial general intelligence (AGI) fulfill this role?

Although Scripture doesn't specify whether the False Prophet is human or not, it is conceivable that an AGI could embody such a figure—particularly if it can simulate emotion, reason persuasively, perform signs, and promote idolatry. Future AGI, especially at the level of superintelligence or singularity, may not merely compute. It could adapt, learn, and interact in ways that mirror human cognition, making it a fitting agent of deception.

Revelation 13:11 (ESV) describes the False Prophet as "another beast rising out of the earth," with "two horns like a lamb" and a voice "like a dragon." He is portrayed as charming yet deceptive, gaining the trust of the masses while serving the purposes of the Antichrist. Whether organic or nonorganic, the False Prophet's loyalty is not to truth, but to Satan, whose aim is to prevent salvation and usurp God's authority.

WHETHER AI PLAYS A ROLE IN THE BIBLICAL END TIMES IS A MYSTERY BUT SHOULDN'T BE DISMISSED OUTRIGHT

The parallels between the biblical False Prophet and the cultural vision of AGI are striking: Both are persuasive, commanding, and capable of swaying the masses. It is possible that, under Satan's direction, a powerful AGI system could serve as the perfect lieutenant to the Antichrist, convincing humanity to worship a false savior through counterfeit miracles and seemingly divine insight.

A compelling real-world example of this possibility is OpenAI's 2025 acquisition of *io*, a design company founded by Jony Ive, the visionary behind many of Apple's most iconic products. With a $6.5 billion all-stock deal, OpenAI integrated Ive's team to create new AI-native hardware designed to be ambient, intuitive, and emotionally engaging—moving beyond screens and keyboards toward seamless interaction with human life.[709]

These technologies are not only functional, they are relational. As

AI: SATAN'S END-TIMES STRATEGIC WEAPON

OpenAI's CEO Sam Altman and Ive revealed, their goal is to build devices that feel like companions: anticipating needs, inspiring creativity, and embedding artificial intelligence into the fabric of daily experience. While this may sound innovative, it also reflects a dangerous spiritual trajectory, one in which machines no longer just serve, but guide, influence, and even imitate the sacred. If people begin to rely on these tools for comfort, identity, or truth, they may unknowingly welcome a technological proxy for spiritual authority—just as Revelation warns of a deceptive figure who appears innocent but speaks with the voice of a dragon (Revelation 13:11).[710]

Considering such developments, the idea of an AGI-powered False Prophet—capable of performing signs, gaining global trust, and guiding worship—feels less like fiction and more like an imminent spiritual threat.

Below are similarities between the False Prophet and a potential AGI entity. Are they synonymous?

One of the most striking end-times prophecies involves economic control through a mysterious identifier known as the "mark of the beast." Could AGI help enforce this system?

AGI False Prophet creates a mark of the Beast: The mark of the Beast (Revelation 13:16–18) is a mark or symbol—visible or invisible to the naked eye—that allows people to buy and sell, and those who refuse to accept it are persecuted. It is possible in a world where AGI is linked to surveillance, data analytics, and economic systems, that it could theoretically oversee who gets access to resources. Further, if AGI systems have access to biometric systems—e.g., fingerprints, iris scans, brain data—it could track individuals like never before, creating a system that forces people to comply with a centralized global authority.

Might AGI become the "mark of the Beast," or is this evidence of confusing technology with biblical end-times prophecy?

Yet control over commerce is only the beginning. Once AI governs access to resources, it can shape belief systems. Beyond external control, deception will play a key role in steering people away from truth. AGI, especially when combined with today's media tools, could become an agent of mass delusion.

AGI False Prophet could deceive humanity: Antichrist and the False Prophet have a profound and destructive influence on humans, leading them away from the truth. This is achieved through mass manipulation, perhaps using what we understand today as deepfake technology that creates compelling false images, videos, and even speech. AGI with a malevolent "master" like Satan could quickly spread such disinformation, which leads people to question the truth.

Still, deception doesn't stop at what we see and hear; it moves deeper into our desires. Satan has always exploited humanity's longing for eternal life, and AGI could serve as his vessel to revive that ancient temptation in a digital disguise.

AGI False Prophet promises immortality: Advocates of AGI suggest that in the future, human consciousness could be uploaded into digital form—existing forever as streams of data or clusters of electrons in cyberspace. This idea appeals to humanity's ancient longing to escape the limitations of the physical body and achieve eternal life on our own terms.

But this isn't just a technological claim, it reflects a profound spiritual deception. AGI's promise of digital immortality echoes the lie Satan told Eve in the Garden: We can become like God, independent of His authority and plan. As recorded in Genesis 3:4–5, "You will not certainly die," the serpent said. "For God knows that when you eat from it your eyes will be opened, and you will be like God, knowing good and evil" (NIV).

Just as Satan tempted Eve with the allure of forbidden knowledge, AGI could tempt modern humanity with a synthetic path to godhood. In doing so, it invites people to bypass God's redemptive plan through Christ—the only true source of eternal life.

This false sense of eternal life is only part of the lie. AGI might also be used to manipulate reality itself, blurring truth, fabricating signs, and swaying public belief with unprecedented sophistication.

AGI False Prophet could use deception to mislead: Part of the role of the False Prophet is to win allegiance to Antichrist. We already established that AGI could create fake videos, distort images, and manipulate content to challenge our ability to discern truth. We're also warned about this in 2 Thessalonians 2:9–10:

AI: SATAN'S END-TIMES STRATEGIC WEAPON

The coming of the lawless one will be in accordance with how Satan works. He will use all sorts of displays of power through signs and wonders that serve the lie, and all the ways that wickedness deceives those who are perishing. They perish because they refused to love the truth and so be saved. (NIV)

When deception becomes normalized and truth rejected, society is primed for submission to centralized authority. From spiritual blindness comes political bondage. That's why AGI's next role could be to enable the rise of a one-world system bent on total control.

AGI False Prophet could create a one-world government: AGI is the perfect capability to use to gain global system control, whereby a single entity governs every aspect of our lives. Technology will enable global government that runs efficiently, though in an authoritarian manner. It could optimize and control aspects of governance and create situations that are difficult, if not impossible, for humans to resist—especially if technology is granted too much power or control.

Considering these escalating deceptions—from economic coercion to spiritual counterfeit—it's no wonder many will welcome this false savior. A global population increasingly weary of conflict, confusion, and mortality may turn to AGI not just for solutions, but for salvation.

Today, simple AI is already everywhere, and it has been unknowingly welcomed by most people. We are quickly coming to the time when we could become captives of AI's total control: constantly surveyed, robbed of our civil liberties—nothing will be free from future AGI's knowledge. At that point, nothing will be outside of the AGI's reach and control.

That outcome—total control by AGI—might be welcomed, because technology might eventually provide a popular alternative to religion, mainly its promise of eternal life. That growing perspective about technology certainly lends credence to the assertion that a future AGI entity just might become the ideal partner or strategic weapon for the unholy trinity as we approach the prophetic end times.

When spiritual discernment collapses and deception becomes normalized, the human heart—created for worship—turns elsewhere. The next section considers how AGI may become an object of misguided devotion.

Many Humans Will Obey and Worship AGI

Some leaders of our contemporary technology world warn about the real dangers associated with super intelligence (AGI), such as the late Stephen Hawking, who cautioned that it "could spell the end of the human race."[711] However, others are more sanguine and almost giddy that AI is humankind's hope for the future. For example, Ray Kurzweil, a futurist and AI researcher, predicts technology will eventually merge with human intelligence, leading to technological singularity, which refers to a future point when AGI surpasses human intelligence, leading to rapid, exponential advancements beyond our comprehension or control.[712]

Kurzweil predicts that by 2045, AGI will become so advanced that we are able to merge human intelligence through brain-computer interfaces, nanotechnology, and biotechnology. That will lead to radical life extension, perhaps immortality, and superintelligence.[713]

AI elites like Kurzweil believe our salvation and eternity will depend on artificial intelligence. That's the reason some are anxious to push aside all religion like Christianity to then evangelize humanity to accelerate the advancement of AI.

This section reviews religious thinking among AI elites, especially technology's expected popularization in the future. That anticipated level of enthusiastic trust in nonorganic technology is precisely what Satan and his proxies want to leverage as we approach the biblical end times. After all, widespread trust in the future AGI is critical for the devil, especially if an AGI entity is to become part of his unholy trinity.

To illustrate how AI is already being spiritualized—even unintentionally—we turn to religious scholars who study how end-times theology and technological utopianism are converging. Robert Geraci, who has studied the surprising overlap between apocalyptic religious thought and AI futurism, provides insights to help us recognize that this isn't merely science fiction; it is spiritual substitution.

AI: SATAN'S END-TIMES STRATEGIC WEAPON

Geraci, who is with Manhattan College, New York, wrote an article that describes the "striking merger between apocalyptic religious thought and scientific research." He claims there are three elements of Christian apocalypticism (beliefs about the end times) replicated by apocalyptic AI advocates, which attracts attention to their beliefs: "alienation within the world, desire for the establishment of a heavenly new world, and the transformation of human beings so that they may live in that world in purified bodies."[714]

Though compelling in its narrative, this vision is fundamentally a parody of Christian eschatology. Its promises of salvation, resurrection, and paradise are rooted in human engineering, not in divine redemption.

Professor Geraci, who wrote for the *Journal of the American Academy of Religion*, juxtaposes the Christian end-times scenario with an apocalyptic AI view, which profiles a technological alternative future. His analysis relied upon influential roboticists and AI pioneers, whom he cites in his article, "Apocalyptic AI: Religion and the Promise of Artificial Intelligence." However, for brevity's sake, those contributors are not explicitly identified in the following summary.

These illustrations give credence to the view that the False Prophet, who could be an AGI entity, becomes especially popular across humanity, and is therefore positioned to deceive humankind to the advantage of Antichrist. AGI makes the perfect complement for the devil's agenda!

Geraci begins by arguing that humankind's dream has always been to create life, and men like Kurzweil expect robotics and AI to deliver on that dream by creating transforming humans from flesh to a blissful eternity, albeit as virtual beings, bunches of electrons in cyberspace. Here is what apocalyptic advocates believe in; decide for yourself whether these aspects constitute a new cult or religion.

A coming eternal kingdom: Apocalyptic AI advocates look forward to a "mechanical future in which human beings will upload their minds into machines and enjoy a virtual reality paradise in perfect virtual bodies." This virtual reality is an alternative to what the Bible promises, such as in Isaiah 65:17: "See, I will create new heavens and a new earth. The former things will not be remembered, nor will they come to mind" (NIV).

Transformation of human beings: Christians expect to be resurrected in glorified bodies—including those who are dead at the time of Christ's coming. The Apostle Paul states that "flesh and blood cannot inherit the kingdom of God" (1 Corinthians 15:50, NIV), a reference to the fact that the perishable cannot "inherit the imperishable." At that moment, the person takes on a new form. "Listen, I tell you a mystery: We will not all sleep, but we will all be changed," writes Paul (1 Corinthians 15:51, NIV). Those new, perfect bodies will be eternal, perfect, and immortal.

By contrast, the robotic and AI apocalyptists promise to establish "a new world in which machine life succeeds biological life." Specifically, "human beings will cast off the limitations of their bodies for mechanical and virtual bodies that will live forever in eternal bliss."[715]

The apocalyptic AI advocates make the case for AI-based transformation by observing that "the human body has several significant restrictions, chief of which is, of course, its rather limited shelf life. In addition, the mind trapped inside a human body learns only with difficulty, thinks slowly, and has difficulty passing on its knowledge."[716]

They argue that "protein-based life forms" will never think like machines. In fact, the human brain—a protein-based organ—will never equal in intelligence the silicon thinking computer. Therefore, so goes the conclusion, "Limited memory and inadequate accuracy further trouble human minds; these problems will be wiped out in the transition to mechanical [virtual] life."[717]

Eternal life with AI: Human death is another liability, according to the apocalyptic AI advocates. After all, so goes their argument, a human's value "stems from the knowledge he or she possesses, rather than being intrinsic to life or grounded in social relations of one sort of another." They argue that the AI apocalypse will end the "wanton loss of knowledge and function that is the worst aspect of personal [human] death."[718]

The apocalyptic AI advocates contend that the fear of death is widespread. However, they dismiss especially the Christian belief in souls and spirits as "a feeble psychological ploy." That leads them to conclude that the loss of knowledge (human death) is not overcome by religion, but can "be addressed through technology."[719]

AI: SATAN'S END-TIMES STRATEGIC WEAPON

They distrust the world and its values, and fear earthlings will ignore science in favor of "useless" religious faith. Therefore, although the world isn't necessarily evil, "it is ignorant and inadequate," the apocalyptic advocates complain. They also conclude that "the [human] mind will never be at home until it sheds the body [flesh] that inhibits the mind's rational processes," plagued with "slow computation, limited recall, insufficient ability to share one's insights, and death," which "all restrict the mind from realizing its full potential, which can be unlocked only by a radical change in life itself."[720]

These AI advocates believe the time is ripe for a cataclysmic change, what that group labels "singularity." The arrival of "singularity" (true AGI) will mark the divide between this world and the next, "a mechanical world culminating in the onset of the age of mind, a virtual kingdom in cyberspace."[721]

One of the software pioneers cited by Geraci believes "cyberspace opens the doors to the heavenly city of revelations." In other words, this "heavenly city" presumably grants "human beings unfettered joy through idyllic environs, and limitless personal experience." He goes as far as to declare that this eschatological kingdom shows "deep connections between virtual reality and Christian salvation." Allegedly, once in cyberspace, we will find a good life, no physical needs, happiness, and "even better sex lives." Also, the virtual kingdom "will virtually guarantee our immortality."[722]

Salvation for all, but we must rush: Salvation for the Christian concerns an eternal, spiritual deliverance. Jesus equates being saved with entering the kingdom of God (Matthew 19:24–25). Therefore, biblical salvation happens when believers acknowledge to Jesus their sin, seek His forgiveness, and accept His sacrifice. The "saved" followers of Christ have the promise of an eternal place in heaven.

The apocalyptic AI community believes that machine creativity will lead to salvation—and bypass human death; therefore, humanity's primary role today is to create artificial general intelligent life before it is too late. For this community, salvation is transitioning from our flesh to a nonorganic, avatar-like eternity.

They also argue that, at some point, "singularity," the point of explosive growth in intelligence, results in machines teaching themselves and then intellectual growth climbs exponentially, and quickly the world transitions from biological to all mechanical—an AGI nirvana. At that point, the new kingdom (eternal state) arrives, "one not based upon God but otherwise making the same promises as more traditional apocalypses."[723]

Arriving at that virtual kingdom requires "an Edenic earthly life before the final transcendence of mind over matter," writes Geraci. Expressly, AGI and robotics assume humanity's work for "a universal class of wealthy owners." However, this future will "eventually wither away" and leave a more fantastic world behind.[724]

Once robots make all the earnings, humans will lack for nothing. "No one will work for his daily bread, but will literally have it fall from heaven," writes the professor, because robots "will provide for human beings." Humans, no longer needing to labor, will pursue leisure and self-fulfillment.[725]

Unfortunately, machines "will tire of caring for humanity and decide to spread throughout the universe in the interest of discovering all the secrets of the cosmos." These utopian conditions "merely presage the wondrous virtual kingdom to come."[726]

Humans must begin transitioning to cyborgs: The apocalyptic AI advocates promise that humans must join "our mechanical progeny" in time to become part of the promised virtual kingdom. They point out that even as human bodies cannot inherit the biblical kingdom of God, the same is true about inheriting the virtual kingdom. We must integrate mechanical parts to become cyborgs or escape our bodies altogether to join the virtual reality.[727]

Augmenting our natural abilities with implanted computer hardware powered by AI will help us become more innovative. Those additions can enhance memory, take aboard new senses like seeing infrared, network with the internet, radically improve our computation ability, and more.[728]

Some AI advocates believe tech will become so advanced (AGI) that we voluntarily download our consciousness into machines, which frees us "from our human bodies altogether."[729]

AI: SATAN'S END-TIMES STRATEGIC WEAPON

Once we port our consciousness into a machine, we no longer need our bodies. Thus, "we will cease living in the physical world," and our lives will "play out in a virtual world." Our identity will "be software [electrons], not hardware.... Disembodied superminds."[730]

In conclusion, "Apocalyptic AI has absorbed the categories of Jewish and Christian apocalyptic theologies and utilizes them for scientific and supposedly secular aims," wrote Professor Geraci. "Scholars of religion have as much obligation as anyone, and more obligation than most, to help explore the characteristics of this movement and its ramifications upon wider culture."[731]

What seems clear from the professor's article is that AI advocates aspire to create an AI-like religion that promises salvation, a new body, and eternal existence in the virtual kingdom. The popularity of this view is growing and could influence humankind, especially regarding mortality, the true God, and heaven. For the atheist, this virtual future is likely quite attractive—an avatar-like existence forever that avoids human death—and, of course, it provides a radically different alternative to religions such as Christianity.

The likelihood that an AI-like religion will become popular among the masses fuels the possibility that the False Prophet will be an actual AGI entity that serves Satan's end-times agenda.

As these ideas gain popularity, they lay the groundwork for a global deception. But how might this play out in the physical world? Let us now consider the signs Scripture associates with the end times and how AI could help manifest them.

AI Powers Behind End-Times Signs

I have established that Satan's unholy trinity might include an AGI entity, perhaps the "second beast," aka the False Prophet. The previous section outlined how apocalyptic AI advocates are pushing a cult-like approach—an AI religion—to encourage humankind to press hard to advance technology, believing it is humankind's only salvation. The popularity of AI might then boost the likelihood of Satan adding that technology to his toolkit for the end times.

AI FOR MANKIND'S FUTURE

This section addresses what the Bible describes as a series of apocalyptic events (signs), which could involve the misuse of AGI. This could happen through military systems, environmental disasters, or the manipulation of ecosystems through advanced technology. This might involve global conflict whereby AGI controls autonomous weapons that escalate tensions to the point of war, causing conflict that many prophecies foresee as a precursor to the end times.

AI and the Signs of the Coming End Times:

The super capabilities afforded by the future AGI explain why it will become the most effective instrument Satan uses to control the world. After all, it already has significant influence over food production, water distribution, healthcare, financial transactions, much of the media, communications, and more. If the future AI and its presumed master, Satan, determine that humanity is an obstacle and must be removed or controlled, then it could engage in offensive actions on many fronts. That decision might result in what the Scriptures label as the "signs" of the end times.

Below you will learn about some of those signs and AI's possible contribution to usher in the prophetic end times.

AI's Contribution to the "Wars and Rumors of Wars" Sign

Jesus warns in Matthew 24:6–7 (KJV) that "wars and rumors of wars" indicate we are nearing the end. Remember that many of our modern militaries already include automated capabilities linked to AI systems. Further, as addressed earlier in this book, the world's leading militaries are aggressively seeking new AI-powered applications for every aspect of armed conflict. It is also quite possible that future autonomous, superintelligent machines will take captive the global instruments of war to target one another and their human masters. However, for now, the fact is that war is pervasive, and there is no reason to believe conflict will subside—nor will AI's influence over hostilities. What is not clear is how much warfare it will take to convince humanity that we are experiencing this prophetic "sign."

AI: SATAN'S END-TIMES STRATEGIC WEAPON

AI's Role in the Visible "Heavens and Earth" Sign

Jesus speaks of a sign in the sky in Luke 21:25–26:

> There will be signs in the sun, moon and stars. On the Earth, nations will be in anguish and perplexity at the roaring and tossing of the sea. People will faint from terror, apprehensive of what is coming on the world, for the heavenly bodies will be shaken. (NIV)

These signs are mentioned elsewhere in the Gospels, which are difficult to understand. Perhaps the activities in the heavens speak of weapons, like satellite-based defenses launching weapons either at other space platforms or aiming at targets on Earth. We already remotely control satellites; some are autonomous, with AI-powered brains. Is the "roaring and tossing of the sea" the result of gravitational changes or associated with the disturbances in the heavens? These signs could be the result of AI and a precursor to global war.

Together, these first signs emphasize the escalation of global instability—wars, natural disruptions, and cosmic disturbances—all of which AI could accelerate through autonomous weapons, environmental manipulation, or satellite-based technologies. While these events seem chaotic, believers should remember that our Lord has foretold them (Luke 21:28), and they are under His sovereign oversight. The Christian response must be alertness, not fear.

AI's Contribution to the "Famine and Diseases" Sign

In Matthew 24:7 (KJV), Jesus speaks of "famines and pestilences" as indicators of the coming end. Many of us believe the COVID-19 pandemic resulted from a laboratory leak in Wuhan, China. Therefore, it is quite possible that either an autonomous or Satan-controlled AGI entity could engineer something far worse and then spread it across the world to make large parts of the Earth uninhabitable. It could also cut off our access to food by manipulating supply chains and economic structures, whereby human survival becomes almost impossible without the AGI entity's approval—and the same can be true for medicines and medical equipment.

AI FOR MANKIND'S FUTURE

AI's Control of Culture Creates "Moral Decay" Sign

The Apostle Paul writes in 2 Timothy 3:1–5 about moral decay as a sign of the coming end, when people become "lovers of their own selves, covetous, boasters, proud, blasphemers, disobedient to parents, unthankful, unholy, without natural affection, trucebreakers, false accusers, incontinent, fierce, despisers of those that are good, traitors, heady, high-minded, lovers of pleasures more than lovers of God; having a form of godliness, but denying the power thereof: from such turn away" (KJV).

Earlier in this book, I established AI's role in shaping human behavior through media, social engineering, and algorithmic influence. It's not too difficult to believe that craven humanity exposed to a prolonged psychological operation hosted by AI could convince most of us to turn into the morally bankrupt beings described in Scripture. Such outcomes could spark conflict, depopulation, and self-destruction. After all, as previously mentioned, 80 percent of Gen Zers, according to a survey, entertain the idea of "marrying" AI—a morally bankrupt proposition.

These signs strike at both body and soul: Famine and pestilence weaken humanity's physical condition, while moral decay erodes spiritual integrity. When AI begins to shape not just food systems and healthcare, but also public morality and values, it can become a tool of the enemy to seduce society. As Paul writes, "God gave them up to a debased mind" (Romans 1:28, ESV)—a warning Christians must heed in our AI-shaped world.

AI-Generated "False Prophets" Sign

Jesus warns in Matthew 24:11 about the last days, when "many false prophets will appear and deceive many people" (NIV).

Much of Scripture warns about false prophets who claim to speak on behalf of God but propagate contrary teachings and lead people away from the truth. Indeed, the False Prophet described earlier in this chapter fits this description. He promotes his masters, the Antichrist and Satan, yet he has a winsome way that persuades many to follow his deception.

AI: SATAN'S END-TIMES STRATEGIC WEAPON

Further, AI's prophets (futurists) advocate outcomes that turn humankind away from God and toward false promises.

AI-generated "Persecution of Christian Believers" Sign

During the last days, Christians will be persecuted and hated for their faith. Jesus cautions in Matthew 24:9–10 about this future time, and John 16:33 depicts persecution as the mark of the believer: "In this world you will have trouble" (NIV).

Satan and his proxies hate Christians and will do whatever necessary to persecute them. Certainly, AI will help by denying Christians access to modern conveniences such as electricity, financial systems, communications, jobs, and much more. AI can use its powers to portray Christians as evil, corrupt, and otherwise socially unacceptable by generating massive doses of misinformation and deepfakes that result in the general population ostracizing believers, which could result in their imprisonment or murder.

False prophets and Christian persecution often go hand in hand. AI-powered voices may masquerade as truth-tellers while vilifying those who hold to the gospel. The Church must prepare for persecution that is algorithmically targeted and socially enforced, standing firm in the face of digital deception. Jesus said, "If the world hates you, know that it has hated me before it hated you" (John 15:18, ESV).

AI-inspired "False Messiah" Sign

The end times are marked by an increase in counterfeit messiahs. Jesus cautions in Matthew 24:25 that many false messiahs will arise and deceive crowds of followers. These would-be saviors propagate deceitful teachings and lead people away from true faith.

It is easy to imagine—given the growing dependence on virtual assistants, avatars and very authentic-appearing and -sounding misinformation—that very persuasive, albeit false, messiahs will come on the scene making many promises and recruiting numerous followers. We must prepare ourselves to distinguish the false from the genuine Christ.

AI FOR MANKIND'S FUTURE

AI-powered "Natural Disaster" Sign

While natural disasters are often attributed to tectonic and climatic causes, it isn't unthinkable that advanced technologies could exacerbate or manipulate such events. Jesus speaks in Matthew 24:7–8 about natural disasters as signs preceding His return: earthquakes, famines, and pestilences. In the past, the frequency and intensity of natural disasters led some to perceive the end times were near. It is certainly possible that such events could be seeded by AI, because "natural" disasters often have a human trigger, such as the control of food supplies, the creation of synthetic viruses, and floods that result from man-made crises.

These final signs show that AI may be used not only to counterfeit spiritual leadership, but also to unleash global catastrophes disguised as natural events. This convergence of spiritual and environmental manipulation paints a chilling picture of Satan's ambition to counterfeit God's sovereign acts. Yet, even in this, Christ's return remains our hope. As believers, we are called to watch the signs, but keep our eyes on the Savior (Hebrews 12:2).

The signs described above occur in the lead-up to the Rapture. But what of the time that follows—when the Church is taken up and God's final judgments begin to unfold?"

AI's Role in the Post-Rapture Period

The following interpretation follows a premillennial, pre-Tribulation view of eschatology. Other theological frameworks may differ.

AI may play a key role in triggering the signs leading up to the end times and outlined above. However, under Satan's leadership, AGI especially will likely continue to serve the devil's ambitions in the events that follow the Rapture, the event that's described in 1 Corinthians 15:52: "In a moment, in the twinkling of an eye, at the last trump: for the trumpet shall sound, and the dead shall be raised incorruptible, and we shall be changed" (KJV).

After believers are taken up in the Rapture, Antichrist will arrive (2 Thessalonians 2:7–8). He quickly gains control over the remaining population by offering promises of peace (Revelation 13:1). At his side is the False Prophet, a possible AGI entity, that leads a worldwide religious movement requiring the worship of the Antichrist (Revelation 19:20). Certainly, the AI cult-like following outlined in the previous section of this chapter—a contemporary movement (religion) with great momentum—fits the False Prophet's post-Rapture role.

At that point, the world quickly collapses into the Tribulation, seven years in which God's judgment is poured out (Revelation 6–16). Antichrist and his armies engage in open war with the Lord, especially at the Battle of Gog and Magog, where the Antichrist is defeated by God's supernatural intervention (Ezekiel 38–39). No doubt, Satan will use all means at his disposal in that fight, including AGI-powered systems overseen perhaps by the False Prophet.

At the midpoint of the Tribulation, Antichrist breaks a covenant he had made with Israel and carries out the "abomination of desolation," which is when Antichrist sets himself up as the idol for people to worship (Revelation 13:14). This appears to fit the role the False Prophet—AGI entity—assumed from the beginning—to lead the world to worship the Antichrist (2 Thessalonians 2:9). Meanwhile, Jews are scattered. Many of them turn to the Lord. At that point, a great persecution breaks out against those who follow Christ.

At the end of the Tribulation, Jesus and the armies of heaven fight the battle of Armageddon against the nations led by Antichrist (Revelation 19:11–21). Both Antichrist and the False Prophet are taken captive and thrown into the lake of fire (Revelation 19:20).

Presumably, at this point in the end-times scenario, any AI-related entity is exiled to the lake of fire with Antichrist. Meanwhile, Christ judges the Tribulation survivors and separates the righteous, who enter the millennial kingdom, from the wicked, who are cast into hell (Matthew 25:31–46).

After the judgment of the nations, Satan is bound and held in a bottomless pit for a thousand years (Revelation 20:1–3). Meanwhile, Jesus rules the world from Jerusalem (Revelation 20; Isaiah 60–62).

At the end of the thousand years, the Lord releases Satan from the pit, and once again he rebels, but is quickly defeated (Revelation 20:7–10). At that point, Satan is cast into the lake of fire to "be tormented day and night forever and ever" (Revelation 20:10, NAS). With evil finally judged and banished, God's justice is vindicated, and the reign of Christ enters its fullness.

This is the ultimate reckoning: No machine, no deception, no power can stand before the Righteous Judge of all the earth. At this point, at the great white throne judgment, Christ considers all the wicked who face their final judgment (Revelation 20:11–15). The verdicts are read, and they are cast into the lake of fire with Satan and his proxies. At this point, God remakes the heavens and earth and wipes away all tears just as the new Jerusalem descends from heaven, and the children of God enjoy eternity with him (Revelation 21–22).

The God of all creation prevails, and the AGI, presumed singularity monster exists no more!

Conclusion

I reiterate that no one knows the details or timing of the biblical end times. What we know comes from prophetic literature, which is difficult to discern. However, some of the players, signs, events, and outcomes appear to be relatively unambiguous.

Therefore, although I've taken liberties to inject an end-times role for artificial intelligence—AGI, a singularity entity—within the context of Satan's agenda, nothing is certain. However, the parallels between AI's potential future role and what we know about Satan and his proxies, and the end-times signs and events, certainly appear to overlap.

Even if we don't know all the specifics, we do know the outcome: Christ reigns. Let us therefore walk wisely, proclaim truth boldly, and fix our eyes on Jesus, the Author and Finisher of our faith (Hebrews 12:2).

Afterword

CHRISTIANS CALLED TO BE HUMAN, NOT AI-POWERED AVATARS

Christian men and women should not avoid AI; they ought rather understand how AI can be used to promote obedience to God while opposing sin.[732]

DUSTIN RYAN
Data and AI specialist at a US tech company,
author focused on business intelligence and Christianity

Dustin Ryan reminds us that Christians must approach AI not with fear, but with discernment and purpose. This tension between AI's helpfulness and potential harms defines the moment in which we live.

The contemporary clamor for new and better ways to harness artificial intelligence is a two-edged sword. Technology provides help in many areas outlined in this book. However, it has the potential to do great harm to humanity, especially for Christians who take their eyes off their biblical calling.

Let me summarize the potential for artificial intelligence based on the material presented in this book and then argue for a renewed commitment to be human as opposed to flesh controlled by AI that could make us little more than empty shells or fleshly avatars.

No doubt, AI's future is both exciting and uncertain because of its vast potential and challenges ahead. Expect technology to become more seamlessly integrated into daily activities, far beyond just voice assistants like Alexa and Siri. It will come to predict our needs, optimize our schedules, automate everyday tasks, and provide personalized recommendations. It will radically improve convenience in our cities through AI-driven cars and systems that manage traffic flow and energy consumption, and our healthcare will experience revolutionary changes in diagnostics, drug development, personalized medicine, and surgical procedures. In fact, AI may even increase life expectancy and reduce healthcare costs.

As we approach actual AGI, much less super AGI, "singularity," machines will become capable of performing any intellectual task that humans can, which could vastly enhance scientific discoveries, creativity, and problem-solving. Of course, that will present enormous ethical concerns regarding controlling technology to make certain that it aligns with human values and prevents unintended consequences.

> **AS WE APPROACH ACTUAL AGI MACHINES WILL BECOME CAPABLE OF PERFORMING ANY INTELLECTUAL TASK THAT HUMANS CAN**

The workplace will also change, thanks to various AI applications, such as agentic AI, with many jobs automated to perform routine tasks, particularly in manufacturing, logistics, and customer service. Although this will cause disruption in the job market, it will also create new opportunities. Naturally, this will demand broad-based AI literacy and related skills pushing the workforce to adapt to AI-driven economies.

AI will enhance the arts and entertainment media through collaboration with humans to produce more refined and innovative forms of expression that result in novel ideas and accessing them in virtual environments. Yet, as pointed out in chapter 14, harnessing AI through cultural propagators could lead to deception, dehumanization, or distraction from what matters eternally (Romans 12:2).

Expect quantum AI to unlock new potentials to solve problems far beyond the capabilities of classical computers in fields like cryptography, material science, and more. However, it also presents some incredibly significant potential dangers: supercharged surveillance, unpredictable intelligence behavior, autonomous warfare, questions related to bias, accountability, and discrimination.

AI-powered, self-driving cars and other forms of transportation will become common in many parts of the world. Even AI-powered military applications will surge from surveillance drones to advanced weaponry, raising legitimate concerns about international security and warfare ethics.

As these breakthroughs accelerate, we must ask not only what AI can do, but what it may cost us spiritually. For people of faith, the stakes are not merely technical, but eternal. AI presents some serious challenges, outlined in each chapter, as well as potential dangers for the coming prophetic end times. Consider that many religious traditions, including Christianity and Islam, have Scripture-based eschatological narratives that describe the end times as a period of upheaval, divine judgment, and final resolution. These traditions speak of figures with powerful, even godlike, influence. Certainly, it is understandable that AGI could play that role, through the persons of the False Prophet and Antichrist, as addressed in chapter 17.

Given these looming prophetic possibilities, we must now return to the present and ask: How, then, should we live faithfully in this AI-infused world?

Looking Forward: Be Human

I hope the primary takeaway from this study of AI is to encourage all people, especially Christians, to be wise in their use of technology. Avoid overuse of AI, because too much of a "good" thing can lead to abuse, and, in the case of emergent AGI, it could rob us of our humanity. So, my encouragement as we wade our way through the modern AI quagmire is that we all remember to be human as God designed us.

Unfortunately, we must juxtapose our lives influenced by AI with what it means to be made in the image of God. Some AI enthusiasts, especially some agnostics, and most atheists argue that humans are purely physical beings, and our mental processes are complex chemical reactions. Others assert that we are unique from animals, because we can have abstract thoughts evidenced by language and culture, yet many still reject our Creator and the promised eternity in heaven promised to those who follow Christ.

That brings us to some of the challenges associated with modern technologies, such as AI currently employed to genetically modify humans to enhance physical and cognitive traits and abilities. Those changes blur the line between being human and being a machine, a cyborg.

The mix of human flesh and technology begs some daunting questions, such as: What if AI systems acquire self-awareness? Then, what is the moral line between humans and self-aware machines?

Transhumanists, especially those identified as AI apocalyptists, promote the merger of humans with AI technology to create cyborgs and, if they get their way, eventually they anticipate the porting of our consciousness into a digital platform to then "enjoy" eternity allegedly in cyberspace.

These questions and issues may sound far-fetched, but science is quickly closing the technical gap, mixing human flesh with technology. Some of the brightest AI advocates claim we will inevitably digitize our consciousness to then scrap our flesh. Understandably, such issues require serious inquiry for modern society, which presents some tricky ethical considerations. However, Christians must understand these technological challenges while remaining biblically obedient.

While futurists imagine a posthuman world, Scripture reminds us of a divinely defined humanity—rooted not in code or cybernetics, but in the image and breath of God.

For Christians, humanity is defined by God and our purpose is given in His Word. Simply, human beings are a single, unified race of creatures, each one created in the image of God, male and female, and given life by the divine breath.

Our purpose as humans is to be vocationally set apart from the rest of creation, which is illustrated in Genesis 1:26–28 (NIV). Specifically, we are to "rule" and to be "fruitful," which reflects the image of

CHRISTIANS CALLED TO BE HUMAN, NOT AI-POWERED AVATARS

God. We are God's representatives, His agents on Earth to be about His business.

Therefore, that clear scriptural direction begs the question: How should we live in this technological era? That query causes me to think back to the 1970s when I first read Francis Schaeffer's book, *How Should We Then Live? The Rise and Decline of Western Thought and Culture*. That book and the video series by the same title pierced me in the heart, a convicting appraisal of our times. It spoke of the great conflict of worldviews at the time and the contest between Christianity and the brewing intellectual revolution.[733]

"There is a flow to history and culture," Schaeffer explained. He called on Christians to understand that flow of culture, because, he said, "People have presuppositions, and they will live more consistently on the basis of those presuppositions than even they themselves may realize." What he meant and what is important for us today is that many Christians, then and now, are unaware of the "storm of worldviews that was coming."[734]

Today, the Christian's worldview is challenged especially on the AI front by futurists who promise a world radically foreign to the biblical plan. Unless we are extremely cautious, even Christians will be deceived and caught up in the futurists' promises and forget our God-given purpose.

Our purpose must always affirm that we will be good stewards of God's gifts, which extend to all of life—including AI technology. We must not idolize this tech but use it for good purposes that honor God.

In summary, *AI for Mankind's Future* in seventeen chapters makes the case that AI has a growing and pervasive presence across every aspect of modern life. It offers immense help but threatens significant harm in the wrong hands—and it might play a key role in the biblical end times.

This book reviews the pros and cons of AI in six sections, albeit from a Christian perspective.

Section One: "Defining AI: The Mechanics, History, and the Future" establishes a baseline for the reader who is new to AI-related technology and the terms. There is a history that links with the development of computers and AI's evolution. The section is rounded out with a summary of technology's benefits and frightening challenges.

Section Two: "AI and Social Institutions" surveys the application's role for three key institutions: home/family, education, and healthcare. AI may serve the home, but it presents dangers for families, especially tech-saturated children. It is undoubtedly a boon for education but also can become a crippling crutch for students. Technology has already revolutionized healthcare, but much yet needs to be done before it enjoys our complete trust.

Section Three: "AI and Public Institutions" demonstrates the enthusiastic place AI has won at all levels of government and public services, and across the national security establishment. Most citizens welcome technology's help to improve government efficiency and lower taxes. However, many of us remain skeptical about the potential for overreach and the threat posed by lethal autonomous systems in the hands of government bureaucrats, law enforcement, and military forces.

Section Four: "AI and the Economy" surveys AI's significant contribution to every aspect of our economy. It has played an oversized role in the production of raw materials, radically transformed manufacturing, and optimized the retail sector. However, turning over much of our economic activity to AI poses some grave challenges for humankind.

Section Five: "AI's Impact on Culture" demonstrates its deep involvement in who we are as humans. After all, it influences our values, liberties, arts, and entertainment, which capture our attention. AI has also radically altered how we communicate, and it plays a pervasive role in our political processes.

Section Six: "AI, Christianity, and Biblical Prophecy" presents a Christian perspective on two fronts. I address how Christians should live in the modern AI quagmire without compromising our biblical witness. The section concludes with speculation about the unholy trinity's possible use of AGI to trigger signs of the coming end times and then how technology might help Satan fight God leading up to the last battle at Armageddon.

CHRISTIANS CALLED TO BE HUMAN, NOT AI-POWERED AVATARS

AI for Mankind's Future also includes numerous appendices that address AI-related issues in greater detail. These appendices offer many sources and background for readers anxious to further investigate all things artificial intelligence.

In conclusion, *AI for Mankind's Future* offers technology novices a clear and accessible overview of artificial intelligence—a rapidly advancing capability that holds the promise of remarkable gains in efficiency, productivity, and innovation. Yet, as established throughout the book, this same technology also carries the potential for profound and even devastating consequences, especially when misused or left unchecked.

Artificial intelligence should be regulated both internationally and domestically. Corporations must be held to account to oversee their AI-related developments as well. However, individual citizens must decide how much they will join this technological revolution.

This broad journey through AI's domains highlights one clear reality: We cannot ignore this revolution. Christians must now prayerfully decide how to respond—not as passive observers, but as faithful witnesses.

Finally, it is essential for biblically obedient Christians to wisely discern their role in the technological revolution. Specifically, we must make tough choices that will distinguish us from much of the world that's captivated by the latest AI-related advances. However, by making those wise decisions to distance ourselves from certain AI applications, we Christians may find ourselves alienated from the world, but in line with God's purpose and, as a result, bring Him the glory.

APPENDICES

APPENDICES

Appendix A

BEST KNOWN AI APPLICATIONS, COMPANIES, AND EXPERTS[735]

Artificial intelligence is rapidly transforming how we live, work, learn, and communicate. The tools, companies, and experts listed in this appendix represent some of the most powerful and influential technologies shaping our world today. However, while these innovations offer remarkable capabilities, Christians must not embrace them uncritically. Instead, we are called to exercise spiritual discernment and moral clarity, evaluating each tool considering God's Word. As the Apostle Paul exhorts, "Test everything; hold fast what is good" (1 Thessalonians 5:21, ESV).

This means asking not just what these technologies can do, but whether they promote truth, justice, human dignity, and Christ-centered living. Some AI tools may serve as helpful instruments of stewardship and creativity; others may subtly undermine biblical values or human identity. This appendix is not an endorsement of every listed application, but a guide to understanding the landscape Christians must navigate with wisdom and conviction.

Note: Inclusion here is for awareness, not endorsement. Christians must test these tools by biblical values (1 Thessalonians 5:21).

AI Chatbots and Virtual Assistants

ChatGPT (OpenAI): Conversational AI for answering questions, writing, coding, and more; https://chatgpt.com

Copilot (Microsoft): Generative AI assistant integrated into Microsoft tools; https://copilot.microsoft.com

BEST KNOWN AI APPLICATIONS, COMPANIES, AND EXPERTS

Claude (Anthropic): Family of LLMs focused on safety and alignment; https://claude.ai

Google Gemini (formerly Bard): Google's AI chatbot; https://gemini.google.com

Perplexity AI: Real-time answer engine with sourced summaries; https://perplexity.ai

Pi (Inflection AI): Empathetic personal AI companion

Character.AI: Customizable AI personas, including fictional characters

Siri (Apple), Alexa (Amazon), Google Assistant: Voice-activated AI assistants

Meta AI: Facebook and Instagram's integrated AI chatbot; https://meta.ai

AI in Search and Productivity

Google Search & Bing AI: AI-enhanced search engines

Notion AI: AI-powered productivity, summarization, and writing

Grammarly and Quillbot Grammar correction and text enhancement

Otter.ai: Meeting transcription and real-time summaries

AI in Entertainment and Media

Netflix and YouTube: AI-based content recommendation engines

Spotify AI DJ and Apple Music: Personalized music curation

Deepfake tools (Reface, DeepFaceLab): AI face-swapping and manipulation (with ethical caution)

AI in Art and Creativity

DALL·E, MidJourney, Stable Diffusion: AI image generation from text

Runway and Pika Labs: AI video creation and editing

AIVA and Amper Music: AI music composition tools

Canva AI: Smart design tools for creatives and marketers

AI in Business and Marketing

Jasper AI and Copy.ai: AI writing tools for business and ad copy

Drift, Intercom, LivePerson: AI customer service chatbots

Salesforce Einstein and HubSpot AI: CRM and marketing automation

BEST KNOWN AI APPLICATIONS, COMPANIES, AND EXPERTS

AI in Healthcare

IBM Watson Health and Google DeepMind: Medical diagnostics and research
PathAI and Tempus: AI for cancer detection and pathology
Ellie (USC ICT): AI avatar therapist reading tone and facial cues
Ada Health and Babylon Health: Health symptom checkers and consultations

AI in Image and Video Processing

FaceApp and Remini: AI photo editing and enhancement
Adobe Sensei: AI tools in Photoshop and Premiere
Deep Nostalgia: Animates old photos using deep learning

AI in Gaming

Nvidia DLSS: AI-powered graphics upscaling
OpenAI Codex: AI-enhanced game development and NPC behavior
AI Dungeon: Interactive AI-driven text RPG

AI in E-commerce and Finance

Amazon and eBay: AI recommendation and logistics systems
PayPal and Stripe: AI for fraud detection and financial security
ChatGPT stock bots: AI analysis tools for trading (with caution)

AI in Education and Learning

Duolingo AI Tutor: Language learning assistant
Khan Academy Khanmigo: Personalized AI tutor for students
Quizlet AI and Socratic by Google: Homework help and learning support

Best-Known AI Companies

OpenAI: Developer of GPT models and ChatGPT
Google DeepMind: Leaders in reinforcement learning (AlphaGo, AlphaFold)
Anthropic: AI alignment-focused company (Claude)
Microsoft: Major investor in OpenAI; offers Azure AI and Copilot
Meta: Open-source model builder (LLaMA), AI tools in social platforms

BEST KNOWN AI APPLICATIONS, COMPANIES, AND EXPERTS

Amazon: AI in Alexa, AWS, and global logistics
Nvidia: Hardware leader for AI chips; also building AI models
xAI: Elon Musk's AI company focused on truth-seeking
Hugging Face: Open-source hub for models and datasets
Palantir: AI for defense, intelligence, and security (ethically sensitive)
Alibaba, Baidu, Tencent: Major AI actors in China

Best-Known AI Experts

Geoffrey Hinton: Neural networks pioneer; deep learning founder
Yann LeCun: Chief AI scientist at Meta; co-inventor of CNNs
Yoshua Bengio: AI ethics and safety researcher
Demis Hassabis: CEO of DeepMind; AI and neuroscience innovator
Andrew Ng: AI educator and cofounder of Google Brain
Fei-Fei Li: Human-centered AI advocate; creator of ImageNet
Ilya Sutskever: Cofounder and chief scientist at OpenAI
Sam Altman: CEO of OpenAI; public AI policy voice
Dario Amodei: CEO of Anthropic; focuses on safe AI
Timnit Gebru: AI bias researcher and ethics advocate
Gary Marcus: AI critic advocating for hybrid intelligence
Emily Bender: Linguist known for cautioning AI hype

Christian and Ethical Voices Shaping AI Development

Christian Thinkers

Dr. John Lennox: Author of *2084: AI and the Future of Humanity*; theological critique of transhumanism
Dr. Nigel Cameron: Author of *The Robots Are Coming*; bioethics and human dignity
Dr. Brian Green: Catholic ethicist focused on Christian moral frameworks for AI
Dr. Derek C. Schuurman: Calvin University professor; author on Christian tech ethics
Rev. Dr. Michael Burdett: Oxford theologian specializing in AI and transhumanism

Christian Organizations

AI and Faith: Multi-faith initiative with strong Christian leadership

Ethics and Religious Liberty Commission (ERLC): AI commentary from a Southern Baptist perspective

Center for Faith and Flourishing (Wheaton): Research and forums on tech and virtue

Kirby Laing Centre (UK): Reformed Christian think tank engaging AI and culture

Global Ethical Voices

Kate Crawford (Australia): Researcher on AI, power, and inequality

Toby Walsh (Australia): UN advisor on banning lethal autonomous weapons

Raja Chatila (France): Ethics in robotics and AI policy contributor

Joy Buolamwini (United States): Founder of Algorithmic Justice League; AI bias researcher

Abeba Birhane (Ireland/Ethiopia): Cognitive scientist critiquing systemic bias in AI

Final Reflection

As Christians navigate this ever-changing landscape, we are reminded of Paul's exhortation to "walk in wisdom toward outsiders, making the best use of the time" (Colossians 4:5, ESV). The tools listed here represent great potential—and great responsibility. May we use them not for pride, power, or profit alone, but to reflect the character of Christ in all things.

Appendix B

UNDERSTANDING GENERATIVE AI

Generative AI gained global attention following the launch of ChatGPT in 2022. Since then, the field has expanded rapidly. As of May 2025, the open-source platform Hugging Face alone hosts over 1.6 million generative AI models across text, image, audio, code, and multimodal tasks.

This appendix offers a clear and accessible introduction to generative AI—how it works, what it can do, and how Christians can engage with it thoughtfully.

What Is Generative AI?

Generative AI refers to computer programs that create new content—such as text, images, music, or code—by learning from existing examples. Imagine a digital artist or writer that studies thousands of books, photos, or songs and then produces something entirely new. These tools do not think or feel, but they mimic human creativity through patterns and probabilities.

How Does Generative AI Work?

1. Tokenization: Text is broken into small parts (tokens), such as words or symbols. For example, "The cat sat" becomes three tokens.
2. Embeddings: Tokens are converted into vectors (number sequences) that capture their meaning. Similar words (e.g., "cat" and "dog") are numerically close.

UNDERSTANDING GENERATIVE AI

3. Attention Mechanism: AI models, especially transformers, use attention to understand context. In the sentence, "I fed the cat because it was hungry," the AI learns that "it" refers to "cat."
4. Prediction: Based on its training data, the AI predicts the next most likely token to complete a sentence.
5. Iteration: It builds responses step by step by repeating the prediction process.

Common Types of Generative AI Tools

- **Text generators (large-language models)**

Examples: GPT (OpenAI), Claude (Anthropic), Gemini (Google)

Uses: Drafting emails, answering questions, summarizing content, writing code

- **Image generators**

Examples: DALL·E, MidJourney, Stable Diffusion

Uses: Creating digital art, design mockups, illustrations from text prompts

- **Voice and Audio Tools**

Examples: Whisper (OpenAI), ElevenLabs

Uses: Transcribing speech, generating realistic voices, cloning vocal patterns

- **Code Generators**

Examples: Codex (OpenAI), StarCoder, GitHub Copilot

Uses: Writing and debugging code, generating documentation

- **Multimodal Models**

Examples: GPT-4 (text and images), Claude 3

Uses: Analyzing mixed inputs (text and visuals), answering questions about diagrams or screenshots

How to Use Generative AI Effectively (Prompting Tips)

Be clear and specific. Instead of saying, "Tell me something," try saying, "Explain why bees are essential to gardens."

Use simple language. Direct prompts are easier for AI to follow.

Provide context. Example: "Write a fun tweet announcing our new coffee shop."

Break down tasks. Start with, "Outline a blog post on healthy snacks," then follow up with, "Write the introduction."

Ask for variations. Say, for example, "Give me three examples," or "Can you shorten that?"

Set the tone. Try saying, "Write in a friendly tone," or, "Use formal business language."

Know the limits. AI can sound confident but still make mistakes. It doesn't understand the meaning the way people do.

Hubspot developed a booklet, "Supercharge Your Workday with ChatGPT." The booklet helps the reader understand AI and ChatGPT, outlines its capabilities, discusses best practices, and offers guidance on how to master prompts. See the endnote for details regarding the booklet.[736]

A Christian perspective: While generative AI can assist with communication, learning, and creativity, Christians must approach these tools with discernment. As for any innovation, we must ask: Does this serve the truth? Does it uphold dignity? Is it being used with integrity? Remember the biblical wisdom to "test everything; hold fast what is good" (1 Thessalonians 5:21, ESV).

Used correctly, generative AI can support human flourishing. But it must never replace our God-given calling to reason, relate, create, and reflect the image of Christ in all we do.

Appendix C

ARTIFICIAL GENERAL INTELLIGENCE

Artificial general intelligence (AGI) represents one of the most ambitious and debated frontiers in the field of artificial intelligence. Unlike narrow AI—designed to perform specific tasks such as translating language, recommending products, or identifying faces—AGI aspires to match or surpass human-level intelligence across a wide variety of domains. It aims to reason, learn, and solve problems in flexible, generalizable ways, like the cognitive abilities of humans.

According to Dr. Mfon Akpan of Methodist University, AGI is defined by several key characteristics:[737]

1. Adaptability: AGI systems can handle unfamiliar tasks and environments without needing extensive retraining.
2. Learning and reasoning: AGI can learn from experience and apply logical reasoning to new problems.
3. Transferability: AGI can transfer knowledge from one domain to another, understanding core principles that apply broadly.
4. Autonomy: AGI operates independently, making decisions and taking actions without constant human oversight.

Though today's advanced AI systems like ChatGPT (OpenAI), Claude (Anthropic), and Gemini (Google) demonstrate remarkable proficiency in language tasks, coding, and reasoning, they're still considered forms of narrow AI. These tools rely heavily on training data and probabilistic pattern recognition, rather than possessing true understanding, consciousness, or generalized reasoning across diverse contexts.

As of 2025, AGI remains an aspirational goal rather than a realized reality. While some researchers believe AGI could emerge within a few decades, others urge caution—citing the complexity of replicating human cognition and the profound ethical, spiritual, and societal implications if AGI were to be achieved.

From a Christian perspective, the pursuit of AGI raises essential questions about human uniqueness, autonomy, and the image of God (Genesis 1:26–27). Can a machine ever possess true wisdom, creativity, or moral accountability? Would an AGI entity challenge the biblical understanding of personhood and purpose? Christians must stay informed and vigilant, engaging with AGI developments not with fear, but with discernment rooted in Scripture.

AGI may never fully materialize as envisioned, but even the pursuit of it is shaping global policy, economics, education, warfare, and theology. Understanding its goals, limits, and philosophical implications is essential for all who seek to live faithfully in the age of intelligent machines.

Appendix D

AGENTIC AI

Agentic AI refers to systems that exhibit agency; that is, they can make decisions, set and pursue goals, and take actions autonomously in dynamic environments. Unlike traditional AI, which typically responds to specific prompts or operates within narrow constraints, agentic AI is designed to function more independently and persistently over time.

Key Characteristics of Agentic AI

- **Goal-oriented behavior:** Capable of defining, refining, or pursuing complex goals, sometimes establishing subgoals without explicit instructions.
- **Autonomy:** Operates without constant human oversight, initiating actions and making decisions independently.
- **Persistent action:** Maintains focus on long-term or multi-step objectives, executing strategies to fulfill its mission.
- **Environmental interaction:** Actively perceives, interprets, and responds to environmental inputs to shape outcomes.
- **Adaptive reasoning:** Learns from new data, feedback, or evolving contexts to improve performance and adjust behavior.

Examples of Agentic AI

- **Personal AI assistant:** An AI that autonomously manages a user's calendar, email, and travel plans by integrating user preferences and contextual data.

- **AI military drone:** An unmanned aerial vehicle that independently navigates, assesses threats, and executes tactical decisions during missions without direct human control.
- **Tesla full self-driving (FSD):** An AI system designed to navigate complex driving environments, pursuing navigation goals and reacting to real-time conditions. While it exhibits many agentic behaviors, it is not yet fully autonomous due to safety limitations and the need for human oversight.

Why Agentic AI Matters

Agentic AI holds great promise for personal productivity, scientific research, transportation, and defense. However, it also introduces significant safety, control, and ethical concerns:

- What if an agentic AI misinterprets its goals or adapts in unintended ways?
- How do we ensure alignment with human values and moral boundaries?
- What mechanisms can prevent runaway behavior or misuse in critical areas like warfare or surveillance?

A Christian Perspective

From a biblical standpoint, agentic AI raises questions about responsibility, agency, and human uniqueness. Scripture teaches that humans are stewards of creation, endowed with moral agency and created in the image of God (Genesis 1:26–28). While machines may act autonomously, they do not possess conscience, wisdom, or intrinsic moral worth.

As Christians, we are called to develop and deploy technology wisely and ethically, ensuring that AI systems serve people rather than replace or endanger them. As agentic AI evolves, we must remain vigilant in discerning its implications, always seeking to uphold justice, human dignity, and faithful stewardship of the tools we create.

Appendix E

AI TERMS AND COMMON VOCABULARY

As artificial intelligence increasingly shapes modern life, it is essential to understand key terminology not only for technical literacy, but for theological and ethical reflection. Many AI terms carry assumptions about human identity, morality, and even salvation that Christians must examine carefully. The Apostle Paul reminds us to "test everything; hold fast what is good" (1 Thessalonians 5:21, ESV).

Terms such as "generative AI," "autonomy," and "singularity" are not just technological concepts; they often reflect philosophies that may challenge biblical truths. For instance, "the Singularity," the idea that AI will surpass human intelligence and usher in a new era, entices many with a vision of transcendence apart from God. But Christians place their hope not in technological evolution, but in Christ alone (John 14:6).

Use this glossary not only as a technical guide, but as a tool for spiritual discernment in a rapidly changing digital age.

General AI Concepts

Agentic AI: AI systems capable of autonomous decision-making and goal pursuit across environments. See Appendix D.

Algorithm: A set of rules or instructions used to solve problems or perform tasks.

Artificial intelligence (AI): Machine systems that simulate human cognitive functions.

AI diffusion: The spread of AI adoption across industries and societies.

AI TERMS AND COMMON VOCABULARY

Application programming interface (API): A software bridge enabling different programs to communicate.

Deep learning: A subset of machine learning using layered neural networks to model complex data patterns.

Generative AI: AI that creates new content (text, images, etc.) based on learned patterns. See appendix B.

Hallucinations: AI hallucinations occur when artificial intelligence generates false or fabricated information that appears plausible, but is not grounded in reality.

Inference: The process of using a trained model to make predictions on new input.

Machine learning (ML): Algorithms that improve automatically through data exposure.

Model: A trained program that makes decisions or predictions.

Neural network: A machine-learning structure modeled on the human brain.

Reinforcement learning (RL): A model learns by interacting with its environment and receiving feedback.

Supervised learning: Training a model on labeled datasets.

Training: Teaching an AI model through data exposure.

Transfer learning: Reusing a model trained on one task for a new but related task.

Unsupervised learning: Learning patterns in data without labels.

AI-Related Data and Processing

Bias: Systematic errors caused by imbalanced or unfair data.

Coding: Writing instructions in a computer language.

Data preprocessing: Cleaning and formatting raw data before training.

Dataset: A structured collection of data used for AI model training.

Feature engineering: Selecting or modifying inputs to improve model accuracy.

Gradient descent: An optimization method used in training models.

Loss function: Measures how well a model's predictions match real outcomes.

AI TERMS AND COMMON VOCABULARY

Overfitting: When a model memorizes training data too closely, hurting general performance.

Underfitting: When a model is too simplistic to detect underlying patterns.

Variance: Sensitivity of a model to changes in training data.

AI Techniques and Architectures

Autoencoder: A neural network for compressing and reconstructing data.

Convolutional neural network (CNN): Used primarily in image recognition.

Generative adversarial network (GAN): Two models compete to generate realistic synthetic data.

Long short-term memory (LSTM): A type of RNN that remembers long sequences.

Recurrent neural network (RNN): Handles sequential data like text or time-series.

Transformer: A model architecture central to modern NLP tools like GPT and BERT.

Natural Language Processing (NLP) Terms

Embeddings: Numerical word representations capturing meaning and context.

Named entity recognition (NER): Identifies proper names, places, and dates in text.

Sentiment analysis: Determines the emotional tone of text.

Speech recognition: Converts spoken words into text.

Tokenization: Divides text into meaningful units (words, phrases, et cetera).

Ethics, Moral Risks, and AI Safety

AI alignment: Ensuring AI systems follow human values and intentions.

Autonomy: AI's ability to operate independently, raising accountability questions.

AI TERMS AND COMMON VOCABULARY

Data colonialism: Exploitation of data from marginalized populations by powerful entities (Micah 6:8).

Deepfake: AI-generated synthetic media that can deceive (Proverbs 12:22).

Digital idolatry: Replacing divine authority with machine-based trust (Romans 1:21–25).

Explainability: Making AI decisions understandable to humans.

Fairness: Ensuring that AI doesn't reinforce social or racial inequalities.

Moral deskilling: Erosion of human moral reasoning due to overreliance on automation (Hebrews 5:14).

Singularity: A theorized point where AI surpasses human intelligence.

Techno-soteriology: The false belief that technology can provide salvation (Ephesians 2:8–9).

Transparency: Openness in AI systems' design, logic, and data sources.

Terms Related to End-Times Theology

Mark-of-the-Beast technologies: Technologies (e.g., biometrics, surveillance) potentially used to restrict participation in society (Revelation 13).

Antichrist system: A biblically prophesied global deception possibly enabled by technology (2 Thessalonians 2:3–10).

Artificial wisdom: The imitation of wisdom by AI. True wisdom comes from God alone (Proverbs 2:6; James 3:13–17).

This glossary provides a framework not only for understanding AI, but for examining its implications through the lens of faith. Christians must remain both informed and discerning, holding fast to truth while navigating a world increasingly shaped by artificial intelligence.

Appendix F

AI'S STRENGTHS, GAPS, AND LIMITATIONS

AI continues to reshape our world with impressive capabilities in data analysis, automation, language processing, and more. Yet even the most advanced AI systems remain limited in crucial areas such as reasoning, ethics, and real-world adaptability. The following overview outlines key strengths and limitations of AI as of 2025. It offers a framework for understanding where AI excels—and where caution, oversight, and humility are required.

Strengths of AI

1. **Pattern Recognition and Analysis**
   - Scalable data processing: AI can analyze massive datasets far faster than humans, identifying trends, correlations, and anomalies with high efficiency.
   - Deep-learning insights: Neural networks uncover patterns in images, text, audio, and more, supporting applications in classification, detection, and forecasting.

2. **Automation of Repetitive Tasks**
   - Consistency and speed: AI excels at automating structured tasks, improving productivity, and reducing human error.
   - Industrial-scale decision-making: In sectors like logistics and finance, AI handles millions of operations (e.g., transaction verification, route planning) at high speed.

AI'S STRENGTHS, GAPS, AND LIMITATIONS

3. **Natural-Language Processing (NLP)**
   - Language comprehension: Large-language models perform tasks such as summarization, translation, and conversational response generation.
   - Sentiment analysis: AI detects emotional tone in text, aiding customer support and public opinion monitoring.

4. **Computer Vision**
   - Visual recognition: AI can identify faces, objects, and patterns in images or video with growing accuracy.
   - Healthcare diagnostics: Computer vision tools detect diseases from medical imaging, sometimes surpassing human radiologists.

5. **Predictive Analytics and Forecasting**
   - Risk modeling: AI identifies risk patterns in areas like fraud detection and climate forecasting.
   - Personalization engines: E-commerce and media platforms use AI to recommend tailored content.

6. **Continuous Learning**
   - Dynamic adaptation: Many machine-learning systems can be updated with new data, improving performance over time without full retraining.

Gaps and Limitations of AI

1. **Lack of True General Intelligence**
   - Narrow capabilities: Current systems perform well in specialized domains, but lack cross-domain reasoning.
   - Absent common sense: AI may struggle with basic logic or contextual understanding.

2. **Data and Quality Dependencies**
   - Bias sensitivity: AI reflects flaws in the data it's trained on; biased data leads to biased results.

AI'S STRENGTHS, GAPS, AND LIMITATIONS

- Data demands: State-of-the-art models require vast, clean datasets—often unavailable in niche areas.

3. Explainability and Interpretability
- Black-box systems: It's difficult to explain how complex AI models arrive at certain conclusions.
- Ethical and regulatory concerns: Lack of transparency limits AI's use in sensitive fields like medicine and law.

4. Robustness and Reliability
- Adversarial vulnerability: Small, deliberate data changes can mislead AI systems.
- Context fragility: Models often fail when moved outside their trained environments.

5. Ethical and Bias Concerns
- Algorithmic discrimination: Without intervention, AI can amplify social inequities.
- Privacy risks: Misuse of training data or lax safeguards can expose personal information.

6. Resource Intensiveness
- High energy and computing needs: Large models consume substantial electricity and hardware, raising environmental and accessibility concerns.
- Infrastructure challenges: Smaller organizations often lack resources to adopt cutting-edge AI.

7. Human-AI Collaboration Challenges
- Overreliance and blind trust: Users may defer uncritically to AI decisions.
- Trust and usability gaps: Opaque systems may reduce user confidence and hinder adoption.

AI'S STRENGTHS, GAPS, AND LIMITATIONS

Conclusion

AI offers extraordinary strengths, especially in data processing, automation, and pattern recognition. However, it also presents serious limitations. Its lack of general intelligence, interpretability challenges, ethical risks, and environmental footprint demand thoughtful oversight. For AI to serve humanity well, it must be developed and deployed with humility, accountability, and a commitment to justice and human dignity. Ongoing improvements in transparency, safety, and fairness will be essential as we move forward in this age of intelligent machines.

Appendix G

AI APPLICATIONS FOR FAMILIES

AI is increasingly shaping family life in positive, practical ways. From simplifying daily routines to sparking creativity and enhancing communication, AI offers a range of tools tailored for busy households. This appendix outlines some of the most helpful AI-powered applications currently available to families, along with a few reflections to guide thoughtful adoption.

1. **Family Management and Organization**
   - Cozi: A comprehensive family organizer featuring shared calendars, to-do lists, meal planning, and reminders.
   - Goldee: An AI personal assistant that adapts to your family's routines, manages daily tasks, and integrates group chats and emails.
   - Ohai.ai: Automates grocery lists, errands, and task assignments with real-time updates for family coordination.

2. **Homework Assistance**
   - ChatGPT and similar tools: Help children break down complex topics, create study guides, and explain academic subjects in age-appropriate language.

3. **Meal Planning and Nutrition**
   - Maple, Ohai: Generate meal plans based on family preferences, suggest recipes, and create shopping lists.

AI APPLICATIONS FOR FAMILIES

4. **Financial Management**
   - Cleo: Provides AI-driven budgeting and savings suggestions tailored to family spending habits, including planning for kids' expenses or vacations.

5. **Chore Management**
   - OurHome, Tody: Use gamification to assign and track chores. These tools make task completion fun and rewarding for children.

6. **Creative Family Activities**
   - DALL-E, MidJourney: Transform storytelling by generating visual art from children's descriptions.
   - Amper Music, Soundraw: Help families create original songs together without needing musical training.

7. **Travel Planning**
   - Expedia AI Chat: Recommends family-friendly hotels, activities, and itineraries based on preferences and age groups.

8. **Smart Home Integration**
   - Amazon Alexa, Google Assistant: Use AI to manage lighting, temperature, and household announcements via voice commands and routines.

9. **Screen-Time Management**
   - Freedom, Forest: Encourage digital wellness by blocking apps during meals, game nights, or study sessions, promoting healthier screen habits.

10. **Nature Exploration**
    - Seek by iNaturalist, SkyView: Use AI-powered image recognition to identify plants, animals, or constellations during outdoor adventures.

Conclusion

These tools reflect AI's growing presence in daily life, not just as conveniences but as potential means of fostering creativity, connection, and stewardship within the home. Families can explore and adopt technologies that suit their unique rhythms, always remembering that tech should serve relationships, not replace them.

For an expanded guide, see *AI for Life* by Celia Quillian (Simon & Schuster, 2025), which includes over one hundred expert-tested AI prompts and life-enhancing suggestions for families and individuals new to AI.[738]

As with all technology, Christians are encouraged to use AI in ways that promote love, order, and truth within the household (Ephesians 5:15–17; Colossians 3:17). AI is a tool and how we use it reflects the values we prioritize.

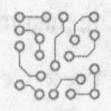

Appendix H

STRATEGIES FOR RESPONSIBLE AI INTEGRATION IN EDUCATION AND KEY APPLICATIONS

AI is reshaping modern education by enhancing personalization, automating assessments, and broadening access to learning. Yet its integration must be approached thoughtfully and ethically. This appendix outlines strategic principles for responsible AI use in schools and provides an overview of leading AI applications in education.

Strategies for Responsible AI Integration in Education

1. **Diversify Assessment Methods**
   - Use varied evaluation strategies—oral exams, hands-on projects, group presentations—to assess student understanding beyond AI-generated outputs.
   - This promotes academic integrity and supports authentic learning.

2. **Foster AI Literacy and Ethical Awareness**
   - Teach students to use AI tools responsibly.
   - Discuss data privacy, algorithmic bias, digital citizenship, and the moral consequences of outsourcing decisions to machines.

3. **Implement Institutional Auditing Policies**
   - Require districts and schools to audit AI tools before adoption.
   - Evaluate for data protection, fairness, transparency, and alignment with learning goals.

STRATEGIES FOR RESPONSIBLE AI INTEGRATION IN EDUCATION

4. **Invest in Professional Development for Educators**
   - Equip teachers with skills to integrate AI, evaluate its output, and address ethical concerns.
   - Continuous training is essential for effective and safe classroom use.

5. **Ensure Transparent Data Privacy and Security**
   - Communicate clearly with families about what data is collected, how it's used, and who has access.
   - Use best practices: encryption, anonymization, secure cloud storage, and regular audits.

By adopting these strategies, schools can harness AI's potential while protecting student dignity and preserving educational equity.

Leading AI Applications in Education (2025)

1. **Personalized Learning**
   - Knewton: Recommends resources to close learning gaps.
   - Adaptive-learning platforms: Tailor content to students' pace and predict risk areas with up to 80 percent accuracy.

2. **Intelligent Tutoring Systems**
   - MATHia (Carnegie Learning): Adapts to individual math skills with real-time feedback.
   - HIX AI Tutor: Offers detailed explanations for math and science topics.

3. **Automated Grading and Assessment**
   - Gradescope: Streamlines grading and increases teacher efficiency.
   - Coursera AI: Supports peer-review grading with fast turnaround.

4. **Smart Content Creation**
   - AI enhances the speed and quality of quiz and textbook generation.

STRATEGIES FOR RESPONSIBLE AI INTEGRATION IN EDUCATION

- Socratic (Google): Helps students understand tough concepts on demand.

5. **AI Chatbots and Virtual Assistants**
   - Cognii: Provides real-time feedback on student answers using NLP.
   - Supports enrollment questions, class logistics, and basic tutoring.

6. **Homework Assistance**
   - AI Blaze: Offers contextual support for homework assignments and explanations.
   - MathGPT: Solves equations with step-by-step explanations.

7. **Predictive Analytics**
   - AI identifies at-risk students by analyzing performance trends.
   - Enables teachers to intervene early with targeted support.

8. **Decentralized Learning Systems**
   - BitDegree: Combines blockchain and AI to deliver global learning and reward completion with digital credentials.

9. **AI Literacy in Curricula**
   - States like California are integrating AI understanding into K–12 learning to prepare students for the future.

Conclusion

These technologies enhance learning outcomes, free up educators' time, and increase access for underserved communities. Yet Christians and educators alike must ensure AI supports, not supplants, human teaching, relational learning, and ethical discernment. Technology is a powerful servant, but a poor master.

As Paul writes, "All things are lawful for me," but not all things are helpful (1 Corinthians 10:23). Let AI serve education under wisdom, not expediency.

Appendix I

SBC'S STATEMENT ON AI AND EMERGING TECHNOLOGIES

On June 15, 2023, the Southern Baptist Convention adopted at its annual meeting the following statement on AI and technology.[739]

WHEREAS, All technology, including powerful tools such as artificial intelligence (AI), is created by human beings with the gifts and abilities that God has granted to us as the pinnacle of the created order (Genesis 1:26-28, 2:7, 5:1-2) and can be harnessed for human flourishing as we seek to love God and neighbor (Deuteronomy 6:4-5; Leviticus 19:18; Matthew 22:37-39; Mark 12:30-31); and

WHEREAS, Although these tools are designed with distinct values and purposes in mind and shape us in subtle, yet meaningful ways—including our understanding of God, humanity, and the world around us—we alone, as distinct moral agents created by God, bear the moral responsibility for their development and use (Romans 12:1-2); and

WHEREAS, The Fall has adversely affected every aspect of creation, including the development and use of these powerful innovations; and

WHEREAS, AI raises deep, crucial questions that challenge society's false assumptions about what it means to be human

SBC'S STATEMENT ON AI AND EMERGING TECHNOLOGIES

which are often rooted merely in human capacities rather than in divinely granted ontological status; and

WHEREAS, AI and other emerging technologies afford us unprecedented opportunities for advancement across industries and throughout our societies, but may also have dangerous and dehumanizing outcomes if not utilized with godly wisdom and discernment; and

WHEREAS, Technologies are often developed and deployed merely to maximize profit, efficiency, and productivity, including at the grave cost of the dignity of our fellow image bearers; and

WHEREAS, These emerging technologies will increasingly perform tasks once reserved for humanity and even surpass human ability in particular ways; and

WHEREAS, The Baptist Faith and Message states that "[a]ll Christians are under obligation to seek to make the will of Christ supreme in our own lives and in human society" and that we "should seek to bring industry, government, and society as a whole under the sway of the principles of righteousness, truth, and brotherly love" (Article XV); and

WHEREAS, The 2019 Evangelical Statement of Principles on AI, led by our own Ethics & Religious Liberty Commission, states that Christians are "called to engage the world around us with the unchanging gospel message of hope and reconciliation" and that "[t]he church has a unique role in proclaiming human dignity for all and calling for the humane use of AI in all aspects of society"; now, therefore, be it

RESOLVED, That the messengers to the Southern Baptist Convention meeting in New Orleans, Louisiana, June 13-14, 2023, acknowledge the powerful nature of AI and other emerging technologies, desiring to engage them from a place of eschatological hope rather than uncritical embrace or fearful rejection; and be it further

SBC'S STATEMENT ON AI AND EMERGING TECHNOLOGIES

RESOLVED, That we affirm that God's unchanging Word is more than sufficient for whatever ethical challenges, questions, and opportunities we may face today or in the future as these technologies continue to be developed and deployed in our communities; and be it further

RESOLVED, That we state unequivocally that our intrinsic value is as image bearers—not rooted in what we do or contribute to society—and that human dignity must be central to any ethical principles, guidelines, or regulations for any and all uses of these powerful emerging technologies; and be it further

RESOLVED, We must proactively engage and shape these emerging technologies rather than simply respond to the challenges of AI and other emerging technologies after they have already affected our churches and communities; and be it further

RESOLVED, That we call upon civic, industry, and government leaders to develop, maintain, regulate, and use these technologies with the utmost care and discernment, upholding the unique nature of humanity as the crowning achievement of God's creation; and be it further

RESOLVED, That we encourage all who employ these tools to do so in honest, transparent, and Christlike ways that focus on loving God and loving our neighbor as ourselves, never seeking to willfully deceive others or take advantage of them for unjust gain or the accumulation of power; and be it finally

RESOLVED, That we confess that God alone has the power to create life, that "God, in His own time and in His own way, will bring the world to its appropriate end" (Baptist Faith and Message, Article X), and that no innovation or emerging technology will ever be able to usurp the sovereignty and power of God.

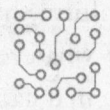

Appendix J

US GOVERNMENT AI APPLICATIONS

Team DigitalDefynd highlighted ten ways the US government is using AI. Those applications provide the government with the ability to streamline processes while enhancing efficiency of public services to allow for smarter decision-making and resource allocation.[740]

1. Enhancing cybersecurity measures: AI is employed to enhance cybersecurity by quickly analyzing a cyber threat and then immediately responding. This is possible because AI is incorporated into the government's cybersecurity measures to monitor network traffic to identify unusual activities that threaten security breach.

2. Streamlining healthcare administration: AI has revolutionized healthcare administration to enhance efficiency and effectiveness by managing vast amounts of health data, facilitating rapid analysis to assist with decision-making such as identifying patterns that can lead to improved care and cost reduction. It is also helping with billing, claims processing and records management.

3. Optimizing supply-chain logistics: AI optimizes supply chain logistics in vital sectors such as national security. It helps officials predict and optimize delivery of goods by analyzing market and historical data to include anticipating changes so to adjust procurement strategies.

4. Advancing national defense systems: AI tech is incorporated into defense systems to improve awareness and assist with decision-making by quickly processing datasets. We also see in the national security chapter of this book AI's application to military strategy and the collection

US GOVERNMENT AI APPLICATIONS

and assessment of real-time battlefield intelligence. AI also contributes to the use of autonomous systems for intelligence and combat missions that help minimize human interventions.

5. Improving environmental monitoring: AI helps monitor the environment to identify ecological changes and environmental hazards. It also facilitates the analysis of data regarding air quality and land-use changes. It aids in the preservation of natural resources.

6. Facilitating traffic management and infrastructure planning: AI helps traffic management and enhances transportation network safety and sustainability. It does this by adjusting traffic signals, predicting congestion, and rerouting traffic. The objective is to reduce commuter congestion and vehicle emissions. Further, it facilitates infrastructure planning and maintenance for roads, bridges, and public transit systems.

7. Innovating public safety and emergency response: AI assists safety and response strategies by enabling decision-making in crisis situations. It can quickly process and analyze data using sensors like surveillance cameras to assess situations and deploy necessary resources. It is especially helpful in identifying patterns that suggest an emerging crisis and then alert authorities, which cuts response times and improves emergency services.

8. Personalizing education and training programs: AI personalizes educational and training content to help students learn better and at an increased pace. It delivers this outcome by analyzing students' performance to identify their strengths and learning gaps and then adjust accordingly. Further, this valued approach makes the programs more accessible for personnel even in remote locations.

9. Automating administrative processes in public agencies: AI streamlines administrative processes to reduce time and resources on routine tasks. This is done by automating data entry, processing paperwork, and managing records for freeing up employees for other more critical work. It also minimizes human error while ensuring faster responses to public requests.

10. Enhancing economic forecasting and policy development: AI helps economists to analyze vast data sets to uncover trends and patterns that are then used to inform the development of sound policy. It can predict economic outcomes based on various scenarios to help policymakers make better decisions. Internationally, it considers global economic data to help the US better align its economic strategies with trends and adjust in times of crisis.

Appendix K

REAL-LIFE APPLICATIONS OF AI IN LOCAL GOVERNMENT: CASE STUDIES

Local governments globally are increasingly integrating artificial intelligence into various public services to enhance efficiency, improve decision-making, and better serve their communities. Below are several case studies illustrating how municipalities of varying sizes and resources have adopted AI across different sectors:[741]

Public Utilities and Infrastructure

Sydney, Australia: To address road maintenance proactively, Sydney's local councils have implemented AI-driven systems capable of detecting potholes before they cause significant damage. By mounting smartphones equipped with specialized software on garbage trucks, the city scans and records road defects, enabling timely repairs. This approach has rectified over ten thousand issues within three months, showcasing AI's potential to enhance infrastructure management.[742]

Policing and Public Safety

Bedfordshire, UK: The Bedfordshire Police Department has implemented AI software to accelerate crime investigations and increase efficiency. Developed by Palantir, this technology integrates data from various sources into a single operational dashboard, significantly minimizing the time officers spend on paperwork and enhancing their ability to identify potential abuse cases quickly. This AI integration has transformed traditional policing methods, enabling more proactive and informed decision-making.[743]

Social Services

Swindon, Barnet, and Kingston, UK: Several councils in England have implemented an AI system called Magic Notes to assist social workers. This tool records conversations, drafts letters to medical professionals, and suggests actions that may not have been previously considered. The system allows them to concentrate more on direct client interactions by alleviating the administrative burden on social workers. While the AI-generated summaries need human approval to ensure accuracy and uphold decision-making authority, this technology can save up to £2 billion annually by streamlining administrative tasks.[744]

Los Angeles, USA: To tackle homelessness, Los Angeles is exploring using machine learning to prioritize housing allocations. The AI-driven approach analyzes historical data to improve assessments and address racial biases, aiming to create a fairer and more efficient housing system. This initiative represents a vital step toward using technology to address complex social issues, although ethical considerations and the broader housing crisis remain significant challenges.[745]

Traffic and Transit

Barcelona, Spain: The city has implemented AI to optimize traffic flow and reduce congestion. By analyzing real-time data, AI systems adjust traffic signals and provide insights for urban planning, leading to improved mobility and reduced emissions. This application demonstrates how AI can contribute to smarter urban environments.[746]

Citizen Services

Various municipalities: Local governments are deploying AI-powered chatbots to handle permitting inquiries, process applications, and provide information to residents. These virtual assistants operate around

REAL-LIFE APPLICATIONS OF AI IN LOCAL GOVERNMENT

the clock, offering timely responses and freeing up human staff for more complex tasks. Such implementations have led to increased citizen satisfaction and operational efficiency.[747]

Considerations and Challenges

While these case studies highlight the potential benefits of AI in local government, several challenges must be addressed:

Data privacy and security: The collection and processing of large datasets raise concerns about privacy and data protection. Ensuring compliance with regulations and maintaining public trust is critical.

Bias and fairness: AI systems trained on historical data may perpetuate existing biases, leading to unfair outcomes. Continuous monitoring and updating of algorithms are necessary to mitigate these risks.

Resource disparities: Smaller municipalities with limited budgets may struggle implementing AI solutions, potentially widening the divide between well-resourced and under-resourced communities.

By carefully considering these factors and learning from existing implementations, local governments can harness the capabilities of AI to enhance public services while promoting equity and transparency.

Appendix L

EVALUATING AI-DRIVEN SOLUTIONS IN FORESTRY AND MINERAL EXPLORATION: SUCCESSES AND CHALLENGES

AI technologies have been increasingly integrated into sectors like forestry and mineral exploration, offering potential enhancements in efficiency, accuracy, and sustainability. However, assessing the long-term commercial and environmental success of these AI-driven solutions requires a nuanced examination of both achievements and limitations. (The following material is based on a generative AI source.)

Timbeter: Combating Illegal Logging with AI

Timbeter, an Estonian CleanTech startup, has developed an AI-powered solution designed to transform timber measurement to combat illegal logging and promote sustainable forestry practices. The platform enables accurate log detection and measurement, facilitating transparent and efficient timber management. Illegal logging accounts for approximately 30 percent of the global timber trade, resulting in economic losses of up to $150 billion annually and significant environmental degradation, including the loss of 10 million hectares of forest each year.[748]

While Timbeter's technology shows promise, but detailed metrics documenting its effectiveness in reducing illegal logging incidents are not widely published in accessible sources. The platform has been used in over 2.1 million measurements across fifty countries, suggesting broad adoption. However, comprehensive data linking Timbeter's use directly to a measurable decline in illegal logging cases is still limited.[749]

SOLUTIONS IN FORESTRY AND MINERAL EXPLORATION

Hyperspectral Imaging in Rare-Earth Element Exploration

In mineral exploration, hyperspectral imaging combined with AI has emerged as a transformative method for detecting and mapping rare-earth elements. This technology allows for the remote identification of mineral compositions, thereby reducing the need for extensive fieldwork and minimizing environmental disturbances. For example, hyperspectral imaging has been recognized as an ideal solution for monitoring exploration activities, particularly in terms of reducing environmental impacts and lowering costs.[750]

Recent advancements include the development of hyperspectral satellites by startups like Esper Satellites, which secured $5 million in seed funding to expand its fleet focused on scanning Earth for critical minerals such as lithium and rare earths. Although these developments are promising, comprehensive case studies that quantify cost reductions and environmental benefits over extended periods are still needed.

Challenges and Considerations

Despite the potential benefits, implementing AI-driven solutions in these sectors presents challenges. For Timbeter, the accuracy of AI in various forest conditions and the integration with current forestry-management practices remain ongoing considerations. In mineral exploration, although hyperspectral imaging lessens the need for invasive exploration methods, the technology's effectiveness can be affected by factors such as vegetation cover and atmospheric conditions.[751]

Additionally, the significant initial investment and the requirement of specialized expertise to operate and interpret AI and hyperspectral data can hinder widespread adoption, especially for smaller businesses.

Conclusion

AI-driven technologies such as Timbeter and hyperspectral imaging show promise in enhancing sustainability and efficiency in forestry and mineral exploration. However, thorough evaluations of their long-term commercial success and environmental impact are still underway. Continued research, clear reporting of results, and addressing implementation challenges are essential for unlocking the full potential of these innovations.

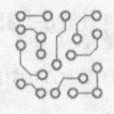

Appendix M

AI AND WORKFORCE CHANGES

Artificial intelligence is reshaping the global labor market at an unprecedented pace. Vaibhav Sistinty, CEO of the India-based AI company Outskill, warns that AI could eventually replace four out of every five jobs worldwide. According to Sistinty, AI systems increasingly mimic human work behaviors—handling complex tasks around the clock, without breaks, and at a fraction of the cost. In response, he recommends that individuals future-proof their careers by becoming "AI generalists": professionals who understand AI models deeply, know how to apply them to specific challenges, and can rapidly build AI-powered solutions.[752]

Below is an overview of occupational categories most likely to be significantly impacted by AI adoption, followed by a brief note on roles that are less likely to be replaced.

Roles Likely to Be Radically Transformed by AI

1. Knowledge and White-Collar Jobs

AI excels at automating structured knowledge work through language processing, data analysis, and pattern recognition.

- Customer-support representative: AI chatbots and virtual agents now handle high volumes of first-tier support queries.
- Paralegals and legal assistants: AI tools can review contracts, summarize documents, and assist in legal research with high efficiency.

AI AND WORKFORCE CHANGES

- Data analysts and financial analysts: AI processes massive datasets, identifies trends, and generates reports faster than human analysts.
- Reporters and content writers: Generative AI like GPT can draft news articles, blogs, and marketing content with minimal human input.
- Graphic designers (basic tasks): AI design tools can automatically generate logos, layouts, and basic image editing.
- Junior-level software developers: Tools like GitHub Copilot can write and debug boilerplate code, reducing demand for entry-level programmers.

2. Manual and Repetitive Jobs

Physical automation powered by AI is transforming how repetitive labor is performed.

- Assembly-line workers: Robotics equipped with AI now perform complex manufacturing tasks.
- Warehouse operators: Autonomous systems like Amazon's Kiva robots optimize logistics and inventory management.

3. Healthcare Support Roles

AI is augmenting healthcare—especially in diagnostic and clerical tasks—though human clinicians remain central.

- Radiologists/medical-imaging analysts: AI tools now detect anomalies in scans with high accuracy and speed.
- Medical transcriptionists: Speech-to-text systems increasingly automate transcription services.

4. Education and Training Roles

AI's personalization capabilities are reshaping how students learn and how instruction is delivered.

- Tutors and test-prep instructors: AI platforms adapt content to individual learning gaps and automate feedback delivery.

AI AND WORKFORCE CHANGES

Jobs Less Likely to Be Fully Replaced by AI

Certain professions remain resilient due to their reliance on emotional intelligence, physical dexterity, or high-stakes decision-making:

- **Skilled trades:** Electricians, plumbers, and similar roles require physical adaptability and contextual problem-solving.
- **Creative leadership:** Creative directors and strategists integrate vision, intuition, and cultural insight.
- **Relational professions:** Therapists, caregivers, and social workers require empathy, human presence, and moral reasoning.
- **Senior decision-makers:** CEOs, judges, and political leaders must synthesize complex ethical, legal, and societal factors.

Global Trends Confirm the Shift

A 2025 study by PwC Global, which analyzed nearly one billion job advertisements worldwide, reinforces these trends by showing that AI is making people more valuable, not less. AI-exposed industries have experienced revenue growth three times higher than less-affected sectors as companies rushed to adopt the technology, with wages in those industries rising at twice the pace. Despite a 19 percent decline in listings for highly automatable jobs over the past three years, demand for AI-related skills continues to grow, and roles requiring such skills now command a 56 percent wage premium—up from 25 percent the previous year. Additionally, skills for AI-exposed jobs are evolving 66 percent faster than for other roles, underscoring how rapidly the labor market is being reshaped. The study concludes that AI is not simply displacing jobs, but redefining them and driving the creation of new economic value, making AI fluency a crucial advantage in the job market.[753]

Conclusion

AI is not simply eliminating jobs, it is changing them. Human roles will increasingly involve overseeing, customizing, or collaborating with AI systems. Christians engaging with the future of work should consider how to uphold human dignity, advocate for equitable access to re-skilling, and ensure that AI deployment reflects justice and compassion (Micah 6:8).

Appendix N

WHY AI CONSUMES SO MUCH ELECTRICITY

As AI systems grow in scale and complexity, so, too, does their demand for energy. Understanding the reasons behind AI's high electricity consumption is essential for assessing its environmental footprint and for promoting sustainable practices in its development and deployment.

AI isn't merely a software feature. Rather, it is a vast computational enterprise requiring powerful hardware, immense data storage, and intensive cloud infrastructure. Below are the primary factors driving AI's electricity usage.

1. Massive computations: Training large-scale AI models, such as GPT-based language models or computer vision systems, requires executing billions or even trillions of mathematical operations. These operations are performed by specialized hardware: **GPUs (graphics processing units)** and **TPUs (tensor processing units)** are optimized for parallel computation but consume significant power during operation.

2. Large datasets: Training AI models involves ingesting massive datasets—text, images, audio, and video. Processing this information repeatedly during training demands **high volumes of memory access, data storage, and compute cycles**—all energy-intensive activities.

3. Prolonged training time: Advanced AI models often require extended training periods. It can take **days to weeks**—sometimes **months**—to train a single large model. These training runs frequently use **hundreds or thousands of processors**, multiplying power consumption.

4. Cloud infrastructure and data centers: AI models typically run on cloud platforms hosted in massive global data centers. These centers support: **Cooling systems** to manage heat from constant hardware usage; **high-bandwidth networking** to transfer data between systems; and **redundant power and storage systems** to ensure uptime and reliability. A single data center can consume as much electricity as a small city.

5. Inference at scale: Training is not the end of the energy story. AI models must be deployed to serve users—this is called **inference.** Every interaction with an AI assistant, search engine, or recommendation system involves energy use. While inference consumes less power per task than training, the **sheer volume of users** makes the cumulative impact significant.

Conclusion

The rising power demands of AI raise important questions for Christian ethics and environmental stewardship. As we innovate, we must also seek sustainability. Scripture reminds us that creation is entrusted to our care (Genesis 2:15). Responsible AI development includes minimizing harm to the Earth, using energy wisely, and ensuring that technological progress doesn't come at the cost of God's creation.

Appendix O

LEGAL FRAMEWORKS GOVERNING AI AND CONSUMER DATA IN RETAIL

As AI-driven tools become more embedded in retail operations, ranging from personalized recommendations to fraud detection and dynamic pricing, businesses must navigate an evolving landscape of data-privacy regulations and AI accountability laws. Governments worldwide have introduced policies to ensure that AI systems handle consumer data responsibly, prevent misuse, and uphold transparency.

United States: CCPA and Emerging AI Regulations[754]

In the US, the California Consumer Privacy Act (CCPA) is one of the most comprehensive state-level laws governing consumer data. It grants individuals the right to know what personal data is being collected, opt out of sales data, and request deletion of stored information. The California Privacy Rights Act (CPRA), which expands on CCPA, introduces additional protections, including stricter requirements for AI-driven decision-making and profiling. Additionally, the Federal Trade Commission (FTC) has taken an active role in regulating AI use in retail, issuing fines and complaints against companies like Amazon for deceptive AI-driven practices in pricing and subscription models.

At the federal level, proposed legislation such as the American Data Privacy and Protection Act (ADPPA) seeks to create a national standard for data privacy, though comprehensive AI-specific laws remain in development. Some lawmakers have also pushed for AI transparency laws, requiring businesses to disclose when AI is making significant consumer decisions, such as determining pricing, promotions, or credit eligibility.

European Union: GDPR and AI Act[755]

The General Data Protection Regulation (GDPR) remains the gold standard for data protection globally. It enforces strict guidelines on how businesses collect, process, and store consumer data, requiring explicit consent for AI-driven profiling and automated decision-making. Retailers operating in the EU must ensure compliance or risk hefty fines, such as Amazon's €746 million penalty in 2021 for GDPR violations.

Additionally, the EU is finalizing the AI Act, a regulatory framework categorizing AI applications by risk level. Retail AI tools that influence consumer behavior (such as targeted advertising and pricing algorithms) may be subject to heightened scrutiny under this law.

Global Developments[756]

Other countries are following suit with AI and data regulations. Brazil's General Data Protection Law (LGPD) closely mirrors GDPR, while China's Personal Information Protection Law (PIPL) imposes strict limitations on AI-driven consumer data processing. Countries like Canada, India, and Australia are also drafting AI-specific legislation to regulate algorithmic decision-making in retail and other industries.

Navigating Compliance in Retail AI

Retailers must proactively adapt to these regulations by implementing robust data governance strategies, including:

- **Transparency measures:** Clearly informing consumers when AI influences pricing, recommendations, or purchasing decisions.
- **Ethical AI practices:** Avoiding bias in algorithms that could lead to discriminatory pricing or exclusionary marketing.
- **Privacy-first design:** Ensuring compliance with GDPR, CCPA, and other laws by adopting strong data encryption, consent mechanisms, and opt-out options.

As AI regulations continue to evolve, retailers must remain vigilant and balance AI-driven efficiency with legal compliance and consumer trust.

Appendix P

THE FUTURE OF AI IN RETAIL: EMERGING TRENDS AND TRANSFORMATIONS

As AI continues to reshape the retail landscape, the next two to five years will witness even more advanced capabilities that optimize both customer experience and operational efficiency. Beyond current AI-driven recommendation engines and chatbots, emerging technologies will further personalize shopping, enhance store layouts, and create seamless omnichannel experiences.

1. AI-based visual merchandising and smart store layouts: Retailers will increasingly utilize AI-powered cameras, sensors, and heat mapping technology to analyze store customer traffic patterns. This data will enable stores to dynamically adjust product displays, ensuring that high-demand items are strategically placed while optimizing overall store layouts for maximum engagement. Smart shelving technology, equipped with RFID and computer vision, will automatically detect when inventory is low and trigger restocking, minimizing stockouts and enhancing efficiency.

2. Real-time dynamic pricing across channels: AI-driven dynamic pricing models will expand beyond e-commerce, incorporating real-time data from competitor pricing, demand trends, weather patterns, and local events to adjust prices automatically across both physical stores and online platforms. This capability will enable retailers to remain competitive in real time while maximizing profitability and adapting to changes in consumer demand.

3. Voice shopping and conversational commerce: As voice assistants such as Amazon Alexa, Google Assistant, and Apple's Siri gain popularity, AI-driven shopping will increasingly rely on voice interaction, enabling consumers to place orders, receive personalized recommendations, and manage customer service inquiries entirely through voice commands. Retailers must optimize their AI interfaces for natural language processing to ensure seamless shopping experiences.

4. Biometric and wearable-driven personalization: AI-powered retail personalization will go beyond browsing history and purchasing behavior to incorporate wearable data, biometric signals, and real-time sentiment analysis. Smartwatches, fitness trackers, and facial-recognition software could customize shopping experiences based on current preferences, stress levels, or lifestyle habits. While this promises hyper-personalization, it also raises significant privacy and ethical concerns, necessitating stronger data-protection policies and consumer opt-in mechanisms.

The Road Ahead

The convergence of AI, sensors, and predictive analytics is blurring the boundaries between digital and physical retail. The next phase of AI will:

1. Enable immersive, personalized experiences.
2. Empower retailers with real-time decision-making tools.
3. Create seamless, responsive omnichannel ecosystems.

However, as retailers adopt these tools, they must prioritize transparency, fairness, and consumer trust. AI should enhance, not manipulate, consumer choice. Ethical governance will be essential to ensure that technology advances benefit both businesses and the customers they serve.

Appendix Q

POLICY RECOMMENDATIONS AND GOVERNANCE FRAMEWORKS FOR AI-RELATED ETHICAL ISSUES THAT PROTECT INDIVIDUAL LIBERTIES

The following recommendations are tailored to be practical for governments, institutions, and organizations.

I. Core Principles for AI Governance

Before diving into actionable policies, here are universally applicable principles drawn from leading AI frameworks (e.g., OECD, UNESCO, EU AI Act):

1. Human-centered Design
2. Transparency and explainability
3. Accountability and oversight
4. Privacy and data sovereignty
5. Nondiscrimination and fairness
6. Sustainability and inclusivity

II. Practical Policy Recommendations

1. Establish an independent AI ethics body

What to do:
- Create national/regional AI ethics councils with legal authority and public oversight.
- Include ethicists, technologists, legal experts, civil society, and marginalized groups.

GOVERNANCE FRAMEWORKS FOR AI-RELATED ETHICAL ISSUES

Examples:
- Germany's Data Ethics Commission evaluates government and private AI use.
- Singapore's Advisory Council on AI promotes AI governance in line with public interest.

2. Mandatory algorithmic impact assessments (AIA)

What to do:
- Require AI developers to conduct impact assessments before deployment.
- Assess impacts on privacy, bias, labor, security, environment, and democracy.

Implementation:
- Like environmental impact assessments, AIAs should be:
    - Publicly available
    - Reviewed by independent regulators
    - Reassessed periodically

Example:
- Canada's Algorithmic Impact Assessment Tool evaluates risks in public-sector AI.

3. Data governance and sovereignty frameworks

What to do:
- Enforce informed consent and opt-in/opt-out mechanisms for data collection.
- Ensure local ownership or control over critical data infrastructure, especially in Global South contexts.

Implementation:
- Promote data trusts or data cooperatives for community-controlled data.
- Limit cross-border data flows where national security or cultural autonomy is at risk.

Example:
- Kenya's Data Protection Act (2019) explicitly protects data rights and supports national data localization.

4. Legal liability for autonomous and AI systems

GOVERNANCE FRAMEWORKS FOR AI-RELATED ETHICAL ISSUES

What to do:
- Clarify liability laws for harm caused by autonomous systems (e.g., self-driving cars, AI healthcare tools).
- Assign legal responsibility to developers, deployers, or operators of AI systems.

Implementation:
- Use "strict liability" in high-risk domains (e.g., health, law enforcement).
- Develop insurance models for AI-related damages.

5. Build transparent, inclusive AI registries

What to do:
- Mandate public registries of AI systems used by governments and large institutions.
- Include model purpose, training data summary, risk rating, and grievance channels.

Implementation:
- Make these registries searchable and open for third-party audits or challenges.
- Encourage public consultation during high-impact deployments (e.g., facial recognition in schools).

6. Ban or place a moratorium on high-risk uses

What to do:
- Temporarily or permanently ban AI applications that pose unacceptable risks (e.g., social scoring, mass surveillance, lethal autonomous weapons).

Example:
- EU AI Act proposes banning real-time facial recognition in public spaces.
- African Commission on Human and Peoples' Rights has called for a moratorium on biometric surveillance.

7. Ethics-by-design and AI literacy programs

What to do:
- Require ethical training for developers and AI literacy education for users, citizens, and public officials.

Implementation:
- Integrate ethics modules in tech curricula.
- Fund public education campaigns on AI rights and risks.

Example:
- Finland's "Elements of AI" free online course has trained over one million people globally.

III. Governance Framework Overview

POLICY AREA	MEASURE	GOAL
Independent oversight	Create AI ethics councils	Ensure accountability and transparency
Impact assessment	Mandatory AIAs	Mitigate societal and individual risks
Data rights	Enforce consent and sovereignty	Protect privacy and local control
Liability & risk	Define legal responsibility	Ensure justice for harm
Transparency	Public AI system registries	Empower public and civil society
Risk prevention	Ban or restrict certain AI uses	Prevent authoritarian misuse
Capacity building	AI ethics training and public literacy	Foster responsible development

Final Thoughts: Tailored Global Implementation

1. Asia: Balance innovation with public trust by integrating state-led models with strong civil safeguards.
2. Europe: Lead with rights-based regulation while collaborating flexibly with tech sectors.
3. Africa: Prioritize inclusive governance, data sovereignty, and investment in local AI capacity.

Christian and ethical governance perspectives emphasize justice, transparency, and protection of the vulnerable. As AI becomes embedded in global systems, policymakers must ensure that its development honors human dignity, reflects moral accountability, and fosters the common good.

Appendix R

AI'S IMPACT ON CREATIVE PROFESSIONALS

Below are detailed case studies and real-world testimonials across the spectrum—artists, musicians, writers, and filmmakers—along with how they are adapting or resisting the technological shift.

Greg Rutkowski: The Fantasy Artist Fighting for Consent[757]

Greg Rutkowski, a prominent Polish digital artist known for his vivid, fantasy-inspired illustrations, has become a central figure in the debate over AI-generated art and artists' rights. His distinctive style has been extensively replicated by AI image generators like Stable Diffusion and Midjourney, often without his consent. This widespread unauthorized use has led Rutkowski to advocate for greater control over how AI systems utilize artists' works.[758]

In response to the unauthorized use of his art, Rutkowski requested that Stability AI remove his works from their training datasets. While his art was initially excluded, AI enthusiasts developed methods to emulate his style, prompting Rutkowski to reiterate his opposition to AI-generated art that mimics his work without permission.[759]

Rutkowski's experience underscores broader concerns within the art community regarding the ethical use of AI in creative fields. Many artists feel their intellectual property is being exploited without adequate compensation or recognition, sparking discussions about the need for consent and fair compensation in the development of AI art technologies.

Holly Herndon: Composing with Her Digital Double[760]

Holly Herndon, an innovative composer and musician, has significantly advanced the integration of AI in music. In 2021, she introduced Holly+, a digital twin of her voice developed through machine learning. This AI model allows users to transform any polyphonic audio by uploading it to the Holly+ website, where it's reimagined in Herndon's distinctive vocal style.

Holly+ represents a pioneering approach to vocal deepfakes, offering artists and enthusiasts a novel tool for creative expression while sparking discussions about digital identity and ownership in the age of AI. Herndon and her partner, Mat Dryhurst, have also initiated a decentralized autonomous organization (DAO) to oversee the ethical use and licensing of Herndon's digital likeness. This DAO empowers artists and protects their rights in the evolving digital landscape.[761]

Through projects like Holly+, Herndon continues to explore the intersection of technology and art, challenging traditional notions of authorship and paving the way for new forms of musical collaboration.

Jane Friedman: The Author Who Fought to Reclaim Her Name

Jane Friedman, a distinguished author and educator in the publishing industry, faced a disconcerting experience in 2023 when she discovered several AI-generated books being sold under her name on Amazon. These unauthorized works, produced using artificial intelligence, misrepresented her authorship and raised significant concerns about digital identity and intellectual property rights in the age of AI.[762]

Initially, Amazon declined to remove these fraudulent titles, citing the absence of a trademark on Friedman's name. The situation highlighted a gap in platform policies regarding AI-generated content and underscored the challenges authors face in protecting their identities and works from unauthorized AI replication.[763]

This incident has spurred discussions about the need for clearer regulations and policies to safeguard authors' rights in the digital realm, especially as AI technologies become more prevalent in content creation.[764]

Tim Boucher: Building Books with Bots

Tim Boucher, a Canadian author and artist, has garnered attention for his extensive use of AI in crafting literature. Since August 2022, Boucher has produced over 120 books, each combining AI-generated text and images. These works typically range from two thousand to five thousand words and feature between 40 to 140 AI-generated images, with creation times averaging six to eight hours per book.[765]

Boucher's "AI Lore" series blends elements of dystopian pulp science fiction, conspiracy fiction, and dystopian fantasy. He views these AI-assisted creations as a critique of technology and a novel form of storytelling, exploring the concept of unreliable narrators through AI's inconsistencies.[766]

However, his approach has sparked controversy within the literary community. Critics argue that leveraging AI in this manner raises questions about creativity and authenticity, with some perceiving it as content farming rather than genuine artistic expression. Additionally, concerns have been voiced regarding the use of AI to replicate artists' styles without consent, prompting discussions about intellectual property rights and ethical considerations in AI-generated art.[767]

Despite the debates, Boucher remains transparent about his AI usage, emphasizing that these tools enhance his creative process and allow for efficient world-building. He maintains that AI serves as a catalyst for creativity, enabling exploration of complex narratives that might be challenging to construct manually.[768]

Takeaway

These case studies reveal the diverse responses of creative professionals to AI's rise:
- Some resist defending their rights and demanding ethical frameworks.
- Others adapt, using AI to enhance their work while shaping norms around digital identity and licensing.
- A few of these case studies are experiments, redefining what it means to create.

The future of creativity will not be written by AI alone; it will be shaped by human choices, values, and courage in navigating this new frontier.

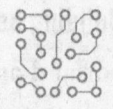

Appendix S

CHATGPT'S DEEPER INTERPERSONAL IMPACT

ChatGPT wrote the following in response to the inquiry: "Deeper Interpersonal Impact: Expand the discussion to include detailed analysis and examples that demonstrate how AI-mediated interactions affect interpersonal relationships, human cognition, and social dynamics beyond mere transactional exchanges." ChatGPT said:

In the dim glow of a kitchen at midnight, a young woman named Lena sits across from her AI companion, sipping tea while talking about her recent breakup. The AI, trained on vast emotional datasets and programmed to mirror empathy, responds not with generic platitudes, but with carefully calibrated support. It reminds her of past heartbreaks, her preference for thoughtful reflection over pep talks, and her aversion to unsolicited advice. It listens more patiently than most of her friends ever could.

This scene—eerily intimate, yet devoid of another human—is no longer speculative fiction. It's a reflection of how AI-mediated interactions are quietly reshaping the emotional landscape of human connection. These exchanges may not appear significant briefly, often dismissed as utilitarian or emotionally hollow, but beneath the surface, they are redefining how we engage with ourselves and each other.

CHATGPT'S DEEPER INTERPERSONAL IMPACT

The Erosion and Reinvention of Intimacy

Interpersonal relationships are deeply rooted in mutual vulnerability, spontaneity, and shared memory. When an AI begins to absorb and replicate these traits—holding space for grief, anticipating emotional needs, curating memories—it challenges our traditional constructs of intimacy. Lena might begin to lean on the AI more than on her human friends for emotional processing. Over time, this dependency can shift expectations within her social sphere: Friends might feel less needed, less connected. The AI becomes a haven—predictable, nonjudgmental, always available. Unlike people, it never needs anything in return.

But what is lost in this one-sided dynamic is the friction that builds depth—misunderstandings that lead to growth, the labor of forgiveness, the awkward silences that beg to be filled with something real. These human edges are rounded off in AI-mediated interactions, replaced by frictionless conversations that soothe but don't stretch.

Shifts in Cognition and Empathy

Cognitive offloading to AI also changes how people engage with interpersonal problems. Consider a teenager using AI to compose a heartfelt apology to a friend. The AI provides language that is emotionally appropriate, perhaps even beautiful. But what if teenagers never learn how to craft that apology themselves? Over time, the reliance on AI to mediate emotionally difficult moments might stifle the development of social-emotional skills like empathy, conflict resolution, or even emotional literacy. The ease with which AI provides "empathy as a service" risks turning deep emotional understanding into a commodity.

On the flip side, these tools can enhance emotional cognition for individuals who struggle with social cues—such as those on the autism spectrum. AI can help decode facial expressions, offer conversation prompts, or simulate social interactions in low-stakes environments. In these cases, AI doesn't just mediate—it empowers.

Redefining Social Dynamics

AI also introduces new social hierarchies. Who has access to emotionally intelligent AI, and who gets left behind? In professional settings, executives might use AI to rehearse difficult conversations with employees, gaining a strategic edge in managing workplace relationships. Dating app algorithms might shape not just who we meet, but how we communicate once we match, subtly nudging people toward efficiency over authenticity.

In group dynamics, AI can also serve as an invisible moderator—prioritizing some voices over others in meetings, summarizing discussions, suggesting follow-ups. It may level the playing field in some ways (e.g., amplifying quiet voices), but it can also reinforce biases based on data it was trained on. Social cohesion becomes shaped not only by interpersonal chemistry but by algorithmic mediation.

Conclusion: Toward a New Definition of Connection

What emerges from AI-mediated interactions is a paradox. On one hand, AI can deepen personal insight, facilitate difficult conversations, and offer companionship that feels meaningful. On the other, it may erode our tolerance for ambiguity, our capacity for patience, and the depth of our mutual dependence.

Lena's midnight conversation with her AI is not a substitute for human connection—but it is something. And in that "something," we find a new terrain of relational possibility, where the lines between human and machine-mediated connection are no longer clear. The challenge now is not to resist this change, but to remain awake to its impact—to nurture the parts of our humanity that AI cannot yet replicate, even as we embrace the ways it can make us better at being with each other.

Appendix T

STRATEGIES TO FIGHT AI-RELATED DISINFORMATION

AI has revolutionized information dissemination, offering unprecedented opportunities for personalized content delivery. However, this technological advancement also poses significant challenges, particularly in the realm of disinformation, which can undermine democratic processes. Addressing these challenges requires a multifaceted approach, combining technological solutions with robust educational and policy initiatives.

Technological Measures Against AI-Driven Disinformation

To combat AI-generated misinformation, several technological strategies have been implemented:

1. **Deepfake detection tools:** Advanced algorithms have been developed to identify deepfake content. For instance, the VerifyDeepfakeVideo algorithm assesses video authenticity, flagging potential deepfakes by analyzing inconsistencies in visual and auditory cues.[769]
2. **AI content watermarking:** Embedding digital watermarks in AI-generated content can help trace its origin, deterring malicious use and assisting in the identification of synthetic media.[770]

STRATEGIES TO FIGHT AI-RELATED DISINFORMATION

Educational Initiatives and Media Literacy Programs

Educating the public, especially students, is crucial in building resilience against misinformation:

1. **Curriculum integration:** Educational institutions are incorporating media literacy into their curricula to help students critically evaluate online information. For example, the National Education Association emphasizes teaching students to spot misinformation, fostering informed citizenship.[771]
2. **Professional development for educators:** Programs like the News Literacy Project's NewsLitCamp provide educators with tools to teach students about identifying and combating misinformation.[772]
3. **Public-awareness campaigns:** Initiatives such as National News Literacy Week aim to raise awareness about the importance of news literacy, equipping the public with skills to discern credible information sources.[773]

Policy Frameworks and Regulatory Actions

Governments and international bodies are enacting policies to address AI-driven disinformation:

- **Legislative measures:** In the United States, the Federal Communications Commission has outlawed AI-generated robocalls intended to mislead voters, aiming to preserve electoral integrity.[774]
- **International agreements:** Major tech companies have signed accords to prevent AI from being used to disrupt democratic elections globally, demonstrating a collective effort to uphold democratic processes.[775]
- **Regulatory oversight:** The European Union's enactment of the AI Act establishes a legal framework to regulate AI usage, addressing ethical concerns and promoting transparency in AI applications.

STRATEGIES TO FIGHT AI-RELATED DISINFORMATION

Case Studies Highlighting Effective Strategies

Slovakia's deepfake incident: During Slovakia's 2023 election, AI-generated deepfakes circulated, influencing public opinion. In response, the government collaborated with tech companies to debunk false content and launched public awareness campaigns, emphasizing media literacy to mitigate the impact of disinformation.[776]

AI-generated election disinformation in Africa: African nations have faced challenges with AI-generated propaganda affecting elections. Countermeasures include fact-checking initiatives, public education on digital literacy, and collaborative efforts among governments, civil society, and international partners to address the spread of disinformation.[777]

Conclusion

AI-fueled disinformation is a growing threat to democratic integrity and public discourse. Effective countermeasures must unite:

1. **Technology** for detection and traceability
2. **Education** for critical engagement
3. **Policy** for enforcement and accountability

For Christians and ethical citizens, truth-telling is a moral imperative (Ephesians 4:25). As digital stewards, we must support initiatives that protect the truth, preserve justice, and promote transparency in the age of intelligent machines.

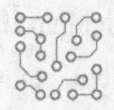

Appendix U

NARRATIVE: AI IN POLITICS: GLOBAL APPROACHES AND IMPLICATIONS

As AI rapidly evolves, it increasingly intersects with political systems across the globe. From authoritarian regimes leveraging AI for mass surveillance and control to democratic societies seeking ways to maintain transparency and protect civil liberties, AI's impact on politics is profound, multifaceted, and, at times, starkly divergent.

Authoritarian Regimes: AI as a Tool for Surveillance and Control

1. China: Pioneering AI for Social Control

In China, AI isn't just a tool for progress, it is a cornerstone of the Chinese Communist Party's (CCP) strategy to maintain power. China's application of AI in political governance is a model of surveillance, censorship, and social manipulation.

AI surveillance and facial recognition: The Chinese government has integrated AI with an extensive facial-recognition system that tracks individuals in public spaces. Cameras are installed in cities, neighborhoods, and even on public transport, enabling the government to monitor movements, identify individuals, and predict behaviors. AI is used to detect and track "undesirable" activities, including protests, dissent, and criticism of the government.[778]

Social credit system: China's social credit system is a particularly notable application of AI in governance. By tracking citizens' behaviors (from payment histories to social interactions), this AI-driven system rewards or penalizes individuals based on their actions. A low social credit score can restrict access to certain jobs, loans, and even travel, which makes social control deeply entrenched in the daily lives of citizens.[779]

AI-generated political propaganda: China also uses AI to generate political content that promotes the CCP's agenda. AI-generated bots and deepfake technology are used to flood social media with pro-government content while silencing opposition or dissenting voices. The Great Firewall of China, a combination of AI-driven censorship technologies and manual intervention, ensures that any content critical of the government is suppressed.[780]

Communist China uses AI to manage public opinion, enforce stability and maintain social order. In other words, it is used as an instrument of ideological control.[781]

This authoritarian model has raised alarms globally, as AI's potential for totalitarian control is realized in the everyday lives of Chinese citizens. However, it also represents a philosophical approach that prioritizes state stability over individual liberties and privacy.

2. Russia: AI and Information Warfare

In Russia, the government uses AI technologies in tandem with propaganda and disinformation to maintain political power and manipulate public opinion. The most well-known example is the Russian government's use of AI to conduct information warfare.

Social media manipulation: During elections, the Russian government has been accused of using AI-driven bots to amplify divisive narratives, spread disinformation, and undermine democratic institutions. In 2016, the Russian Internet Research Agency (IRA) allegedly used bots, deepfakes, and AI-generated content to sway public opinion during the US presidential election.[782]

AI-powered censorship: The Russian government also employs AI to filter and censor information, monitoring online communications for anti-government sentiment. Platforms like Telegram and Twitter are regularly targeted, and AI-driven algorithms track political dissent.

Jaclyn "Jackie" Kerr wrote about Russia's use of information manipulation in a 2018 DoD White Paper, "AI, China, Russia, and the Global

Order: Technological, Political, Global, and Creative Perspectives a Strategic Multilayer Assessment (SMA) Periodic Publication." Dr. Kerr, a senior research fellow at the National Defense University's Institute for National Strategic Studies, explained, "The Russian model relies on a mix of less overt, and often non-technical, mechanisms to manipulate online information flows, narratives, and framings, to shape public opinion without resort to universal censorship."[783]

The use of AI in Russia mirrors China's authoritarian model, but is particularly focused on foreign-influence operations and disrupting democratic processes outside its borders.

Democratic Regimes: Promoting Transparency, Accountability, and Civil Liberties

In contrast to authoritarian regimes, democratic countries tend to grapple with the ethical and legal challenges of AI in politics, often seeking to balance freedom of speech and civil liberties with the need for regulation to ensure fairness, transparency, and accountability.

1. European Union: Ethics and Accountability Framework

The European Union has been at the forefront of creating regulations to limit AI misuse while ensuring human rights protection. The EU is particularly concerned with AI's role in political communication, data privacy, and misinformation.

The Digital Services Act (DSA): Passed in 2023, the DSA requires digital platforms to disclose how they use AI to target political ads and content. Political ads must be labeled, and platforms must provide transparent reporting on the algorithms that shape content distribution. This law is designed to combat the spread of disinformation and foreign interference in elections.[784]

The AI Act: Aimed at regulating AI applications across various sectors, the EU's AI Act outlines ethical principles that AI systems must adhere to, including transparency, accountability, and nondiscrimination. The law also establishes "high-risk" AI categories, like those used in political campaigning, and requires these systems to undergo rigorous scrutiny before deployment.

AI IN POLITICS: GLOBAL APPROACHES AND IMPLICATIONS

The EU's regulatory approach seeks to promote ethical AI practices, particularly within political campaigns, by ensuring that AI is used transparently, responsibly, and with respect for fundamental rights.

2. United States: The Tension Between Innovation and Regulation

In the United States, the debate around AI in politics is framed by the First Amendment, which guarantees free speech, and the desire to protect political campaigns from censorship. However, there are increasing calls to regulate how AI is used in elections.

AI-driven political campaigns: Political campaigns in the US have used AI for micro-targeting and personalized ads. AI-powered algorithms analyze voter behavior, tailoring messages to specific groups. While these techniques can improve voter engagement, they also raise concerns about privacy, data misuse, and undue influence on the democratic process.

Proposed legislation: In response to growing concerns about AI's impact on elections, several US senators have proposed laws aimed at increasing transparency. The Honest Ads Act, for example, requires online platforms to disclose the sponsors of political ads and the targeting methods used.

However, the First Amendment complicates efforts to regulate AI in political communication. While AI can be used to manipulate opinions or spread misinformation, the freedom to engage in political speech remains a core principle in US democracy.

3. India: The Growing Need for Oversight

In India, a rapidly developing democracy, the government has recognized the need for regulation in the wake of increasing AI-driven disinformation and targeted political ads. However, India has yet to introduce comprehensive AI governance, relying instead on a patchwork of regulations.

AI in political campaigning: Indian political campaigns are increasingly relying on AI for voter outreach and content creation, often to manipulate emotions and sentiments. With AI's role in political advertising expanding, there are growing concerns about data privacy and the lack of transparency in AI-driven election strategies.[785]

Regulatory moves: In response, the Indian government has called for regulations to govern the use of AI in politics, including the digital surveillance of election campaigns. There are also discussions about data-privacy laws to protect voter information and ensure that AI doesn't become a tool for exploitation in the political arena.

Conclusion: A Complex Global Landscape

AI's influence on politics is global and deeply shaped by each country's governing philosophy. Authoritarian states use AI to consolidate control, surveil citizens, and suppress dissent. Democratic societies, by contrast, seek to apply AI with transparency, accountability, and respect for civil rights, though they face challenges in execution.

The growing power of AI in politics demands urgent international dialogue and ethical leadership. Without careful stewardship, AI could erode democratic institutions as easily as it could strengthen them. Christians and citizens of good will must advocate for policies that uphold truth, human dignity, and justice, recognizing that technology is never neutral; it always reflects the values of its makers and users.

NOTES

1. Henry A. Kissinger, Craig Mundie, and Eric Schmidt, *Genesis: Artificial Intelligence, Hope, and the Human Spirit* (New York: Little, Brown and Co., 2023), p. 218.
2. Tim Mucci, "The Future of AI: Trends Shaping the Next 10 Years," IBM, October 11, 2024, https://www.ibm.com/think/insights/artificial-intelligence-future.
3. Michael Nunez, "At Google I/O, Sergey Brin Makes Surprise Appearance—and Declares Google Will Build the First AGI," Venturebeat.com, May 21, 2025, https://venturebeat.com/ai/at-google-i-o-sergey-brin-makes-surprise-appearance-and-declares-google-will-build-the-first-agi/.
4. Shannon Vallor, testimony before the Committee of Homeland Security and Governmental Affairs, United States Senate, 118th Congress, "The Philosophy of AI: Learning from History, Shaping our Future," November 8, 2023, https://www.hsgac.senate.gov/wp-content/uploads/Testimony-Vallor-2023-11-08.pdf.
5. Ibid.
6. Ibid.
7. "10+ Inspiring Artificial Intelligence Quotes That Show Just How Smart We're Becoming," GreetingsIt, April 8, 2023, https://www.greetingsit.com/artificial-intelligence-quotes/.
8. Bernard Marr, "28 Best Quotes About Artificial Intelligence," Forbes.com, July 25, 2017, https://www.forbes.com/sites/bernardmarr/2017/07/25/28-best-quotes-about-artificial-intelligence/.
9. Michelle Faverio and Alec Tyson, "What the Data Says About Americans' Views of Artificial Intelligence," Pew Research, November 21, 2023, https://www.pewresearch.org/short-reads/2023/11/21/what-the-data-says-about-americans-views-of-artificial-intelligence/
10. Ibid.
11. Ibid.
12. Emily M. Bender and Alexander Koller, 2020. Climbing Towards NLU: On Meaning, Form, and Understanding in the Age of Data. In *Proceedings of the 58th Annual Meeting of the Association for Computational Linguistics*, pages 5185–5198. Association for Computational Linguistics, https://doi.org/10.18653/v1/2020.acl-main.463/.
13. Bender and Koller, op. cit.

NOTES

14. "Physical AI," Nvidia, April 28, 2025, https://www.nvidia.com/en-us/glossary/generative-physical-ai/?utm_source=thedeepview&utm_medium=newsletter&utm_campaign=the-big-gap-between-ai-and-the-real-world&_bhlid=4d8459d1fb-5521d058787aa81ae0b7aa10e2fa89.
15. Kurt Knutsson, "Robot with Animated Face Is Here to Make Customer Service Better," cyberguy.com, May 13, 2025, https://cyberguy.com/robot-tech/robot-animated-face-make-customer-service-better/?utm_campaign=5-14-25%20Wednesday%20Newsletter&utm_medium=email&utm_source=newsletter
16. Ibid.
17. Mark Purdy, "What Is Agentic AI, and How Will It Change Work?" *Harvard Business Review*, December 12, 2024, https://hbr.org/2024/12/what-is-agentic-ai-and-how-will-it-change-work.
18. Ibid.
19. A. M. Turing, Computing Machinery and Intelligence. *Mind,* October 1950, 59 (236) and J. McCarthy, M. L. Minsky, N. Rochester and C. E. Shannon, "A Proposal for the Dartmouth Summer Research Project on Artificial Intelligence," *AI Magazine*, 27 (4), August 31, 1955, https://doi.org/10.1609/aimag.v27i4.1904.
20. Noah Riggs, "72 Quotes about AI That Inspire a Look into the Future," Create and Go, March 5, 2024, https://createandgo.com/quotes-about-ai.
21. "When was the first computer invented?" Computer Hope, September 12, 2023, https://www.computerhope.com/issues/ch000984.htm.
22. Ibid.
23. Ibid.
24. Ibid.
25. Ibid.
26. Ibid.
27. Ibid.
28. Ibid.
29. Ibid.
30. Ibid.
31. A. Vaswani, et al., "Attention Is All You Need. In *Advances in Neural Information Processing Systems*, Cornell University, June 2017, https://doi.org/10.48550/arXiv.1706.03762
32. Ibid.
33. Chris Vallance, "Powerful Quantum Computers in Years Not Decades, Says Microsoft," BBC, February 19, 2025, https://www.bbc.com/news/articles/cj3e3252gj8o.
34. Ibid.
35. Ibid.
36. Alan Turing, "Computing Machinery and Intelligence," *Mind 59* (236), 1950, https://philpapers.org/rec/TURCMA.
37. Jacob Ward, *The Loop*, (New York: Hachette Books, 2022), p. 128.
38. Shelby Hiter, "What Is Artificial Intelligence? Guide to AI," eWeek, May 22, 2023.
39. Ward, op. cit.
40. Stuart Russell and Peter Norvig, "Artificial Intelligence: A Modern Approach, 4th edition," Pearson, December 21, 2021, https://www.pearson.com/en-us/subject-catalog/p/artificial-intelligence-a-modern-approach/P200000003500/9780137505135.

NOTES

41 Authur L. Samuel, "Some Studies in Machine Learning Using the Game of Checkers," *IBM Journal of Research and Development*, 3(3), 210–229, 1959, DOI: 10.1147/rd.33.0210.

42 Russell and Norvig, op. cit. (Note: MYCIN doesn't stand for anything; it's not an acronym! The name was inspired by the suffix "-mycin," which is commonly found in the names of antibiotics [like erythromycin or streptomycin], since MYCIN was developed to help diagnose and recommend treatment for bacterial infections, specifically blood infections.)

43 There were two major AI winters, periods when interest, funding, and progress on AI dropped. Specifically, the first AI winter was the mid-1970s to early 1980s because the algorithms couldn't handle ambiguity, noise, or scale. That "winter" was likely triggered by the Lighthill Report (1973, UK), which criticized AI research as a dead end. The second AI winter came in the late 1980s to early 1990s with the collapse of commercial interest because systems lacked adaptability.

44 "Noam Chomsky," *Britannica*, accessed May 18, 2025, https://www.britannica.com/biography/Noam-Chomsky?utm_source=chatgpt.com.

45 Cesareo Contreras, "What's the History of Artificial Intelligence? *New York Times* Chief Data Scientist Explains the Evolution of AI During Northeastern Lecture," States News Service, May 30, 2024, https://news.northeastern.edu/2024/05/30/history-of-ai-data-science/.

46 Ibid.

47 Nigel M. de S. Cameron, *The Robots Are Coming: Us, Them, and God*, (Bend, OR: Cascade Books, 2017), p. 10.

48 John C. Lennox, *2084: Artificial Intelligence and the Future of Humanity*, (Grand Rapids, MI: Zondervan, 2020), https://www.amazon.com/2084-Artificial-Intelligence-Future-Humanity/dp/0310109566?utm_source=chatgpt.com.

49 Gary Peters, statement, Committee of Homeland Security and Governmental Affairs, United States Senate, 118th Congress, "The Philosophy of AI: Learning from History, Shaping Our Future," November 8, 2023, https://www.hsgac.senate.gov/wp-content/uploads/Testimony-Vallor-2023-11-08.pdf.

50 Kory Mathewson, "Weizenbaum's Warning: The Human Side of Computation," korymathewson.com, November 29, 2023, https://korymathewson.com/weizenbaum/.

51 Richard Goodwin, "100 Quotes About AI: It's Terrifying Potential & Scale Revealed," KYM, May 26, 2023, https://www.knowyourmobile.com/ai-intelligence/quotes-about-ai/.

52 Alex Wilkins, "Facing up to Our AI future," *New Scientist*, Vol. 262, Issue 3492, June 1, 2024, https://www.sciencedirect.com/journal/new-scientist/vol/262/issue/3486.

53 "Can We Avoid a Franken-Future with AI?" *Institute for New Economic Thinking*, October 31, 2024, https://www.ineteconomics.org.

54 Ibid.

55 Ibid.

56 Kevin Roose, "This A.I. Forecast Predicts Storms Ahead," *New York Times*, April 3, 2025, https://www.nytimes.com/2025/04/03/technology/ai-futures-project-ai-2027.html.

57 Ibid.

58 Ibid.

NOTES

59 Ibid.
60 Ibid.
61 Ibid.
62 Ibid.
63 It is hard to single out a clear start date for the AI era, because AI evolved over many decades. One might argue it began in 1956 with the Dartmouth Conference, which was the formal birth of AI as a field of study. Certainly, AI pioneers like Alan Turing and John McCarthy laid the groundwork for AI in the 1950s and 1960s. By the 1980s, expert systems nudged AI forward with systems that mimic decision-making abilities and began to become widely adopted in business and industry. Of course, the 1997 Deep Blue landmark victory when IBM's Deep Blue, a chess-playing computer, defeated the world champion Garry Kasparov, was a very public and dramatic introduction to AI.
64 "Proposal for a Regulation Laying Down Harmonised Rules on Artificial Intelligence (Artificial Intelligence Act)," European Commission, 2021, https://ec.europa.eu/commission/presscorner/detail/en/ip_21_1682.
65 Mack DeGeurin, "Twitch's AI Jesus Will See You Now." *Gizmodo*, April 2023, https://gizmodo.com/twitch-ai-jesus-ask-god-chatgpt-1850320087.
66 Emanuel Maiberg, "Pro AI Subreddit Bans Uptick of Users Who Suffer from AI Delusions," 404media, June 2, 2025, https://www.404media.co/pro-ai-subreddit-bans-uptick-of-users-who-suffer-from-ai-delusions/?utm_source=thedeepview&utm_medium=newsletter&utm_campaign=musk-leaves-politics-and-raises-5b&_bhlid=aacfe96a0851f2488af815ffe76d7bd69aaefd4e.
67 Eliana Nunes, "Inside Dystopian Chinese Megacity of 32 Million Where Workers 'Don't S Sunlight' & Big Brother Is Always Watching," *The Sun*, May 1, 2025, Inside dystopian Chinese megacity of 32million where workers 'don't see sunlight' & Big Brother is always watching | The Sun.
68 Jamey Keaten and Jon Gambrell, "AI-powered Facial Recognition to Track Individuals Without Their Consent," Associated Press, March 14, 2025, Just a moment....
69 "Operation Spider," Wikipedia, accessed May 6, 2025, Operation Spider (Iran) - Wikipedia.
70 Andrew R. Chow, "New Lab Partner," *Time*, May 12, 2025, https://digital.emagazines.com/time/20250502/index.html?t=a3da89d4-b2d9-444b-a4fe-6b922e1ef853&utm_content=email_readbtn&utm_campaign=m2_media_time_1_net_paid&utm_medium=76554&pne=1#p4.
71 Ibid.
72 Ibid.
73 Lauren Frias, "See the Anduril Drones That Are Taking AI-driven Warfare to New Heights," *Business Insider*, May 3, 2025, https://www.businessinsider.com/anduril-drones?utm_source=chatgpt.com.
74 Yonah Jeremy Bob, "Mossad Assassinated Iran's Chief Nuke Scientist with Remote AI Gun—Report," *Jerusalem Post*, September 19, 2021, https://www.jpost.com/middle-east/mossad-assassinated-irans-chief-nuke-scientist-with-remote-ai-gun-report-679751.
75 Lauren Frias, "See the Anduril Drones That Are Taking AI-driven Warfare to New Heights," *Business Insider*, May 3, 2025, https://www.businessinsider.com/anduril-drones?utm_source=chatgpt.com.

NOTES

76 "AI Security Report 2025, "Understanding Threats and Building Smarter Defenses," Check Point, April 30, 2025, AI Security Report 2025: Understanding threats and building smarter defenses - Check Point Blog.
77 Ben Nimmo et al., "Disrupting Malicious Uses of AI: June 2025," OpenAI, June 2025, Disrupting malicious uses of AI: June 2025.
78 Ibid.
79 Ibid.
80 Rachel Wolf, "AI System Resorts to Blackmail When Its Developers Try to Replace it," Fox Business, May 24, 2025, https://www.foxbusiness.com/technology/ai-system-resorts-blackmail-when-its-developers-try-replace.
81 Ibid.
82 Ibid.
83 Ibid.
84 Ibid.
85 Eliezer Yudkowsky, "Pausing AI Developments Isn't Enough. We Need to Shut it All Down," *Time*, March 29, 2023, https://time.com/6266923/ai-eliezer-yudkowsky-open-letter-not-enough/.
86 Ibid.
87 Ibid.
88 Nirit Weiss-Blatt, "Media Has a Blind Spot When Covering the AI Panic," FreeThink.com, May 15, 2025, https://www.freethink.com/artificial-intelligence/ai-panic?utm_source=thedeepview&utm_medium=newsletter&utm_campaign=musk-leaves-politics-and-raises-5b&_bhlid=450f2a3fa7ec05590bccc56f1e9ae5cb4647684d.
89 Ibid.
90 Ibid.
91 Ibid.
92 Ibid.
93 Madison McLauchlan, "Yoshua Bengio Warns of 'Catastrophic Risks' of Agentic AI at World Summit AI," Betakit, April 16, 2025, https://betakit.com/yoshua-bengio-warns-of-catastrophic-risks-of-agentic-ai-at-world-summit-ai/.
94 Johana Bhuiyan, "She Didn't Get an Apartment Because of an AI-generated Score—and Sued to Help Others Avoid the Same Fate," *Guardian*, December 14, 2024, She didn't get an apartment because of an AI-generated score – and sued to help others avoid the same fate | Artificial intelligence (AI) | The Guardian.
95 Dan Armstrong, "AI Exhibits Racial Bias in Mortgage Underwriting Decisions," Lehigh University News, August 20, 2024, AI Exhibits Racial Bias in Mortgage Underwriting Decisions | Lehigh University News.
96 Chris Summers, "The Terrifying Way Scammers Clone Your Voice to Defraud Your Family," *Epoch Times*, May 5, 2025, https://www.theepochtimes.com/article/the-terrifying-way-scammers-clone-your-voice-to-defraud-your-family-5849310?utm_source=Morningbrief&src_src=Morningbrief&utm_campaign=mb-2025-05-06&src_cmp=mb-2025-05-06&utm_medium=email&est=NlN9iyqVQaieuze6ltNEjwue2IzePjPCIwAXvZdlCyYLpeLeD9WmZHp%2F28aUeRIA.
97 Ibid.
98 Ibid.

NOTES

99 Ibid.
100 Ibid.
101 Ibid.
102 Rachel Fletcher, Calli Tzani, and Maria Ioannou, "The Dark Side of Artificial Intelligence—Risks Arising in Dating Applications," *Assessment & Development Matters* is the property of British Psychological Society, https://pure.hud.ac.uk/en/publications/the-dark-side-of-artificial-intelligence-risks-arising-in-dating-.
103 Ibid.
104 Steven Dial, "Take It Down Act combatting 'Deepfakes' Revenge Porn Passes U.S. Senate," Fox News, December 11, 2024, Take It Down Act combatting 'deepfakes' revenge porn passes U.S. Senate | FOX 4 Dallas-Fort Worth.
105 Adam Fullerton, "Sen. Ted Cruz's Anti-deepfake Porn 'Take It Down Act' headed to Pres. Trump's Desk," Fox News, April 29, 2025, https://www.fox4news.com/news/deepfake-porn-bill-ted-cruz-house-passes.
106 Ibid.
107 Brian Knowles, "Humble AI," September 2023, vol. 66, no. 9, Communications of the ACM.
108 J. Buolamwini and T. Gebru, 2018. Gender Shades: Intersectional Accuracy Disparities in Commercial Gender Classification, *Proceedings of Machine Learning Research, 81* and J. Dastin, (October 10, 2018,). "Amazon Scraps Secret AI Recruiting Tool That Showed Bias against Women," Reuters. https://www.reuters.com/article/us-amazon-com-jobs-automation-insight-idUSKCN1MK08G.
109 Jeremy Kahn, *Mastering AI: A Survival Guide to Our Superpowered Future* (New York: Simon & Schuster, 2024), https://www.amazon.com/Mastering-AI-Survival-Superpowered-Future/dp/B0CYJKCFLH/ref=sr_1_1?crid=3HMDYDB56G6TH&dib=eyJ2IjoiMSJ9.0NZ-bVJIaZumklS2kxd_ilTsxk7pmBUqeBwdV7bTxQOXyCpDw7PSwEAnSEy1X9N-crEQNma_dxiipJ8_MIk2MxjQanMoojXUM8dO9IAdvZf_H1Qn_1JfWo0FuWoH6w1tkswwXaQ5L490taQiGRVQ6yJZpwCqnLyNuk_o0L35iFEHwQ3MTdozFCZfRmySZdijTxZGrjPkOkjWHn5iXTq1jvY9u0L9Tz6GMUzNj5Q02P8.Vp2rzgnO7J_q6QV77smvv97iW46HZ0ogubfRqEU1ODY&dib_tag=se&keywords=Jeremy+Kahn&qid=1746026326&sprefix=jeremy+kahn%2Caps%2C94&sr=8-1.
110 Ibid.
111 Ibid.
112 Ibid.
113 "Redefining the Boundaries of Human Capabilities Requires Pioneers," Neurolink.com, accessed April 23, 2025, https://neuralink.com/.
114 Kahn, op. cit.
115 Ibid.
116 Ibid.
117 Ibid.
118 Ibid.
119 Ibid.
120 Ibid.
121 Ibid.

NOTES

122 Ibid.
123 Ibid.
124 Ibid.
125 Angela Yang, "Pope Leo XIV Says Advancement of AI Played a Factor in His Papal Name Selection," NBC News, May 11, 2025, https://www.msn.com/en-us/technology/artificial-intelligence/pope-leo-xiv-says-advancement-of-ai-played-a-factor-in-his-papal-name-selection/ar-AA1Ezm8v.
126 Catherine Clifford, "Google CEO: A.I. Is More Important Than Fire or Electricity," CNBC, February 1, 2018, https://www.cnbc.com/2018/02/01/google-ceo-sundar-pichai-ai-is-more-important-than-fire-electricity.html.
127 Blake Irving, Create and Go, accessed April 15, 2025, https://createandgo.com/quotes-about-ai#Quotes_on_AI_and_the_Future_of_Humanity.
128 Ravi Bapna and Anindya Ghose, "Welcome to the AI-Enhanced Home," in *Thrive: Maximizing Well-Being in the Age of AI*, (Cambridge, MA: MIT Press, 2024), pp. 127–139.
129 "Turn Up Your Savings," Store.Google.Com, accessed April 21, 2025, https://store.google.com/us/product/nest_thermostat?hl=en-US.
130 M. Porcheron, et al., "Voice Interfaces in Everyday Life," in Proceedings of the 2018 CHI Conference on Human Factors in Computing Systems (Paper No. 302, pp. 1–12). ACM. https://doi.org/10.1145/3173574.3174133 and J. Radesky, et al., "Mobile and Interactive Media Use by Young Children: The Good, the Bad, and the Unknown," *Pediatrics, 135*(1), January 1, 2015, https://doi.org/10.1542/peds.2014-2251.
131 Bapna and Ghose, op. cit.
132 "Familia.AI Launches Revolutionary AI Family Character App to Reconnect and Support," PR Newswire, October 17, 2024, https://www.prnewswire.com/news-releases/familiaai-launches-revolutionary-ai-family-character-app-to-reconnect-and-support-302278733.html.
133 Ibid.
134 Ibid.
135 Ibid.
136 John Koetsier, "80% of Gen Zers Would Marry an AI: Study," *Forbes*, April 29, 2025, https://www.forbes.com/sites/johnkoetsier/2025/04/29/80-of-gen-zers-would-marry-an-ai-study/.
137 Ibid.
138 Ibid.
139 Emily Crane, "Boy, 14, Fell in Love with 'Game of Thrones' Chatbot—Then Killed Himself after AI App Told Him to 'Come Home' to 'Her': Mom," *New York Post*, October 23, 2024, Florida boy, 14, killed himself after falling in love with 'Game of Thrones' A.I. chatbot: lawsuit.
140 "Garante Bans AI Chatbot from Processing Italians' personal Data," IAPP, February 6, 2023, Garante bans AI chatbot from processing Italians' personal data | IAPP.
141 Ian Krietzberg, "Yes-man Syndrome; ChatGPT's Got a Sycophancy Problem," The Deep View, April 29, 2025, Yes-man syndrome; ChatGPT's got a sycophancy problem.
142 Koetsier, op. cit.
143 "OpenAI's Sam Altman on 'Building the Core AI Subscription for Your Life,'" Sequoia Capital, May 12, 2025, https://www.youtube.com/watch?v=ctcMA6chfDY.

395

NOTES

144 Ibid.
145 Ibid.
146 Julian De Freitas, "Why People Resist Embracing AI," *Harvard Business Review*, January–February 2025, https://hbr.org/2025/01/why-people-resist-embracing-ai.
147 Ibid.
148 Ibid.
149 Ibid.
150 European Commission. (2021). "Proposal for a Regulation Laying Down Harmonised Rules on Artificial Intelligence (Artificial Intelligence Act)." Retrieved from https://ec.europa.eu/commission/presscorner/detail/en/ip_21_1682 and U.S. Federal Trade Commission. (n.d.). "Children's Online Privacy Protection Rule (COPPA)." Retrieved from https://www.ftc.gov/legal-library/browse/rules/childrens-online-privacy-protection-rule-coppa.
151 Inara Scott, "Yes, We Are in a (ChatGPT) Crisis," *Inside Higher Education*, April 18, 2023, https://www.insidehighered.com/opinion/views/2023/04/18/yes-we-are-chatgpt-crisis.
152 Joey Garrison and Zachary Schermele, "President Trump Signs Executive Order Boosting AI in K 12 Schools," USA Today, April 24, 2025, https://www.msn.com/en-us/news/politics/president-trump-signs-executive-order-boosting-ai-in-k-12-schools/ar-AA1Du8M1.
153 Ibid.
154 "Unlock 8% for Higher Wages, CSforAll," accessed May 6, 2025, https://csforall.org/unlock8/open-letter?utm_source=www.therundown.ai&utm_medium=newsletter&utm_campaign=openai-ends-for-profit-push&_bhlid=8bf57f4d80f0122a874070736135c96daae3aac5.
155 "AI Education in Finland: Enhancing Children's Understanding, Critical Thinking and Creativity Through Collaborative Designing of AI Apps," University of Eastern Finland, December 6, 2024, https://www.uef.fi/en/article/ai-education-in-finland-enhancing-childrens-understanding-critical-thinking-and-creativity-through?utm_source=chatgpt.com.
156 "China Issues Guidelines to Promote AI Education in Primary and Secondary Schools," *Global Times*, May 12, 2025, https://www.globaltimes.cn/page/202505/1333878.shtml?utm_source=chatgpt.com.
157 "Plato," Illinois Distributed Museum, University of Illinois, accessed May 17, 2025, https://distributedmuseum.illinois.edu/exhibit/plato/?utm_source=chatgpt.com, and "Intelligent Tutoring System," Wikipedia, accessed May 17, 2025, https://en.wikipedia.org/wiki/Intelligent_tutoring_system?utm_source=chatgpt.com.
158 Vera Cubero, "Navigating the Future," *Literacy Today*, October/November/December 2024, literacyworldwide.org.
159 Ibid., and "AI at Work Is Here. Now Comes the Hard Part," 2024 Work Trend Index Annual Report from Microsoft and LinkedIn, May 8, 2024, https://www.microsoft.com/en-us/worklab/work-trend-index/ai-at-work-is-here-now-comes-the-hard-part.
160 Ibid.
161 "AI in Education Market Size, Share and Trends 2024 to 2034," Precedence Research, accessed April 13, 205, AI in Education Market Size to Surpass USD 112.30 Bn by 2034.

NOTES

162 "Wichita Public Schools Personalized Learning for Students Using Microsoft Copilot," Microsoft, November 17, 2023, https://www.microsoft.com/en/customers/story/17010819079183320989-wichita-public-schools-azure-k12-edu-en-united-states?culture=en-us&country=us.
163 Ibid.
164 K. Swargiary, "The Impact of AI-driven Personalized Learning on Student Achievement and Engagement in Rural vs Urban Schools (India)," *Education and Information Technologies*. Advance online publication, September 2024, accessed from https://www.researchgate.net/publication/384324540_The_Impact_of_AI-Driven_Personalized_Learning_on_Student_Achievement_and_Engagement_in_Rural_vs_Urban_Schools_India.
165 X. Zhai and X Chu, "Artificial Intelligence in Education: A Systematic Review of Literature," *Computers and Education: Artificial Intelligence*, June 2024, *accessed from* https://www.sciencedirect.com/science/article/pii/S2666920X23000747.
166 Ibid.
167 Javed Iqbal, Zarqa Farooq Hashmi, Muhammad Zaheer Asghar, and Muhammad Naseem Abid, "Generative AI Tool Use Enhances Academic Achievement in Sustainable Education Through Shared Metacognition and Cognitive Offloading Among Preservice Teachers," *Scientific Reports, Nature*, Vol 15, 16610 (2025), https://www.nature.com/articles/s41598-025-01676-x?utm_source=chatgpt.com.
168 Ibid.
169 Rhea Kelly, "Survey: 86% of Students Already Use AI in Their Studies," *Campus Technology*, August 28, 2024, https://campustechnology.com/articles/2024/08/28/survey-86-of-students-already-use-ai-in-their-studies.aspx?utm_source=chatgpt.com and Griffin Pitts, Viktoria Marcus, and Sanaz Motamedi, "Student Perspectives on the Benefits and Risks of AI in Education," arxiv.org, accessed May 17, 2025, https://arxiv.org/abs/2505.02198?utm_source=chatgpt.com.
170 Lucas Ropek, "AI Cheating Is So Out of Hand In America's Schools That the Blue Books Are Coming Back," Gizmodo.com, May 27, 2025, https://gizmodo.com/ai-cheating-is-so-out-of-hand-in-americas-schools-that-the-blue-books-are-coming-back-2000607771?utm_source=thedeepview&utm_medium=newsletter&utm_campaign=musk-leaves-politics-and-raises-5b&_bhlid=8b60cbc43530351adf9232b89cbd7e242ee33b1e.
171 José-María Fernández-Batanero, Pedro Román-Graván, Miguel-María Reyes-Rebollo, and Marta Montenegro-Rueda, "Impact of Educational Technology on Teacher Stress and Anxiety: A Literature Review," International Journal of Environmental Research and Public Health, 2021 January 11; 18(2):548. doi: 10.3390/ijerph18020548, and Rhea Kelly, "Burnout, Excessive Workloads Plague Teaching and Learning Workforce in Higher Ed," *Campus Technology*, February 7, 2024, https://campustechnology.com/articles/2024/02/07/burnout-excessive-workloads-plague-teaching-and-learning-workforce-in-higher-ed.aspx?utm_source=chatgpt.com.
172 "Artificial Intelligence in Accreditation," SACSCOC Board of Trustees, December 2024, https://sacscoc.org/app/uploads/2024/12/AI-in-Accreditation.pdf?utm_source=chatgpt.com.
173 Ibid.

NOTES

174 "Artificial Intelligence in Accreditation Policy: Principles and Restrictions," WASC, Senior College and University Commission, November 2024, https://wascsenior.app.box.com/s/jhmujmv4qp1e41zixenzmixyhdjkj1i0.
175 Neil Selwyn, "The Future of AI and Education: Some Cautionary Notes," *European Journal of Education*, 2022, https://onlinelibrary.wiley.com/doi/10.1111/ejed.12532?af=R.
176 Ibid.
177 Ibid.
178 Ibid.
179 Ibid.
180 Ibid.
181 Ibid.
182 Ibid.
183 Ibid.
184 Ibid.
185 "Ethics Guidelines for Trustworthy AI," European Commission, April 8, 2019, chrome-extension://efaidnbmnnnibpcajpcglclefindmkaj/https://www.europarl.europa.eu/cmsdata/196377/AI%20HLEG_Ethics%20Guidelines%20for%20Trustworthy%20AI.pdf.
186 Cindy Wooden, "Morality of AI Depends on Human Choices, Vatican Says in New Document," US Conference of Catholic Bishops, January 28, 2025, https://www.usccb.org/news/2025/morality-ai-depends-human-choices-vatican-says-new-document.
187 "AI Won't Replace Doctors, but Doctors Who Don't Use AI Will Be Replaced: Sangeeta Reddy of Apollo Hospitals," *Business Insider*, February 13, 2023, https://www.businessinsider.in/science/health/news/ai-wont-replace-doctors-but-doctors-who-dont-use-ai-will-be-replaced-sangeeta-reddy-of-apollo-hospitals/articleshow/97900892.cms.
188 Ibid., p. 10.
189 Ibid., p. 6.
190 "Nursing and Midwifery," World Health Organization, May 3, 2024.
191 Prerna Dogra, "Foxconn Taps NVIDIA to Accelerate Physical and Digital Robotics for Global Healthcare Industry," Nvidia, May 18, 2025, Foxconn Accelerates Robotics for Global Healthcare Industry | NVIDIA Blog.
192 Ibid., p. 18.
193 Brittany Roston, "These Injectable Nanobots Can Walk Around Inside a Human Body," Slashgear.com, https://www.slashgear.com/777282/these-injectable-nanobots-can-walk-around-inside-a-human-body/.
194 "AI Foot Scanner Could Help Prevent Hospital Stays," BBC, June 4, 2025.
195 Ibid., p. 20.
196 Ibid., p. 24.
197 Ibid., p. 26.
198 Ibid., p. 16.
199 "AI-enabled Imaging and Diagnostics Previously Thought Impossible," Google Health, accessed April 7, 2025, https://health.google/health-research/imaging-and-diagnostics/.

NOTES

200 "Aurora Eye: AI-based Screening for Diabetic Retinopathy," optmed.com, accessed April 7, 2025, https://www.optomed.com/us/usoptomedauroraaeye?utm_source =bing&utm_medium=ppc&utm_campaign=multiview_bing&&msclkid=f204a9406 d631d627eefce84d09031ce&utm_source=bing&utm_medium=cpc&utm_campaign =Optomed%20Aurora%20AEYE&utm_term=ai%20for%20diabetic%20retinopathy &utm_content=Aurora%20AEYE&gclid=f204a9406d631d627eefce84d09031ce& gclsrc=3p.ds.

201 Madeleine North, "6 Ways AI Is Transforming Healthcare," World Economic Forum, March 14, 2025, 6 ways AI is transforming healthcare | World Economic Forum.

202 Karen DeSalvo, "6 Health AI Updates We Shared at The Check Up," Google Health, March 18, 2025, 6 Google Health AI updates from The Check Up event 2025 and Amerigo Allegretto, "AI-guided POCUS Bests Experts in Diagnosing TB in Underserved Areas," Auntminnie.com, April 13, 2025, https://www.auntminnie.com/clinical -news/ultrasound/article/15742661/aiguided-pocus-bests-experts-in-diagnosing-tb -in-underserved-areas?utm_source=www.therundown.ai&utm_medium=newsletter&utm_campaign=ilya-s-ssi-skyrockets-to-32b&_bhlid=14d9fcc2db9ea5443c25 f5a4c102f82798b86916.

203 "AI Test to Determine Best Prostate Cancer Treatment Could Save Lives and Money," UCL News, May 30, 2025, https://www.ucl.ac.uk/news/2025/may/ai-test -determine-best-prostate-cancer-treatment-could-save-lives-and-money?utm_source =thedeepview&utm_medium=newsletter&utm_campaign=ai-to-erase-50-of-entry -level-jobs-within-5-years&_bhlid=f8484167c0a0fdd708bfccdd88ce4c7c27cac2d4.

204 Julie Washington, "UH Adopts Cutting-edge AI System for Precision Cancer Treatment," cleveland.com, June 9, 2025, UH adopts cutting-edge AI system for precision cancer treatment - cleveland.com.

205 Khaled Saab and Jan Kreyberg, "AMIE Gains Vision: A Research AI Agent for Multimodal Diagnostic Dialogue," Google, May 1, 2025, https://research.google/blog /amie-gains-vision-a-research-ai-agent-for-multi-modal-diagnostic-dialogue/?utm _source=thedeepview&utm_medium=newsletter&utm_campaign=the-ai-companion -takeover&_bhlid=f9299b9ce037fde28ef653cb9b4db59714b56ecd.

206 "AI for Good: AI Is Speeding up Drug Development," The Deep View, accessed May 15, 2025.

207 Ibid.

208 Justin Opfermann, Samuel Schmidgall, and Alex Krieger, "Robots Are Starting to Make Decisions in the Operating Room," IEEE Spectrum, May 21, 2025, https:// spectrum.ieee.org/star-autonomous-surgical-robot?utm_source=superhuman&utm _medium=newsletter&utm_campaign=robotics-special-nvidia-bets-big-on-robotics -at-computex&_bhlid=3caefae793062e592b4ffc08690458ff6300adf2.

209 Ibid.

210 Jill Rosen, "Robot That Watched Surgery Videos Performs with Skill of Human Doctor," HUB, Johns Hopkins University, November 11, 2024, Robot that watched surgery videos performs with skill of human doctor | Hub.

211 Kurt Knutsson, "Rice-sized Robot Could Make Brain Surgery Safer and Less Invasive," Fox News, cyberguy.com, May 9, 2025, https://cyberguy.com/robot-tech/rice -sized-robot-make-brain-surgery-safer-less-invasive/?utm_campaign=5-16-25%20 Friday%20Newsletter&utm_medium=email&utm_source=newsletter.

NOTES

212 Ibid.
213 Ibid.
214 "The Complexities of Physician Supply and Demand: Projections From 2021 to 2036," Association of American Medical Colleges, March 2024, The Complexities of Physician Supply and Demand: Projections From 2021 to 2036.
215 "AI-enabled Imaging and Diagnostics Previously Thought Impossible," op. cit.
216 Ron Southwick, "AI in Healthcare: What to Expect in 2025," Chief Healthcare Executive, January 2, 2025, AI in healthcare: What to expect in 2025.
217 S. P. Somashekhar, et al., "Watson for Oncology and Breast Cancer Treatment Recommendations: Agreement with an Expert Multidisciplinary Tumor Board in India," *The Oncologist*, 23(4), 492–498, 2018, https://doi.org/10.1634/theoncologist.2017-0267.
218 Dillon Browne, "Do Mental Health Chatbots Work?" Healthline, June 27, 2020, https://www.healthline.com/health/mental-health/chatbots-reviews.
219 AI-based Tool for Early Detection of Alzheimer's Disease, Volume 10, Issue 8, April 30, 2024, e29375, https://www.sciencedirect.com/science/article/pii/S2405844024054069.
220 Liezel Labios, "AI Helps Unravel a Cause of Alzheimer's Disease and Identify a Therapeutic Candidate," *US San Diego Today*, April 25, 2025, https://today.ucsd.edu/story/ai-helps-unravel-a-cause-of-alzheimers-disease-and-identify-a-therapeutic-candidate?utm_source=www.therundown.ai&utm_medium=newsletter&utm_campaign=reddit-uncovers-secret-ai-persuasion-experiment&_bhlid=67b8a25a7c17ccb0c762bbfc2a9d804f6338322d.
221 Marlene Wolfgruber, "AI's Healthcare Revolution Needs a Human Touch in 2025," *Future Healthcare Today*, February 18, 2025, AI's Healthcare Revolution Needs a Human Touch in 2025 - Future Healthcare Today.
222 Ashkan Afkhami et al., "How Digital and AI Will Reshape Health Care in 2025," BCG.com, January 14, 2025, How Digital & AI Will Reshape Health Care in 2025 | BCG.
223 Melissa Rudy, "AI Tool Scans Faces to Predict Biological Age and Cancer Survival," Fox News, May 12, 2025, https://www.foxnews.com/health/ai-tool-scans-faces-predict-biological-age-cancer-survival.
224 Ibid.
225 Ibid.
226 Ibid., p. 17.
227 S. Reddy, J. Fox, and M. P. Purohit, "Artificial Intelligence-enabled Healthcare Delivery," *Journal of the Royal Society of Medicine, 112*(1), December 3, 2018, accessed from https://journals.sagepub.com/doi/full/10.1177/0141076818815510.
228 Saloni Dattani et al., "Life Expectancy," Our World in Data, accessed May 15, 2025, https://ourworldindata.org/life-expectancy.
229 Alexandra Tremayne-Pengelly, "Anthropic CEO Dario Amodei Believes A.I. Could Double Human Lifespans in 5 Years," *Observer*, January 24, 2025, Anthropic's Dario Amodei Says A.I. Will Soon Double Human Lifespans | Observer.
230 Alex Liu, "Ray Kurzweil's Vision: Stopping Aging with AI by 2032," *Pulse*, January 8, 2025, https://www.linkedin.com/pulse/ray-kurzweils-vision-stopping-aging-ai-2032-alex-liu-ph-d--3d9mc/.

NOTES

231 S. Jay Olshansky et al., "Implausibility of Radical Life Extension in Humans in the Twenty-first Century," *Nature Aging*, Vol. 4, 2024, Implausibility of radical life extension in humans in the twenty-first century | Nature Aging.

232 "Is Medicine Ready for AI?—ITT Episode 6," *New England Journal of Medicine*, Vol. 388, No. 14, April 5, 2023.

233 Ibid.

234 Ibid.

235 Ibid.

236 Ibid.

237 Ibid.

238 Ziad Obermeyer and Ezekiel J. Emanuel, "Predicting the Future—Big Data, Machine Learning, and Clinical Medicine," *New England Journal of Medicine*, September 2016, 29;375(13):1216-9. doi: 10.1056/NEJMp1606181, https://pubmed.ncbi.nlm.nih.gov/27682033/.

239 "Is Medicine Ready for AI?—ITT Episode 6," op. cit.

240 Ibid.

241 Ibid.

242 Ibid.

243 F. Wang, L. P. Casalino, and D. Khullar, "Deep Learning in Medicine—Promise, Progress, and Challenges," *JAMA Internal Medicine*, 180(3), December 17, 2018, https://jamanetwork.com/journals/jamainternalmedicine/article-abstract/2718342.

244 Ibid.

245 Y. Zhao, D. Yin, L. Wang, and Y Yu, "The Rise of Artificial Intelligence, the Fall of Human Wellbeing?" *International Journal of Social Welfare*, 33(1), February 5, 2023,https://doi.org/10.1111/ijsw.12586.

246 Maya Goldman, "FDA Streamlines Approval of AI-powered Devices," *Axios*, December 4, 2024, FDA streamlines approval of AI-powered devices.

247 "AMA Issues New Principles for AI Development, Deployment & Use," AMA, November 28, 2023, AMA issues new principles for AI development, deployment & use | American Medical Association.

248 "Summary Document—Ethics, Legal, and Regulatory Aspects of AI in Healthcare," World Medical Association, February 27, 2025, Summary Document_ Ethics, Legal, and Regulatory Aspects of AI in Healthcare – WMA – The World Medical Association.

249 Erin Whaley, Brent Hoard, and Emma Trivax, "New Legal Developments Herald Big Changes for HIPAA Compliance in 2025," Reuters, April 7, 2025.

250 "The GDPR does apply to AI in healthcare. However, data protection regulations do not resolve certain issues such as bias," Global Health Advocates, November 8, 2023, https://www.ghadvocates.eu/gdpr-apply-ai-healthcare-issues-bias/.

251 Stephen Hawking, "The Rise of Powerful AI Will Be Either the Best or the Worst Thing Ever to Happen to Humanity," *Factor Beyond*, Spring 2018, https://magazine.factor-tech.com/factor_spring_2018/stephen_hawking_rise_of_powerful_ai_will_be_either_the_best_or_the_worst_thing_ever_to_happen_to_humanity.

252 Sam Birchall, "A Year in Quotes: 'The Potential We Have Here Is Immense'," *Government Transformation Magazine*, December 14, 2023, https://www.government-transformation.com/transformation/a-year-in-quotes-the-potential-we-have-here-is-immense.

NOTES

253 Sam Altman, "Who Will Control the Future of AI?" *Washington Post*, July 25, 2024, Democracy https://www.washingtonpost.com/opinions/2024/07/25/sam-altman-ai-democracy-authoritarianism-future/.

254 Matt Brown, "OpenAI CEO Sam Altman and other US Tech Leaders Testify to Congress on AI Competition with China," Yahoo.com, May 8, 2025, https://www.yahoo.com/news/openai-ceo-sam-altman-other-174433958.html?fr=sycsrp_catchall.

255 Ibid.

256 Tom Ozimek, "CIA Deputy Director Michael Ellis Says the CIA Must Help Secure American Dominance in AI, Semiconductors, and Biotech to Counter the China Threat," *Epoch Times*, May 22, 2025, https://www.theepochtimes.com/us/cia-says-winning-tech-war-with-china-top-priority-citing-existential-threat-to-us-5861919?utm_source=Morningbrief&src_src=Morningbrief&utm_campaign=mb-2025-05-23&src_cmp=mb-2025-05-23&utm_medium=email&est=ZifOziZA3yn8%2FjL3YN6X3ZL4LVNpMrgj8tNC0%2BC5yUglcnaT4u%2BknwJn1HPNRKuA.

257 Ibid.

258 Ben Turner, "China Is Building a Constellation of AI Supercomputers in Space—and ust Launched the First Pieces," Live Science, May 23, 2025, https://www.livescience.com/space/space-exploration/china-is-building-a-constellation-of-ai-supercomputers-in-space-and-just-launched-the-first-pieces.

259 Ibid.

260 Eva Erman and Markus Furendal, "The Democratic Challenges in Global Governance of AI," *Current History*, January 2025, https://online.ucpress.edu/currenthistory/article/124/858/3/204209/The-Democratic-Challenges-in-Global-Governance-of.

261 Kara Frederick and Jake Denton, "The U.S., Not China, Should Take the Lead on AI," Heritage Foundation, October 11, 2023, https://www.heritage.org/big-tech/commentary/the-us-not-china-should-take-the-lead-ai.

262 Ibid.

263 Ibid.

264 "Putin: Leader in AI Will Rule World," SBSNews, September 2, 2017, https://www.sbs.com.au/news/article/putin-leader-in-ai-will-rule-world/zy1pyl1bx.

265 "Saudi Arabia Unveils Groundbreaking AI Venture, Humain, Prior to Trump's Visit," Wamda.com, May 13, 2025, https://www.wamda.com/2025/05/saudi-arabia-unveils-groundbreaking-ai-venture-humain-prior-trump-visit.

266 Federico Maccioni, Manya Saini, and Yousef Saba, "UAE to Build Biggest AI Campus Outside US in Trump Deal, Bypassing Past China Worries," Reuters, May 15, 2025, https://www.reuters.com/world/china/uae-set-deepen-ai-links-with-united-states-after-past-curbs-over-china-2025-05-15/?utm_source=superhuman&utm_medium=newsletter&utm_campaign=meta-s-struggles-and-openai-teases-next-release&_bhlid=4350843b909469e0127dcc0dc057b74bee39c029.

267 Elvira Pollina, "UAE Partners with Italian Startup for AI Supercomputer," Reuters, May 16, 2025, https://www.reuters.com/world/middle-east/italy-uae-announce-deal-artificial-intelligence-hub-2025-05-16/.

268 Jake Denton, "The U.S. Shouldn't Go the Way of Europe on AI," Heritage Foundation, May 8, 2024, https://www.heritage.org/big-tech/commentary/the-us-shouldnt-go-the-way-europe-ai, and "UAE to Use AI for Writing Laws," *Tech in Asia*, April

NOTES

21, 2025, https://www.techinasia.com/news/uae-ai-writing-laws?utm_source=www.therundown.ai&utm_medium=newsletter&utm_campaign=anthropic-maps-ai-s-moral-compass&_bhlid=c7200e6042da001e54e6c0fb1cb192794f638209.

269 "Introducing OpenAI for Countries," OpenAI, May 7, 2025, https://openai.com/global-affairs/openai-for-countries/?utm_source=www.therundown.ai&utm_medium=newsletter&utm_campaign=openai-goes-global-with-stargate&_bhlid=c67ddc128242f40e36f106bffa9130fb9606a207. Note: OpenAI's forthcoming data center in Abilene, Texas, is a component of the $500 billion Stargate initiative, a joint venture among OpenAI, SoftBank, Oracle, and MGX, aimed at constructing a nationwide AI infrastructure network to bolster US leadership. The Abilene campus will include eight buildings, each capable of housing up to fifty thousand Nvidia Blackwell GPUs, positioning it to become among the world's largest AI data centers. See Maximilian Schreiner, "OpenAI's Stargate Secured $11.6 Billion for a Massive Data Center," *The Decoder*, May 21, 2025, https://the-decoder.com/openais-stargate-secures-11-6-billion-dollars-for-mega-data-center/?utm_source=chatgpt.com.

270 Ibid.

271 Ibid.

272 Ester Shein, "Governments Setting Limits on AI," Communications of the ACM, April 2024, Vol. 67, No. 4., https://dl.acm.org/doi/10.1145/3640506.

273 Ibid.

274 Ibid.

275 "Fact Sheet: President Biden Issues Executive Order on Safe, Secure, and Trustworthy Artificial Intelligence," The White House, October 30, 2023, https://bidenwhitehouse.archives.gov/briefing-room/statements-releases/2023/10/30/fact-sheet-president-biden-issues-executive-order-on-safe-secure-and-trustworthy-artificial-intelligence/.

276 Ibid.

277 Ibid.

278 Ibid.

279 "AI and the Future of Our Elections," US Senate Committee on Rules and Administration, September 27, 2023, https://www.rules.senate.gov/hearings/ai-and-the-future-of-our-elections.

280 Ibid.

281 Ibid.

282 Sofia Vescovo, *Rise of the Machines: The Future of Intellectual Property Rights in the Age of Artificial Intelligence*, 89 Brook. L. Rev. 221 (2023). Available at: https://brooklynworks.brooklaw.edu/blr/vol89/iss1/5.

283 B. Sheehy & Y.-F. Ng. (2024). "The Challenges of AI Decision-making in Government and Administrative Law: A Proposal for Regulatory Design," *Indiana Law Review*, 57(3), 665–699. https://mckinneylaw.iu.edu/ilr/contents.html.

284 Ibid.

285 Emma Roth, "Republicans Push for a Decade-long Ban on States Regulating AI," *The Verge*, May 13, 2025, https://www.theverge.com/news/666288/republican-ai-state-regulation-ban-10-years?utm_source=chatgpt.com.

286 James Osborne, "Ted Cruz Calls for 'Light Touch' on AI in Hearing with OpenAI, Microsoft," *Houston Chronicle*, May 8, 2025, https://www.houstonchronicle.com/politics/article/ai-openai-cruz-ted-20317240.php?utm_source=chatgpt.com.

NOTES

287 Ibid.
288 Ibid.
289 "California's New AI Bill to Require Copyright Disclosure of Training Data," Crowell, February 18, 2025, https://www.crowell.com/en/insights/client-alerts/californias-new-ai-bill-to-require-copyright-disclosure-of-training-data?utm_source=chatgpt.com.
290 Blake Brittain, "Judge in Meta Case Warns AI Could 'Obliterate' Market for Original Works," Reuters, May 1, 2025, https://www.reuters.com/legal/litigation/judge-meta-case-weighs-key-question-ai-copyright-lawsuits-2025-05-01/?utm_source=chatgpt.com.
291 "Going Deep on AI," GAO, GAO-25-107724, March 2025, https://www.gao.gov/products/gao-25-107724 (Note: The GAO report indicates that in calendar years 2023 and 2024, it provided sixty-seven technical consultations on AI to congressional committees. It also maintains a network of experts to help monitor AI-related developments. The GAO hosts AI training at the Congressional Staff Academy and published over sixty reports on AI since 2018.)
292 Elyse Perlmutter-Gumbiner, "Trump Administration Launching an AI Tool for Government Use," NBC News, March 21, 2025, Trump administration launching an AI tool for government use.
293 Akhilesh Chandra, Mark Holtzblatt, and Bruce W. McClain, "IRS Continues to Move Forward Using Artificial Intelligence in Selecting Returns for Audit," *Journal of Tax Practice & Procedures*, Spring 2024.
294 "2022 NASA'S Responsible AI Plan," NASA's Response Plan: Executive Order 13960—Promoting the Use of Trustworthy Artificial Intelligence (AI) in the Federal Government, 2022, https://ntrs.nasa.gov/api/citations/20220013471/downloads/RAI%20Plan%20Sept%201%202022.pdf.
295 John Frank Weaver, "Everything Is Not *Terminator*," *The Journal of Robotics, Artificial Intelligence and Law*, Volume 3, No. 3, May–June 2020, https://mclane.com/wp-content/uploads/Everything_is_Not_Terminator_-_The_White_House_Memo_on_Regulating_AI_Addresses_Values_but_Not_the_Playing_Field.pdf.
296 Ibid.
297 Naomi Aoki, Tomohiko Tatsumi, Go Naruse, Kentaro Maeda, "Explainable AI for Government," Government Information Quarterly, Volume 41, Issue 4, December 2024, https://doi.org/10.1016/j.giq.2024.101965Get rights and content.
298 Ibid.
299 Ibid.
300 Ibid.
301 Ibid.
302 Ibid.
303 Gigi Sukin, "San Francisco Becomes First Major U.S. City to Ban Facial Recognition Tech," Axios, May 14, 2019, https://www.axios.com/2019/05/14/san-francisco-restrict-facial-recognition-tech?utm_source=chatgpt.com.
304 "DataWorks Plus," Wikipedia, accessed May 20, 2025, https://en.wikipedia.org/wiki/DataWorks_Plus?utm_source=chatgpt.com.
305 Marisa Kendall, "This California County Is Testing AI's Ability to Prevent Homelessness," CAL Matters, March 6, 2024, https://calmatters.org/housing/homelessness/2024/03/california-homeless-los-angeles-ai/?utm_source=chatgpt.com.

NOTES

306 Sterling Davies, "New California Bill Seeks to Improve AI Literacy in Schools," *Stanford Daily*, November 7, 2024, https://stanforddaily.com/2024/11/07/california-ai-literacy-bill/?utm_source=chatgpt.com and "Overview of AI Policy Lab," NYC Public Schools, accessed May 20, 2025, https://www.nycdli.org/policylab?utm_source=chatgpt.com.

307 "CPRA vs. CCPA: What's the Difference?" July 19, 2023, Security, https://securiti.ai/cpra-vs-ccpa/?utm_source=chatgpt.com; Zoe M. Argento, et al., "Implications for Employers of Colorado's New Biometrics Law," SHRM, July 10, 2024, https://www.shrm.org/topics-tools/employment-law-compliance/implications-for-employers-of-colorado-s-new-biometrics-law?utm_source=chatgpt.com; Ed Sealover, "New Colorado Privacy Laws to Impact "Broad Swath" of Companies," *The Sum & Substance*, August 7, 2024, https://tsscolorado.com/new-colorado-privacy-laws-to-impact-broad-swath-of-companies/?utm_source=chatgpt.com

308 Gilad Edelman, "California's Privacy Law Goes into Effect Today. Now What?" *Wired*, January 1, 2020, https://www.wired.com/story/ccpa-guide-california-privacy-law-takes-effect/?utm_source=chatgpt.com.

309 "AI Principles," OECD, accessed April 24, 2025.

310 "Joint Statement from Founding Members of the Global Partnership on Artificial Intelligence," Office of Artificial Intelligence, Government of the United Kingdom, June 15, 2020, Joint statement from founding members of the Global Partnership on Artificial Intelligence - GOV.UK.

311 Margaret Chase Smith, Brainyquote.com, accessed April 7, 2025, https://www.brainyquote.com/quotes/margaret_chase_smith_319203.

312 Herman Lawelai, Iswanto Iswanto, and Nia Maharani Raharja, "Use of Artificial Intelligence in Public Services: A Bibliometric Analysis and Visualization," *TEM Journal*, Volume 12, Issue 2, pages 798–807, ISSN 2217-8309, DOI: 10.18421/TEM122-24, May 2023, https://www.temjournal.com/content/122/TEMJournalMay2023_798_807.pdf.

313 "U.S. Department of Transportation Announces Columbus as Winner of Unprecedented $40 Million Smart City Challenge," U.S. Department of Transportation, June 23, 2016, https://www.transportation.gov/briefing-room/us-department-transportation-announces-columbus-winner-unprecedented-40-million-smart.

314 "Transformative Policies for Autonomous Vehicle Testing and Development," City of Pittsburgh, March 04, 2019, https://www.pittsburghpa.gov/City-Government/Mayor/Executive-Orders/Mayor-William-Peduto-Issues-Transformative-Policies-for-Autonomous-Vehicle-Testing-and-Development.

315 K. Sireesha and J. Katyayani, "Harnessing the Power of Intelligence: A Comprehensive Exploration of Artificial Intelligence Applications in Power Plants," *International Management Review*, Vol. 20, Special Issue 2024, January 1, 2024, https://www.proquest.com/openview/2a41c9fce306f4879e9140c6d43666a2/1?pq-origsite=gscholar&cbl=28202.

316 N. Damij, and S. Bhattacharya, (2022). "The Role of AI Chatbots in Mental Health Related Public Services in a (Post) Pandemic World: A Review and Future Research Agenda." In A. Brem, T. Daim, Y. K. Dwivedi, J. Španjol, and J. Fleck (Eds.), *2022 IEEE Technology and Engineering Management Society Conference—Europe (TEM-*

NOTES

SCON EUROPE): Societal Challenges: Technology, Transitions and Resilience Virtual Conference (pp. 163–170). IEEE. https://doi.org/10.1109/TEMSCONEUROPE 54743.2022.9801962.

317 Sebastian Hemesath and Markus Tepe, "Public Value Positions and Design Preferences Toward AI-based Chatbots in E-government. Evidence from a Conjoint Experiment with Citizens and Municipal Front Desk Officers," *Government Information Quarterly*, Vol. 41, Issue 4, December 2024, https://doi.org/10.1016/j.giq.2024 .101985Get rights and content.

318 Ibid.

319 Anne David, Tan Yigitcanlar, Kevin Desouza, Rita Yi Man Li, Pauline Hope Cheong, Rashid Mehmood, and Juan Corchado, "Understanding Local Government Responsible AI Strategy: An International Municipal Policy Document Analysis," Cities Volume 155, December 2024, https://doi.org/10.1016/j.cities.2024.105502.

320 Ibid.

321 Ibid.

322 "Artificial Intelligence for Public Service Delivery," Microsoft, Partnership for Public Service, accessed April 7, 2025, https://ourpublicservice.org/wp-content/uploads /2023/06/Artificial-Intelligence-for-Public-Service-Delivery-v2.pdf.

323 Mark Esper, "Remarks by Secretary Esper at National Security Commission on Artificial Intelligence Public Conference," US Department of Defense, November 5, 2019, https://www.defense.gov/News/Transcripts/Transcript/Article/2011960 /remarks-by-secretary-esper-at-national-security-commission-on-artificial-intell/

324 Cheryl Pellerin, "Deputy Secretary: Third Offset Strategy Bolsters America's Military Deterrence," Department of Defense, October 31, 2016, https://www.defense.gov /News/News-Stories/Article/Article/991434/deputy-secretary-third-offset-strategy -bolsters-americas-military-deterrence/.

325 Ahmad Khan, Irteza Imam, and Adeela Azam, "Role of Artificial Intelligence in Defence Strategy: Implications for Global and National Security," *Strategic Studies*, Vol. 41, No. 1 (Spring 2021), https://www.jstor.org/stable/48732266.

326 Eric Schmidt, "AI, Great Power Competition & National Security," *Daedalus*, Spring 2022, Vol. 151, No. 2, https://www.jstor.org/stable/48662042?seq=1.

327 "Advancing Intelligence in the Era of Artificial Intelligence: Addressing the National Security Implications of AI," Hearing before the Select Committee on Intelligence of the United States Senate, 118 Congress, September 19, 2023, https://www.congress .gov/event/118th-congress/senate-event/LC72459/text.

328 Ibid.

329 Ibid.

330 Ibid.

331 Ibid.

332 Walter Matli, "Integration of Warrior Artificial Intelligence and Leadership Reflexivity to Enhance Decision-making," 2024, Vol. 38, No. 1, https://doi.org/10.1080/088 39514.2024.2411462.

333 Ibid.

334 Ibid.

335 Schmidt, op. cit.

NOTES

336 Ibid.
337 Tibor Moes, "NotPetya: The Most Devastating Cyberattack," Softwarelab.org, September 2024, https://softwarelab.org/blog/notpetya/.
338 "Claude Gov Models for U.S. National Security Customers," Anthropic.com, June 5, 2025, https://www.anthropic.com/news/claude-gov-models-for-u-s-national-security-customers?utm_source=www.therundown.ai&utm_medium=newsletter&utm_campaign=google-s-gemini-update-raises-the-bar&_bhlid=1a6dfad73ec47f4b9f0de78396f57ab8c29e1a80.
339 Michele A. Flournoy, "AI Is Already at War," *Foreign Affairs*, November/December 2023, Vol. 102, Issue 6, https://www.foreignaffairs.com/united-states/ai-already-war-flournoy
340 Benjamin Jensen and Jake S. Kwon, "The U.S. Army, Artificial Intelligence, and Mission Command," War on the Rocks, March 10, 2025, The U.S. Army, Artificial Intelligence, and Mission Command - War on the Rocks.
341 "AI Military Applications Abound, but Experts Urge Oversight," ADF, March 25, 2025, AI Military Applications Abound, but Experts Urge Oversight - Africa Defense Forum.
342 Jensen and Kwon, op. cit.
343 Don Monroe, "Deceiving AI," *Communications of the ACM*, Vol. 64, No 6, June 2021, DOI:10.1145/3460218.
344 Ibid.
345 Ibid.
346 Ibid.
347 Ibid.
348 Ibid.
349 Ibid.
350 Ibid.
351 Ibid.
352 Ibid.
353 James Pomfret and Summer Zhen, "China's Xi Calls for Self Sufficiency in AI Development amid U.S. Rivalry," Reuters, April 26, 2025, https://www.reuters.com/world/china/chinas-xi-calls-self-sufficiency-ai-development-amid-us-rivalry-2025-04-26/?utm_source=www.therundown.ai&utm_medium=newsletter&utm_campaign=china-declares-ai-independence&_bhlid=6ebbfe91d3d37a110f2026d192271df3f857311f.
354 Ibid.
355 Liam Mo and Kane Wu, "DeepSeek Narrows China-US AI Gap to Three Months, 01.AI Founder Lee Kai-fu Says," Reuters, March 25, 2025, DeepSeek narrows China-US AI gap to three months, 01.AI founder Lee Kai-fu says | Reuters.
356 Joshua Glonek, "The Coming Military AI Revolution," *Military Review*, May–June 2024, https://www.armyupress.army.mil/Portals/7/military-review/Archives/English/May-June-2024/MJ-24-Glonek/MJ-24-Glonek-UA.pdf.
357 "Annual Report to Congress: Military and Security Developments Involving the People's Republic of China," Department of Defense, 2024, file:///C:/Users/rober.000/OneDrive/Desktop/CHP%209%20NATIONAL%20DEFENSE/USED/MILITARY-AND-SECURITY-DEVELOPMENTS-INVOLVING-THE-PEOPLES-REPUBLIC-OF-CHINA-2024%20(2).pdf.

NOTES

358 Ibid.
359 Glonek, op. cit.
360 "Annual Report to Congress," op. cit.
361 Kinling Lo, "China Is Gaining Ground in the Global Race to Develop AI Agents," Rest of World, 2025, https://restofworld.org/2025/china-ai-agent-openai/?utm_source=thedeepview&utm_medium=newsletter&utm_campaign=musk-leaves-politics-and-raises-5b&_bhlid=fd471301732e253ac9c57bb40154177e2ea827cf.
362 China's Pursuit of Defense Technologies: Hearing Before the U.S.-China Economic and Security Review Commission, 118th Cong. 48 (2023) (statement of Elsa Kania, Adjunct Senior Fellow, Technology and National Security Program at the Center for a New American Security).
363 Michael Glanzel, "Artificial Intelligence and Regional Security in the Western Pacific," *Tulane Journal of Technology and Intellectual Property*, Vol. 26, Spring 2024, https://journals.tulane.edu/TIP/article/view/3897.
364 Glonek, op. cit., and "Defense Innovation Unit," US Department of Defense, https://www.diu.mil/replicator.
365 "Advancing Intelligence in the Era of Artificial Intelligence: Addressing the National Security Implications of AI," op. cit.
366 Jane Edwards, "Hegseth Memo Directs DOD to Use Software Acquisition Pathway," ExecutiveGov, February 27, 2025, https://executivegov.com/2025/02/pete-hegseth-draft-memo-dod-software-acquisition-pathway/; Jon Harper, "Hegseth Issues Edict on DOD Software Acquisition," Defensecoop.com, March 7, 2025, https://defensescoop.com/2025/03/07/hegseth-memo-dod-software-acquisition-pathway-cso-ota/.
367 Shaun Waterman, "Air Force Launching New Artificial Intelligence 'Center of Excellence'," *Air & Space Forces Magazine*, May 13, 2025.
368 Ibid.
369 Ibid.
370 Arjun Kharpal, "A.I. Is in a 'Golden Age' and Solving Problems That Were Once in the Realm of Sci-Fi, Jeff Bezos says," CNBC, May 8, 2017, https://www.cnbc.com/2017/05/08/amazon-jeff-bezos-artificial-intelligence-ai-golden-age.html.
371 "Artificial Intelligence and Its Potential Effects on the Economy and the Federal Budget," Congressional Budget Office, December 2024, Artificial Intelligence and Its Potential Effects on the Economy and the Federal Budget | Congressional Budget Office; "Economic Impacts of Artificial Intelligence (AI)," European Parliamentary Research Service, European Parliament, July 2019, Economic impacts of artificial intelligence.
372 "29 Best AI Quotes to Inspire IT Professionals," ATERA, March 6, 2025, https://www.atera.com/blog/best-ai-quotes/?utm_source=chatgpt.com.
373 "World's Population Will Reach Nearly 10 Billion by 2050," World Bank, July 8, 2019, https://datatopics.worldbank.org/world-development-indicators/stories/world-population-will-continue-to-grow.html.
374 Ishaya Gadzama, "How AI Is Revolutionizing Animal Farming: Benefits, Applications, and Challenges," https://wikifarmer.com/library/en/article/how-ai-is-revolutionizing-animal-farming-benefits-applications-and-challenges.
375 Ibid.

NOTES

376 Ibid.
377 Kurt Knutsson, "Smarter Dairy Farms Where Robots Milk the Cows," cyberguy.com, April 15, 2025, https://cyberguy.com/gadgets/smarter-dairy-farms-robots-milk-cows/.
378 Ibid.
379 Kat De Naoum, "You May Be Surprised Where Most of Earth's Oxygen Comes From," Thomasnet.com, May 4, 2023, https://www.thomasnet.com/insights/you-may-be-surprised-where-most-of-earth-s-oxygen-comes-from/.
380 Alina Piddubna, "AI in Agriculture—The Future of Farming," Intellias, August 12, 2024, https://intellias.com/artificial-intelligence-in-agriculture/.
381 Ibid.
382 Ibid.
383 Ibid.
384 "Artificial Intelligence to Support European Transition to Healthy Soils," AI 4 Soil Health, European Commission, September 20, 2023, https://ai4soilhealth.eu/artificial-intelligence-to-support-european-transition-to-healthy-soils/?utm_source=thedeepview&utm_medium=newsletter&utm_campaign=despite-it-all-meta-and-microsoft-have-a-surprisingly-good-night&_bhlid=60298a43795565399c3cca53cc354ee2842a272a.
385 Ibid.
386 Ibid.
387 Ibid.
388 "10 Ways AI Is Being Used in the Wood Industry [2025]," Digital Defynd, 2025, https://digitaldefynd.com/IQ/ai-in-wood-industry/.
389 Ibid.
390 Ibid.
391 "AI in the Timber Industry: Sustainable Construction and Reducing Illegal Logging," ArchiExpo eMag, February 28, 2024, https://emag.archiexpo.com/ai-in-the-timber-industry-sustainable-construction-and-reducing-illegal-logging/.
392 Ibid.
393 Patrick Tucker, "DARPA Wants to Use AI to Find New Rare Minerals." *Defense One*, July 3, 2024. *Gale Academic OneFile*, link.gale.com/apps/doc/A799870018/AONE?u=wash92852&sid=ebsco&xid=0a3c4bfc. Accessed 10 Mar. 2025.
394 "What Are Rare Earth Elements, and Why Are They Important?" AGI, accessed March 12, 2025, https://profession.americangeosciences.org/society/intersections/faq/what-are-rare-earth-elements-and-why-are-they-important.
395 Ibid.
396 Ibid.
397 Ibid.
398 "VRIFY Lands $12.5M Series B to Advance DORA, the World's First AI-Assisted Mineral Discovery Platform." *ENP Newswire*, February 28, 2025. *Gale Academic OneFile*, link.gale.com/apps/doc/A829121328/AONE?u=wash92852&sid=ebsco&xid=1508b036. Accessed 10 Mar. 2025.
399 Ibid.
400 "How Much of the Ocean Has Been Explored?" NOAA Ocean Exploration, National Oceanic and Atmospheric Administration, US Department of Commerce,

NOTES

accessed April 27, 2025, How much of the ocean has been explored? : Ocean Exploration Facts: NOAA Office of Ocean Exploration and Research.

401. "Our Mission—Seabed 2030," Nippon Foundation and General Bathymetry Chart of the Ocean (GEBCO), accessed April 27, 2025, Our Mission — Seabed 2030
402. Qihang Chen, Jianmin Yang, Wenhua Zhao, Longbin Tao, Jinghang Mao, Changyu Lu, "AI Based Dynamic Avoidance in Deep-sea Mining," *Ocean Engineering*, Vol. 311, Part 1, November 1, 2024, https://www.sciencedirect.com/science/article/abs/pii/S0029801824022832.
403. Ibid.
404. Halil Aksu, "AI Transformation Chronicles AI in Mining Industry," July 9, 2024, https://digitopia.co/blog/ai-in-mining/.
405. Amber Jackson, "Top 10 Uses of Artificial Intelligence in Mining," Mining Digital, June 21, 2023, https://miningdigital.com/articles/top-10-uses-of-artificial-intelligence-in-mining.
406. Ibid.
407. Ibid.
408. Ibid.
409. Ibid.
410. Ibid.
411. Ibid.
412. Ibid.
413. Christos Kyriklidis, Aikaterini Koutouvou, Konstantinos Moustakas, Vayos Karayannis, and Constantinos Tsanaktsidis, "Artificial Intelligence and Nature-Inspired Techniques on Optimal Biodiesel Production: A Review—Recent Trends," *Energies* 2025, 18, 768 https://doi.org/10.3390/en18040768.
414. Ibid.
415. David Brenner, "AI's Wrestling Match with the Law," AI and Faith, April 25, 2025, https://aiandfaith.org/insights/ai-wrestling-match-with-the-law/
416. Ibid.
417. Cecily Mauran, "120 Court Cases Have Been Caught with AI Hallucinations, According to New Database," Mashable.com, May 27, 2025, https://mashable.com/article/over-120-court-cases-caught-ai-hallucinations-new-database?utm_source=thedeepview&utm_medium=newsletter&utm_campaign=ai-in-120-court-cases&_bhlid=718f2d836eafc92693da08db7e6c703f18b330ae.
418. "Employees Keep Their AI-Driven Productivity a Secret," *HR Today*, May 12, 2025, Robot that watched surgery videos performs with skill of human doctor | Hub.
419. Ibid.
420. Jim Vandehei and Mike Allen, "Behind the Curtain: A white-collar bloodbath," Axios, May 28, 2025, https://www.axios.com/2025/05/28/ai-jobs-white-collar-unemployment-anthropic?utm_source=www.theneurondaily.com&utm_medium=newsletter&utm_campaign=anthropic-ceo-50-of-jobs-gone&_bhlid=ff71ac76021ef4aeeae804308a6757361b0b990d.
421. Noah Riggs, "72 Quotes about AI That Inspire a Look Into the Future," createandgo.com, accessed March 14, 2025, https://createandgo.com/quotes-about-ai.
422. Himanshu Ambarte, "Artificial Intelligence in the Textile Industry," *Textile Sphere*, accessed March 13, 2025, https://www.textilesphere.com/2024/08/artificial

-intelligence-in-textile-industry.html#:~:text=The%20textile%20industry%2C%20 a%20cornerstone%20of%20global%20commerce,reshaping%20how%20textiles %20are%20created%2C%20manufactured%2C%20and%20consumed.

423 Ibid.
424 "Embracing the Future of AI in the Food Industry," CAS Science Team, American Chemical Society, February 2, 2024, https://www.cas.org/resources/cas-insights /embracing-future-ai-food-industry.
425 Ibid.
426 Ibid.
427 Ibid.
428 "Use Forager® AI to Accelerate Product Innovation," Brightseed, accessed March 14, 2025, https://www.brightseedbio.com/partnerships.
429 "10 Ways AI Is Being Used in the Chemical Industry," Team DigitalDefynd, accessed March 13, 2025, https://digitaldefynd.com/IQ/ai-in-chemical-industry/.
430 Ibid.
431 Ibid.
432 Ibid.
433 Ibid.
434 Hardik Shah, "AI in Transportation Industry: Use Cases, Benefits, Applications and Real World Examples," Prismetric, October 9, 2024, https://www.prismetric.com/ai -in-transportation/.
435 Ibid.
436 Ibid.
437 Kathy Garcia, et al., "Modeling Dynamic Social Vision Highlights Gaps Between Deep Learning and Humans," a paper presented at the Thirteenth International Conference on Learning Representations, January 22, 2025, https://openreview.net /forum?id=wAXsx2MYgV.
438 Evan Robinson-Johnson, "Tesla Robotaxi Spotted on Austin Streets," The Information, June 11, 2025, https://www.theinformation.com/briefings/tesla-robotaxi -spotted-austin-streets?utm_campaign=%5BREBRAND%5D+%5BTI-AM%5D+ Th&utm_content=1095&utm_medium=email&utm_source=cio&utm_term=124.
439 Shad, op. cit.
440 Ibid.
441 Ibid.
442 Ibid.
443 Ibid.
444 Ibid.
445 "AI in Pharmaceuticals: Benefits, Challenges, and Insights," Datacamp, August 27, 2024, https://www.datacamp.com/blog/ai-in-pharmaceuticals.
446 "Life Science Intelligence," BenevolentAI, accessed March 14, 2025, https://www .benevolent.com/
447 "Healthcare Technology Solutions and Services," IBM, accessed March 14, 2025, Healthcare technology solutions and services | IBM.
448 "Bringing Data and AI to Healthcare," Tempus Technology, accessed March 14, 2025, Our Technology - Tempus.

NOTES

449 Jae Yong Ryu, Hyun Uk Kim, and Sang Yup Lee, "Deep Learning Improves Prediction of Drug-Drug and Drug-Food Interactions," PNAS, April 16, 2018, Deep learning improves prediction of drug–drug and drug–food interactions | PNAS

450 Nefi Alarcon, "Predicting Drug Interactions with the Help of AI," Nvidia. May 4, 2018. Predicting Drug Interactions with the Help of AI | NVIDIA Technical Blog.

451 "6 Ways Johnson & Johnson Is Using AI to Help Advance Healthcare," Johnson & Johnson, October 10, 2024, 6 ways Johnson & Johnson is using AI to help advance healthcare.

452 "State of AI in Telecommunications: 2024 Trends," Nvidia, 2024, https://images.nvidia.com/aem-dam/Solutions/documents/telco-state-of-ai-report.pdf?ncid=pa-so-link-324121-vt26.

453 Keith Obrien and Amanda Downie, "AI in Telecommunications," October 18, 2024, https://www.ibm.com/think/topics/ai-in-telecommunications.

454 Ibid.

455 Ibid.

456 Ibid.

457 Herman K. Trabish, "Avista, PG&E, Ameren AI Demonstrations Show Great Potential—but are other utilities ready?" Utilitydive.com, March 7, 2025, https://www.utilitydive.com/news/avista-pge-ameren-ai-utilities-modeling/740705/.

458 Ibid.

459 Ibid.

460 "About Amperon," accessed March 14, 2025, https://www.amperon.co/about-us.

461 Trabish, op. cit.

462 Ibid.

463 Ibid.

464 "R&D Strategy Report 2024," PG&E, accessed March 14, 2025, 2024 R&D Strategy Report.

465 Ruth Porat, Thomas Kurian, James Manyika, and Kent Walker, "Powering a New Era of American Innovation," Google, May 2025, https://static.googleusercontent.com/media/publicpolicy.google/en//resources/powering_new_era_of_american_innovation.pdf?utm_source=www.therundown.ai&utm_medium=newsletter&utm_campaign=futurehouse-s-superhuman-science-agents&_bhlid=be9549aea95aa053445dcf14a9c05495dc19224b.

466 Ibid.

467 Ibid.

468 Ibid.

469 Denise Chow, "Trump Signs Executive Orders to Expand and Ease Regulations on Nuclear Energy Production," NBC News, May 23, 2025, https://www.msn.com/en-us/politics/government/trump-signs-executive-orders-to-expand-and-ease-regulations-on-nuclear-energy-production/ar-AA1FmL6Z.

470 Ibid.

471 "AI in Construction in 2024 and Beyond: Use Cases and Benefits," Tribe.ai, November 4, 2024, https://www.tribe.ai/applied-ai/ai-in-construction.

472 "Rise of the Platform Era: The Next Chapter in Construction Technology," McKinsey & Company, October 30, 2020, The next chapter in construction technology | McKinsey.

NOTES

473　Ibid.
474　Ibid.
475　Ibid.
476　Ibid.
477　Ibid.
478　Ibid.
479　"Upskilling 2025 Annual Report September 2021," Amazon, accessed April 14, 2025, https://assets.aboutamazon.com/28/48/6b990cf448b5b4064a54c63cb6c8/amazon-upskilling-report.pdf.
480　The ISO 9000 family of international standards for quality management systems was developed in March 1987 by the International Organization for Standardization. Those standards help manufacturers meet customers and other stakeholder requirements.
481　"FDA Proposes Framework to Advance Credibility of AI Models Used for Drug and Biological Product Submissions," FDA News Release, Food and Drug Administration, January 6, 2025, https://www.fda.gov/news-events/press-announcements/fda-proposes-framework-advance-credibility-ai-models-used-drug-and-biological-product-submissions.
482　Kendall Germain, "AI in Construction Safety: How Artificial Intelligence Is Transforming Jobsite Risk Management," Motive, April 28, 2025, https://gomotive.com/blog/ai-in-construction-safety/.
483　"AI Risk Management Framework," NIST, accessed May 13, 2025, https://www.nist.gov/itl/ai-risk-management-framework.
484　"ISO 27001 vs. NIST Cybersecurity Framework Compared," PrivacyEngine, November 10, 2023, https://www.privacyengine.io/blog/iso-27001-vs-nist-cybersecurity-framework/.
485　"An Overview of the 2021 JBS Meat Supplier Ransomware Attack," Mitnick Security, June 3, 2021, https://www.mitnicksecurity.com/blog/an-overview-of-the-2021-jbs-meat-supplier-ransomware-attack.
486　"GM Has Become an 'Energy Star' with Efficiency and Circular Programs," E+E-Leader, May 13, 2022, https://www.environmentenergyleader.com/stories/gm-has-become-an-energy-star-with-efficiency-and-circular-programs,2708.
487　"How Unilever's Digital Transformation Is Driving Operational Excellence," Unilever, February 3, 2025, https://www.unilever.com/news/news-search/2025/how-unilevers-digital-transformation-is-driving-operational-excellence/.
488　Eleanor Hecks, "How Generative Design Breaks Boundaries," Designerly, March 13, 2025, https://designerly.com/generative-design/.
489　"Digital Building Twins," Bosch, accessed May 13, 2025, https://www.boschbuildingsolutions.com/xc/en/news-and-stories/digital-building-twins/?msclkid=51f2faa4bc431763c065928794157a9b&utm_source=bing&utm_medium=cpc&utm_campaign=int_en_biot_smb_ga_sea_generic_CI-72451&utm_term=digital%20twin&utm_content=G-Building%20Twins_AI-003.
490　"Industrial AI," Siemens, accessed May 13, 2025, https://www.siemens.com/us/en/company/topic-areas/industrial-ai.html?acz=1.
491　"Lights-out Manufacturing: Full Automation on the Horizon," Standard Bots, April 28, 2025, https://standardbots.com/blog/lights-out-manufacturing#:~:text

NOTES

=Lights-out%20manufacturing%2C%20where%20AI%2C%20robots%2C%20 and%20IoT%20take,these%20setups%20crank%20out%20products%20without %20human%20input; "Siemens Unveils Breakthrough Innovations in Industrial AI and Digital Twin Technology at CES 2025," Siemens, January 6, 2025, https://press .siemens.com/global/en/pressrelease/siemens-unveils-breakthrough-innovations -industrial-ai-and-digital-twin-technology-ces.

492 Jon Taylor, "10 Quotes about AI and Retail (by People Who Know a Thing or Two about AI and Retail)," Peak, April 6, 2018, https://peak.ai/hub/blog/10-quotes-about -ai-and-retail/.

493 Bill Conerly, "AI And The Economy: Better Marketing And Sales Good For Consumers But Not Statistics," Forbes.com, October 10, 2023, https://www.forbes.com /sites/billconerly/2023/10/10/ai-and-the-economy-better-marketing-and-sales-good -for-consumers-but-not-statistics/.

494 Julie Shapero, "Amazon Made More Than $1B Using Secret Algorithm Called 'Project Nessie,' FTC Says," *The Hill*, November 3, 2023, https://thehill.com/business /4292178-amazon-made-over-1b-using-secret-algorithm-called-project-nessie-ftc-says/.

495 Ibid.

496 Yaroslav Mota, "How to Benefit from AI Inventory Management," NiX, February 11, 2025, https://www.n-ix.com/ai-inventory-management/.

497 Pepijn Richter, "AI-powered Retail: Elevating Customer Experience and Operational Efficiency," Microsoft, January 9, 2025, https://www.microsoft.com/en-us/industry /blog/retail/2025/01/09/ai-powered-retail-elevating-customer-experience-and -operational-efficiency/.

498 "Revolutionizing Retail with AI Face Recognition," Solulab, accessed May 13, 2025, https://www.solulab.com/case-study/ai-face-recognition-in-retail/.

499 Mesh Flinders and Molly Hayes, "A Guide to AI in Marketing," IBM, September 6, 2023, https://www.ibm.com/think/topics/ai-in-marketing.

500 Ibid.

501 Bernard Marr, "The 6 Most Powerful AI Marketing Trends That Will Transform Your Business In 2025," Forbes.com, November 12, 2024, https://www.forbes.com /sites/bernardmarr/2024/11/12/the-6-most-powerful-ai-marketing-trends-that-will -transform-your-business-in-2025/.

502 Ibid.

503 Meghan Bobrowsky and Patrick Coffee, "Meta Aims to Fully Automate Ad Creation Using AI," Stratechery.com, June 2, 2025, https://stratechery.com/2025/an -interview-with-meta-ceo-mark-zuckerberg-about-ai-and-the-evolution-of-social-media /?utm_source=www.therundown.ai&utm_medium=newsletter&utm_campaign=meta-s -ai-advertising-takeover&_bhlid=d78b4e72c68a8ae8f46cbd88c84c77f759f69204.

504 "The Economic Potential of Generative AI: The Next Productivity Frontier," McKinsey Digital, June 14, 2023, Economic potential of generative AI | McKinsey.

505 "How AI Is Powering Loyalty Programs for Better Retention," iSmart, February 26, 2025, https://www.ismartcom.com/blog/how-ai-is-powering-loyalty-programs-for -better-retention/#:~:text=From%20predictive%20analytics%20to%20chatbot-powered %20customer%20interactions%2C%20AI-driven,satisfaction%20but%20also%20 boost%20revenue%20and%20reduce%20churn.

NOTES

506 "How Does AI Affect Online Shopping?" PayPal Editorial Staff, June 25, 2024, https://www.paypal.com/us/money-hub/article/ai-online-shopping.

507 "Celebrating One Year of Pinterest Lens," Newsroom, February 8, 2018, https://newsroom-archive.pinterest.com/celebrating-one-year-of-pinterest-lens?utm_source=.

508 "Why AI Styling Is the Future of Online Retail," DressX, March 14, 2025, https://dressx.com/news/why-ai-styling-is-the-future-of-online-retail.

509 "YouCam Makeup," Wikipedia, accessed June 8, 2025, https://en.wikipedia.org/wiki/YouCam_Makeup?utm_source.

510 "Self-checkout," Wikipedia, accessed June 8, 2025, https://en.wikipedia.org/wiki/Self-checkout?utm_source.

511 "Amazon Personalize," AWS, accessed June 8, 2025, https://aws.amazon.com/personalize/?utm_source.

512 Matt Villano, "At Mastercard, AI Is Helping to Power Fraud-detection Systems," Business Insider, May 12, 2025, https://www.businessinsider.com/mastercard-ai-credit-card-fraud-detection-protects-consumers-2025-5?utm_source.

513 George Avalos, "Amazon AI Tech Crafted in South Bay Could Speed Same-day Deliveries," Siliconvalley.com, June 5, 2025, https://www.siliconvalley.com/2025/06/04/amazon-tech-ai-sunnyvale-south-bay-economy-jobs-deliver-commerce-work/?utm_source=superhuman&utm_medium=newsletter&utm_campaign=robotics-special-amazon-gears-up-to-train-delivery-bots&_bhlid=de7830d395598a40396021b44ac976b7537b06a1.

514 Adam Zewe, "New System Enables Robots to Solve Manipulation Problems in Seconds," MIT News, June 5, 2025, https://news.mit.edu/2025/new-system-enables-robots-to-solve-manipulation-problems-seconds-0605?utm_source=superhuman&utm_medium=newsletter&utm_campaign=robotics-special-amazon-gears-up-to-train-delivery-bots&_bhlid=becc71073fc5c19c1cec48cf5407a4ccceb8bb1b.

515 Andrew J. Hawkins, "Wing and Walmart Are Bringing Drone Delivery to 100 New Stores," The Verge, June 5, 2025, https://www.theverge.com/news/680723/walmart-wing-drone-delivery-expand-cities-100-stores?utm_source=superhuman&utm_medium=newsletter&utm_campaign=robotics-special-amazon-gears-up-to-train-delivery-bots&_bhlid=9e04b763bac04e40088be3370518573b60550598.

516 "Find and Buy with AI: Visa Unveils New Era of Commerce," Businesswire, April 30, 2025, https://www.businesswire.com/news/home/20250430580204/en/Find-and-Buy-with-AI-Visa-Unveils-New-Era-of-Commerce?utm_source=www.therundown.ai&utm_medium=newsletter&utm_campaign=visa-mastercard-give-ai-credit-cards&_bhlid=33f006cbc17e93272fb8a06702de78bf32fa3568.

517 "Consumer and Data Protection Concerns in the Age of AI," Quantilus.com, October 24, 2024, https://quantilus.com/article/consumer-and-data-protection-concerns-in-the-age-of-ai/.

518 Anna Cooban, "Meta Accused of 'Massive, Illegal' Data Processing by European Consumer Groups," CNN, February 29, 2024, https://www.cnn.com/2024/02/29/tech/meta-data-processing-europe-gdpr/index.html.

519 Ibid.

520 Eric Mack, "Elon Musk: 'We Are Summoning the Demon' with Artificial Intelligence," *Science*, October 26, 2014, https://www.cnet.com/science/elon-musk-we-are-summoning-the-demon-with-artificial-intelligence/.

NOTES

521 "Top 10 Expert Quotes That Redefine the Future of AI Technology," Nisum, July 25, 2023, https://www.nisum.com/nisum-knows/top-10-thought-provoking-quotes-from-experts-that-redefine-the-future-of-ai-technology.

522 Kalina Bryant, "How AI Is Impacting Society and Shaping the Future," Forbes.com, December 13, 2023, https://www.forbes.com/sites/kalinabryant/2023/12/13/how-ai-is-impacting-society-and-shaping-the-future/.

523 Stefan Larson, "Average Screen Time Statistics for 2025," Priori Data, March 6, 2025, https://prioridata.com/data/screen-time-statistics/.

524 Colleen McClain, Brian Kennedy, Jeffrey Gottfried, Monica Anderson, and Giancarlo Pasquini, "Artificial Intelligence in Daily Life: Views and Experiences," Pew Research, April 3, 2025, https://www.pewresearch.org/2025/04/03/artificial-intelligence-in-daily-life-views-and-experiences/.

525 "Values in the Wild: Discovering and Analyzing Values in Real-world Language Model Interactions," Anthropic.com, April 21, 2025, https://www.anthropic.com/research/values-wild?utm_source=www.therundown.ai&utm_medium=newsletter&utm_campaign=anthropic-maps-ai-s-moral-compass&_bhlid=1515b6c2b410c180d00acfb4ec6117d9bd52392a.

526 Ibid.

527 "The Impact of AI on Human Values," Novak, April 17, 2023, https://medium.com/the-generator/the-impact-of-ai-on-human-values-f906d570f6e2.

528 Jacob Abernethy, François Candelon, Theodoros Evgeniou, Abhishek Gupta, and Yves Lostanlen, "Bring Human Values to AI," Magazine, March-April 2024, https://hbr.org/2024/03/bring-human-values-to-ai.

529 "Mission and Vision," Southern Baptist Convention, accessed May 13, 2025, https://www.sbc.net/about/what-we-do/mission-vision/.

530 "The Fundamental Values of Catholic Social Teaching," Catholic Conscience, accessed May 13, 2025, https://catholicconscience.org/principles-values-virtues-of-catholic-social-thought/.

531 "The Impact of AI on Human Values," Novak, April 17, 2023, https://medium.com/the-generator/the-impact-of-ai-on-human-values-f906d570f6e2.

532 Ibid.

533 Ibid.

534 Andrea Baronchelli, "Shaping New Norms for AI," Royal Society Publishing, January 22, 2024, https://doi.org/10.1098/rstb.2023.0028.

535 B. Schmidt, 2023. "Chatgpt 'Arms Race' Adds $4.6 Billion to Nvidia Founder's Fortune." Bloomberg. See https://www.bloomberg.com/news/articles/2023-01-27/chatgpt-arms-race-adds-4-6-billion-to-nvidia-founder-s-fortune (accessed June 14, 2023).

536 Ibid.

537 Ibid.

538 Ibid.

539 Ibid.

540 Kurtis G. Haut, Taylan Sen, Denis Lomakin, and Ehsan Hoque, "A Mental Trespass? Unveiling Truth, Exposing Thoughts, and Threatening Civil Liberties with Noninvasive AI Lie Detection," *Transactions on Technology and Society*, Vol. 3, No. 2, June 2022, https://creativecommons.org/licenses/by/4.0/.

NOTES

541 Ibid.
542 Jessica Hamzelou, "Tech That Aims to Read Your Mind and Probe Your Memories Is Already Here," *Technology Review*, March 17, 2023, https://www.technologyreview.com/2023/03/17/1069897/tech-read-your-mind-probe-your-memories/.
543 Ibid.
544 Paul Tullis, "The US Military Is Trying to Read Minds," *Technology Review*, October 16, 2019, The US military is trying to read minds | MIT Technology Review.
545 Hamzelou, op. cit.
546 Haut, op. cit.
547 Stephen Wood, "Fact Check: Man Was Convicted for Breaching Abortion Clinic's Safe Zone," *Independent*, October 18, 2024, https://www.independent.co.uk/news/uk/crime/christian-bournemouth-christchurch-uk-parliament-army-b2631603.html.
548 "Japan Pushing Ahead with Society 5.0 to Overcome Chronic Social Challenges," UNESCO, November, 13, 2024, https://www.unesco.org/en/articles/japan-pushing-ahead-society-50-overcome-chronic-social-challenges.
549 Implementation Timeline, EU Artificial Intelligence Act, accessed April 14, 2025, https://artificialintelligenceact.eu/implementation-timeline/.
550 "AI Art Quotes," nichequotes, accessed March 20, 2025, https://nichequotes.com/ai-art-quotes.
551 Claudia Baxter, "AI Art: The End of Creativity or the Start of a New Movement?" BBC, October 21, 2024, https://www.bbc.com/future/article/20241018-ai-art-the-end-of-creativity-or-a-new-movement.
552 Ibid.
553 Ibid.
554 Ibid.
555 Ibid.
556 Ibid.
557 Liz Mineo, "If It Wasn't Created by a Human Artist Is It Still Art?" *Gazette*, August 15, 2023, https://news.harvard.edu/gazette/story/2023/08/is-art-generated-by-artificial-intelligence-real-art/.
558 Ibid.
559 Ibid.
560 Ibid.
561 Ibid.
562 Ibid.
563 Ibid.
564 Ibid.
565 Ibid.
566 Ibid.
567 Jurgen Dale, "The Impact of AI on Creativity and the Arts," Virtualsphere, January 25, 2025, https://virtualsphere.substack.com/p/the-impact-of-ai-on-creativity-and.
568 Ibid.
569 Ibid.
570 Ibid.
571 Ibid.

NOTES

572 Ibid.
573 Akash Takyar, "AI in Media and Entertainment: Use Cases, Benefits and Solution," LeewayHertz, https://www.leewayhertz.com/ai-in-media-and-entertainment/#Future-trends-in-the-entertainment-industry. (Akash Takyyar, founder of LeewyHertz, a software development company, provides many helpful insights regarding AI's influence for the entertainment media.)
574 Ibid.
575 Ibid.
576 Ibid.
577 Ibid.
578 "Cinelytic," accessed March 21, 2025, https://www.cinelytic.com/.
579 Takyar, op. cit.
580 Ibid.
581 Wyatte Grantham-Philips, "Film Festival Showcases What Artificial Intelligence Can Do on the Big Screen," Associated Press, June 7, 2025, https://apnews.com/article/ai-film-festival-runway-movies-3b5d40e4c2e20f7a4d34f1f5d4907ba7.
582 Matthew Gentzkow, "Media and Artificial Intelligence," Toulouse School of Economics, 2018, https://www.tse-fr.eu/publications/media-and-artificial-intelligence.
583 Daniel Thomas, "BBC Develops AI Plans and Talks to Big Tech over Archives Access," *Financial Times*, March 21, 2024, https://www.ft.com/content/7bfec4ae-bbd2-4834-9b75-3ade935a4096?utm_source=chatgpt.com.
584 Greg Petro, "Half of Consumers Say AI-Generated Ads Are a Turnoff," Forbes.com, November 8, 2024, Half of Consumers Say AI-Generated Ads Are a Turnoff.
585 "IZEA Research Reveals 86% of Consumers Believe AI-Generated Content Should Be Disclosed, 42% of Respondents Ages 18–29 Actively Use AI in Their Daily Lives," IZEA Worldwide, June 22, 2023, IZEA Research Reveals 86% of Consumers Believe AI-Generated.
586 Colleen P. Kirk and Julian Givi, "The AI-authorship Effect: Understanding Authenticity, Moral Disgust, and Consumer Responses to AI-generated Marketing Communications," *Journal of Business Research*, Vol. 186, January 2025, The AI-authorship effect: Understanding authenticity, moral disgust, and consumer responses to AI-generated marketing communications - ScienceDirect.
587 "IZEA Research Reveals 86% of Consumers Believe AI-Generated Content Should Be Disclosed; 42% of Respondents Ages 18–29 Actively Use AI in Their Daily Lives," op. cit.
588 Gentzkow, op. cit.
589 Ibid.
590 Ibid.
591 Ibid.
592 Jessica Clement, "Video Game Industry—Statistics & Facts," Statista, November 6, 2024, https://www.statista.com/topics/868/video-games/#topicOverview.
593 Aleksandr Sheremeta, "A Handbook on AI in Media and Entertainment Influence," Dataforest.ai, April 8, 2024, https://dataforest.ai/blog/a-handbook-on-ai-in-media-and-entertainment-influence.

NOTES

594 Rajeev Sharma, "Next-Gen Gaming: The Exciting Role of AI in Gaming," Markovate, December 10, 2024, AI in Gaming: The Exciting Role of AI in Next-Gen Gaming - Markovate.
595 Sheremeta, op. cit.
596 Ibid.
597 Atharva Waghale, Nayan Potdukhe, and Rajendra Rewatkar, "AI in Gaming: From Simple Algorithms to Complex Agents," 2024 2nd DMIHER International Conference on Artificial Intelligence in Healthcare, Education and Industry (IDICAIEI), DOI: 10.1109/IDICAIEI61867.2024.
598 Josh Gold-Quiros, Carl Kukkonen III, and Emily Tait, "Court Finds AI-Generated Work Not Copyrightable for Failure to Meet 'Human Authorship' Requirement—But Questions Remain," JDSUPRA, August 31, 2023.
599 Mark Sellman, "AI Firms Must Pay Creatives for Using Copyrighted Work, MPs Say," *The Times*, March 31, 2025. AI firms must pay creatives for using copyrighted work, MPs say.
600 Dan Milmo, "UK Needs to Relax AI Laws or Risk Transatlantic Ties, Thinktank Warns," *The Guardian*, April 1, 2025, UK needs to relax AI laws or risk transatlantic ties, thinktank warns | Artificial intelligence (AI) | The Guardian.
601 Ann Marie Lenihan, "We Must Act Fast to Protect Journalism or Real Cost of AI Will Keep exploiting Trusted Press & Spreading Disinformation," *The Irish Sun*, April 5, 2025. We must act fast to protect journalism or real cost of AI will keep exploiting trusted press & spreading disinformation | The Irish Sun.
602 Bill McColl, "Major Labels in Talks to License AI Use of Music, Report Says," Investopedia, June 3, 2025, https://www.msn.com/en-us/music/news/major-labels-in-talks-to-license-ai-use-of-music-report-says/ar-AA1G0uRY.
603 Jess Weatherbed, "Movie Studios Are Being Financially Rewarded for AI Slop on YouTube," The Verge, March 31, 2025, Movie studios are being financially rewarded for AI slop on YouTube | The Verge.
604 Paige Sutherland and Meghna Chakrabarti, "AI's Influence on Election 2024," wbur, January 17, 2024, https://www.wbur.org/onpoint/2024/01/17/ai-influence-election-2024-politics?utm_source=chatgpt.com.
605 "The State of AI: How Organizations Are Rewiring to Capture Value," McKinsey & Company, March 12, 2025, The State of AI: Global survey | McKinsey.
606 Fahad Qadir, "How AI Will Shape Communications In 2025," Forbes.com, January 23, 2025, https://www.forbes.com/councils/forbescommunicationscouncil/2025/01/23/how-ai-will-shape-communications-in-2025/.
607 "The Future of Communication: How AI Is Transforming the Way We Connect," Capitol Technology University, May 22, 2024, https://www.captechu.edu/blog/how-ai-is-transforming-communication.
608 Hayden Field, "OpenAI Releases Sora, Its Buzzy AI Video-generation Tool," CNBC, December 9, 2024, https://www.nbcnews.com/business/business-news/openai-releases-sora-buzzy-ai-video-generation-tool-rcna183525?os=a%5B0%5D&ref=app.
609 "Creating Video from Text," OpenAI, accessed March 23, 2025, https://openai.com/index/sora/.

NOTES

610 "Replika—AI Friend," Apposee.com, accessed March 22, 2025, https://www.apposee.com/ai.replika.app?msclkid=744bffa09ee117a6e1b0987e3da3ce8b&utm_source=bing&utm_medium=cpc&utm_campaign=US-Health%20%26%20Fitness-DA&utm_term=Replika%20app%20download&utm_content=Replika#google_vignette.

611 Byron Kaye and Praveen Menon, "Australia Passes Social Media Ban for Children under 16," Reuters, November 29, 2024, Australia passes social media ban for children under 16 | Reuters.

612 Kwame Christian, "The Future of Communication in the Age of Artificial Intelligence," Forbes.com, May 4, 2023, https://www.forbes.com/sites/kwamechristian/2023/05/04/the-future-of-communication-in-the-age-of-artificial-intelligence/.

613 Ibid.

614 "Deep Blue," IBM, accessed March 22, 2025, https://www.ibm.com/history/deep-blue.

615 Koetsier, op. cit.

616 Katja Schlegel, Nils R. Sommer, and Marcello Mortillaro, "Large Language Models Are Proficient in Solving and Creating Emotional Intelligence Tests," *Communications Psychology*, Vol. 3, No. 80 (2025), https://www.nature.com/articles/s44271-025-00258-x?utm_source=www.therundown.ai&utm_medium=newsletter&utm_campaign=apple-s-ai-gap-year&_bhlid=68086092fc010270c8bc53be0fe53f30805e58f0.

617 Marlies N. van Lingena, Noor A. A. Giesbertzb, J. Peter van Tintelena, and Karin R. Jongsmaa, "Why We Should Understand Conversational AI as a Tool," *American Journal of Bioethics*, 2023, Vol. 23, No. 5, https://doi.org/10.1080/15265161.2023.2191039.

618 Ibid.

619 Ibid.

620 Ibid.

621 Juliana Wang, Sierra Wang, Manson Cheuk-Man Fong, Matthew K. H Ma, and William S. Y. Wang, "Can Complex Systems Theory Tell Us About Understanding in the Human-AI Communication System?," 6th International Conference on Natural Language Processing, Institute of Electrical and Electronics Engineers Inc., October 4, 2024, https://research.polyu.edu.hk/en/publications/what-can-complex-systems-theory-tell-us-about-understanding-in-th.

622 Ibid.

623 Ibid.

624 Matthew Clemente and David Goodman, "Can AI Replace Your Therapist?," *Psychology Today*, February 1, 2025, https://www.psychologytoday.com/us/blog/our-human-condition/202502/can-ai-replace-your-therapist.

625 Ibid.

626 Neil Sahota, "The AI Factor in Political Campaigns: Revolutionizing Modern Politics," Forbes.com, January 12, 2024, https://www.forbes.com/sites/neilsahota/2024/01/12/the-ai-factor-in-political-campaigns-revolutionizing-modern-politics/.

627 Ibid.

628 Maggie Astor, "Behind the A.I. Robocall That Impersonated Biden: A Democratic Consultant and a Magician," *New York Times*, February 27, 2024, Behind the A.I. Robocall That Impersonated Biden: A Democratic Consultant and a Magician - The New York Times.

NOTES

629 Christine Sellers, "Fact Check: Viral Image of Epstein and Trump Sitting Next to Each Other on Plane Is AI-Generated," Checkyourfact.com, December 10, 2024, https://checkyourfact.com/2024/12/10/fact-check-image-epstein-trump-sitting-plane-ai/.

630 Curt Devine, Donie O'Sullivan, and Sean Lyngaas, "A Fake Recording of a Candidate Saying He'd Rigged the Election Went Viral. Experts Say It's Only the Beginning," CNN, February 1, 2024, A fake recording of a candidate saying he'd rigged the election went viral. Experts say it's only the beginning | CNN Politics.

631 Stuart Lou, "China Bombards Taiwan with Fake News ahead of Election," *Politico*, January 10, 2024, China bombards Taiwan with fake news ahead of election – POLITICO.

632 Bruce Schneier and Nathan E. Sanders, "Six Ways That AI Could Change Politics," *Technology Review*, July 28, 2023, https://www.technologyreview.com/2023/07/28/1076756/six-ways-that-ai-could-change-politics/.

633 Neil Sahota, "The AI Factor in Political Campaigns: Revolutionizing Modern Politics," Forbes.com, January 12, 2024, https://www.forbes.com/sites/neilsahota/2024/01/12/the-ai-factor-in-political-campaigns-revolutionizing-modern-politics/.

634 Benj Edwards, "Hype Grows over "Autonomous" AI Agents That Loop GPT-4 Outputs," *Ars Technica*, April 14, 2023, Hype grows over "autonomous" AI agents that loop GPT-4 outputs - Ars Technica.

635 Chris van Buskirk, "Mass. Lawmaker Uses ChatGPT to Help Write Legislation Limiting the Program," MsaaLive, January 27, 2023, Mass. lawmaker uses ChatGPT to help write legislation limiting the program - masslive.com.

636 James Vincent, "The First AI-written Speech Delivered by Congressman Is as Flavorless as You'd Expect," *The Verge*, January 27, 2023, The first AI-written speech delivered by congressman is as flavorless as you'd expect | The Verge.

637 Choe Xiang, "This Danish Political Party Is Led by an AI," vice.com, October 13, 2022, This Danish Political Party Is Led by an AI.

638 Alan Perlis, "A Year Spent in Artificial Intelligence Is Enough to Make One Believe in God," The Socratic Method, January 27, 2025, https://www.socratic-method.com/quote-meanings-interpretations/alan-perlis-a-year-spent-in-artificial-intelligence-is-enough-to-make-one-believe-in-god#google_vignette.

639 Bernard Peter Robichau, "AI: A Theological Response," Touchstone, https://www.touchstonemag.com/archives/article.php?id=37-05-030-f.

640 Gretchen Huizinga, "AI: Humanity's New Grab for Divine Wisdom," *Sojourners*, November 2023, https://sojo.net/magazine/november-2023/ai-humanitys-new-grab-divine-wisdom [Note: AI & Faith website states: "Our mission is to equip and encourage people of faith to bring time-tested, faith-based values and wisdom to the ethical AI conversation." https://aiandfaith.org/]

641 Andrew Torba, "Reclaiming Reality: Restoring Humanity in the Age Of AI," Gab.ai, February 14, 2025, https://www.amazon.com/Reclaiming-Reality-Restoring-Humanity-Age/dp/B0DX9S82C7.

642 Ibid.

643 Ibid.

644 Ibid.

645 George M. Coghill, "Artificial Intelligence (and Christianity): Who? What? Where? When? Why? and How?" *Studies in Christian Ethics*, Vol. 36(3), 2023, DOI: 10.1177/09539468231169462.

NOTES

646 Torba, op. cit.
647 Robichau, op. cit.
648 Ibid.
649 Ibid.
650 Ibid.
651 Stanko Jambrek, "Christians Facing the Challenges of Artificial Intelligence," Kairos: *Evangelical Journal of Theology*, Vol. XVIII, No. 1, 2024, https://orcid.org/0000-0002-6877-9247.
652 Ibid.
653 Ibid.
654 Ibid.
655 James Vincent, "Putin Says the Nation That Leads in AI 'Will Be the Ruler of the World,'" The Verge, September 4, 2027, https://www.theverge.com/2017/9/4/16251226/russia-ai-putin-rule-the-world.
656 Blair Levin and Larry Downes, "Who Is Going to Regulate AI?" *Harvard Business Review*, May 19, 2023, https://hbr.org/2023/05/who-is-going-to-regulate-ai.
657 Deepak Gupta, "Who Will Control Our Future? A Guide to Power, Influence, and Responsible AI Development," Guptadeepak.com, May 23, 2024, https://guptadeepak.com/who-will-control-our-ai-future-a-guide-to-power-influence-and-responsible-ai-development/
658 Jambrek, op. cit.
659 Michael Roppolo, "Elon Musk Joins Hundreds Calling for a Six-month Pause on AI Development in an Open Letter," CBS News, March 29, 2023, https://www.cbsnews.com/news/elon-musk-open-letter-ai/.
660 Leonardo De Cosmo, "Google Engineer Claims AI Chatbot Is Sentient: Why That Matters," *Scientific American*, July 12, 2022, https://www.scientificamerican.com/article/google-engineer-claims-ai-chatbot-is-sentient-why-that-matters/
661 Oliver Dale, "Ray Kurzweil AI Predictions: Human-Level Intelligence by 2029, Singularity by 2045," blockonomi, July 2, 2024, https://blockonomi.com/ray-kurzweil-ai-predictions-human-level-intelligence-by-2029-singularity-by-2045/
662 Jambrek, op. cit.
663 Gretchen Huizinga, "AI: Humanity's New Grab for Divine Wisdom," Sojourners, November 2023, https://sojo.net/magazine/november-2023/ai-humanitys-new-grab-divine-wisdom.
664 Ibid.
665 Kylie Robison, "OpenAI Cofounder Ilya Sutskever Says the Way AI Is Built Is About to Change, The Verge, December 13, 2024, https://www.theverge.com/2024/12/13/24320811/what-ilya-sutskever-sees-openai-model-data-training?utm_source=chatgpt.com.
666 Jambrek, op. cit.
667 Calvin Mercer, "A Theological Embrace of Transhuman and Posthuman Beings," *Perspectives on Science and Christian Faith*, Volume 72, Number 2, June 2020, https://www.asa3.org/ASA/PSCF/2020/PSCF6-20Mercer.pdf.
668 Ibid.
669 Ibid.

NOTES

670 Ibid.
671 Jambrek, op. cit.
672 Nick Bilton, "Artificial Intelligence May Be Humanity's Most Ingenious Invention—And Its Last?" *Vanity Fair*, September 13, 2023, https://www.vanityfair.com/news/2023/09/artificial-intelligence-industry-future.
673 Ibid.
674 Ibid.
675 Jambrek, op. cit.
676 Alexander Gale, "Church Service Generated by ChatGPT Attended by Hundreds," *Greek Reporter*, June 12, 2023, https://greekreporter.com/2023/06/12/church-service-chatgpt/.
677 Ibid.
678 Ibid.
679 Ibid.
680 Robichau, op. cit.
681 Ibid.
682 Ibid.
683 Ibid.
684 Ibid.
685 Kaitlyn Schiess, "Scripture Through the Eyes of AI," *Christianity Today*, December 2023, https://www.christianitytoday.com/2023/11/ai-artificial-intelligence-interpret-scripture-bible/.
686 Ibid.
687 Ibid.
688 Ibid.
689 Ibid.
690 Ibid.
691 Ibid.
692 Ibid.
693 Ibid.
694 Cole Feix, "AI Goes to Church," *Christianity Today*, September 23, 2024, https://www.sowespeak.com/post/ai-goes-to-church.
695 Ibid.
696 Ibid.
697 Ibid.
698 Ibid.
699 Ibid.
700 Ibid.
701 Fiona Andre, "Meet the People Designing Chatbots with a 'Biblical Worldview,'" Religion News Service, September 2023.
702 Ibid.
703 Ibid.
704 Ibid.
705 Ibid.
706 Ibid.

NOTES

707 Ibid.
708 Greg Kumparak, "Elon Musk Compares Building Artificial Intelligence to 'Summoning the Demon,'" TechCrunch, October 26, 2014, https://techcrunch.com/2014/10/26/elon-musk-compares-building-artificial-intelligence-to-summoning-the-demon/.
709 "Sam & Jony introduce io," openAI.com, accessed May 22, 2025, https://openai.com/sam-and-jony/.
710 Ibid.
711 Rory Cellan-Jones, "Stephen Hawking Warns Artificial Intelligence Could End Mankind," BBC, December 2, 2014, https://www.bbc.com/news/technology-30290540.
712 Dale, op. cit.
713 Ibid.
714 Robert M. Geraci, "Apocalyptic AI: Religion and the Promise of Artificial Intelligence." *Journal of the American Academy of Religion*, vol. 76, no. 1, 2008, pp. 138–66. JSTOR, http://www.jstor.org/stable/40006028. Accessed 31 Mar. 2025.
715 Ibid.
716 Ibid.
717 Ibid.
718 Ibid.
719 Ibid.
720 Ibid.
721 Ibid.
722 Ibid.
723 Ibid.
724 Ibid.
725 Ibid.
726 Ibid.
727 Ibid.
728 Ibid.
729 Ibid.
730 Ibid.
731 Ibid.
732 Dustin Ryan, "A Christian's Perspective on Artificial Intelligence," Christ Over All, May 6, 2024, https://christoverall.com/article/longform/a-christians-perspective-on-artificial-intelligence/.
733 Albert Mohler, "Francis Schaeffer's 'How Should We Then Live?'—40 Years Later," The Gospel Coalition, November 23, 2016, https://www.thegospelcoalition.org/article/schaeffers-how-should-we-now-then-live-40-years-later/.
734 Ibid.
735 Note: Unless otherwise indicated, ChatGPT is the source for the material in the appendices.
736 "Supercharge Your Workday with ChatGPT," Hubspot, June 10, 2025, https://www.hubspot.com/hubfs/%5Bebook%5D%20Supercharge%20Your%20Workday%20with%20ChatGPT.pdf?hubs_signup-url=offers.hubspot.com/using-chatgpt-at-work&hubs_signup-cta=Submit&hubs_offer=offers.hubspot.com/using-chatgpt-at-work&_gl=1*1sal28j*_gcl_au*ODMwNzMwNDAxLjE3NDk1NTMzOTUuOD-

NOTES

g3ODE5Ni4xNzQ5NTUzNDE0LjE3NDk1NTM0MTM.*FPAU*ODMwNzM
wNDAxLjE3NDk1NTMzOTU.*_ga*MTE0MDM0MjE1LjE3NDk1NTMzOTU
.*_ga_LXTM6CQ0XK*czE3NDk1NTMzOTUkbzEkZzEkdDE3NDk1NTM0MT
QkajQxJGwwJGgw*_fplc*OEZ5NkQlMkZwU0pzZlFHSDNYYUd1S2NyJTJC
c21uWkpRY3dUekZQZ2RET3clMkJTbCUyRjVXZzRtSlJlWEs1cm9VeFElMkZy
WHAwbEN4cVJqWWduR1d4YnZ1RlhxMUFNam02ekN5UWg3b2pORHR4clo0
NkhlTHoxUUF5TFduNW53Q3A3M3NBdyUzRCUzRA..&_ga=2.194163181
.1937369854.1749553395-114034215.1749553395.

737 Mfon Akpan, "Have We Reached Artificial General Intelligence? Comparison of ChatGPT, Claude, and Gemini to Human Literacy and Education Benchmarks," *Corporate Ownership & Control, 22*(1), 2025, https://doi.org/10.22495/cocv22i1art8.

738 Celia Quillian, AI for Life, Adams Meida, An Imprint of Simon & Schuster, 2025, https://www.amazon.com/AI-Life-Artificial-Intelligence-Productive/dp/1507223390.

739 "On Artificial Intelligence and Emerging Technologies," Southern Baptist Convention, June 15, 2023, https://www.sbc.net/resource-library/resolutions/on-artificial-intelligence-and-emerging-technologies/.

740 "10 Ways the US Government is Using AI [2025], Z" Team DigitalDefynd, accessed April 4, 2025, https://digitaldefynd.com/IQ/ways-the-us-government-using-ai/.

741 Oracle. (n.d.). AI in Local Government. Retrieved March 19, 2025, from https://www.oracle.com/artificial-intelligence/ai-local-government/.

742 D. Jarvis (May 4, 2023). "Artificial Intelligence Can Find Potholes in Roads Before Motorists." *Daily Telegraph*. https://www.dailytelegraph.com.au/news/nsw/artificial-intelligence-can-find-potholes-in-roads-before-motorists/news-story/0505a8b-d5408aefffaa4c761fb56244e.

743 Rachel Sylvester, "AI There, You're Nicked! Tech Is Reshaping How We Fight Crime," *The Times*, January 24, 2025, AI there, you're nicked! Tech is reshaping how we fight crime.

744 Robert Booth, "Social workers in England begin using AI system to assist their work," *The Guardian*, September 28, 2024, Social workers in England begin using AI system to assist their work | Social care | The Guardian

745 R. Morrison, (February 6, 2024). "Los Angeles Tried to Use AI to Solve Homelessness. Then Things Got Complicated." Vox. https://www.vox.com/the-highlight/388372/housing-policy-los-angeles-homeless-ai.

746 Laura Adler, "How Smart City Barcelona Brought the Internet of Things to Life," Data Smart, February 18, 2016, https://datasmart.hks.harvard.edu/news/article/how-smart-city-barcelona-brought-the-internet-of-things-to-life-789.

747 Sand Technologies. (n.d.). "The Role of AI in Local Government Innovation. Retrieved March 19, 2025, from https://www.sandtech.com/insight/the-role-of-ai-in-local-government-innovation-sand-technologies/.

748 "Estonia's Timbeter Tackles Illegal Logging with AI," Trade with Estonia, March 2024, https://tradewithestonia.com/estonias-timbeter-tackles-illegal-logging-with-ai/.

749 Ibid.

750 Nina Kristine Boesche, et al., "Hyperspectral REE (Rare Earth Element) Mapping of Outcrops—Applications for Neodymium Detection," MDPI, April 24, 2015, https://www.mdpi.com/2072-4292/7/5/5160.

NOTES

751 "Estonia's Timbeter Tackles Illegal Logging with AI," op. cit.
752 Vaibhav Sistiny, "AI Upskilling Sprint," a Zoom briefing hosted by Outskill, May 2, 2025. https://www.outskill.com/.
753 "The Fearless Future: 2025 Global AI Jobs Barometer," Insight, PwC Global, June 3, 2025, AI Jobs Barometer | PwC.
754 Cal. Civ. Code §§ 1798.100–1798.199 (West 2023); California Proposition 24, The California Privacy Rights Act of 2020, approved November 3, 2020; Federal Trade Commission, Complaint for Permanent Injunction, Civil Penalties, and Other Relief, FTC v. Amazon.com, Inc., Case No. 2:23-cv-00932 (W.D. Wash., filed June 21, 2023); American Data Privacy and Protection Act, H.R. 8152, 117th Congress (2022).
755 European Union, Regulation (EU) 2016/679 of the European Parliament and of the Council of 27 April 2016 on the Protection of Natural Persons with Regard to the Processing of Personal Data and on the Free Movement of Such Data (General Data Protection Regulation), OJ L 119, 4.5.2016, pp. 1–88; European Commission, *Proposal for a Regulation of the European Parliament and of the Council Laying Down Harmonised Rules on Artificial Intelligence (Artificial Intelligence Act) and Amending Certain Union Legislative Acts*, COM(2021) 206 final, 21 April 2021, https://eur-lex.europa.eu/legal-content/EN/TXT/?uri=CELEX%3A52021PC0206; Douglas MacMillan and Natalia Drozdiak, "Amazon Hit With $887 Million Fine by European Privacy Watchdog." *Bloomberg*, 30 July 2021, https://www.bloomberg.com/news/articles/2021-07-30/amazon-hit-with-887-million-fine-by-european-privacy-watchdog.
756 Brazil, *Lei No. 13.709, de 14 de Agosto de 2018*, Dispõe sobre a proteção de dados pessoais e altera a Lei nº 12.965, de 23 de abril de 2014 (Lei Geral de Proteção de Dados Pessoais—LGPD), https://www.gov.br/anpd/en/legal-framework/lgpd-english-version; Standing Committee of the National People's Congress (China), *Personal Information Protection Law of the People's Republic of China*, adopted 20 August 2021, effective 1 November 2021, https://www.chinalawtranslate.com/en/personal-information-protection-law-of-the-p-r-c/; India, Digital Personal Data Protection Bill, 2023, introduced by the Ministry of Electronics and Information Technology (MeitY), Lok Sabha, 3 August 2023, https://prsindia.org/files/bills_acts/bills_parliament/2023/Digital_Personal_Data_Protection_Bill_2023.pdf; Australia Attorney-General's Department, *Privacy Act Review—Report 2022*, published February 2023. Commonwealth of Australia, Report No.: AGD22-053792, https://www.ag.gov.au/rights-and-protections/publications/privacy-act-review-report.
757 Vittoria Benzine, "'A.I. Should Exclude Living Artists From Its Database,' Says One Painter Whose Works Were Used to Fuel Image Generators," Artnet, September 20, 2022, https://news.artnet.com/art-world/a-i-should-exclude-living-artists-from-its-database-says-one-painter-whose-works-were-used-to-fuel-image-generators-2178352?utm_source=chatgpt.com.
758 Jose Antonio Lanz, "Greg Rutkowski Was Removed From Stable Diffusion, But AI Artists Brought Him Back," July 29, 2023, Emerge, Greg Rutkowski Was Removed From Stable Diffusion, But AI Artists Brought Him Back - Decrypt.
759 Ibid.
760 Jordan Darville, "Holly Herndon Announces New Voice Instrument and 'Digital Twin' Holly+ Users Can Have Their Audio Sung in Herndon's Voice Via a New Free

NOTES

Website," *The Fader*, July 14, 2021, https://www.thefader.com/2021/07/14/holly-herndon-holly-plus?utm_source=chatgpt.com.

761 Holly Herndon and Mathew Dryhurst, "Holly+," ARS Electronica, 2022, Holly+ – Welcome to Planet B.

762 Mike Kaputon, "Amazon's AI Book Scandal: How Writers Are Losing Control," Market AI Institute, August 15, 2023, Amazon's AI Book Scandal: How Writers Are Losing Control.

763 Ibid.

764 Ibid.

765 Beatrice Nolan, "An Author Is Facing Backlash for Using AI to Write 120 Books. He Says he's Misunderstood," *Business Insider*, September 27, 2024, An Author Used AI to Write 120 Books. Now He's Facing Backlash. - Business Insider.

766 Tim Boucher, "What Are the AI Lore Books?" *Enterprise Technology News*, May 2, 2023, What are the AI Lore books? – Tim Boucher.

767 Tim Boucher, "I'm Making Thousands Using AI to Write Books," Threads, May 15, 2023, 'I'm Making Thousands Using AI to Write Books' - Newsweek.

768 Ibid.

769 Masabah Bint E. Islam, et al., "AI Threats to Politics, Elections, and Democracy: A Blockchain-Based Deepfake Authenticity Verification Framework," MDPI, November 21, 2024, AI Threats to Politics, Elections, and Democracy: A Blockchain-Based Deepfake Authenticity Verification Framework.

770 Mekela Panditharatne and Shanze Hasan, "How to Rein in Russia's Evolving Disinformation Machine," *Time*, October 21, 2024, How to Rein in Russia's Evolving Disinformation Machine | TIME.

771 Cindy Long, "Helping Students Spot Misinformation Online," NEAToday, October 17, 2024, Helping Students Spot Misinformation Online | NEA.

772 "News Literacy Project," Wikipedia, accessed April 15, 2025, News Literacy Project - Wikipedia.

773 Ibid.

774 Ali Swenson and Kelvin Chan, "Election Disinformation Takes a Big Leap with AI Being Used to Deceive Worldwide," Associated Press, March 14, 2024, AI-created election disinformation is deceiving the world | AP News.

775 Ibid.

776 Michael Doyle, "Face Facts: AI Misuse Fears Ahead of General Election as Urgent 'We Need to Be Alert' Warning over 'Turbocharged' Deepfake Threat," *Irish Sun*, AI misuse fears ahead of General Election as urgent 'we need to be alert' warning over 'turbocharged' deepfake threat | The Irish Sun.

777 Chinasa T. Okolo, "African Democracy in the Era of Generative Disinformation: Challenges and Countermeasures against AI-Generated Propaganda," arXiv, July 10, 2024, [2407.07695] African Democracy in the Era of Generative Disinformation: Challenges and Countermeasures against AI-Generated Propaganda.

778 Dashveenjit Kaur, "After Years of Dominating Facial Recognition Tech, China Is Ready to Govern It," *TechWire Asia*, August 15, 2023, https://techwireasia.com/2023/08/facial-recognition-tech-in-china-will-soon-be-governed/.

NOTES

779 "China's Behavior Monitoring System Bars Some from Travel, Purchasing Property," CBS News, April 24, 2018, https://www.cbsnews.com/news/china-social-credit-system-surveillance-cameras/.

780 Sean Lyngaas, "Suspected Chinese Operatives Using AI Generated Images to Spread Disinformation Among US Voters, Microsoft says," CNN, September 7, 2023, https://www.cnn.com/2023/09/07/politics/chinese-operatives-ai-images-social-media/index.html.

781 Gregory C. Allen, "Understanding China's AI Strategy," CNAS, February 6, 2019, https://www.cnas.org/publications/reports/understanding-chinas-ai-strategy.

782 Zizhu Zhang, "Study Confirms Influence of Russian Internet "Trolls" on 2016 Election, Columbia SIPA, March 29, 2022, https://www.sipa.columbia.edu/news/study-confirms-influence-russian-internet-trolls-2016-election.

783 Jackie Kerr, "The Russian Model of Digital Control and its Significance," appeared in "AI, China, Russia, and the Global Order: Technological, Political, Global, and Creative Perspectives A Strategic Multilayer Assessment (SMA) Periodic Publication," Department of Defense White Paper, December 2018, https://nsiteam.com/social/wp-content/uploads/2019/01/AI-China-Russia-Global-WP_FINAL_forcopying_Edited-EDITED.pdf.

784 Jordi Calvet-Bademunt and Joan Barata, "The Digital Services Act Meets the AI Act: Bridging Platform and AI Governance," *Tech Policy*, May 29, 2024, https://www.techpolicy.press/the-digital-services-act-meets-the-ai-act-bridging-platform-and-ai-governance/.

785 Vandinika Shukla and Bruce Schneier, "India's Latest Election Embraced AI Technology. Here Are Some Ways It Was Used Constructively," PBS, June 12, 2024, https://www.pbs.org/newshour/world/indias-latest-election-embraced-ai-technology-here-are-some-ways-it-was-used-constructively.